Complex Rivalry

Complex Rivalry

THE DYNAMICS OF
INDIA-PAKISTAN CONFLICT

Surinder Mohan

University of Michigan Press
Ann Arbor

For questions or permissions, please contact um.press.perms@umich.edu

Published in the United States of America by the University of Michigan Press
Manufactured in the United States of America
Printed on acid-free paper

First published October 2022

A CIP catalog record for this book is available from the British Library.

Library of Congress Cataloging-in-Publication data has been applied for.

ISBN 978-0-472-07559-1 (hardcover: alk. paper)
ISBN 978-0-472-05559-3 (paper: alk. paper)
ISBN 978-0-472-22063-2 (e-book)

Library of Congress Control Number: 2022942054

To my parents, Kamla and Om Parkash Sharma
  For idealism and unconditional love

To my brothers, Sunil Dutt and Satish Kumar
  For courage and selfless contribution to my life

To Dr. A.P.J. Abdul Kalam (1931–2015)
  For motivation and giving wings to the "fire"

Contents

Digital materials related to this title can be found on the Fulcrum platform via the following citable URL: https://doi.org/10.3998/mpub.12195673

Figures

Tables

Foreword

The India-Pakistan conflict is one of the most protracted and violent conflicts in global history after World War II. Amid a plethora of literature striving to explain the causes, dynamics, and prognosis of this conflict, *Complex Rivalry: The Dynamics of India-Pakistan Conflict* promises to make a mark. Scholarly research on this conflict has hitherto deployed different theoretical frames ranging from an ideological lens that traced its raison d'être to India's partition in 1947, which morphed into a lasting bilateral conflict rooted in mutually incompatible nation-building strategies pitching India's secular nationalism against Pakistan's Muslim (and later, Islamic) nationalism. The most pervasive and abiding frame is, however, offered by the power politics model of the realist paradigm that has continually re-invented itself over time. This imaginary has variously sought to explain the long-standing India-Pakistan conflict as an enduring contestation for power and status within and beyond South Asia and presents even the Kashmir conflict as a territorial dispute between the two neighboring countries. Simply put, both explanations remain incomplete without each other, and yet large parts of the theoretically informed literature on the India-Pakistan conflict fall short in accounting for the missing pieces of the puzzle because they remain bound by the choices of their respective theoretical frames. Surinder Mohan breaks new ground in attempting a multivariate inquiry cutting across different international relations (IR) paradigms by developing and deploying a rivalry-based hub-and-spokes framework, which he terms a "complex rivalry model," for understanding the India-Pakistan case.

The core strength of the book is that it lets the field speaks for itself and on its own terms, in that it does not countenance any of the dominant theoretical paradigms—realism, liberalism, or constructivism—to singly determine the inclusion or exclusion of any variables for this study. Backed by a rich, detailed, and nuanced account of empirical data, it offers a comprehensive analysis of the complex, multi-layered, and constantly evolving nature of this rivalry. This study belongs to the new genre of IR literature that challenges the old knowledge divides wherein theories were primarily devised by scholars in the global North and data for testing was generated by those located in the global South. Though much has been written about the dynamics of interstate rivalries, what makes this book different is Surinder Mohan's attempt to re-formulate the theoretical premise and parameters of this phenomenon based on the insights drawn from his field research rather than the other way around. The "hub" and the "spokes" provide a macro and micro frame, respectively, for taking into account the constantly evolving temporal factors, and the interactions between the two offer an effective explanatory frame, imparting a long shelf life to this book, mainly for its promising predictive value. Another virtue of this well-researched book is that it lays down various possible trajectories and provides a comprehensive framework of rivalry transformation in three systematic phases, referred to as "steps to peace," which the leadership of India and Pakistan must pursue to explore the path of peace-building and make headway to a promising transformation and stable peace in the long run.

The US withdrawal from Afghanistan, the return of the Taliban regime with Pakistan's support, and China's growing influence in South Asia are poised to recast the geo-politics and geo-economics of this region in the near future, making this study vital for both scholars and practitioners of international diplomacy.

Navnita Chadha Behera

Professor, Department of Political Science, University of Delhi

Former Vice-President, International Studies Association (2019–20)

Acknowledgments

Scholars who engage in research need many kinds of support—intellectual, financial, and emotional. I have been extremely fortunate as numerous individuals and institutions have helped me during the fourteen years of research and writing, and I want to express my appreciation.

At the outset, I would like to thank the Department of Political Science, University of Delhi, for all its wonderful support during the writing of the PhD dissertation from which this book is derived. Navnita Chadha Behera, my dissertation advisor; the late Indra Nath Mukherji of Jawaharlal Nehru University; L. Premashekara of Pondicherry University; and Chandan Sharma of IIM-Lucknow were particularly helpful in promoting my development as a researcher. They have given me the utmost freedom to think, question, and use different theoretical lenses as tools of investigation at different points in time; this book would not have been written without that freedom and support base. I am also thankful to Shibashis Chatterjee, Rajesh Rajagopalan, and Anjoo Sharan Upadhyay, my dissertation examiners, for their valuable feedback and encouragement. I thank them all.

While pursuing my master's degree, two outstanding studies gave me intellectual inspiration and brought a phenomenal change in my thinking: John A. Vasquez's *The War Puzzle* and Paul F. Diehl and Gary Goertz's co-authored work *War and Peace in International Rivalry*. I wish to acknowledge the authors of both volumes—although they do not know me nor have they seen this book—for their profound impact on my thinking and ideas.

This book on rivalry benefited from the valuable feedback of the anonymous reviewers at the University of Michigan Press. Their productive interventions and suggestions not only helped me to rethink and reshape some of the key ideas, but also widened my intellectual horizons and understanding of the field. I am also indebted to Springer Nature, Oxford University

Press and the Japan Association of International Relations, and Wiley-Blackwell for granting permission to use materials that appeared, respectively, in "Military Capabilities and Regime Type: The Emergence of India-Pakistan Rivalry," *International Politics* 56, 1 (February 2019): 49–69; "Ideology, Territorial Saliency, and Geographic Contiguity: The Beginning of India-Pakistan Rivalry," *International Relations of the Asia-Pacific* 16, 3 (September 2016): 371–407; and "Transforming the Line of Control: Bringing the 'Homeland' Back In," *Asian Politics and Policy* 5, 1 (January 2013): 51–75. Thanks are due as well to the editors and anonymous reviewers of these journals whose observations and suggestions helped me to shape the ideas in the early stage of research.

Over the years of writing, I presented parts of the book at the following universities and institutions: University of Delhi, Jawaharlal Nehru University, University of Kerala, University of Mumbai, Pondicherry University, University of the Punjab (Lahore), and the Kerala International Center. I thank the organizers and many anonymous individuals for asking important questions that forced me to think harder. I am thankful to Ajay Dharshan Behera who helped me to arrange meetings and interviews in New Delhi and Lahore and made it possible for me to attend seminars organized by the Pakistan Studies Programme, Academy of International Studies, at Jamia Millia Islamia during 2010–13. For their interviews and suggestions, I am thankful to Mani Shankar Aiyar, Pawan Anand, the late Shujaat Bhukari, Mathew Joseph C., Zafar Choudhary, Lakho Devi, the late Brigadier Gurmeet Kanwal, Asgar Ali Karbalai, Ambassador Vivek Katju, Mohammad Akram Mirza, the late Kuldip Nayar, Ambassador G. Parthasarathy, the late Ram Payari, Rikhi Ram, the late Sukh Ram, the late Prem Swaroop, and Achin Vanaik.

I am also grateful to the many people who supported me during the field trip to Pakistan in October 2015. Particularly, I am thankful to Shahid H. Kardar, the vice chancellor of Beaconhouse National University (Lahore) and the former finance minister of Punjab and governor of the State Bank of Pakistan, for hosting and helping me to arrange my visa and interviews with researchers, academics, journalists, diplomats, and retired armed forces personnel in Lahore and Islamabad. I am also grateful to Aamir Rafique (University of the Punjab in Lahore) for arranging my accommodations and meetings with intellectuals, and facilitating access to the fine institutions and libraries of the city. I am also thankful to Muhammad Awais, who accompanied me in Lahore and managed my travel schedules flawlessly despite the last-minute changes in interview timings. In Islamabad, Ayesha Siddiqa was generous with her time and gave me introductions to those I wished to interview. Her answers to my questions not only provided new insights but also set the stage for intellectual discussions with the key area experts. In Pakistan, for their interviews and suggestions, I am thankful to Lt. Gen. Asad Durrani, Ghazi Salahuddin, Imtiaz Gul, Pervez Hoodbhoy, Akmal Hussain, General Jehangir Karamat, Ambassador Aziz Ahmed Khan, Ambassador Iqbal Ahmad Khan, Ijaz Khan, Ambassador Shahryar Mohammad Khan, Ambassador Shahid Malik, Lt. Gen. Talat Masood, Sajjad Naseer, A.H. Nayyar, Ambassador Ashraf Jehangir Qazi, Rasul Baksh Rais, Ahmed Rashid, the late Ibn Abdur Rehman, Mohammad Waseem, and the late Mohammad Ziauddin.

Over the years, I have accumulated debts of gratitude to a number of people. My heartfelt thanks to their grinding efforts: Sakuntla and Sushma Gupta, Mulakh Raj, Bhan Singh, Ved Parkash Kapoor, Chaman Lal Sharma, Satya Devi Sharma, Kasturi Lal Sharma, Sneh Bala Sharma, Joyti Parkash Harnal, Kuldeep Raj Gupta, the late Prem Lata Bushe, Prem Parkash, Vinod Sharma, Pritam Shoor, Vinod Kumari, the late Nand Lal Isher, the late Ram Payari Sudan, Om Parkash Saraf, Kundan Lal Khajuria, Sudesh Gupta, Suresh Kumar Sharma, Brij Mohan, Ghanshyam Sharma, Pushap Raina, M.L. Dogra, Dalbir Singh, Tejinder Kaur, Sunil Sharma, B. Krishnamurthy, D. Sambandhan, H. Kalpana, Nikhila H., the late Savita Pandey, the late Amar Nath Khajuria, the late Baldev Raj Sharma, Kaliaperumal, and Tamil Amma.

I am also thankful to my friends who have provided me indispensable support over the years: Josukutty C. Abraham, Wasim Ahmad, Syed Rizwan Ahmed, K. Aurobinda Babu, Banasmita Bohra, Parteek Chibber, Biju Koonathan, Rupak Kumar Jha, K. Ananda Kumar, Ritesh K. Mishra, Dharshan Ojha, Sahil Pathania, Vineeth R.S., Anjan Kumar Sahu, Ashwani Sharma, Gourav Sharma, Yogesh Sharma, Prakash Singh, Cyril Vasudevan, Tango da Gama, and the late Kivthee. In many ways, I am indebted to my childhood friend Joginder Singh, who stood by me in sunshine and in shade.

On my home front, I am profoundly grateful to my family members. My sister and brother-in-law, Kamlesh and Chaman Lal Sharma, for their boundless interest and contribution in my studies. Childhood motivators, Sanjeev Kumar Saraf and Ravi Kumar Verma, for their extraordinary support and guidance that made my "drift" to academics possible. I am indebted to my *bhabhis*, Asha and Neeta, for their consistent encouragement and meaningful support over the last two decades. My thanks go to Meroline and Alfred Naveen Lobo and my mother-in-law, Mary Lobo, for their unfailing cooperation and assuming those responsibilities which I was supposed to shoulder.

Sabina, my guide since master's, and now my sister-in-law as well, inculcated research interest and values well before I entered the field of research. This helped me to remain focused and grounded even when I switched universities to complete my cherished project: my doctoral thesis. Thanks are due as well to Nigel Monteiro, my co-brother, Mary and Robert D'Souza, Felix Saldanha, Dr. Glenn Fernandes, Dr. Annie Rajaratnam and Dr. Sujaya V. Rao for playing meaningful roles when the situation on the personal front appeared critical in 2019–21. For her unconditional care and passionate queries about the status of the book project, Sr. Noel Saldanha deserves a special mention. Last, but not least, I fondly remember my father-in-law, the late Apoline L.V. Lobo, who had spend almost half of his life in the Afro-Asian conflict zones and acquired an alternative understanding of cooperation and conflict.

A special note of thanks go to my nieces and nephews, Shivani, Abhishek, Anjali, Raghav, Aman, Divya, Aavantika, Anushka, Aaditi, Arvind, Sara, Amartya, Keshav, Mark, and Aaron, whose innocent questions, concerns, and probing encouraged me to keep going when my enthusiasm waned. My son, Aaditya, deserves my apologies for not being able to join "his world" ever since his birth in his maternal hometown—I hope he will forgive me for my prolonged absence and unintended ignorance. I wish to acknowledge my wife, Susanna, for her sustained and extraordinary support both as an individual and fellow researcher.

I acknowledge the help of people at the University of Michigan Press for making this book a reality. Elizabeth Demers, editorial director and the senior acquiring editor for political and social science, showed much interest in the project from the outset. Mary Hashman, the production editor, Haley Winkle, editorial associate, Anita Hueftle, copyeditor, Devon Thomas, indexer, and their colleagues supervised all phases of the project and did a superb job of steering the book to publication.

Finally, I am grateful to the hearty encouragers who believed in my ideas ahead of time: my idealist parents, Kamla and Om Parkash Sharma; my accommodative and insightful brothers, Sunil Dutt and Satish Kumar; and the platonic motivator who instilled confidence in me, the late Dr. A.P.J. Abdul Kalam. Together they gave me confidence to choose a path of my choice, to think with heart, and to avoid opportunism, that made the real difference. For all that and more, this book is dedicated to them.

Surinder Mohan
University of Jammu
February 17, 2022

CHAPTER I

Introduction

International Relations Theory
and the India-Pakistan Rivalry

Since their independence, India and Pakistan have been engaged in a seemingly permanent hostility which makes their long-standing duel one of the most intractable and unresolved interstate conflicts of the present times. The two countries' competing claims to the Muslim-majority state of Jammu and Kashmir (J&K/Kashmir)[1] is the real bone of contention which plays a fundamental role in shaping their clashing ideologies, national security interests, and policy perspectives. In other words, the unresolved ethno-territorial issue of the partition, Kashmir, is the core dispute between India and Pakistan which is so intertwined in their national ideologies and security narratives that it incites their leadership to take armed recourse. For this reason, coupled with their ideational-reputational concerns, distrust, and hostility, India and Pakistan never hesitated to take advantage of each other's internal and external vulnerabilities and engage in high-magnitude armed conflicts that include four wars—the First Kashmir War (1947–48), the Second Kashmir War (1965), the Bangladesh War (1971), and the Kargil War (1999)—and more than half a dozen severe armed crises which almost spiraled out of control and ended just short of all-out war.[2]

Over time, the two states have pursued the practices of power politics—such as joining alliances, engaging in military buildups and power balancing, and acquiring nuclear weapons—to maximize their security choices and demonstrate their will to use force to achieve political goals or deter threats in Kashmir and elsewhere. Overall, these security-enhancing measures, coupled with pressures from nationalist groups and domestic hardliners, have compounded the two adversaries' security dilemmas that compel them to pursue foreign policies imbued with militarism and political rhetoric. By and large, this approach shaped their political leadership and government officials' policy choices—for instance, to handle Kashmir by employing unilateral solutions or aggressive means—which gradually linked one issue with another at the dyadic level and formed what John Vasquez calls "a vicious cycle of disagreement-negative acts-hostility" (1993: 80). Against this setting, India and Pakistan's continued military engagement and reactionary outlook toward each other's political-security exposures eventually evolved into a competitive nuclear and missile race.

Though nuclear weapons' massive destructive power deterred both adversaries from entering into all-out wars, as nuclear optimists have predicted, this phenomenon neither stabilized the region nor succeeded in establishing a robust nuclear deterrence between them. In fact, far from inducing stability, as S. Paul Kapur (2008) argues, the acquisition of nuclear weapons has provided the revisionist party, Pakistan, a compelling incentive to continue the low-intensity confrontation in Kashmir without fearing a major retaliatory action from the superior adversary, India. Over the last couple of decades or so, the two adversaries' nuclear engagement and ever-expanding missile competition substantiates that the nuclear factor has not only stabilized this rivalry but also taken it to a different strategic plane, which has brought about a dramatic transformation in their differences over the Kashmir issue.[3]

In order to gain a broader understanding of the India-Pakistan rivalry, apart from its origin and maturity, this book examines several baffling and inter-related questions: What makes this rivalry persist, unlike several rivalries that terminated with the end of the Cold War? How have the great powers, alliance politics, and power capabilities shaped this rivalry? Why does power asymmetry not favor the dominant state, India, imposing its will on the weaker opponent—Pakistan? Has the nuclearization of South Asia stabilized the India-Pakistan rivalry? If so, how? How do conflict triangulations at the regional and extra-regional levels (that is, India-Pakistan-Afghanistan, China-India-Pakistan, and India-China-United States) contribute to the India-Pakistan rivalry? Can structural and temporal changes transform or terminate this rivalry? If yes, what are they? Scholars have made attempts to address these questions; however, in doing so, their accounts are largely drawn to the realist scholarship which dominates the field of international relations (IR). Though the realist paradigm offers us much for the understanding of different aspects of interstate rivalries, the answers offered in the context of the India-Pakistan rivalry are not comprehensive. Hence, apart from understanding the shortcomings of the leading IR paradigms, the purpose of this book is to offer a multivariate cross-paradigmatic framework to address the case in question—the India-Pakistan rivalry.

THE ARGUMENT

A substantial body of research has sought to explain how the conflict between India and Pakistan originated and developed over time, offering multiple perspectives including an emphasis on nationalism along with the ethno-religious and cultural factors on the one hand and the power politics model of the realist paradigm on the other. However, a multivariate inquiry cutting across different IR paradigms to understand the India-Pakistan case has yet to be attempted in a serious and systematic fashion—a gap this book seeks to address by developing and deploying a rivalry-based hub-and-spokes framework. This framework, also termed the "complex rivalry" model, draws on and deploys a range of variables from the leading IR paradigms while making use of tools offered by comparative politics. The objective is to develop a better analytical framework for explaining the formation and development of the India-Pakistan rivalry, as well as discussing hitherto unexplored conditions and different scenarios for a possible transformation or termination of the rivalry. By not limiting its theoretical toolkit to any single paradigm, this study is unique in its approach and better positioned to debate and answer baffling questions that the single-paradigm-based studies address rather inadequately and in isolation.

Many theoretical studies, if not most, tend to explain dyadic relationships in an episodic manner by focusing on specific events, such as military crises or wars, and thereby neglect the dynamic implications of various domestic, regional, and international factors that play a key part in shaping the course of the India-Pakistan rivalry. The proposed inter-paradigmatic hub-and-spokes framework seeks to fill this gap by taking into account most such factors (and events) in a holistic manner. It offers an explanation of the life cycle of India-Pakistan rivalry in four sequential phases: initiation, development, maintenance, and a possible transformation/termination. Empirically, the "hub" and the "spokes" provide a macro and micro frame, respectively, for taking into account the evolving structural and temporal factors, and their constant interaction in the context of each other offers an effective explanatory frame, which has a predictive value as well.

In addition, the complex rivalry model holds explanatory value for understanding India-Pakistan relations partly because of its conceptual advantages: it is not restricted to the realist worldview and is open to insights from liberalism—particularly economic interdependency and the democratic peace theory—as well as the constructivist school, as it takes into account conflicts arising out of identity and ideological issues of divergent, if not antithetical, nation-building strategies of India and Pakistan, and critical theory by injecting a sense of self-reflexivity in its analysis. In doing so, it contests some elements of different theoretical perspectives while supporting others in a bid to overcome their shortcomings to offer an effective theoretical and empirical account of the India-Pakistan rivalry.

I argue that five specific conditions underlie the evolution of the Indo-Pakistani conflict into a "complex rivalry": (1) its survival in spite of experiencing two political shocks, that is, the Bangladesh War and the end of the Cold War; (2) its linkage, or conflict triangulation, with other rivalries at different points in time; (3) the inclusion of the nuclear factor in the conflict, which fundamentally altered the dynamics of the rivalry by injecting stability; (4) the dyadic stability in the militarized disputes and hostility level despite changes in the regime type, that is, from non-democratic periods to the periods of joint democracy; and (5) the dyad's involvement in a multi-layered conflict pattern, that is, disagreement on several issues simultaneously, with a tendency to link-and-accumulate new issues. I also argue that the fundamental incompatibility between India's and Pakistan's foreign policy objectives, their often opposing regional alignments and strategic postures, and their different political systems favor the persistence of this rivalry with little prospect of its early transformation or termination. Breaking this deadlock and mitigating India and Pakistan's long-standing differences requires both sides to restructure and reorganize their national priorities, so that their respective policy makers understand each other's position and make efforts to secure domestic support to implement risky policies while exploring the possibilities of conflict resolution and rivalry transformation.

INTERNATIONAL RELATIONS THEORY AND THE INDIA-PAKISTAN RIVALRY

In this short survey, I explore the leading IR paradigms to highlight their shortcomings and silence in explaining various angularities associated with the India-Pakistan rivalry. The core premises of each paradigm have much to offer us for understanding the relationship between clashing interests, power capabilities, and adversarial policies in the India-Pakistan context and interstate rivalries in general. Another purpose of this survey, beyond demonstrating that one paradigm is better than another, is to develop a background to propose a multivariate cross-paradigmatic model of rivalry—discussed at length in Chapter 3—and lay the foundation of the India-Pakistan case on it. To begin this exercise, let us consider the dominant paradigm of IR, realism, first.

Realism

The philosophical origin of the realist theories—classical, structural/defensive, offensive, and neoclassical—draws on the Hobbesian view of the "state of nature" that exists in absence of a sovereign authority (Hobbes [1651] 1951).[4] Though these are systemic theories and most effective in dealing with the system structures or problems, they are also relevant to understand the dynamics of conflictual dyads. The emphasis of classical realism is on the role of "power" and "human nature"—as a source of aggressive behavior, conflict, and war. It asserts that to maintain peace in the system or subsystems, a relative equality in power among states or alliance blocs is essential because it prevents any single state or bloc from emerging as hegemon (Carr 1940; Morgenthau [1967] 2001). In his classic study, *Man, the State, and War*, Kenneth Waltz (1959) outlined a three-image organization of international relations: the first image stresses the role of individual decision-makers (*human nature*), the second image focuses on the causal developments at the level of domestic politics or socio-economic systems (*the state*), and the third image explains the nature of the international system (*anarchy*). He argues that the third image, the anarchic nature of the international system and the endless competition for power and security, is the major cause of the outbreak of war:

> The third image describes the framework of world politics, but without the first and second images there can be no knowledge of the forces that determine policy; the first and second images describe the forces in world politics, but without the third image it is impossible to assess their importance or predict their results. (Waltz 1959: 238)

Therefore, according to Waltz, "there is a constant possibility of war in a world in which there are two or more states each seeking to promote a set of interests and having no agency above them upon which they can rely for protection" (1959: 227). Against this backdrop, Waltz gives importance to the possession of military power that generally draws states into a "security dilemma" in which one state's security enhancement ends up in security reduction of the other (see Jervis 1976). Instead of maximizing power and security, as Waltz (1959, 1979) and John Mearsheimer (2001) contend, the realist practice mostly "constructs a zero-sum world" that makes the international system vulnerable (Vasquez 1993: 118).[5]

Some scholars argue that "history is much more open and radically indeterminate than is being supposed" by the realists "as a struggle for power" (Vasquez 2004: 195). What Waltzian neorealism sees as structural and eternal is actually a social construction, argues Alexander Wendt (1987, 1999). "The term 'anarchy,'" Wendt argues, "itself makes clear why this must be so: it refers to an absence ('without rule'), not a presence; it tells us what there is not, not what there is. It is an empty vessel, without intrinsic meaning. What gives anarchy meaning are the kinds of people who live there and the structure of their relationships" (1999: 308–9). From another standpoint, as Vasquez argues, "power politics behavior is a series of steps to war, not to peace. It is one of the great contradictions of the history of the modern global system that while the theory of power politics has been offered as the only realistic path to attain and secure peace, the practices of power politics have been associated with the outbreak of war" (1993: 86). In this dominant state-centric concept, Jack Levy and William Thompson note, the weakness lies in "the limited variation in anarchy across time and across international systems, and hence its inability to explain the enormous variation in war and peace over time and space" (2010: 32). Likewise, Kal Holsti questions the realist explanation of international politics:

> If war is rooted in a Hobbesian psychology, why has Sweden not been involved in a war since 1721? . . . [I]f anarchy (the main system characteristic) remains the most important permissive cause of war, then why do we find war-free regions such as South America, North America, and Western Europe? (2009: 371)

Apart from these shortcomings, Waltzian neorealism takes only major powers into consideration and ties minor powers' relations to their actions. Though a majority in the field affirm that the Waltzian thesis—which defines the structure of the international system in terms of three characteristics: anarchy, functional homogeneity of units, and the distribution of capabilities (Waltz 1979: 79–101)—has profound strength to offer explanation of conflicts across the system, it faces shortcomings in explaining the dyadic contentions among minor powers which are largely steered by their internal settings rather than exclusively shaped by the external conditions and anarchical environment as Waltz suggests. This draws our attention to the fact that a significant number of interstate conflicts are not shaped or driven by those conditions that Waltzian neorealism projects with certainty.[6] Some scholars argue that realism has limitations for explaining the occurrence of war in bipolar and multipolar settings (Copeland 2000; Vasquez 1993, 2004). For example, Vasquez maintains that

> [realism] does not provide an accurate explanation of the causes of war and of peace because the consequences it predicts for its policies do not occur. The scientific inaccuracy of realism is evident in the fact that the practices it recommends for dealing with a war-threatening situation do not lead to peace but to war; indeed they often increase the prospect of war. This indicates that the underlying theory of war and peace from which these practices are derived is flawed. (1993: 89)

To enhance security in the nuclearized world, Waltz (1981) contends that the prospects of peace may increase if "more" states will acquire nuclear weapons—Bruce Bueno de Mesquita and William Riker's (1982) Correlates of War (COW) data-based study (1945–1976) also maintains that a system where all states possess nuclear weapons may be less dangerous than a system with partial possession. Here realism faces a fundamental problem because, as Rajesh Basrur notes, "nuclear weapons raise serious objections to the central concept of power. If nuclear war is not a viable option, then what does power mean?" (2008: 6). This puzzle brings realism to the crossroads: "At one extreme," as Patrick Jackson and Daniel Nexon observe, "lies the claim that anarchy produces a certain logic approximating a natural necessity; at the other, the denial that there is anything natural or necessary about claims associated with anarchy" (2009: 924).

Further, to "assay" more about the nature, logic, and cause of rivalries, such as the Indo-Pakistani and the Israeli-Palestinian, the neorealist propositions may be examined by employing Carl von Clausewitz's understanding that "theory must constantly pass the test of reality" (quoted in Paret 1992:

103). By following Clausewitz, I find Karl Popper's (2002) falsification method—for instance, the universality of a conjecture that "*all* swans are white"—as a starting point to highlight the limitations of structural theories like realism (and others),[7] especially in the Indo-Pakistani context. However, Waltz (2003b) disapproves such falsification methods to evaluate theories. To test theories, he argues, one should take "hard cases" which are capable of confounding the existing confirmations. Given its unique ability to survive and contradict key realist propositions, in my view, the India-Pakistan rivalry does qualify under this criterion, for four reasons.

First, the realists posit that long-term power conflict between asymmetric competitors is quite unlikely, as the weak side cannot withstand the powerful adversary for long with wide capability differences. Therefore, the likelihood of such conflicts transitioning into protracted conflicts/rivalries is minimal or most unlikely. But the Indo-Pakistani asymmetric conflict, a hard case, challenges the realist conformations as some of its key propositions even fail to pinpoint what drives this mismatched dyadic conflict, particularly when India holds a more than six-fold capability edge against Pakistan (see *Military Balance* 2022). As a result of imbalance in the dyadic power capability, the realist proposals suggest, India should have been the instigator of war or disputes against the weaker adversary, Pakistan, to settle its unresolved issues. However, the case is otherwise. Despite India's greater power, Pakistan has not only successfully maintained the rivalry since its inception but is also responsible for three of four major wars and a majority of the militarized disputes with its superior rival (see Tables 4.1, 5.1, 6.1, and 7.1). Against this setting, this book contends that though the realist paradigm does provide limited insights to the development of India-Pakistan rivalry, it fails to explain why Pakistan frequently aims for objectives far in excess of what its limited capabilities permit. In simple words, why is this asymmetric conflict prolonging? It seems by overemphasizing the role of asymmetric factors and undermining the role of those factors outside its domain, mainly those that constitute the liberal and the constructivist paradigms, the realist paradigm is not able to fully grasp what drives this asymmetric conflict ceaselessly.

Second, the main focus of the realist paradigm is on "power" (Mearsheimer 2001; Morgenthau [1967] 2001; Waltz 1979). However, the nuclearization of South Asia handicaps the realist "power" concept in two ways: first, if nuclear weapons make war obsolete, then the key variables on which the conception of "power" rests become meaningless; and second, in a hypothetical case, if a nuclear war broke out, would "power" favor the stronger nuclear state against the weak nuclear adversary? Mearsheimer's (2001) offensive realism, which shares insight with A.F.K. Organski's (1958) hegemonic power transition theory, contends that maximizing power is the best means to increase security, that is, by achieving hegemony. Mearsheimer's argument again has limitations: first, it argues for a few states which are *capable to attain hegemony* in the system, thus it has a motivated bias; and second, attaining absolute security is almost impossible. Moreover, the logic of power maximization, based on the worst-case assessments, might have relevance against non-nuclear weak states, but its chance to hold correct against nuclear powers is questionable. Against this backdrop, the activation of offensive realism under the protective shield of nuclear weapons against even a weak nuclear state might provoke the weaker state to initiate a pre-emptive strike against the stronger nuclear rival, thereby upending the latter's security maximization efforts and rendering it insecure (by losing valuable assets or experiencing immense destruction)—a concern also shared by defensive realists. In short, the very centrality of "power" to attain stability in the realist paradigm has pushed it to a state of *self-denial*.

Third, the realist framework ignores the role of domestic politics and other internal processes in shaping the course of interstate conflicts or rivalries, instead emphasizing anarchy and the distribution of capabilities as an ordering principle in the international system. On this basis, only external developments decide the fate of states as they compel states to struggle persistently to acquire more power in the anarchic system (or subsystems) (Waltz 1979: 65–72). Looking at the pattern of power distribution in South Asia, it is evident that the region is marred with unresolved conflicts and recurrent militarized disputes despite having an established hegemonic order. The Indo-Pakistani intractable conflict over the unresolved ethno-territorial Kashmir dispute is a case in point. Surprisingly, the realists offer no coherent answer to this puzzle, particularly about its resolution, but they firmly advocate the practices of power politics to handle it. Actually, the Kashmir dispute comprises multiple factors that range from domestic/internal settings to external factors; thus, ignoring any factor or any aspect of these factors leads to a distorted understanding of this dispute and the India-Pakistan rivalry. In this respect, a multivariate framework based on the realist power distribution and liberal and constructivist notions holds better explanatory power to understand and explain these aspects of this rivalry.

Fourth, the realist paradigm assumes that non-major states have mini-

mal impact on the international system because of their weak status. "The
fates of all the states . . . in a system are affected much more by the acts and
the interactions of the major ones than of the minor ones," writes Waltz
(1979: 72). In contrast, India's and Pakistan's patterns of militarized
behavior—conventional, subconventional, and nuclear—underscore their
capability to disturb or destabilize the regional or systemic balance; hence
there is no compelling basis for believing that non-major states' acts and
interactions have no system-transforming potential or consequences (see
Batcher 2004; Toon et al. 2019).

Since 1998, the overt nuclearization of South Asia has vested the two
non-major states with such destructive capability that the survival of many
states hinges on their actions—reports suggest that Pakistan's rapidly
expanding nuclear arsenal might assist it to become "the world's fifth-largest
nuclear weapon state" within a decade or so (see Kristensen, Norris, & Diamond 2018: 348). Over a century ago, long before the discovery of nuclear
weapons, Rabindranath Tagore, an Indian philosopher, forewarned the policy makers of major states about the emergence of such a situation in the
near future. He said, "[T]imes of trouble are sure to come to all nations when
the weak can bring fatal disaster to the stronger," especially through their
"endless bullfight" (quoted in Guha 2009: xlii; Tagore [1917] 2009: 53). Since
1990, consistent with the Tagorian and contrary to the Waltzian thesis, the
eruption of armed crises between India and Pakistan in the shadow of
nuclear weapons underscores their potential to destabilize the regional and
global balance. During the Kargil War, for the first time after the Cuban Missile Crisis, the world came close to a cataclysmic situation when India and
Pakistan had readied "their nuclear arsenals for possible deployment" (Riedel 2002: 8; see Chengappa 2000: 437; V. Malik 2006: 259–60; Talbott 2004:
161–62). Had it taken a nuclear turn, the situation of South Asia, and beyond,
certainly would have been far more disastrous than the Hiroshima-Nagasaki
tragedy of World War II.[8]

Moving backwards, during the Bangladesh War of 1971, long before the
nuclearization of South Asia, India and Pakistan's bullfight had almost
drawn the two superpowers into a large-scale clash (see Kissinger 1979: 900–
901). On a similar note, Michael Brecher's empirical study also questions, if
not falsifies, Waltzian understanding by establishing that the Bangladesh
War had a major impact on the regional subsystem and the international
system (2008: 194–95).[9] Apart from this, the devastating defeat and disintegration of Pakistan, which led to the formation of Bangladesh, altered the US

hold over the South and Southeast Asian regions as it lost a geopolitical and strategic edge against its archrival: the Soviet Union.[10] This shows how the armed interactions of two non-major states, India and Pakistan, question the validity of the realist argument.

In brief, it can be argued that a considerable part of realist propositions do not fully grasp the nature, gravity, and path of the India-Pakistan rivalry. In other words, a "hard" and "highly complex" India-Pakistan case goes against the underlying tenets of realism.

Power Transition Theory

Organski's (1958) *power transition theory* is a hegemonic realist theory but it is quite the opposite of its realist counterpart *balance of power* (e.g., Claude 1962; Waltz 1979; Wright 1964). Both theories revolve around a central proposition: whether the condition of power equality increases or decreases the peace in the system. The power transition theory posits that the dominant power, the most powerful state, creates and maintains a structure—the status quo—through which it regulates international behavior to extend its own long-term interests. Generally, the weak powers ally with the leading state and receive economic and security benefits for being satisfied with the existing order. However, the system includes some dissatisfied states which are relatively weak to challenge the dominant state or waiting for a more opportune moment to thwart the status quo. The proponents of power transition theory question the utility and veracity of anarchy:

> Power transition sees the international order not as anarchical at all, but as hierarchically organized in a manner similar to the domestic political system. Actors accept their position in the international order and recognize influence based on differences in the power distribution among nations. This fundamentally different assumption separates power transition from preceding realist models. (Kugler & Organski 1989: 172)

The power transition theory posits that power preponderance has a higher likelihood to ensure peace in the system than does power parity. The probability of war is greater when the capability of a dissatisfied ascendant state roughly begins to match the dominant state in the system. Dissatisfaction with the existing order motivates the rising challenger to restructure the system in accordance with its interests; thus the challenger initiates war or major crises of far-reaching consequences (Gilpin 1981; Organski 1958; Organski & Kugler 1980; Thompson 1988). Precisely for this reason, contrary to the balance of power theory, the proponents of power transition theory argue that "the ultimate basis of power is the demographic potential of a state" (Lemke 2002: 26). However, Brecher's (2008: 268–69) study compares the power transition and balance of power hypotheses and finds that the balance of power–based structure is "the least unstable" and the power transition–based structure is "the least stable."[11] On the other hand, Daniel Geller's (1993) findings emphasize that unstable power parity (in terms of military capability) is almost twice as likely to be associated with war as unstable power preponderance.

A careful study of the history of interstate conflicts also shows a deadlock between parity/war and imbalance/war hypotheses as they support and reject both almost in equal measure. For example, the power transition between the United States and Britain occurred peacefully in the beginning of the twentieth century. Britain did not resist. Similarly, Vasquez notes, Russia surpassed France at the end of 1890 and instead of war they formed an alliance (1993: 102). Dale Copeland's (2000) analysis depicts another grim picture of power transition. He argues that out of six major wars from 1600 to 1945, the power transition hypothesis failed five times (Copeland 2000; for a detailed criticism, see Vasquez 1993: 103–5). Similarly, the balance of power theory failed to explain why World War I occurred when the two opposing alliances were roughly equal. Additionally, it fails to answer a two-and-a-half-millennia-old Greek puzzle: why Sparta and Athens fought the Peloponnesian War when they were roughly equal (for detailed criticism see Bremer 1992; Garnham 1976; Geller 1993, 2000; Geller & Singer 1998; Mihalka 1976). In short, as for other realist theories, a major limitation of the power transition theory is that it needs a pre-existing condition, that is, an existing rivalry, to predict the outcome of war. From these examples, it is clear that where the balance of power theory holds correct, the power transition encounters problems, and vice versa.[12]

Though the power transition theory is considered a systemic theory, Douglas Lemke (2002) has applied it in the regional sub-systems, which he calls "local hierarchy" or "local status quo." According to Lemke (2002), those regions dominated by single predominant powers tend to be more stable and peaceful in comparison to those that include several nearly equal powers. The preponderant state's capability and superiority in the local hierarchy discourages relatively inferior local challenger(s) from resorting to aggression or any such move which has potential to reverse the status quo. In this sense, the power transition theory can operate between two states at the dyadic and regional levels and explain a given rivalry's potential transition or rate of change.

Upon its application in the South Asian region, the power transition propositions face issues with regard to the Indo-Pakistani rivalry. First, Pakistan has never attained even a rough equality against India throughout its lifetime but it initiated three wars and more than three-fourths of the total militarized disputes that occurred between the two states (see Tables 4.1, 5.1, 6.1, and 7.1).[13] Second, India's dominant power status in its local hierarchy (South Asia) does not help it to enforce, if not institute, peace in the region. Third, the power transition theory predicts that the stronger state wins the war; thus the weak states refrain from initiating one until they attain a rough parity against the dominant rival. But this proposition is not consistent with the case of Indo-Pakistani rivalry as Pakistan's acts have contradicted this proposition thrice against its stronger rival. Fourth, some scholars argue that by acquiring nuclear capability in 1998, Pakistan has attained parity against India and that is why it initiated the Kargil War.[14] If nuclear weapons have assisted Pakistan to attain power parity with its much bigger neighbor, India, then the power transition theory confronts a twofold problem: (1) How does it explain this dyad's pre-1998 rivalrous relationship that witnessed three wars—two initiated by Pakistan—and several armed disputes in the absence of nuclear weapons and under sheer military disparity? (2) Why does the revisionist nuclear Pakistan refrain from challenging the status quo opponent, India, in the post–Kargil War period? These puzzles can baffle the proponents of power transition theory (as well as the proponents of balance of power and nuclear deterrence). From this discussion, it may be surmised that most of the power transition claims confront difficulty in grasping the complexity of the India-Pakistan conflict.

However, the power transition hypothesis receives overall support in India-to-Pakistan relations, except in one instance.[15] As a dominant regional power, India is satisfied with the favorable status quo; thus it refrains from initiating wars. Additionally, this theory seems to have some validity in the post-Kargil period in terms of conventional aspects as India's steady growth in the economic, military, and political domains has left Pakistan far behind. However, a look at the issue from another view underscores that this observation may have limitations of its own because the post–Kargil War stability might be independent of those variables over which the power transition lays its claim, or other conditions might be in action for such relative *stability*: (1) Pakistan's engagement in the Af-Pak region against the terrorist outfits and its collaboration with China with regard to the China-Pakistan Economic Corridor (CPEC), both of which have significantly engaged it and diverted its attention away from Kashmir; (2) its internal political discord and economic turmoil; and (3) the United States' and international organizations' consistent pressure, as well as other conditions. These conditions seem to have had a considerable impact on Pakistan's post-9/11 revisionist policy—particularly after the initiation of the US-led global war against terrorism, which diverted Pakistan's resources and attention away from Kashmir by engaging it in unstable border areas of the Af-Pak region—rather than the narrative offered by the power transition paradigm, India's consistent economic growth and power capabilities have scaled up its dominance against Pakistan at the dyadic and regional level.

Deterrence

The theory of deterrence posits that relative power equality between states facilitates deterrence; the possession of significant military capabilities establishes peace by increasing the costs and risks of aggression (Jervis 1976).[16] In other words, "wars occur when deterrence fails—when one side either lacks the military capabilities to threaten a sufficiently costly response to aggression, or when its threat lacks credibility" (Levy & Thompson 2010: 30). The focus of this theory is on explaining deterrence failure or success (that is, war or no-war) during the eruption of a dyadic conflict rather than on "what happens after deterrence," which places it in the group of event theories (Diehl & Goertz 2000: 79).[17] To attain peace, the proponents of deterrence argue that states must not appease or encourage the aggressor and must remain prepared for war by employing coercive strategies and engaging in military buildups. In the backdrop of hard power projection, it is important to understand why general optimism toward nuclear deterrence is problematic. Nuclear deterrence is a theory of war prevention and not one that offers viable conditions for enduring peace, but this aspect has gotten limited attention in the literature. By relying on the logic of credible threats of massive destruction, the theory of nuclear deterrence largely confines itself to war prevention scenarios and emphasizes establishing peace by increasing nuclear stockpiles and relying on the ultimate firepower or terror of nuclear weapons.

For the nuclear deterrence theorist, the state of absence of war is "peace" and nuclear weapons' massive destructive capability ensures such a peace in the anarchic international system. But to maintain such an absence in inter-state relations or at the dyadic level, the nuclear-armed states have to continuously balance each other's capabilities, which ironically does not allow the weaker side to surrender any earlier than it otherwise might have done—Pakistan against India is a case in point. The phenomenon of balancing capabilities immunizes the parties by preparing them to absorb more damage before they can be forced to give up. Additionally, while stressing the war prevention aspect, nuclear optimists are silent on the state and durability of peace resulting from *effective* nuclear deterrence. Mere war prevention cannot be considered a sufficient condition to attain peace, so the plausibility of nuclear deterrence as a comprehensive theory might remain under scrutiny until it explains both war and peace—more specifically, peace not as a reflex scenario of war threats—and helps us understand the non-Western cases without replicating or imposing the Cold War experiences. For such reasons, and others associated with the notions of nuclear deterrence and postures, Lawrence Freedman questions the validity of the widely propagated nuclear deterrence theory and nuclearized stability in the present times:

> We need to think about the meaning of stability when there is mutual danger but not assured destruction, when the small arsenals are more in play than the large, and when the underlying political relations are in a constant state of flux and the potential for miscommunication is high. Regional actors do not naturally take their cues from the erstwhile great powers, and they expect proposals for any new order to speak to their distinctive cultures and traditions. This is why we need a new theory. (Freedman 2009: 29)

However, apart from reputational apprehensions, it is correct that nuclear weapons' destructive power and their catastrophic impact on human civilization have compelled the nuclear states to respect and preserve the tradition of nuclear non-use in the anarchic world (see Tannenwald 2007; Paul 2009), but sustaining the tradition in the volatile South Asian region remains doubtful in light of both second-generation nuclear states' contentious political behavior and threatening nuclear postures that include India's punitive limited war strategy—the "Cold Start"—and Pakistan's counter-measure of maintaining a "full-spectrum deterrence" capability. In this context, the February 2019 cross-border retaliatory air strikes confirm that the two nuclear-armed states are not hesitant to cross what nuclear optimists generally recognize as "red lines," which further casts doubt on whether India and Pakistan would be able to honor the tradition of nuclear non-use in a future crisis or war.[18] Such risky and unprecedented behavior makes this dyad an outlier case to re-examine the notions associated with nuclear deterrence or optimism with regard to nuclear states' rational behavior under the protective shield of nuclear weapons. Given the operational limitations and nuclear behavior of India and Pakistan, it is fallacious to claim that (1) nuclear weapons enhance regional (or global) security; (2) nuclear-armed states' existent nuclear postures increase stability; and (3) nuclear weapon states will be more cautious in their interactions and will never engage in war (see Narang 2013; Vanaik 2015).

From the context of rivalry approach, the deterrence theory confronts six issues. First, its arguments are heavily dependent on the capabilities of the defender state. Second, it has limitations in explaining why weak states initiate wars against powerful defenders (Paul 1994). Third, successful deterrence has a tendency to prolong the rivalry; thus it inhibits the prospects of conflict resolution (George & Smoke 1989). Fourth, on the pretext of enhancing security, it contributes to the stability of rivalry in both ways: through war avoidance and peace avoidance. Fifth, the militarized dispute is a given condition in deterrence theory; thus it starts in the middle (that is, during the maturity of a rivalry) by skipping the important phase of rivalry initiation. And sixth, the deterrence studies fail to provide a comprehensive framework to explain the impact of past interactions on adversaries' present or future relationship (Diehl & Goertz 2000). In sum, the major limitation of nuclear deterrence, as a war prevention theory, is that by avoiding war it does not institute peace. Additionally, though deterrence might institute temporary peace by promoting and activating coercive strategies, which generally compel rivals to remain ready for any eventuality, deterrence cannot avoid war or crisis threat. Hence, it strengthens the cycle of rivalry preservation or stabilization. These drawbacks underline how deterrence theory ignores other aspects of interstate conflicts, for instance, the causes of recurring militarized disputes and the beginning and termination of dyadic conflicts. To overcome these limitations, particularly in the India-Pakistan case, a rivalry-based framework is useful because deterrence works differently in the context of rivalry, and the rivalry-based framework provides sufficient room to raise and examine a new set of questions which is not possible within the deterrence framework.

Constructivism

Since Waltz's publication of *Theory of International Politics*, no theory wrestled with the Waltzian realism as efficiently as the constructivist theory did, particularly Wendt's (1999) *Social Theory of International Politics*. Wendt writes that realists are of "the view that the culture of international life does not depend on what states do, and IR scholars should therefore take that culture as given—reify it—and focus on helping states do the best that they can within it" (1999: 377). In contrast, he argues, "anarchic systems have no structure or logic, but rather that these are a function of social structures, not anarchy. Anarchy is a nothing, and nothings cannot be structures," thus "there is no such thing as a 'logic of anarchy'" (Wendt 1999: 309, 247). Putting it differently, Wendt (1992) argues that "anarchy is what states make of it." In other words, he implies that what neorealists see as structural and eternal is in reality a social construction, that is, state interactions, that decides what kind of system should prevail and not vice versa—as Waltzian realism maintains. He criticizes the realist theory for the dubious and status quo-ist nature of realism:

> The kind of knowledge produced by [realism] is useful for solving problems within the existing system, but not for changing the system itself. The result is that problem-solving theory has the practical effect in the real world of helping to reproduce the status quo, and in this way Realism, despite its claim of objectivity, becomes a normative as well as scientific theory. (Wendt 1999: 377)

Wendt argues that anarchy can have at least three types of structures, which dominate the system on the basis of "three cultures of anarchy"— enmity, rivalry, and friendship—that depict variations in the structure of anarchy between states' relationships. To understand the India-Pakistan case, Wendt's characterization of "three cultures of anarchy"—the Kantian culture of friendship; the Lockean culture of rivalry; and the Hobbesian culture of enmity—has potential to explain this conflict systematically. The Hobbesian culture is based on Hobbes's principle of "the war of all against all," under which the use of violence has no limitation. It emphasizes that the international system is anarchic where all states struggle to maximize their security (by arming against one another) on the basis of preconceived images of mutual enmity. The Lockean culture recognizes the sovereignty of "other," and in doing so, it curtails the Hobbesian culture (that the fittest survives and thrives in the system). Though the use of violence is considered under the Lockean culture to advance a particular objective or interest, it moves away from the Hobbesian practice of kill or be killed by recognizing competitors as "rivals." The Kantian culture advances the idea of formation of "security community," in which the use of violence vanishes while securing interests. Thus, on the basis of shared knowledge and without resorting to military power, mutual security and coexistence is the highest aim of this culture.

It seems that the Wendtian logic, "anarchy is what states make of it," has relevance to understand the India-Pakistan conflict—as both countries share a common socio-political background which has a profound impact on the evolution of their post-partition political behavior and policies. The structural variations in their anarchic culture have shaped their bilateral relationship differently. Against this setting, the two states' armed coexistence and violent relationship can be explained effectively by employing Wendt's three cultures of anarchy—which contends that "the high death rate of the Hobbesian culture creates incentives to create a Lockean culture, and the continuing violence of the latter, particularly as the forces of destruction improve in response to its competitive logic, creates incentives in turn to move to a Kantian culture" (Wendt 1999: 311). "Once a Lockean culture has been internalized," claims Wendt, "there is little chance of it degenerating into a Hobbesian one, and similarly for a Kantian into a Lockean" (1999: 312).

In the India-Pakistan case, Duncan McLeod (2008) and Shibashis Chatterjee (2008) have applied Wendt's constructivist approach. McLeod notes that despite "theological differences," a Kantian logic of friendship existed between different religious communities during the pre-colonial and colonial periods in the Indian subcontinent (2008: 29). But the imperialist European powers had disturbed this "socio-cultural phenomenon" by politicizing the subcontinent's culture, that is, by introducing liberal institutions and separating religion from the polity, which was not conducive to the diverse pasts and practices of different religious communities of the subcontinent (McLeod 2008: 33). Consequently, the liberal polity communalized the two majority communities—the Hindus and the Muslims—by promoting ideological differences through the Indian National Congress and the Muslim League. Finally, it tore down the Kantian friendship by pushing the subcontinent to a Lockean rivalry. Later, based on the colonial period's ideological differences, it promoted and justified the partition of unified India and the foundation of two sovereign states, India and Pakistan. This way both India and Pakistan entered into a Lockean rivalry after their independence and subsequently fought the wars of 1947–48 and 1965 over the future status of Kashmir, a Westphalian reality. During the 1971 war, the two adversaries made a clear departure from the Lockean rivalry by moving from the "status quo to a Hobbesian position of kill or be killed" over East Pakistan (McLeod 2008: 101). Subsequent to the 1971 war, the Hobbesian position further consolidated under the nuclear shield, as this dyad has not taken necessary initiatives to attach meaning to nuclear deterrence and limit the nuclear threat as the superpowers had during the Cold War. That is why both are locked in a Hobbesian anarchy.

Likewise, Chatterjee writes that "the India-Pakistan conflict runs much deeper as it is about their mutually invalidating claims of what constitutes nationhood that put them on contradictory trajectories, which makes their biographies antithetical," and "rules out sympathetic understanding of each other's positions, constraints, commitment and problems" (2008: 192). Against this backdrop, the two states' hostile relationship "is neither historical nor predetermined" but a product of presupposed beliefs and images of one another that determines their policies and constructs their social relationship (Chatterjee 2008: 192). The post-colonial formation of nation-states, Chatterjee maintains, created a wedge between the Hindu and the Muslim communities of undivided India by building their state identities on territorial paradox, a Westphalian reality, which is sustaining their conflict despite their shared culture, tradition, ethnicity, and the like. Thus the realist notions of material capabilities (symmetric/asymmetric), argues Chatterjee, are not real factors that drive this conflict.

Taking all the assumptions together, the Wendtian constructivism put forward a strong case which has potential to explain the India-Pakistan conflict more fully. Though constructivism accurately explains the genesis of the Indo-Pakistani conflictual relationship through the Kantian and the Lockean cultures, it confronts a serious problem in the Hobbesian culture. Under the shadow of nuclear weapons, the Wendtian understanding emphasizes that the two South Asian adversaries are locked in a Hobbesian anarchy and have adopted "a kill or be killed" position against each other. In other words, Wendt means that once the Hobbesian anarchy is socially formed or internalized, the rival states generally start behaving in such a manner that the resulting interactions compel them to act as existential threats to each other. From this standpoint, under the Hobbesian anarchy, India and Pakistan are doing exactly the same by maximizing their nuclear and missile capabilities to harm each other.

However, it is noteworthy that constructivism encounters difficulty to explain why nuclear India and Pakistan are avoiding war(s) after adopting the Hobbesian culture and not pursuing "war" as a strategy to end their conflict once and for all. In short, why did more opportune events under the Hobbesian anarchy—the Brasstacks crisis of 1986–87, the Kargil War of 1999, the twin armed standoff of 2001–2, the 2008 Mumbai terrorist attacks, and the 2019 post-Pulwama military standoff—fail to facilitate or convince both states to adopt "killing" strategy? Do unimaginable consequences of nuclear destruction, one of the important realist propositions, pose a serious challenge to the constructivist understanding, or is it something else? To break this deadlock and overcome its limitation with regard to the current state of India-Pakistan rivalry, the constructivist paradigm has to explain more.

The short theoretical survey undertaken above shows that all the leading IR paradigms have something to say about interstate rivalries; however, despite their strengths and established position in the field, each has limitations for offering a comprehensive explanation of the India-Pakistan rivalry. In general, most of the IR paradigms provide event-driven explanations, as they ignore some essential aspects of the interstate behavior and treat each conflict (or war) as a "war" or "no-war" event; this leads them to explain the occurrence and sustenance of rivalries in intervals. On the other hand, the rivalry approach—as a process theory—overcomes these limitations by identifying and knitting together all "war" and "no-war" events, which provides adequate support for investigation and generalization of interstate rivalries. For this reason, relying on a single IR paradigm does not bring to light processes and relationships that deserve intensive investigation for a comprehensive explanation of hard cases like the India-Pakistan rivalry.

To overcome the shortcomings of the leading IR paradigms and the area studies scholarship (which is also largely event driven), a multivariate cross-paradigmatic approach is required to develop an effective analytical framework which would provide an appropriate and logical structure as well as guide the research strategy to probe the causes of rivalry in depth and more fully. The rivalry approach not only enables this study to raise new questions and develop a number of possible explanations about the India-Pakistan conflict, but also provides an opening to consider the issues of peace and conflict resolution—an area rarely explored in the literature on the subject. More precisely, it enables the study to refine/refute key generalizations and generate new and different knowledge about the India-Pakistan rivalry. It also provides a window for value addition in the field by rendering contextual space to develop a multivariate model, an exercise undertaken in Chapter 3, which has potential to cut across the paradigmatic barriers and establish generalizations about the wider population of rivalries to which the case of India-Pakistan belongs. Against this background, I adopt the rivalry approach as a multivariate pathway to provide a basis to understand how different aspects of the India-Pakistan rivalry have assumed meaning and how the two adversaries have evolved their policy responses in due course. With regard to this, a systematic and elaborative exercise has been carried out in Chapters 2 and 3.

ORGANIZATION OF THE BOOK

This book starts with an introduction to the topic. After deploying the argument of the study, it provides a brief critique of the leading IR paradigms and highlights their limitations with regard to the India-Pakistan case. Chapter 2 provides an in-depth and extensive review of the rivalry conception. Rather than focusing on rare events such as wars, the chapter seeks to understand the dynamics of most dangerous dyads of interstate conflict by categorizing eight different rivalry models in three separate schools. In doing so, it examines how the emerging subfield of interstate rivalries challenges the event-driven research by establishing that the "conflict events" between the states are not independent of one another; they are in fact interlinked over time and space. Explicitly, the rivalry approach, as a process theory, establishes an explanatory path to rivalry onset, development, and termination.

Chapter 3 proposes a "hub-and-spokes"–based "complex rivalry" model by adopting a framework underpinned by the conception of rivalry. This model shows how the interplay and fusion of three structural factors—ideology, territorial salience, and geographical contiguity—give rise to a situation that forms a "hub," which influences the peripheral temporal factors (the "spokes") and vice versa. Such a situation evolves an interactive bilateral mechanism that can be better interpreted through a hub-and-spokes framework. By situating the India-Pakistan relations in this framework, the complex rivalry model shows how consistent interactions between the hub and the spokes brought in centripetal and centrifugal stress on the dyad by unfolding a process of change—that is, the gradual augmentation in hostility and accumulation of grievances—which eventually locked the two feuding states into a long-standing rivalry.

Chapter 4 operationalizes the complex rivalry model in practice to (1) understand if territorial salience and geographical contiguity have had any effect on the origins of the India-Pakistan rivalry and (2) identify how the international strategic factors, differing regime types, and domestic politics brought adversaries closer to the recognition of a long-term rivalry. It shows that ideology, territorial salience, and geographical contiguity have indeed played a crucial role to form one of the most complex and dangerous rivalries since the end of World War II, but to claim that ideology was the sole guiding force to initiate the India-Pakistan rivalry, without taking into account the pivotal role of territorial salience and geographical contiguity, probably does not hold. After the partition of India, it explains, the presence or absence of the structural factors have had a profound impact on India's and Pakistan's decision-making, mainly in terms of whether to escalate or de-escalate their armed contention over Junagadh, Kashmir, and Hyderabad. Further, it shows how the structural factors played a key role to influence the peripheral temporal factors in the early phase of the conflict and collectively moved the cartwheel of India-Pakistan rivalry. Due to a weaker hub, particularly non-existent geographical contiguity, Pakistan was unable to challenge India militarily over Junagadh and Hyderabad. In contrast, Kashmir's compatibility with the hub-and-spokes framework not only motivated the Pakistani leadership to engage India militarily but also made the newly formed country a revisionist party in a very short period, from 1947 to 1958.

Chapter 5 analyzes the period of intense rivalry from 1959 to 1972 and explains how the specific effects of past interactions have regulated India's and Pakistan's actions. It describes how the First Kashmir War did not meet India's and Pakistan's definitive aims and how this stalemate led both sides to engage in more militarized disputes in the succeeding years. Repeated confrontations also failed to resolve Kashmir to either side's satisfaction as the leadership on both sides was unwilling to make concessions on the territory in dispute—Kashmir—because of its intrinsic value and ideological-reputational concerns. These patterns of conflictual behavior, particularly the 1965 war, further contributed to deepening the rivalry between the two states. This chapter then describes how the development of an enemy image activated the domestic political scene on each side by attracting the attention and interest of important hardliners in the government, the political opposition, and the mass public. The restraining forces were not ready to accept their governments' conciliatory actions toward the rival, especially a negotiated compromise on Kashmir that would alter their national positions. In addition, the international strategic factors, different regime types, and domestic politics also began to affect the dynamics of the rivalry. Instead of assisting the rival parties to reach a negotiated resolution, the great powers have complicated the rivalry by providing Pakistan external support—especially in terms of weapons, finance, and diplomatic maneuverings—that reduced its recovery time from the previous defeats and prepared it for future armed challenges. As a result, the two adversaries increasingly pursued coercive policies rather than diplomatic means meant to manage or settle the rivalry. Consistent pursuit of the practices of power politics led India and Pakistan to confront each other repeatedly over Kashmir and fight a decisive war in 1971. Although the war tilted the regional power balance toward India, the end of the rivalry remained out of sight.

Chapter 6 describes how a relatively de-escalated rivalry, particularly after the disintegration of Pakistan in 1971, again escalated with the Soviet invasion of Afghanistan in 1979. In the aftermath of the Bangladesh War, though Pakistan did stop challenging India as its political leadership perceived conflict as a costly and inefficient activity against the strong rival, the compromised peace allowed it to focus on material capability while setting the home in order. From this standpoint, Pakistan's post-war commitment toward a peaceful bilateral relationship was clearly grounded on its immediate security concerns; once comparative advantages began to tilt toward it during the Afghanistan War (1979–89), Islamabad was no longer hesitant to revive its traditional revisionist policy and pursue military options against India to secure its political goals. In addition to Pakistan's qualitative muscle, its nuclear program and threatening military stance, which intensified the secessionist movement in the Indian Punjab, compelled New Delhi to employ aggressive policies to pressure Islamabad—for instance, the occupation of the Siachen Glacier and the initiation of the Brasstacks military exercise. The chapter explains how mutual adoption of tactics intended to coerce each other led the two states to follow a path of distrust and hostility, which considerably reversed the decade-long de-escalation and relative peace. Finally, Chapter 6 explores why the South Asian rivalry remained dormant during 1972–80 and why it began to escalate in the early 1980s and assumed a severe confrontational form thereafter.

Chapter 7 recounts how the systemic shift and favorable political conditions in Kashmir, coupled with the increasing nuclear stress, emboldened the Pakistani decision-makers to pursue the militaristic course to wrest Kashmir from India in the post–Cold War years. Findings of this chapter draw considerable support from internal and external shocks and the rivalry linkage propositions—particularly the global war against terrorism, the India-Pakistan rivalry in Afghanistan, and the impact of power capabilities on the structure of the rivalry. From the standpoint of the hub-and-spokes framework, it explains how the alignment of structural and temporal factors and their concerted interactions tilted the dyadic balance toward Pakistan in the early post–Cold War years and later, after the Kargil War, how the regional power positions reversed drastically with the temporal factors' stress on the structural factors. Two key changes explain this shift: (1) the global expansion of terrorism and the US-led reactive war against it, which collided with Pakistan's militaristic interests; and (2) India's stable polity and increasing economic integration with the objectives of globalization. These developments significantly influenced the great powers' viewpoint as well as their approach toward the Indo-Pakistani dyad, with the international community becoming more open to acknowledging and accommodating India's concerns, which eventually strengthened its position in the regional and extra-regional hierarchy. Though India's fast-growing capabilities and increasing international clout have pressured Pakistan to desist from frequent militaristic provocations in Kashmir, particularly from channeling a political-cum-armed movement, the prospects of rivalry transformation or termination are still bleak. While emphasizing this aspect, the chapter describes how the nuclear factor has transformed the South Asian rivalry by aiding Pakistan to exploit the nuclear threat to pressure India to negotiate over Kashmir.

Finally, the focus of Chapter 8 is on rivalry transformation and attaining stable peace. It analyzes whether any change in the internal and external dynamics is possible that could help create conducive conditions to transform or terminate the India-Pakistan rivalry. Using the hub-and-spokes framework, the chapter examines the relative position and interplay of select structural and temporal factors to see whether they provide any window of opportunity to reshape India-Pakistan relations in the near term. It underscores that the fundamental incompatibility between the adversaries' foreign and security policies, strategic postures, regional alignments, and political systems have a high likelihood to result in persistence of the India-Pakistan rivalry with few prospects for an early transformation or termination. To break this deadlock and mitigate their long-standing differences, it is proposed, the two adversaries must reframe their national priorities and goals so that the new situation or combinations of conditions would assist their policy makers to implement risky policies and make headway to a promising transformation. In the end, this chapter provides a detailed schema of rivalry transformation in three sequential phases, referred to as "steps to peace," which offer an in-depth explanation of how the Indo-Pakistani rivalry can be peacefully resolved and stable peace attained at the dyadic level.

CHAPTER 2

The Existing Conceptualizations of Rivalry

INTRODUCTION

Since the end of the Cold War, a subfield focusing on interstate rivalries has emerged as an important branch of study in IR. Rather focusing on rare events, such as war, this research program seeks to understand the dynamics of what many scholars perceive to be the most dangerous dyads of interstate conflict: *enduring rivalries*. The rivalry literature defines "enduring rivalries" as consistently frequent and highly hostile international armed conflicts between the same pair of states for an extended period of time (Bennett 1996; Diehl & Goertz 2000; Hensel 1999; Maoz & Mor 2002). This subfield challenges the event-driven research by establishing that "conflict events" between the states are not independent but interlinked over time and space. Rivalry approaches, as process theories, seek to explain the onset of rivalries, their development, and their eventual termination.

Scholars have studied a wide range of dyadic conflicts and offered different theoretical and empirical characterizations of interstate rivalries (Bennett 1996, 1997a, 1997b, 1998; Diehl & Goertz 2000; Goertz & Diehl 1992, 1993, 1995a, 1995b; Hensel 1999; Maoz & Mor 2002; Thompson 1995, 2001). In general, they argue that states develop differences as a result of their incompatible foreign policy goals and contested issues, and often their inability to resolve these differences leads them to engage in serious militarized interstate disputes (MIDs) which eventually lock them into severe and long-standing duels called enduring rivalries (Diehl & Goertz 2000; Goertz & Diehl 1992; Hensel 1999). "An enduring rivalry," Goertz and Diehl write, "is a hostile and competitive relationship in which each side views the other as posing a significant threat to its own interests. In such a relationship, rivals expect that disputes, crises and even war will continue into the future"

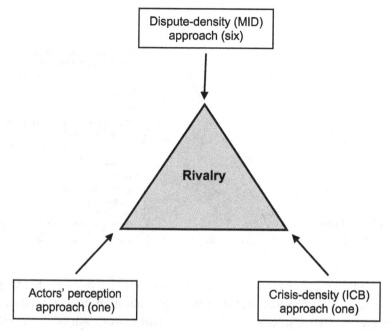

Figure 2.1. Rivalry identification: Three schools of rivalry approaches

(1995b: 299). Development of such a mistrusting, competitive, and hostile relationship further "sets the stage for escalating tensions in a dispute," which mostly "culminate in war" (Goertz 1994: 210).

Though the literature employs different methods to identify rivalries, there is considerable agreement over their characterization. To measure and conceptualize rivalries, the rivalry literature can be divided into three broad schools: (1) dispute density; (2) actors' perception; and (3) crisis density (see Figure 2.1). They differ in terms of identification, number of disputes, initiation and termination criteria, length, frequency, and severity of the rivalry. The six approaches based on density of disputes (specifically, MIDs) broadly identify rivalries as isolated-, proto-, and enduring rivalries (Bennett 1996, 1997a, 1997b, 1998; Diehl & Goertz 2000; Goertz & Diehl 1995a; Hensel 1999; Klein, Goertz, & Diehl 2006; Maoz & Mor 2002). A second school focuses on actors' perception and issue disagreement and identifies conflictual pairs as "strategic rivalries" (Colaresi, Rasler, & Thompson 2007; Thompson 1995, 2001). The crisis-density approach forms a third school and classifies rivalries by using the International Crisis Behavior (ICB) dataset (Hewitt 2005). Scholars associated with each of these schools and approaches have devel-

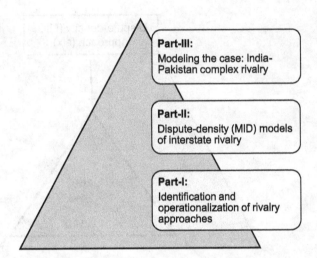

Figure 2.2. Pyramid
approach

oped unique sets of cases that support their own conception of rivalry. Therefore, their disagreement on rivalry identification, which requires a number of MIDs or international crises in a particular length of time or criteria involving the role of actors' perceptions and issues, makes the concept of "rivalry" a subject of considerable debate.

All rivalry approaches address various issues related to dyadic conflicts, such as how rivalries initiate (Diehl & Goertz 2000; Goertz & Diehl 1995a; Hensel 1999, 2001; Maoz & Mor 2002; Stinnett & Diehl 2001), how the future behavior of rivalries is affected by the outcomes of recurrent militarized disputes (Bennett 1996, 1997b, 1998; Leng 1983, 2000; Maoz & Mor 1998), how they terminate (Colaresi 2001; Diehl & Goertz 2000; Goertz & Diehl 1995a; Kydd 2000; Schultz 2005), and how similarities or differences in the regime characteristics affect the behavior of rivalries (Bennett 2006, 1997a; Colaresi, Rasler, & Thompson 2007; Conrad & Souva 2011; Hensel, Goertz, & Diehl 2000; Rasler & Thompson 2001; Russett & Oneal 2001).

As shown in Figure 2.2, I adopt a pyramid (bottom-up) approach to lay out the theoretical framework of this study in three parts. Part 1 deals with definitions and identifications of rivalry—enduring, strategic, and interstate—by delving into eight conceptualizations broadly divided into three schools, as mentioned above: dispute-density, actors' perception, and crisis-density (Bennett 1996, 1997a, 1997b, 1998; Colaresi, Rasler & Thompson 2007; Diehl & Goertz 2000; Goertz & Diehl 1995a; Hensel 1999; Hewitt

2005; Klein, Goertz, & Diehl 2006; Maoz & Mor 2002; Thompson 1995, 2001). Part 2 focuses only on two of six dispute-density (or MID-based) approaches, that is, the punctuated equilibrium and the evolutionary models. These models have been given priority over others to examine how much their "static" and "evolutionary" characteristics resonate with the background conditions of the case undertaken here, the India-Pakistan rivalry, which is dominated by misperceptions, hostility, and hatred with little cooperation. The objective of this study is to explore both models and examine their level of consistency and applicability, singular or amalgamated, with the India-Pakistan case so that a case-specific rivalry framework—in association with other conditions—can be developed to examine the full life cycle of the rivalry in question.

The next chapter develops an operational model called complex rivalry, which seeks to explain the dynamics of India-Pakistan rivalry, as part 3 of my approach. In short, the purpose of this chapter is primarily to lay down the foundation to develop a complex rivalry model.

COMPETING CONCEPTUALIZATIONS OF THE RIVALRY APPROACH

The rivalry literature follows different methods to identify rivals and interstate rivalries. As a logical corollary, there are various conceptual and working definitions of rivalries that yield different empirical results on account of different compilations of rivalry lists. Interestingly, the India-Pakistan rivalry figures in all with some variations in severity, frequency, and time span. Here, I review all eight rivalry approaches divided into three separate schools as shown in Figures 2.1 and 2.3.

The First School: Dispute-Density (MID) Approaches

One of the first attempts to define rivalry and offer a theoretical framework was made by Paul Diehl and Gary Goertz, who empirically compared several pairs of states engaged in dyadic contests at any time between 1816 and 1991 (Diehl & Goertz 2000; Goertz & Diehl 1992, 1993, 1995a). They classified severe dyads as *enduring* by focusing on how many disputes within a given time period are necessary to establish or operationalize a meaningful rivalry. Characterized as a dispute-density approach, enduring rivalry exclusively

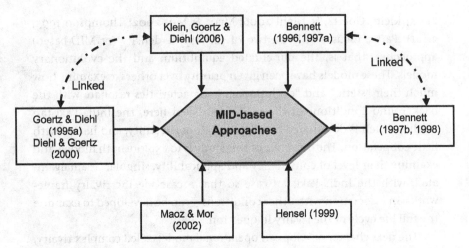

Figure 2.3. Dispute-density/MID–based approaches

relies on the repeated incidences of MIDs as listed in the COW database (Gochman & Maoz 1984; D. Jones, Bremer, & Singer 1996). The COW project defines MIDs as

> united historical cases of conflict in which the threat, display or use of military force short of war by one member state is explicitly directed towards the government, official representatives, official forces, property, or territory of another state. Disputes are composed of incidents that range in intensity from threats to use force to actual combat short of war. (D. Jones, Bremer, & Singer 1996: 163)

Goertz and Diehl argue that "rivalries can exist without an arms race, or a power transition, but they cannot exist without crises or disputes" (1995b: 305). By developing systematic procedures for identifying rivalries of varying durations and frequencies, they classify rivalries on a three-point ordinal scale: "isolated," "proto," and "enduring" (Diehl & Goertz 2000: 42–50). The rationale for this classification is mainly to distinguish severe long-term rivalries from those which are less conflictual or which fade out after initial armed disputes. The sporadic or isolated rivalries are those rival pairs that resort to one or two MIDs before fading out quickly in a few years. This category comprises 76 out of a total 1,166 rivalries examined in their study (Diehl & Goertz 2000). Pairs of states that experience two to four MIDs with a gap of no more than ten years between disputes are classified as proto-rivalries. They fall between isolated and enduring rivalries and comprise 19 percent of rivalries. Finally, enduring rivalries are those pairs which resort to five to six or more MIDs within twenty to twenty-five years. On the basis of this criterion, Diehl and Goertz (2000) have identified sixty-three enduring rivalries in the global arena. For Diehl and Goertz, a rivalry cannot be "enduring" until a set of states follow a consistent dispute-recurring behavior that prolongs their conflict for a long period. Thus, once feuding pairs build up or enter into enduring rivalry, their conflictual engagement lasts for decades.

Diehl and Goertz (2000) define rivalries in a post hoc manner in which earlier conflicts are considered as part of enduring rivalry if a particular pair engages for a long period of time. In other words, a rivalry begins with the occurrence of the first MID between adversaries. According to Goertz and Diehl, enduring rivalry comprises three conceptual components: (1) severity of competitiveness, that is, a minimum of at least six MID incidences; (2) time, that is, a minimum time frame of at least twenty or twenty-five years for dispute occurrence; and (3) spatial consistency, that is, no gaps in the rivalry longer than fifteen years (Diehl & Goertz 2000; Goertz & Diehl 1992, 1993). For an enduring rivalry to be considered terminated requires a minimum period of ten to fifteen years without any militarized dispute after the last dispute. Altogether, Goertz and Diehl define conflicts between the same pair of states that involve multiple militarized disputes, at least five to six, over a period of twenty years as enduring rivalries (see Table 2.1).

However, the timing of conflicts between rivals also plays a role in determining the initiation and termination dates of rivalries. In most MID-based formulations, the initiation date of the first MID in the sequence usually marks the initiation date for the rivalry. To identify a clear rivalry termination date is a challenging task because there is no distinct and clearly observable event that marks the end of rivalry and the beginning of peace between the rivals. Therefore, for rivalry termination, Diehl and Goertz require a long period of peace coupled with absence of a militarized conflict for ten to fifteen years (2000: 38, 46). To know about the exact timing of termination, they draw a parallel with a patient's cure from cancer. Precisely when a patient becomes free from cancer is uncertain because its complete termination is not observable; that is why the patient has to wait for a period of time, with sufficient evidence against symptoms, for the disease to be considered completely eliminated (Diehl & Goertz 2000: 46). Likewise, a fading-out period without new disputes is a prerequisite to determine the termination period of a given rivalry. Sometimes rivals sign a formal treaty to resolve their disputes, but rivalry may resume if they again resort to militarized disputes before the period stipulated for rivalry termination. Diehl and Goertz report that during 1816–1991 around 40 percent of militarized disputes and over half of interstate wars occurred within the context of enduring rivalry (2000: 61–64). They found that severe enduring rivalries are less than 3 percent of all rivalries, but they generate almost one-third of militarized disputes and carry a 59 percent chance of resorting to war during their rivalrous relations (Diehl & Goertz 2000: 60–62).

Diehl and Goertz's (2000) original dataset on international rivalries remains one of the best-known and most utilized measurements of rivalry and has been further reformed and updated by James Klein, Gary Goertz, and Paul Diehl (2006).[1] In this study, the conceptualization of rivalries is refined in two ways. First, the previous classification of rivalries—isolated, proto-, and enduring rivalries—have been re-conceptualized into two general categories of conflicts: "isolated conflicts" and "rivalries." They merged proto- and enduring rivalries into a single category, "rivalries," by ruling out their previous dispute-density criteria (that is, two to four MIDs in ten years for proto-rivalries, and more than five MIDs in twenty years for enduring rivalries). Furthermore, they maintain that isolated conflicts are of short duration since they die out after one or two MIDs and are, therefore, not rivalries at all (Klein, Goertz, & Diehl 2006: 333–34, 337). In the new conceptualization, a particular dyad needs a minimum threshold of three or more MIDs in order to be regarded as a rivalry over the entire period from 1816 to 2001. Since this conceptualization accommodates "shorter and longer rivalries and rivalries with more and fewer disputes," it generates a list of 290 rivalries (115 are enduring and 175 are proto-rivalries) (Klein, Goertz, & Diehl 2006: 340)—four and a half times larger than the previous list of 63 (Diehl & Goertz 2000).

A second essential feature of the new conceptualization is that it makes headway toward a qualitative approach by adopting a wider definition of rivalry which gives less importance to the timing and number of disputes by identifying rivalries based on the inter-relation of issues across recurring disputes. In addition, this formulation, unlike the actors' perception approach proposed by Michael Colaresi, Karen Rasler, and William Thompson (2007), stresses that rivalries can exist among states that do not consider each other as "enemies" (Klein, Goertz, & Diehl 2006). Regarding the rivalry termination, the new dataset retained the old measurement of ten to fifteen years

TABLE 2.1. Identification of rivalries: General and case specific

	Part I: General				Part II: Case Specific		
	Initiation Criteria				The India-Pakistan Rivalry		
Rivalry Approaches	Min. MIDs	Min. Years	No. of Rivalries	Termination Criteria	Rivalry Life	Rivalry Duration	Total MIDs
Diehl & Goertz (2000)	5–6	20	63	10–15 years after the last MID	1947–1991	44	40
Klein, Goertz, & Diehl (2006)	3	N/A	290	10–15 years after the last MID	1947–2001	54	43
Bennett (1996, 1997a)	5	25	34	A formal agreement	1947–	44+	40
Bennett (1997b, 1998)	6	20	61	Settlement of issue in contention and no MID in next 10 years	1967–	34+	15
Hensel (1999)	6	–		15 years after the last MID	1952–	–	35
Maoz & Mor (2002)	6	10	117	Belief stabilization and satisfaction with the status quo	1952–1991	40	35
Colaresi, Rasler, & Thompson (2007)	N/A	N/A	173	Change in decision makers' perceptions and policy	1947–	–	N/A
Hewitt (2005)[1]	3	20	31	15 years after the last crisis	1947–2001	54	11

1. Hewitt (2005) follows Brecher and Wilkenfeld's (1997) ICB database, which counts crises rather than MIDs. The ICB (2016) database counts fourteen crises between India and Pakistan.

after the last MID between the same pairs. Since the new dataset changes the old parameters of rivalry measure and operationalization, its use in case studies might create some confusion. To address this issue, Klein, Goertz, and Diehl suggest that

> scholars [can] . . . undo or reformulate the dataset to their own needs and preferences. For example, other scholars could easily identify enduring rivalries using the old time-density criteria from the dyadic files we compiled for each rivalry; thus, they could reproduce the categories of isolated, proto-, and enduring rivalries or create their own divisions of the rivalry continuum. They might also decide to divide rivalries that we combined for issue reasons. (2006: 339–40)

Like Diehl, Goertz, and Klein's two different dispute-density approaches, a third and fourth stream of rivalry identification came from Scott Bennett's work (1996, 1997a, 1997b, 1998). For rivalry formation, Bennett's (1996, 1997a) conceptualization requires five MIDs over a period of twenty-five years and employs an issue settlement criterion for rivalry termination. This formulation identifies thirty-four interstate rivalries in the international system. Regarding the importance of issues in rivalry dynamics, Bennett maintains that "there must be some connection or overlap between the issues at stake in various disputes between the rivals . . . that makes a rivalry somehow different from simply a dyad with many conflicts" (1996: 160). Probably for this reason, Bennett (1997b) focuses more on the importance of issues to understand the dynamics of severe rivalries. Paraphrasing James D. Morrow, he defines an *issue* as "a policy or set of policies of a government that has international implications and for which all the actors' preferences concerning the outcome are single-peaked" (Morrow 1986, quoted in Bennett 1997b: 230). Thus the "issue" forms a vital linkage between disputes in an ongoing rivalry. According to Bennett:

> The underlying theoretical connection (or perhaps assumption) between issues and rivalries is that disputes do not simply happen but rather occur because state leaders are trying to achieve certain goals that come into conflict. When goals conflict and leaders choose to use or threaten to use force, a militarized dispute occurs. Without some conflicting goals that constitute the issues at stake (and rivalries might include either one or several overlapping issues), repeated disputes would not occur. (1997b: 231)

The dual nature of Bennett's conceptualization puts it at odds with Diehl and Goertz's (2000) rivalry conception, which stresses the frequency of MIDs within a particular time period. However, Klein, Goertz, and Diehl's (2006) new conceptualization adopts the dual character of Bennett's and other approaches. In this duality, Bennett's operationalization oscillates between MIDs and underlying disputed issues. He defines interstate rivalry as

> a dyad in which two states disagree over the resolution of some issue(s) between them for an extended period of time, leading them to commit substantial resources (military, economic or diplomatic) toward opposing each other, and in which relatively frequent diplomatic or military challenges to the disputed status quo are made by one or both of the states. (Bennett 1996: 160)

Bennett (1996, 1997a) requires a threshold of five militarized disputes over a period of twenty-five years between the same rivals that have disagreements over the same issues for a long period of time. In this case, rivalry terminates (1) if rival states stop using armed threats against the other over issues of conflicting goals, and/or (2) both or one party either compromises over the issues of conflict or surrenders their earlier claims. Hence, unlike Diehl and Goertz's (2000) criteria of a "political shock" or absence of a MID in ten to fifteen years, Bennett (1996) requires a formal agreement on conflicting issues for rivalry termination. "Once a settlement has been truly accepted by state leaders," writes Bennett, "rivalries are likely to remain settled due to (1) the reputation costs of reneging on an international agreement, and (2) the domestic costs of switching policy again and being forced to build a new supporting coalition" (1997a: 371). Diehl and Goertz acknowledge that this model has potential to pinpoint the end of rivalries but, they contend, "it does perhaps miss the conclusion of rivalries that 'wither' away without final resolution" (2000: 38). Having acknowledged the impact of domestic factors on rivalry termination, that is, the existence of a relationship between polity change and the end of rivalries, Bennett (1996, 1997a) refines the rivalry termination condition. Akin to Goertz and Diehl's (1995a) proposal, he proposes that a rivalry ends when (1) rival states possess regime similarity, that is, a rivalry involves democratic states, (2) change in regimes occurs, and (3) rival states move toward democratization (Bennett 1997a). Thus for Bennett, democracy is an important condition to end the ongoing rivalries.

Bennett (1997b, 1998) advances a second rivalry identification procedure which identifies sixty-one enduring rivalries in world politics. It adopts Goertz and Diehl's (1995a) identification for rivalry formation that requires six MIDs in a twenty-year period. In this approach, unlike Goertz and Diehl's conceptualization, a rivalry begins only after it is fully established, that is, twenty years after the first MID,[2] and ends when the issue in contention is settled and no more militarized disputes occur in the following ten years (see Table 2.1). For Bennett, however, the absence of militarized disputes does not necessarily mean that rivals' disagreements have been resolved. In addition to the dispute termination, Bennett requires the resolution of issues under dispute through a formal agreement or renunciation to demarcate the end of rivalry. This conceptualization creates a new measure of rivalry termination that considers government leaders' public statements and the rival states' formal documents, which establishes a significant relationship between polity change and the rivalry termination (Bennett 1997b, 1998). According to Bennett's findings, democratic dyads have a higher probability of ending rivalry than mixed regimes, that is, democracy-autocracy dyads.

A fifth identification of rivalry comes from Paul Hensel's study whose central focus is on militarized interstate rivalries that represent "a longstanding, competitive relationship between two or more actors" (1999: 176). Hensel's evolutionary approach is precisely "based on the premise that rivalry rather than being inevitable or predetermined by structural conditions is a dynamic concept and comes into being over time as the cumulative result of interactions between two states" (1998, also see 1999: 183). Therefore, Hensel's general notion of rivalry does not initially differentiate between "enduring rivalries" and other categories of rivalries, "isolated" and "proto." He argues that adversaries do not perceive each other as enemies in the early stages, but frequent eruption of armed disputes, increased threat perceptions, and hostility in the course of their conflictual relationship transform them into enduring rivals. This underlines how Hensel's (1999) rivalry formulation differs with Diehl and Goertz's (2000) and Bennett's (1996) formulations. However, like John Vasquez (1993), he maintains that "disagreement over stakes that are considered to be highly salient might be expected to lead the relevant policymakers to adopt a more suspicious or more hostile stance toward their adversary" (Hensel 1999: 187), which may affect dyads' future foreign policy decision-making.

In Hensel's conception, a full-fledged rivalry between two adversaries requires three conditions: (1) "a competitive relationship over one or more stakes"; (2) "each perceives that the other has hostile intentions and poses a significant security threat"; that is, threat perception; and (3) a competitive relationship with established history and an expectation of conflict in the foreseeable future (1999: 176). In Hensel's conceptualization, the length of rivalries depends on two factors: complicated issues and the outcome of previous disputes, with the latter generally influencing the likelihood and timing of dispute recurrence. These factors affect rivals' policy, perceptions, and choices; thus they are vital to understand "the dynamics that lead to enduring rivalry and the differences between rivalries" (Hensel 1999: 178).

Hensel shows that rivalries follow evolutionary patterns in their progression in which early militarized disputes decide whether an enduring rivalry will be formed or a confronting relationship will die out. According to him, rivalries gradually evolve into enduring rivalries, that is, after indulging in a number of armed disputes, and are not based on the initial militarized confrontations between adversaries. To become enduring rivals, adversaries must pass less severe "early" and "intermediate" phases before entering the "advanced" phase (which requires six MIDs). According to him, more than 54 percent of armed disputes occurring in the early phase have a probability to lead to the next dispute, and the rate of disputes between rivals increases in the later phases of rivalries. As dyadic rivalries intensify in the intermediate and advanced phases, Hensel finds a dramatic increase in the likelihood of dispute recurrence, that is, 71 percent and 89 percent, respectively (1999: 191). After attaining maturity, that is, from the intermediate stage onwards, rivals view each other as enemies and confrontations between them become more frequent and severe—including wars—until rivalry withers away (see Vasquez 1993). Hensel reports that dyadic rivals that match in relative capabilities, especially military, and are non-democratic have an increased likelihood to experience recurrent MIDs. When rivalries intensify after a long conflictual history, not only does the probability of occurrence of every single future dispute become higher than the preceding one, but also their future armed scuffles become "increasingly difficult to avoid"—such "specific characteristics of their past confrontations can hasten or reverse this movement toward rivalry" (Hensel 1999: 175). In short, Hensel believes that only mutual negotiations (and their fruitful outcomes) and democracy can check the eruption of future armed disputes between the confronting states.

The sixth dispute-density approach has been offered by Zeev Maoz and Ben Mor (2002). Their alternative conceptualization is grounded on the structure of interactions between rival states that leads them to form rivalry, intentionally or unintentionally, by pursuing "incompatible goals" (Maoz & Mor 2002: 4; see Maoz 1982: 12–16). They characterize enduring rivalry as "a *persistent, fundamental* and *long term* incompatibility of goals between two states . . . [which] manifests itself in the basic attitudes of the parties toward each other, as well as in recurring violent or potentially violent clashes over a long period of time" (Maoz & Mor 2002: 4–5, emphasis in original). This conceptualization has "strategic" and "evolutionary" undercurrents which are based on "a bargaining process in which the perceptual and behavioral aspects of interactions are interrelated" (Maoz & Mor 2002: 6). It characterizes four dimensions of a rivalry: a specific set of unresolved major issues; strategic perception, that is, hostile intentions and planning against one another; psychological hostility; and most importantly, frequent and severe militarized confrontations (Maoz & Mor 2002: 5).

Maoz and Mor's (2002) identification of enduring rivalry also requires a conflictual dyad that indulges in six or more MIDs in a ten-year (or longer) time span. Along with a systematic differentiation between rivalrous and non-rivalrous relations, their dynamic approach characterizes three steps in a rivalry cycle: "emergence," "evolution," and "termination." Further, they divide the population of rivalrous dyads into a threefold typology: peaceful dyads and proto- and enduring rivalries—which is similar to Diehl and Goertz's (2000) three-point classification (isolated-, proto-, and enduring rivalries).

Maoz and Mor's conceptualization generates a list of 117 (8.9 percent) enduring rivalries which are involved in over 51 percent of total MIDs and 39 percent of all wars (2002: 232). On an average, enduring rivals resort to one MID in three and a half years, a recurrence rate almost sixfold higher than other categories. Maoz and Mor's (2002) findings are almost identical to those of Diehl and Goertz (2000). They point out that enduring rivalries are less than 6 percent of total rivalries but their constant indulgence in severe and repeated conflicts over an extended period makes them dangerous dyads—they contributed to almost half of interstate wars since 1816.

Maoz and Mor (2002) further found that different rivalry dyads have different lock-in patterns. They note that 10.7 percent of dyads get locked into enduring rivalries from the onset. Around 40 percent of dyads establish enduring rivalries in the second phase of their ongoing rivalries and only 7.6 percent of dyads become enduring in their last iteration. They also report the remaining 42.7 percent of dyads are unidentifiable; when they acquire enduring status is not verifiable (Maoz & Mor 2002: 278). This important finding bridges a difference between Diehl and Goertz's (2000) and Hensel's (1999) studies, whose claims are paradoxically opposite to each other: the former argue that rivalries take a static path and the latter contends that rivalries take a gradual path. Furthermore, by establishing interdependence between the "evolutionary process" and "experiential learning and bargaining," Maoz and Mor's (2002) game-theoretic study contributes to Hensel's (1999) and Russell Leng's (2000) approaches, which maintain that rivalry development is an evolutionary process and once adversaries interlock in it they are affected by the outcome of the preceding disputes and draw lessons from that experience to shape their future policies. Like Vasquez (1993) and Daniel Geller and David Singer (1998), Maoz and Mor (2002) note that the pattern of rivalry between two adversaries can survive if the weaker side roughly matches the relative capabilities of a superior adversary. In a given rivalry, once this balance tilts in favor of a superior adversary, there are chances that rivalry could be dislodged or enter into an abeyance phase.

For rivalry termination, they believe that learning from past disputes induces considerable fluctuations in the rivals' belief. As long as rivals preserve such fluctuations, the rivalries will remain intact. Maoz and Mor's (2002) preference change is directly related to adversaries' satisfaction or dissatisfaction with the prevailing status quo. If any rival is dissatisfied with the status quo then the rivalry is likely to continue, and if both sides are satisfied with the status quo after their confrontation then the rivalry is likely to head toward termination (Maoz & Mor 2002: 262–63, 286). Once misperceptions or beliefs stabilize, they believe, the probability of rivalry termination increases by many fold. Similarly, joint democracies and domestic politics play a considerable role in shaping the direction of rivalry. For instance, democratic dyads are more likely to be satisfied with the status quo than non-democratic ones. This indicates that similar democratic regimes increase the prospect of peace by reducing the frequency of disputes.

The Second School: Actors' Perception Approach

The actors' perception approach criticizes the dispute-density approaches on the basis of their over-dependence on feuding pairs' militarized behavior within a specific time frame (Thompson 1995). To recognize states as rivals, this conceptualization rests heavily on actors' *perceptions* rather than militarized actions or disputes, which differentiates it from the dispute-density approaches. This distinct feature brings it into another school called "strate-

gic rivalries" that combines competitors' status and perceptions by analyzing their diplomatic histories (Colaresi, Rasler, & Thompson 2007; Thompson 1995, 2001). In other words, this approach needs rivals to identify and
recognize each other as adversaries without necessarily engaging in frequent
militarized disputes. It maintains that the dispute-density approaches evaluate rivalry by distinguishing states that engage in frequent and infrequent
conflicts rather than identifying rivalry *per se*. Colaresi, Rasler, and Thompson (2007) argue that utmost stress shall be given to the importance of rivalry
rather than its duration. This means their thrust is more on primary security
threats (actors' perceptions) which are permanent sources of conflict rather
than those having secondary relevance (militarized disputes). In doing so,
the proponents of actors' perception reverse the priorities set by a sizable
majority in the field.

The identification of strategic rivalries challenges the dispute-density
formulation on three counts: (1) by identifying rivalries in terms of decision-
makers' perceptions as opposed to the number of disputes between given
states within a specific period; (2) by differentiating predominantly positional and predominantly spatial rivalries as two basic types; and (3) by categorizing positional rivalries with respect to their geo-political milieu
(dyadic, regional, global, and global-regional) (Thompson 1995). While differentiating spatial rivalries from positional, Colaresi, Rasler, and Thompson
write,

> there is no reason to assume that spatial and positional rivalries "work" the
> same way. They are likely to follow different courses—especially in terms of
> initial formation and conflict escalation patterns—because they are subject
> to different pressures, motivations, and decision-making considerations.
> (2007: 197)

Spatial rivalries mostly evolve between contiguous weak states with sym-
metric capabilities and over disputed territory. According to Thompson
(1995), since territorial stakes between rivals can be resolved in a concrete
manner, spatial rivalries are shorter and less dangerous in comparison to
positional rivalries.[3] However, territorial rivalries' shorter life span does not
mean that their disputes can be resolved easily and with more eminent regu-
larity. In contrast, positional rivalries occur between major powers with
roughly symmetrical positions at the systemic or subsystemic level. Though
these rivalries have a lower frequency, they tend to be more dangerous than

spatial rivalries (Thompson 1995: 205). Vasquez's (1996a) study also supports Thompson's (1995) distinction between spatial and positional rivalries; however, he emphasizes that relative equality is a prerequisite of both kinds of rivalries.

By giving emphasis to militarized disputes, Colaresi, Rasler, and Thompson argue, the dispute-density approaches generate a calculated bias toward higher capability states which repeatedly pressure weaker states; for instance, some non-rivalrous strong dyads might meet the empirical criteria of six disputes and some authentic non-militarized weak dyads may remain neglected (2007: 51–52). They further point out that the different dispute-density approaches have different rivalry operationalization; for example, Bennett's (1997b, 1998), Maoz and Mor's (2002), and Diehl and Goertz's (2000) approaches do not have common beginning and termination criteria for rivalries (see Table 2.1). For the beginning of rivalries, Bennett (1997b, 1998), Hensel (1999), and Maoz and Mor (2002) need five or six disputes in a twenty-year time span, which significantly differs from Klein, Goertz, and Diehl's (2006) criteria to establish a rivalry. Indeed, all rivalry identification lists have distinct criteria for rivalry termination (Table 2.1). Colaresi, Rasler, and Thompson contest Bennett's termination criteria—that is, formal agreements between adversaries followed by a dispute-free ten years—as it does not assure a permanent end of rivals' perceptions of one another (2007: 56–58). They also criticize Diehl and Goertz's (2000) and Klein, Goertz, and Diehl's (2006) termination points as excessively fast. For this reason, the proponents of actors' perception approach argue that the dispute-density approaches disagree with each other more than they agree.

To identify dyadic rivalries, Klein, Goertz, and Diehl's (2006) dataset delves into militarized disputes and codes 290 rivalries in the international system. In contrast, Colaresi, Rasler, and Thompson's (2007) dataset concentrates on the rivals' diplomatic history and their leaders' perceptions to code 173 rivalries. This mismatch between the two largest datasets shows a significant difference in rivalry identification. From Klein, Goertz, and Diehl's (2006) list, 183 cases of rivalries do not qualify in Colaresi, Rasler, and Thompson's (2007) list and similarly 67 of the latter's dyadic rivalries do not find a place in the former's list. The 67 strategic rivalries that Klein, Goertz, and Diehl (2006) do not identify comprise 39 percent of Colaresi, Rasler, and Thompson's (2007) cases, and the 183 (enduring) rivalries that the latter does not identify comprise 63 percent of the former's data. In brief, as shown in Table 2.1, a comparative look at all rivalry lists indicates a considerable disagreement between the two approaches—they only agree on 23 dyadic rivalries, which are 6.5 percent of a total 355 cases.

The Third School: Crisis-Density (ICB) Approach

The crisis-density approach follows procedures originally advanced by the dispute-density approaches for identifying dyadic rivalries—however, its focus is on the density of conflict sequences, in terms of frequency of crises between two states over a specified period (Hewitt 2005: 184). To define rivalry, the crisis-density approach relies exclusively on the recurring interstate crises between the same set of states—as recorded by the ICB database (Brecher & Wilkenfeld 1997)—rather than the militarized disputes of the COW database. The ICB's operational definition for a "protracted conflict" requires "at least three international crises between the same pair of adversaries over one or more recurring issues during a period of at least five years" (Brecher & Wilkenfeld 1997: 6). For establishing a "protracted conflict," Michael Brecher and Jonathan Wilkenfeld consider the ICB criteria as a necessary, but not a sufficient, condition. Though Joseph Hewitt's (2005) approach is based on the ICB, it takes a different course for its "protracted conflict" conceptualization, whereas Brecher and Wilkenfeld (1997) consider both multilateral and dyadic interstate conflicts. Hewitt's focus is only on the dyadic formulation to identify particular pairs of states that are "involved in prolonged conflicts featuring recurrent crises" (2005: 184).

Though the crisis-density approach follows the dispute-density's formulation of enduring rivalries to develop the crisis-density model, it produces "a different population of rivalries than one based on MIDs," as it requires different levels of severity, intensity, and durability of crises between rivalrous states. "Even when," Hewitt maintains, "the crisis-based approach identifies the same rivalries as a MID-based approach, the estimated initiation and termination dates will probably be different" (2005: 186). Following Diehl and Goertz's (2000) criteria, the crisis-density approach marks the first crisis date as the initiation of the rivalry and requires a peaceful period of a minimum of fifteen years after the last crisis for termination. But unlike the dispute-density approach's criteria of five to six MIDs in fifteen to twenty-five years without any gap in a rivalry of more than fifteen years, it requires fewer international crises to establish an enduring rivalry.

To qualify as enduring crisis-density rivals, the feuding dyads require a minimum threshold of three crises over twenty years without breaking points between crises longer than specified by the crisis intensity require-ment. In the 1918–2001 period, Hewitt found a total of 778 crisis dyads form-ing 417 rivalries. He reports 257 dyads experienced just one crisis and 88 dyads experienced only two crises, all of which he regarded as isolated rival-ries by following Diehl and Goertz's (2000) classification. A limited number of rivalries experienced three (29 rivalries) or more crises (43 rivalries). His study reports that rivalries with one crisis die out before three years and those with two crises sustain over six years. Only 17.2 percent of rivalries experience three or more crises and generally surpass ten years. Thus the lat-ter set of rivalries has the highest possibility to form a strong lock-in posture that lasts an average forty-four years (that is, 11–55 years). The crisis-density approach identifies 345 isolated rivalries, 41 proto-rivalries, and 31 enduring rivalries (Hewitt 2005: 189–90).

The crisis-based rivalry identification has two main issues with the dispute-density approaches: (1) occurrence of MIDs outside North American and European regions go unreported due to poor media presence, and (2) inclusion of several low-level disputes in the MID dataset "that pose little discernible risk for interstate military hostilities" (Hewitt 2005: 186). These two issues, under- and over-coverage of several low-profile disputes, tend to increase the likelihood of data manipulation, which poses questions for the authenticity of the MID dataset. Hewitt believes that low-level disputes nei-ther pose a dangerous threat to rivals' existence nor increase the likelihood of violent militarized conflicts. According to him, "[A]rmed conflicts that qualify as crises are significantly more severe than MIDs that do not qualify as crises" (Hewitt 2005: 186). Almost 75 percent of crises qualify as MIDs, but approximately the same percentage of MIDs do not experience a crisis.

Though the crisis-based definition relies on the dispute-density approach, it does share some traits with the actors' perception approach that conceptualizes dyadic rivals as "strategic rivals" and defines them as those "actors [that] regard each other as (a) competitors, (b) the source of actual or latent threats that pose some possibility of becoming militarized, and (c) enemies" (Thompson 2001: 560). More specifically, the ICB project shares these traits with strategic rivalries. Rooted in the ICB formulation, the crisis-density approach by design also shares the same traits in defining enduring crisis-density rivalries. Moreover, the crisis-based formulation, like that of strategic rivalries, requires no armed confrontation between adversaries to regard them as rivals. Though these similarities connect this approach with strategic rivalries, as Hewitt writes, there is a high possibility "that an even greater percentage of the strategic rivalries fail to experience an international crisis" (2005: 192).

On the other hand, the crisis-density approach follows a framework parallel to that of dispute-density approaches by paying close attention to crisis severity, durability, and intensity, but it selects rivalries with higher levels of hostility and armed action. Therefore, a considerable disagreement on some rivalries is inevitable between the dispute-density and the crisis-density approaches. In contrast, an agreement with regard to the same set of rivalries is quite likely between the crisis-density and the actors' perception approaches; hence it identifies fewer of the enduring dispute-density rivalries. Additionally, several enduring rivalries "[do] not experience enough international crises to qualify as an enduring crisis-density rivalry" (Hewitt 2005: 192). Hence, Hewitt's approach converges as well as diverges with the dispute-density and the actors' perception approaches. Precisely for this reason, Hewitt claims that the crisis-density approach acts as a mediator between the actors' perception and the dispute-density approaches. How far empirical tests support the crisis-density's "intermediating" role is a question that needs further investigation.

Debating Rivalries: A Comparative Analysis

After examining the rivalry approaches, it is evident that within the dispute-density school, nearly all conceptualizations generally support each other's rivalry identifications. Diehl and Goertz's (2000) study maintains that rivalries originate and terminate abruptly; that is, states lock in enduring rivalries from their first MID and dislodge *only* after experiencing a political shock. A sustained rivalry of a given pair of conflictual states, they argue, requires continuous involvement in militarized disputes, at least six in twenty years. Their study is also supported by Maoz and Mor's (2002) findings, that rivals develop hatred before the sixth MID and lock in enduring rivalry from their fifth dispute onward. In addition to supporting Diehl and Goertz's findings, Maoz and Mor (2002) also stress structural components of rivalry evolution. Likewise Bennett's (1996, 1997a, 1997b, 1998) work supports Diehl and Goertz's (2000) rivalry formulation with minor differences in their beginning and termination criteria for rivalries.

Only Hensel (1999) has a fundamental issue with Diehl and Goertz's (2000) rivalry formulation. He contends that before lock-in to enduring rivalry, the adversarial states must experience several disputes in the early and intermediate phases to heat up their conflictual relationship. So, opposite to Diehl and Goertz's (2000) abrupt lock-in path, he argues that the feuding pairs of states gradually develop rivalry. One of the core manifestations in both formulations is that they require a similar threshold of MIDs, therefore, the principal difference between them is the process rather than the context of rivalry. For Diehl and Goertz, rivalries remain static throughout their lifetime till they terminate, and Hensel argues that rivalries gradually develop with the passage of time. However, Goertz and Diehl (1998) found no support for Hensel's gradualist model, in which armed disputes turn frequent and severe in the later phase of rivalry. Maoz and Mor's (2002) conceptualization bridges this gap by showing that some dyadic rivalries follow Diehl and Goertz's (2000) static path (abrupt lock-in and termination) while others follow Hensel's gradualist path and some in fact show indeterminate lock-in patterns. Therefore, the evidence for both patterns is mixed thus far. In this situation, the possibility to accept or reject a particular rivalry formulation is subject to the nature of the study in general and the genesis of rivalrous dyads in particular.

It is noteworthy that by pinpointing the role of power capabilities in rivalry dynamics, as Vasquez (1993, 1996a, 1996b) and Geller (1993) have shown, Maoz and Mor (2002) support the propositions of power transition theory. However, Colaresi, Rasler, and Thompson (2007) differ and argue that it is quite unlikely that a dyadic rivalry would emerge between unmatched pairs like India and Nepal, China and Kazakhstan, or Israel and Lebanon. Yet some dyads characterized by unequal capabilities, for example, the Indo-Pakistani, the Sino-Taiwanese, the Sino-Vietnamese, and the Israeli-Jordanian, are engaged in long-standing rivalries. Colaresi, Rasler, and Thompson argue that more than power capabilities, the decision-makers' policy orientation and "their perceptions of sources of threat and who their enemies are" matters more (2007: 32). Ironically, their approach also stipulates that rivals should regard each other as competitors, which implies that the adversaries shall have roughly similar capabilities. Though the actors' perception and the crisis-density approaches differ from the dispute-density approaches in identification criteria and methodology, the rivalry scholarship has a common view of rivalry characterization in general, that is, militarized confrontations between rivals, a deep sense of threat perception, and expectation of consistent dispute occurrence in future. This common spirit of rivalry scholarship is central to Vasquez's conceptualization which keeps a unified essence of all approaches and defines rivalry as "a relationship characterized by extreme competition, and usually psychological hostility, in which the issue positions of contenders are governed primarily by their attitude toward each other rather than by the stakes at hand" (Vasquez 1996a: 532).

DISPUTE-DENSITY (MID) MODELS OF INTERSTATE RIVALRY

After comparing the leading rivalry conceptualizations, it is important to note that despite offering general support in certain areas, they significantly differ in their frameworks and applications. Therefore, for conceptual and methodological reasons, they cannot be applied together in a case study nor can any case study adopt all of them to offer a comprehensive explanation of the rivalry context. Against this backdrop, I adopt only two dispute-density approaches to examine the trajectory of the India-Pakistan rivalry. More specifically, I undertake a brief review of "static" and "gradual" dispute-density models, that is, Diehl and Goertz's punctuated equilibrium and Hensel's evolutionary models, respectively. Though other dispute-density approaches also have potential to explain the India-Pakistan rivalry, they are not considered here because the genesis and evolution of the case in question shows much consistency with the conditions and propositions of the punctuated equilibrium and the evolutionary models. The former posits that rivalries originate and end abruptly, and the latter argues that rivalries evolve over time after accumulating grievances through their long history of conflicts.

The Punctuated Equilibrium Model

Diehl and Goertz's (2000) punctuated equilibrium model has its intellectual roots in Niles Eldredge and Stephen J. Gould's biological theory called punctuated equilibrium, which stresses that "the development of species is a very slow process, characterized by long periods of stability with little or no change and interrupted by brief periods of rapid change" (Goertz & Diehl 2000: 202). By inferring insights from Eldredge and Gould's theory and employing them to contextualize interstate rivalries, Diehl and Goertz's (2000) punctuated equilibrium model likewise posits that once rival states are engaged in enduring rivalries, they follow relatively stable phenomena for decades until they are dislodged by massive political shocks (as illustrated by Figure 2.4). The model suggests that to begin a rivalry, there must be some

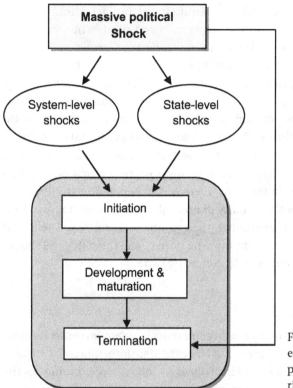

Figure 2.4. Life cycle of enduring rivalries: The punctuated equilibrium model

sudden political disruption in the adversaries' local, regional, or global environment which could disrupt or challenge the status quo. Once established, as Geller (1993) also shows, rivalries are difficult to disrupt because their own mechanism provides them stability.

Diehl and Goertz's (2000) conceptualization revolves around the concept of "basic rivalry level," a re-formulation of Edward Azar's (1972) "normal relations range," which proposes that each pair of countries has an average level of cooperative or hostile interactions around which their relations vary. Drawing from Azar (1972), Diehl and Goertz's (2000) concept expects conflict patterns within the rivalry relationship to fluctuate around the basic rivalry level at the outset and thereafter remain consistent until the rivalry terminates. Once the basic rivalry level is established in the early phase, it does not disrupt easily because the rivalry pattern stabilizes over time. To disrupt the stability, rivalries require dramatic shocks at the systemic or nation-state level. The punctuated equilibrium model, however, does not claim that a majority of militarized disputes within a rivalry will remain the same over time. It expects some variation in severity and duration from the basic rivalry level across different disputes, such as full-scale interstate wars, but in general it proposes stability in the rivals' conflictual behavior. Diehl and Goertz (2000) argue that the influence of exogenous factors is mainly responsible for initiation and termination of rivalries, which further determine their basic rivalry level. More specifically, they identify political shocks—endogenous (nation-state) and exogenous (systemic or subsystemic)—as a necessary condition to start or end rivalries because they bring dramatic changes in the international system or its subsystems. These alterations, therefore, have potential to create new rivalries by disrupting the stability of non-militarized dyads and to terminate ongoing ones by disrupting their conflictual stability. Diehl and Goertz's model further explains how the system- and the state-level shocks impact rivalries, as detailed in the following two subsections.

System Shocks

According to the punctuated equilibrium model, system-level shocks influence rivalries in at least three ways. First, the transformation of the global environment in which states interact opens a window of opportunity for the initiation of new rivalries and termination of the ongoing ones. For example, the end of World War II transformed the international system by dismantling the Eurocentric power structure and evolving a new bipolar rivalry under the United States' and the Soviet Union's supremacy. Similarly, the sudden shock of the end of the Cold War not only terminated the Soviet-American rivalry but also simultaneously set the stage for initiation of many new rivalries and a new unipolar system dominated by the sole surviving superpower—the United States.

Second, system-level shocks may dramatically change the territorial sovereignty bases of the system. Multiple territorial alterations within the system or its subsystems can help the ongoing rivalries to end their competition or push new pairs of states to engage in rivalrous relationship. In other words, inclusion of new sovereign states disrupts the systemic (and subsystemic) balance and induces spirals of pressure over the ongoing rivalries, compelling some pairs to terminate their long-standing conflicts while simultaneously creating a window for initiation and growth of new conflicts.

Third, system-level shocks dramatically alter the distribution of capabilities among major states, which may end the ongoing rivalries and begin new ones by changing their bilateral and multilateral equations. For example, after the end of World War II, the alliance formations and their dramatic rearrangements had redistributed power to new political units that drastically changed the pre-war Eurocentric structure into a Cold War–spearheaded bipolar system. Similarly, the end of the Cold War not only broke apart the Soviet Union's patron-client relationship with developing states but also resulted in the termination of many proxy conflicts in the absence of superpowers' sustained military-economic support, while others, like Kashmir, took a violent turn.

State Shocks

Diehl and Goertz (2000) report that the state-level shocks affect rivalries in at least four ways. First, the formation of independent states poses a dramatic shock to the immediate neighborhood. This development may mark the beginning of rivalry between the parent and the seceding state or between either or both of them with their neighboring states. In an ongoing rivalry, the territorial partition of one state might alter the dyad's power equations, increasing the possibility of unfavorable conditions for one or both adversaries, and may force the weaker side to give up the competition. In such cases, generally the newly independent state aligns with the rival(s) of the parent state for its survival, security, and international legitimacy as the parent state (and neighbors) oppose its independence and maintain pressure on it to return to the status quo ante. In some cases, the powerful state sees the newly independent state as an easy target that motivates its ruling elites to take advantage of the new state's weakness. For this reason, the punctuated equilibrium model proposes that new states have higher prospects to become involved in rivalries soon after gaining independence. Key examples are the Israeli-Palestinian, the Indo-Pakistani, and the North Korean–South Korean rivalries.

Second, the possibility of termination of an ongoing rivalry increases if a civil war–prone state diverts its resources and attention to internal conflict(s). Under such circumstances, the weak state might prefer to terminate its ongoing rivalry to ensure its immediate survival and long-term interests rather than compromising with domestic secessionist forces. On the other hand, it may seek legitimacy or public support or even try to distract attention from its lingering domestic problems by initiating conflict against an external enemy or engaging in an advantageous new rivalry with other state(s).

Third, regime change in an ongoing rivalry also creates an opportunity to terminate the rivalry. Unlike the security studies and the democratic peace scholarship, the punctuated equilibrium model maintains that major policy shifts usually occur with the emergence of new leadership and a change in the quality of governance; both significantly impact the course of dyadic relationships. The emergence of radical regimes often prompts their leadership to take unique actions, which may affect the rival parties' domestic and foreign policies and, in turn, increase the possibilities of initiation of new and termination of ongoing rivalries (see Cox 2010). Transformation of the post-war Franco-German relationship is a case in point. The new political environment not only resolved the two adversaries' seventy-five-year-old territorial dispute over Alsace-Lorraine, but also helped transform the European political system by involving a series of reformative steps that resulted in the formation of a highly progressive multi-state organization: the European Union (EU).

Finally, when a regime transition leads to the formation of a joint-democratic dyad (or a non-democratic one), it impacts the behavior of an ongoing rivalry. Though the punctuated equilibrium model recognizes the peacemaking effect of joint democracy, such a positive association may not be immediate and may vary depending on adversaries' history of conflict—this is also consistent with Hensel's (1999) evolutionary approach. Findings of these models (and others) support the democratic peace theory's central proposition that joint democracy increases the prospects of peace between conflictual pairs or reduces hostility level in established rivalries (see Rummel 1979, 1995; Russett & Oneal 2001).

The Evolutionary Model

Hensel's (1999) evolutionary model of rivalries mainly draws from English natural scientist Charles Darwin's evolutionary theory of natural selection, which proposes that a given set of species or system can change over time through a series of historical events and processes that lead these species or system to a particular state, like the development of new features of species or an entirely new species, or emergence of a new environmental balance for a species. In contrast to Diehl and Goertz's (2000) static approach, which assumes that the rivalry context remains stable throughout the life cycle of

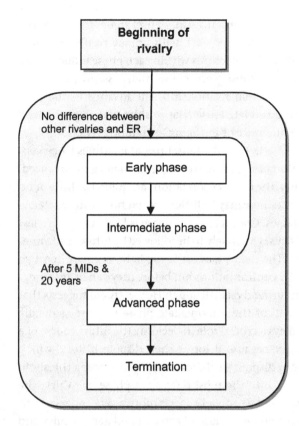

Figure 2.5. Life cycle of enduring rivalries: The evolutionary model

rivalries, Hensel's (1999) evolutionary model posits that rivalries develop and change over time in response to interactions between the rival states. It proposes that conflict patterns systematically vary throughout the rivalry process, and dispute recurrence is much more likely in the advanced phase than in the initial two phases (as illustrated by Figure 2.5). Leng's (2000) study supports Hensel's (1999) findings that adversaries adopt increasingly coercive behavior over time; however, Goertz and Diehl's (1998) volcano model found no such support. In brief, the evolutionary model proposes an unfolding process of change in dyadic relationships over time, that is, with the gradual increase and addition of issues in the conflict.

While Diehl and Goertz's (2000) model assumes that "enduring" rivalries show from the outset a distinct conflict pattern, which is more dangerous than those of "isolated-" or "proto-" rivalries, Hensel's (1999) model suggests that Diehl and Goertz's distinctions between isolated-, proto-, and enduring rivalries are not self-evident. Instead, Hensel argues that potential rivalries pass through different phases, each with unique conflict patterns and characteristics. Events and interactions within each phase influence the outbreak and severity level of subsequent confrontations and help determine whether a given conflictual relationship will advance to the next phase. Mainly these steps formulate tense relationships and compel adversaries to follow an uncertain future by engaging in enduring rivalries.

Similar to Diehl and Goertz (2000), Hensel (1999) identifies three general phases in the evolution of rivalries: early, intermediate, and advanced. In the early phase of rivalry, the two states' relations are guided by little or no history of past conflicts, and there may be little expectation of future interactions to guide their strategies. Conflict in this phase is likely to involve less coercive bargaining and thus is less likely to be followed by future confrontations than other phases. The next phase, intermediate, begins when two adversaries engage in a few confrontations but before they can be meaningfully described as true enduring rivals. Although Hensel (1999) suggests that the approximate time span of the intermediate phase is short, generally three to five disputes, it plays a crucial role in deciding the future course of a dyad's conflictual behavior because it forms their dispute history, which increases the probability of dispute escalation. Once rivals cross a threshold of five disputes, they enter into the most dangerous phase of rivalry: the advanced phase. The evolutionary model expects more severe and recurrent militarized disputes in this phase because of the accumulated hostility and grievances from the past, which increases substantial threat perception, competition, and expectation of more disputes between rivals in the future (Hensel 1999: 184–85).

In some respects, the evolutionary model follows Vasquez's (1993) understanding that the conflictual relationships begin because of the way states handle their contentious issues. Hensel describes how two distinct types of evolutionary influences—"general" and "specific" effects—push rivals through different phases of rivalry (1999, 2001). In "general expectation," as rivals begin to accumulate a longer conflictual history, they undergo more armed disputes, which further deteriorate their relations. This in turn aggravates the feeling of hostility, distrust, and enmity between adversaries and thereby brings them closer to recognition of a long-term rivalry (Hensel 1998). Apart from general expectation, the "specific effects" of past interactions, such as the severity levels and the outcomes of past confrontations, contribute to establish the rivalry. The evolutionary model posits that if militarized disputes do not meet rivals' definitive aims, that is, a complete victory or such like, then the attained stalemates increase the possibility of hostility and distrust between them "without resolving any of their disputed issues to either side's satisfaction" (Hensel & Diehl 1998: 8). In contrast, a dispute that ends in a negotiated compromise is more likely to help resolve issues between adversaries or, at least, assist them in creating a more trusting environment (see Bennett 1996, 1997a, 1997b). Similarly, a dispute that ends in a decisive victory for one side is likely to reduce the level of conflict in its immediate aftermath as the defeated side requires time to recover or prepare for another challenge at a more appropriate moment.

In short, between the specific and the general effects, the evolutionary model sees rivalry developing out of adversaries' earlier interactions. In each case, the impact of these evolutionary factors is likely to be greater when the history of past conflicts activates the domestic political scene on each side by attracting the attention and interest of important domestic actors in government, political opposition, and the mass public. An activated political scene prolongs the rivalry by rewarding the leaders' aggressive behavior and punishing conciliatory actions toward the rival (Hensel 1998).

In sum, the evolutionary model expects rivalries to intensify over time and turn more hostile and violent in due course, particularly in the advanced phase. It also recognizes the impact of "general" and "specific" effects on adversaries' relations, as they influence the evolution of feuding pairs toward or away from enduring rivalries.

CONCLUSION

After an extensive review of all rivalry approaches, I briefly examine the two dispute-density models—punctuated equilibrium and evolutionary—which propose different paths of rivalry formation and progression in time and space. The punctuated equilibrium model posits that following a dramatic political shock, the feuding states quickly lock into enduring rivalry and remain engaged in it for decades until dislodged by some kind of shock. This model assumes a given rivalry as an "enduring rivalry" from the beginning of the first militarized dispute between the two states. Put differently, the rivalry context shows no change from the onset of rivalry right up to its termination, so those rivalries that begin with a political shock—such as the Indo-Pakistani and the Israeli-Palestinian—can be effectively examined by employing this model. On the other hand, Hensel's (1999) evolutionary approach maintains that rival states gradually transform their hostile relationships into enduring rivalries and their hostilities escalate over time. In other words, the evolutionary model requires a few disputes between adversaries to heat up their conflictual interactions before they begin to behave like enduring rivals. This model is suitable for those rivalries that come into existence in the absence of political shocks, for example, the Chilean-Peruvian and the Soviet-American rivalries.

From the viewpoint of applicability, both models suggest that the Indo-Pakistani rivalry largely follows a static path rather than the gradualist one. From the very outset of their conflictual relationship, that is, following an abrupt lock-in, India and Pakistan began to behave like enduring rivals. Since then, the two states have maintained a stable conflict pattern with high levels of hostility—unlike the evolutionary model proposal that the conflict pattern turns severe only in its advanced phase. Moreover, the India-Pakistan rivalry is an outcome of multi-dimensional "endogenous" and "exogenous" factors covered in the punctuated equilibrium model, rather than only "endogenous" conditions specified in the evolutionary model. Despite its congruence with the punctuated equilibrium model, the India-Pakistan rivalry also shows some conformity with the evolutionary model, for instance, in (1) the impact of past interactions on the dyad's future disputes and (2) the role of domestic politics in rivalry formation and maintenance. Incorporation of these aspects in the Indo-Pakistani case, coupled with the notions of a gradualist path, helps to examine the severity of militarized disputes, the accumulation of hostility and grievances, and the impact of past confrontations on the formation and sustenance of the subcontinental rivalry.

On the whole, the comparison of both models suggests that the genesis, the nature, and the course of the India-Pakistan rivalry is largely congruent with the punctuated equilibrium model; however, incorporation of some elements from Hensel's conceptualization certainly helps to make the study more exploratory and robust. For both theoretical and methodological reasons, I therefore infer insights from both models to develop a case-specific model, the "complex rivalry," to provide an alternative and comprehensive explanation of the India-Pakistan rivalry. This exercise is undertaken in the next chapter.

CHAPTER 3

Conceptualizing the Indo-Pakistani Complex Rivalry

A Hub-and-Spokes Framework

INTRODUCTION

From the popular academic debates on the India-Pakistan conflict, three views can be synthesized. Some scholars view this conflict as stemming from Muhammad Ali Jinnah's "two-nation theory," which they say provided many Muslim politicians a much-needed platform to claim and justify that the Muslims were a separate nation within India. From his outline of the theory in 1940 onward, it was internalized as a belief and a tool to claim that the Muslim community's political rights cannot be reconciled under the post-independence Hindu domination; therefore, a separate sovereign entity shall be carved out of united India for the Muslims of the subcontinent. From this view, the roots of the Indo-Pakistani animosity can be traced back to the divergent state-building goals of the Indian National Congress and the All-India Muslim League (hereafter, the Congress and the Muslim League, respectively) that put the two political entities on contradictory trajectories and actuated a series of hostile and reactionary moves that fueled communal divide in the country. Consequently, the country-wide massive communal currents formed a chaotic and envious atmosphere which made India's bifurcation inevitable. After the partition, the validation and internalization of the same logic, the religious nationalism, drove India and Pakistan to evolve a long-term animosity. "What had been a societal security problem of religious conflict between the Muslim League and the Congress Party," as Barry Buzan and Ole Waever have noted, "was transformed into an interstate, military-political one between an Islamic Pakistan and a secular, multicultural, but dominantly Hindu India" (2003: 101).

In a second view, the conflict stems from historical myths and illusions that fuel hatred, fear, hostility, and intolerance on one or both sides and are still prevalent in India and Pakistan. On the basis of this view, the India-Pakistan rivalry can be understood as a thousand-year Hindu-Muslim conflict—beginning with Muslim Turks' invasion of Punjab and the subsequent establishment of Islamic rule over the populous Gangetic Plain. It is hard to believe that Hindu-Muslim religious differences alone are a sufficient condition to explain various aspects of this rivalry. It is well established in the literature that pre-partition India had witnessed Hindu-Muslim coexistence for centuries without widespread violence; however, low-intensity communal conflicts were part of their collective history. In this sense, on the basis of religious discord, the outbreak of communal violence during the partition is not a sufficient cause, though a powerful one, to offer a comprehensive explanation of the formation and persistence of the India-Pakistan rivalry. Moreover, identity-based explanations overemphasize—in a monolithic and monotonic manner—the role of religion and communal clashes in the India-Pakistan case and undermine other factors that play a key part in giving momentum to this rivalry.

In a third view, the Indo-Pakistani rivalry is a tragedy that stems from the internalization of power politics practices and the formation of security dilemma. According to this view, neither side can secure itself without making the other insecure; the result is an endless struggle between them for power and security.

It seems that of the three explanations, the last one is the strongest. The first two have relevance to understand the causes of partition, but their application to analyzing the overall Indo-Pakistani rivalry, though both sound compelling, suffers from flaws. In my view, the Indo-Pakistani rivalry is a complex and problematic conflict which must be viewed in a more complicated manner, not in a simplistic way as the religion- and nationalism-based scholarship does. With this objective in mind, in this chapter I first sketch the background conditions of the India-Pakistan contention and then conceptualize the case study by proposing a hub-and-spokes framework, also called the "complex rivalry" model, to offer a different understanding and explanation of the subcontinental rivalry. By adopting the rivalry conception, this model represents an attempt at theoretical, historical, and interpretative analysis to provide an account of the India-Pakistan rivalry from its inception to the present that betters our understanding of how this rivalry came into existence and why it persists despite experiencing two major political shocks. In the second half of the chapter, I operationalize the complex rivalry model to provide an explanation of the India-Pakistan rivalry in four different thematic phases and lay out the conceptual foundation on which the rest of the book's chapters are built.

THE INDO-PAKISTANI COMPLEX RIVALRY:
A HUB-AND-SPOKES FRAMEWORK

Since 1947, India and Pakistan have locked their horns in an unending rivalry. The conflict pattern of the subcontinental rivalry shows that its origin is associated with the interplay of multifaceted endogenous and exogenous factors. Scholarly debates tend to claim that the Indo-Pakistani rivalry stems from the two states' clashing and antithetical ideologies, which mainly rest on their competing claims to the predominantly Muslim state of J&K (A. Ahmed 1997; Z. Bhutto 1969; Cohen 2004; Ganguly 2002; S. Gupta 1966; Nasr 2005; Varshney 1991). For the Indian state, the Muslim-majority Kashmir is important to affirm its secular ideology and identity. Surrendering its sole Muslim state on religious grounds to Pakistan, it is argued, would problematize its relationship with its own largest minority community, Muslims. For Pakistan, which was created on the basis of the two-nation theory as a homeland for the Muslims of the Indian subcontinent, its nationhood and identity remain incomplete until it wields complete control over the entire state of J&K. That is why, since the partition, the Pakistani elites have made the acquisition of the state a core national interest and relentlessly pursued the policy of irredentism and revisionism. In short, according to this scholarship, the fundamental cause of the origins of the South Asian rivalry is the two states' antithetical ideologies: India's secular character clashes with the principle of Pakistan's ideology as a homeland for the Muslims and vice versa—hence ceding their claim on Kashmir undermines the rationale of their nation-statehood. Their mutually invalidating state-building approaches, it is argued, produce underlying conditions that form the base and comprehend the dynamics of this rivalry.

These perspectives represent the view that Kashmir's ideological prominence for the survival of both states' "national identity" sufficiently explains why this rivalry came into existence and remains intact so far. In directing considerable attention to the ideological aspect of the India-Pakistan contention, a sizable majority in the field tends to neglect the underlying role of "salient territory" and "geographical contiguity" in this rivalry. Ideology, it is argued, played the most important role to initiate and sustain the rivalry during the formative years of independence, and other factors were either secondary or were mere symptoms, not causes, of India and Pakistan's rivalrous progression.

I differ with such preponderant analyses and argue that, along with ideology, Kashmir's territorial salience and geographical contiguity to Pakistan have also played a fundamental role in interlocking India and Pakistan into a rivalrous relationship. Once these three structural factors—ideology, territorial salience, and geographical contiguity—conjoined and evolved into a unified whole in the India-Pakistan case, the ensuing causal process gave rise to the formation of a stronger "core" or "hub" under conditions of extreme differences and hostility that keep the "hub" under constant stress, complicate the disputants' contradicted interests, and thereby dominate their relations. Against this setting, the structural factors' interactions and interdependencies permeate the Kashmir issue to such an extent that it has become a principal contention between India and Pakistan and, in doing so, these core factors draw in and influence temporal factors on the periphery—that is, "international strategic factors"[1] and "key internal settings"[2]—and, in turn, get affected by them. The perpetual interactions and interdependencies between the structural and temporal factors, between which there exists a causal connection, intertwines them in a dynamic process that can be better explained by developing a hub-and-spokes framework—in which the structural "ideology-territory-contiguity" factors act as a "hub" and the temporal factors as "spokes." This framework carefully blends different variables and aspects to provide a theoretical explanation as to why the Indo-Pakistani rivalry came into being and how a highly structured mechanism has sustained it ever since its origin (as illustrated by Figure 3.1).

From the standpoint of the hub-and-spokes framework, in other words, the India-Pakistan conflictual relationship can be conceptualized as a dynamic process in which the structural and temporal factors constantly interact in the context of each other. They form a centripetal and centrifugal stress by unfolding a process of change, that is, the gradual increase in hostility and accumulation of grievances, which escalates the disputants' oppressive behavior and engages them in an intractable conflict: the complex rivalry. This theoretical framework helps to understand the full life cycle of the India-Pakistan rivalry by looking at it afresh through the lens of rivalry

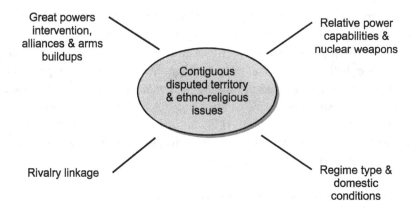

Figure 3.1. Complex rivalry: A general hub-and-spokes framework

conception and establishing a causal connection between the structural factors (hub)—associated with their central contention, the Kashmir issue—and the temporal factors on the periphery (spokes).

After locating and examining the interlinkages and the influence of the structural and temporal factors on the adversarial states' policies/political behavior, I propose a hub-and-spokes "complex rivalry" model to offer an alternative understanding of the India-Pakistan rivalry—which also has potential to explain other rivalries and emerge as a general model (as illustrated by Figure 3.1). This model shows how the structural "contiguous ethno-territorial" factors constituting the "hub" and the temporal factors as "spokes" coordinate and evolve a realpolitik-driven intrinsic interplay which arduously engages India and Pakistan in power politics practices and shapes their relationship as an extreme competition (as illustrated by Figure 3.2).

Before proceeding to conceptualize the model, it is important to define the interstate dyadic contention termed here as "complex rivalry." The proposed definition largely adheres to the general criteria of rivalry literature which expects adversaries to cross a threshold of five to six militarized disputes in a decade and so to qualify as a rivalry. However, it is important to mention here that merely fulfilling the common criteria of a given number of militarized disputes is not sufficient to analyze the rival parties' policy choices, threat perceptions, and the complexity of issues that embroil them in a relationship characterized by extreme competition. Therefore, this study defines "complex rivalry" to cover a versatile interplay of factors that have key roles in shaping the trajectory of dyadic conflicts. Taking these considerations into account, I define a *complex rivalry* as *a highly competitive and hostile relationship between the same pair of states over some issue(s) of intrinsic value or ideological-reputational concern for an extended period. In such a relationship, one or both of the states adopt increasingly coercive behavior and oppose the status quo by frequently engaging in policy and militarized disputes rather than reposing their confidence in diplomatic means to negotiate their issue differences.*

In the next two subsections, the foundation of the proposed complex rivalry model has been laid as a two-part conceptualization: (1) general interpretation and (2) specific interpretation.

Complex Rivalry: A General Interpretation

In a general interpretation, the complex rivalry model explains the context of rivalry by deploying the hub-and-spokes framework from the standpoint of a rivalry paradigm (as illustrated by Figure 3.1). In other words, this model places the rivalry conceptualization in the hub-and-spokes framework to explain the context of a given rivalry in two parts, that is, by (1) contextualizing the contiguous ethno-territorial disputes and the rivalry, and (2) establishing a linkage between the peripheral temporal factors and the rivalry.

Contextualizing the Hub: Contiguous Ethno-territorial Disputes and the Rivalry

Among all the contentious disputes, territorial disputes are considered to be highly "salient" and "sensitive" issues over which rivals can go to any extent to secure their interests or objectives (Garnham 1976; Hensel 1996, 2000; Hill, 1945; Holsti 1991; Huth 1996, 2000; Huth & Allee 2002; Kocs 1995; Leng 1983; Luard 1970; Most & Starr 1989; Quackenbush 2010; Senese & Vasquez 2003, 2008; Vasquez 1993, 1995; Walter 2003; Wiegand 2011). According to Paul Hensel, "Territory is often seen as highly salient for three reasons: its tangible contents or attributes, its intangible or psychological value, and its effects on a state's reputation" (2000: 58). Tangible attributes include strategic value, valuable economic resources, a population sharing ethnic affinities with the challenger state, and the like. Intangible stakes mainly refer to the feelings of attachment to the land, ethno-religious links to the territory, or symbolic, nationalistic values based on varied degrees of ideological overlaps (Hooson 1994; Murphy 1991; Sack 1986). Disputes have the greatest possibility of resolution if they are over tangible stakes, as they are divisible, but if they are laden with intangible stakes then chances of compromise are negligible "because their symbolic nature leads to fears about losing a reputation for credibility or of establishing a bad precedent" (Vasquez 1993: 78).

Mostly, intangible stakes make territorial disputes a symbol for a host of other issues and thereby transform these stakes from symbolic to "transcendent stakes," which make territorial disputes irresolvable because they reflect rivals' fundamental differences over values and norms (Vasquez 1993: 78n17). Inclusion of this characteristic in any contentious relationship makes adversaries' professed state-building beliefs or values, over which their statehood rests, entirely antithetical. Thus once ethno-territorial disputes or territorial contests linked with ideological overtones start exerting their influence on a given rivalry, the involved parties begin to question each other's territorial sovereignty by following a dangerous pattern of recurrent militarized disputes (Huth 1996; Rouhana & Bar-Tal 1998). That is why rivalries involving territorial disputes are most difficult to resolve and consistently flare up for a long time until a mutual resolution takes place between the rivals or a unilateral settlement is forced on the weaker side by the stronger through a devastating war (Vasquez 1993).

Apart from the salient characteristics of the disputed territories and adversaries' reputational concerns, "geographical contiguity" is another important factor that makes territorial disputes an underlying cause of militarized disputes and rivalry formation (Hensel 2000; Vasquez 1993, 1996a). "The potential for international violence exists," write Bruce Russett and John Oneal, "when at least one member of a dyad can reach the other with military force. For most states, the ability to do so is determined foremost by geographical proximity" (2001: 100). The opportunity to fight one another and the extended ability to use force closer to home increases the probability of adversaries' involvement in prolonged rivalries (Quackenbush 2006). Hence "the importance of distance is apparent" in rivalry formation and escalation (Russett & Oneal 2001: 100)—as it affects both the opportunity for involvement in armed disputes and the willingness to engage in them (Most & Starr 1989). To put it differently, this relationship can be explained in terms of Kenneth Boulding's (1962) "loss-of-strength gradient." Since the ability to project power declines with distance, any armed confrontation between two states at a great distance from their homelands is less likely because a state involved in an away-from-home dispute is likely to be at a greater disadvantage. As a result of the lack of contiguous territory, many states do not engage in long-distance contentious relationships. This leads us to conclude that disputes over salient contiguous territory with ethno-religious linkage—that is, religious, ethnic, and linguistic affinities of one (or both) rivals with the populace of a disputed territory—have a higher likeli-hood to embroil the disputants in recurrent militarized confrontations and form a protracted conflict or rivalrous relationship than those disputes where only contiguous or non-contiguous territory, or non-contiguous ter-ritory involving a linked ethno-religious population, is in dispute.

Spokes in Action: The Peripheral Temporal Factors and the Rivalry

In the IR scholarship, it is well established that alliances and arms buildup deter severe armed confrontations and increase the prospects of bargain-ing between the adversaries (Diehl 1985; Morgenthau [1967] 2001; Waltz 1979). On the other hand, a considerable literature on alliances and arms races argues that both of these variables play a significant role in rivalry formation and escalation (Bueno de Mesquita 1975, 1978; Geller 1993; Levy 1981; Maoz 2000; Richardson 1960; Sample 1998a, 1998b, 2000; Siverson & Starr 1989; Vasquez 1993; Wallace 1979, 1982). For instance, Karl Deutsch and David Singer note that "[once] a nation enters into the standard coalition, it is much less of a free agent than it was while [un] aligned. That is, alliance partners now exercise an inhibiting effect—or perhaps even a veto—upon its freedom to interact with non-alliance nations" (1964: 392–93). However, the notion and importance of alliance formation varies from member to member. A member can perceive the goal of alliance formation to be different, that is, offensive instead of defensive or vice versa, which mostly leads to misjudgments and in turn intensifies the probability of dispute occurrence (Maoz 2000). Precisely for this reason, aligned states are more likely to experience extreme mili-tarized conflicts than unaligned states—however, geographically contig-uous and highly militarized unaligned rivals generally experience armed disputes (Bremer 1992; Bueno de Mesquita 1981). As opposed to the realist contention that alliances prevent states from indulging in militarized disputes/wars, the conflict research shows their pivotal role therein (Bremer 1992; Geller & Singer 1998; Gibler 2000; Vasquez 1993). The real-ist notions that balance of power between states leads to peace and stabil-ity do not hold up in the context of rivalry. "Once a major state aligns with a weak state," notes John Vasquez, "this can increase the probability of [severe conflicts rather than peace] because when weak allies are led by

hard-liners they will not support compromises that avoid war. Therefore . . . [alliances] put a constraint on conciliatory acts" (Vasquez 1998:
216, cited in Goertz & Diehl 2000: 214). Furthermore, in rivalrous relationships, alliances and contiguous geography "together produce some
powerful underlying necessary conditions"—that is, "opportunity" and
"willingness," respectively—that structure adversaries' dispute initiation
and escalation tendencies (Siverson & Starr 1989: 43–44).

Likewise, the material calculations, such as buildup of an armed superiority, encourage adversaries to resort to militarized disputes and conflict
escalation (Diehl 1985; Richardson 1960; Sample 1998a, 1998b; Vasquez 1993;
Wallace 1979, 1982). The occurrence of World Wars I and II are two examples
of how arms buildups have played a key role in shaping the great powers'
decisions that spiraled into devastating wars. "Over the past 150 years,"
writes Stuart Bremer, "there is no evidence to support the contention that
the possession of military capability in large quantities ensures peace. On
the contrary, the evidence suggests that . . . there is a positive association
between the possession of military capability and its ultimate use" (1980:
79). Increased misperceptions that a rival is increasing its arms to target an
opponent, in turn, compels the opponent to behave in accordance with the
realist calculus (Sample 1998a, 1998b). Consequently, this behavior weaves a
vicious trap of counter-moves which decreases the bargaining space and
shoves the adversaries into spirals of armed confrontations. Another important aspect associated with alliances and arms buildups is the role of great
powers or third parties in interstate dispute escalations. The research shows
that, besides regional destabilization, most third-party arms transfers apparently contribute to imbalance the minor powers' political-military relations
and thereby lead them to form intensive rivalrous relationships (Barringer
1972; Kinsella 1994, 1995, 1998; Kinsella & Tillema 1995; Miller 2007; Sanjian
1999, 2001, 2003).[3] For instance, Richard Barringer's work sheds light on
how major powers played a critical role in aggravating minor powers'
conflicts:

> [I]t is [the major powers] . . . who must be held largely responsible for the
> course of development of [minor powers'] conflicts. In the pursuit of spheres
> of influence and in the name of righteous principles, the great powers have
> generally supplied the public support and the military hardware that are the
> very fuel of local conflict, even while withholding or failing to furnish the
> agencies of impartial accommodation. (1972: 112)

Considerable attention has been devoted to the puzzle of whether power capabilities and parity are responsible for rivalry formation and recurrent armed confrontations. Though the proponents of power parity claim that the parity balances the rivals' capabilities and thus stabilizes their relations (Waltz 1979), the advocates of power preponderance posit that dominance by one side in an interstate relationship curtails the probability of rivalry formation and escalation (Organski & Kugler 1980). Contrary to the Waltzian thesis, it has been noted that states can sustain rivalries if they possess equal relative capability, potential, and will to challenge their opponents regionally or globally (Vasquez 1996a, 1996b). While examining the conflict patterns of rivals, Daniel Geller has also observed that "dynamic balances, capability shifts—and particularly shifts *toward* parity—are associated with higher probabilities of war" (1993: 189; also see Kim 1992; Kim & Morrow 1992). The reason "symmetrical capabilities . . . make rivalry more likely and more enduring" (Thompson 2001: 573) is that "with roughly equal capabilities, the conflicts of interest are likely to persist because it is less likely that one part of the dyad will be able to impose its will on the other actor successfully" (Colaresi, Rasler, & Thompson 2007: 24). Mismatched relative capabilities never place states in a real competition because the stronger side can crush the weaker opponent with ease and thereby neutralize the chances of rivalry formation or escalation (Vasquez 1996a: 533). After the rivalry formation, it is mostly the challenger state's dissatisfaction with the status quo and its consistent attempts to gain parity that increase the probability of rivalry escalation and intensification (Geller 1992; Lemke 2002; Tammen et al. 2000).

Overall, notwithstanding some exceptions, there is a general consensus that greater parity at the dyadic level positively contributes to the rivalry intensification (Diehl & Goertz 2000; Geller 1993; Lemke 2002; Lemke & Werner 1996; Vasquez 1996b). This suggests that an opposite trend can be noticed only when the weaker adversary begins to shift *away* from relative parity—a prerequisite condition for a sustainable relationship—in a dyadic relationship. Such imbalances in the adversaries' capabilities prompt changes in their preferences, which in turn increase chances that rivals may be compelled to end their competition or, at least, move toward its suspension or de-escalation.

Apart from power parity, the "regime type" is another factor which plays a crucial role to determine the nature of interstate relationships, that is, emphasizing friendship, rivalry, or enmity. In the context of rivalry, the

democratic peace research asserts that democratic dyads experience less frequent militarized disputes than non-democratic dyads (Bayer 2010; Bremer
1992, 1993; Diehl & Goertz 2000; Doyle 1986, 2005; Maoz 1997; Rummel
1979, 1995; Russett 1993; Russett & Oneal 2001). The core argument of this
field suggests that there is a correlation between joint democracy and peace,
especially between neighbors, because democracies act differently as a result
of shared political institutions and norms which shape their domestic and
foreign policies (Doyle 1986; Rummel 1979; Russett 1993).[4] Thus they prefer
to resolve their differences by engaging in peaceful negotiations or adopting
alternate conflict resolution approaches rather than resorting to armed confrontations, and these preferences increase the possibility of the resolution
of contentious issues to a large extent (Dixon 1994; Huth & Allee 2002; Maoz
& Russett 1993). From the standpoint of rivalry, it has been argued that joint
democracy not only reduces the levels of hostility between adversaries across
the major regions of the global system (Maoz 1997), but also pacifies them in
their early stages by increasing the time between armed disputes (Bennett
1997a; Goertz, Jones, & Diehl 2005). However, another aspect of rivalries is
that once they are established, a regime change shows little effect on the process of rivalry (Diehl & Goertz 2000). If rival parties' relations are tense, it is
argued, then the collective democratic governance might not impact rivalry
effectively—in fact, sometimes this may increase short-term militarized disputes between the democratic rivals (see Mansfield & Synder 1995). If such a
rivalry involves a territory or a salient contiguous territory involving an
ethno-religious population in dispute, the probability of positive impact of
joint democracy on their established relationship is minimal or very low
(Huth & Allee 2002; Hensel 1996; Hill 1945; James, Park, & Choi'a 2006;
Vasquez 1993).

Overall, the complex rivalry model I propose here—as illustrated by Figure 3.1—posits that contiguous ethno-territorial disputes are highly conflict-
prone but that what makes rivalries most dangerous is their additional linkage with external strategic factors, key internal settings, and the adoption of
power politics practices as a means to shape their relationship. Though the
model emphasizes that the realist calculus increases the possibilities of dispute occurrence, it is not true in every case. For example, arms races and alliance buildups increase such a probability more in those cases where rivals
have a dispute over contiguous territory. Likewise, the contiguous territories
with an affiliated ethnic population further push dyads toward a staunch
rivalry if the adversaries possess rough power parity and link their conten-

tions with other states, rivalries, or alliance systems. Once rivalries are established and adversaries have internalized the realpolitik norms or practices, it
is highly unlikely that even joint democracy or common democratic governance could undo the established pattern of conflict between the adversaries or manage a generous space to negotiate their disagreements and generate conditions for rivalry transformation or termination in the early to
medium term.

Complex Rivalry: A Specific Interpretation

After the general formulation, now the focus is on specific interpretation of
the India-Pakistan rivalry, primarily its intrinsic interplay that determines
the rivalry process over a period of time. Figure 3.2 gives an overview. Here,
the intrinsic process shows how the Indo-Pakistani rivalry became complex
in nature on account of both sides' simultaneous involvement over many
issues, which include different national identities and ideologies, contiguous ethno-territorial dispute involving varied degrees of overlaps, the
regional and extra-regional power positions, and different regime types,
whose diverse interplay influences and drives this dyad in a particular way.

After the shock of partition in 1947, India and Pakistan's issue differences
and clashing foreign policy choices led their decision-makers to handle contentious issues by employing power politics norms. When the two states
failed to resolve their core dispute over Kashmir peacefully, the matrix of
power politics began to link this contiguous ethno-territorial dispute with
their multifaceted internal and external settings, such as contested national
identities and ideologies, the interventions by great powers or third parties
through arms supply and alliance formations, domestic politics, and the
like. By building their relationship largely on realpolitik culture, India and
Pakistan have not only shaped the Kashmir tangle in a complex manner but
also institutionalized their bilateral relationship on the basis of realist
notions. Over time, both sides have consolidated their position by internal-
izing power politics practices and acquiring advanced military capabilities
to achieve their political objectives. These practices induced spirals of conflict and encouraged their leadership to take a series of aggressive actions to
link one issue with another to form what Vasquez refers to as "a vicious cycle
of disagreement-negative acts-hostility" (1993: 80). As a result, the gradual
augmentation in hostility and accumulation of grievances encouraged their
decision-makers to handle the Kashmir issue by employing unilateral solu-

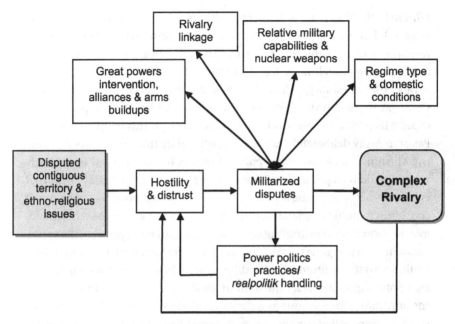

Figure 3.2. Intrinsic process of the Indo-Pakistani complex rivalry: A hub-and-spokes framework

tions offered by the realist paradigm which, in turn, aggravated the rivalry process and drove them to a historical mishandling of Kashmir.

The influence of power politics, coupled with pressure from domestic hardliners and linkages with other rivalries, consistently mounts pressure on the Indian and the Pakistani leadership to engage in arms competition and adopt foreign policies imbued with militarism and political rhetoric. Continuation of such practices led them to construct enemy images of one another and shape the Kashmir dispute as an issue and symbol of national honor and power struggle. Rather than enhancing their security, the possession of advanced military capabilities and alliance buildups brought about a security dilemma in their relationship, under which one side's security enhancement results in security vulnerability to the other. Over the last seven and a half decades, instead of maximizing security, the internalization of the realist norms has charted a zero-sum course in India-Pakistan relations that has made this dyad vulnerable to recurrent militarized disputes rather than increasing any bargaining space to negotiate their issue differences.

Another vital factor that made this rivalrous relationship "complex" pertains to both adversaries' key internal settings, that is, their divergent regime type and domestic politics, which extended the domestic hardliners and the restraining forces sufficient room to play a decisive role to intensify the rivalry. Frequent regime changes in Pakistan, for instance, have increased its democratic instability, which has affected India-Pakistan bilateral relations—as it assisted the Pakistan Army to control the state apparatus and expand its power. However, scholars still debate how this happened: Did the Pakistan Army deliberately subvert the political institutions by not allowing the Muslim League and other political parties to gain ground in the early years? Or did it step into a vacuum created by the weak political forces that eventually accorded it the arbitrator's role in domestic politics—a position it continues to hold? (See Jalal 1995; H.-A. Rizvi 2000.) In the absence of credible political forces controlling the state's policy-making process, the subsequent military regimes have systematically transformed Pakistan into a "military state" by promoting hardline approaches and militarizing the foreign policy. In due course, the military establishment has institutionalized the annexation of Kashmir as a national mission or core objective of Pakistan's foreign policy, which has contributed to three wars, and presented itself as the only institution in the country which has the wherewithal to thwart the perennial Indian threat.

The Pakistan Army's hardline approach has not only undermined the prospects of a peaceful resolution of the Kashmir dispute, in fact, it has also extended ample ground to the domestic hardliners on both sides—whose anti-India and anti-Pakistan postures in the respective countries have carried forward the divisive agenda of the partition—to embark on a path of excessive pressure, especially through the rally-around-the-flag tactics to placate their respective political constituencies. Instead of exploring amicable steps, such as the formation and promotion of credible joint institutions, economic and social engagements, people-to-people contacts, or other such initiatives, which could have created potentially useful bargaining space to negotiate their differences, the two states' excessive focus on the realpolitik approaches have given rise to a situation that guides them to adopt national security and foreign policy practices congruent with the hardliners' viewpoint. The increasing influence of these aspects on their foreign policy making has not only validated the restraining forces' and the hardliners' roles but also made them significant stakeholders in the conflict. Once the hardliners' dominant recommendations, especially in light of security threats, were adopted or followed by the decision-makers as a social practice, India's and Pakistan's policies began to form a vicious cycle of hostility and dispute recurrence. These recurrent crises further created conditions that strengthened the hardliners' position as well as increased a sense of rivalry between the two disputants. Overall, the realpolitik interplay has undermined the prospects of crisis bargaining, particularly through compromise and negotiation, for the leadership of India and Pakistan. Hence, instead of assisting to resolve the disputed issues, the domestic hardliners' orthodox approaches and their gradual accommodation in foreign policy making have headed India and Pakistan into more trouble and eventually made them sworn enemies by stabilizing their rivalrous relations.

Taking all factors together, the intrinsic interplay shows—as illustrated by Figure 3.2—how India and Pakistan engaged in an extreme competition and what mechanisms are at play that complicate their contradictory interests and ceaselessly guide them to resist de-escalation or transformation opportunities and prolong the rivalry with no end in sight.

OPERATIONALIZATION AND THE TIME FRAME OF THE INDIA-PAKISTAN COMPLEX RIVALRY

After the completion of a two-part conceptualization in the preceding section, this section operationalizes the India-Pakistan case by deploying the complex rivalry model and drawing its time frame from its inception onward. To acquire an enduring status, the rivalry approaches generally require a pair of hostile states to engage in six or more militarized disputes in a twenty-year period or come into existence with a political shock of some kind. However, Paul Diehl and Gary Goertz's (2000) model proposes that the political shock is a necessary, but not sufficient, condition to set adversaries to lock in a rivalry. This implies that shocks provide a conducive environment for rivalry initiation, but the probability of rivalry continuation depends on other factors also. Once the rivals recognize their relationship after engaging in initial disputes, they maintain "spatial consistency, duration and militarized competition" throughout the course of their rivalry and complete the rivalry life cycle in three phases: initiation, development, and termination (Diehl & Goertz 2000: 44).

Consistent with the propositions of the punctuated equilibrium model, India's and Pakistan's partition-led independence was the state-level political shock that created specific issue differences between the two states, particularly over the status of Kashmir. This conflictual origin embroiled them in early armed disputes and thereby set off the first stage, the "beginning phase," of their rivalry life cycle (see Figure 3.3). After the accumulation of grievances and hostility from their initial disputes, it was clear that the two states' issue differences and stable conflict pattern would sustain their dyadic contest beyond the beginning phase to the next stage of maturity, that is, the "development phase." Since its advancement to the second phase, the India-Pakistan rivalry has dramatically maintained its rivalrous fixture without making any headway to termination. In other words, this pair's near immunization to endogenous and exogenous shocks, its resistance to change, is not allowing it to move beyond its fixated rivalrous state, particularly toward termination and attaining stable peace.

Though it seems that the trajectory of the India-Pakistan rivalry follows the framework of the punctuated equilibrium model, which maintains that rivalries generally begin and end with political shocks, the proposed complex rivalry model requires certain modifications to encompass a wide range of issues to explain the full life cycle of the subcontinental rivalry in an effective manner. It is correct that the India-Pakistan rivalry came into being with the shock of partition in 1947, but the evidence suggests that it was also strongly affected by the armed violence associated with the rival parties' early actions succeeding the partition. The rivalry literature emphasizes that if new states come into existence by resorting to violence, they pose a high-level military challenge to each other by getting involved in militarized disputes in their post-independence years (see Maoz 1989)—this is precisely what India and Pakistan went through after the shock of partition. Study of these "early actions" is therefore equally important to understand the impact of grievances that augmented the feelings of mutual hostility and enmity and, in turn, intensified the India-Pakistan rivalry over time. Hence, an in-depth analysis of the beginning phase is necessary to examine the two adversaries' contradictory interests, initial disputes, and lessons drawn from them, which shaped their subsequent policies and political behavior.

To classify the duration of the beginning phase, this study modifies the general criterion of a minimum of six militarized disputes—a condition consistent with the standard time-density measurement (D. Jones, Bremer, & Singer 1996)—by incorporating the impact of divergent political systems and domestic politics on the two adversaries' policy choices that yielded thirteen militarized disputes altogether in a period of eleven years following their partition (see Table 4.1). The main objective of this modification is to

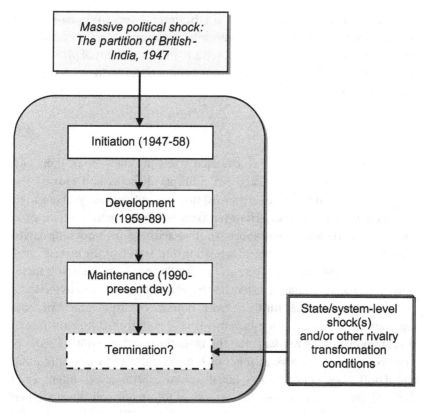

Figure 3.3. Life cycle of the Indo-Pakistani rivalry: The complex rivalry model

grasp the impact of early militarized disputes on the rivalry process rather than stressing the fact that after a certain number of disputes the two states mutually recognized each other as "rivals" or a primary security threat. On the other hand, this modification also approves the evolutionary model's initiation criteria—"early" and "intermediate" phases—which resonates with the punctuated equilibrium model's "isolated conflict" and "proto-rivalry" criteria. From the perspective of punctuated equilibrium, it is correct that India and Pakistan began to view each other as rivals with the shock of violent partition followed by a static conflict pattern, but the inclusion of the evolutionary model's gradualist character helps trace the impact of past grievances and domestic politics on the rivalry maturation. Furthermore, along with the incorporation of qualitative parameters, the modified initiation criterion delineates where this rivalry's "initiation phase" ends and the "development phase" begins. To explain the time frame of the India-Pakistan rivalry, along with the required modifications, a comprehensive exercise follows which traces the life cycle of the rivalry in four sequential phases: "initiation," "development," "maintenance," and a possible "termination" (as illustrated by Figure 3.3).

Initiation of the Rivalry

After coming into existence as sovereign states in August 1947, India and Pakistan simultaneously engaged in multiple disputes and crossed the required threshold of five to six armed disputes within four years of their independence (see Table 4.1). However, as argued earlier, merely fulfilling the common criteria of a given number of militarized disputes is not sufficient to analyze the two states' contentious relationship as well as the diverse interplay of endogenous and exogenous factors. For instance, Pakistan's inclusion in the Western alliance system had triggered an arms race between India and Pakistan after their ninth or tenth militarized dispute. Similarly, the replacement of bureaucratic oligarchy with the military dictatorship in Pakistan brought another fundamental change in the country's political-security practices. Such disruptive changes in the formative years not only influenced both sides' policy choices, but also put in motion several internal and external factors whose versatile interplay eventually consolidated their extreme competition. So, along with the recurrent militarized disputes, it is also important to consider the rivals' crucial policy actions and the impact of resulting outcomes on their interactions that defined the nature and the course of their dyadic relationship. This modification in the initiation phase also enriches the study's qualitative side.

By the "initiation or beginning of rivalry," I mean an early phase of a potential rivalry in which the adversaries shape their relationship by indulging in a number of militarized confrontations. Each confrontation in this phase adds to hostility and grievances from the past, aggravating the outbreak and the severity of the subsequent confrontations. With these modifications, the complex rivalry model demarks the "beginning phase" of the India-Pakistan rivalry as follows: it starts with the political shock of partition and ends with the formation of a robust autocratic-democratic relationship between India and Pakistan in the immediate aftermath of the October 1958 military coup in Pakistan and the initiation of the thirteenth militarized dispute (1947–58).

Development and Maintenance of the Rivalry

To operationalize the complex rivalry model in right fashion, a second modification is required in the development phase. As per the punctuated equilibrium model, the India-Pakistan rivalry is in the second phase and may remain fixated here until the dyad makes headway to termination by experiencing political shocks of some kind. However, this rivalry has experienced two such shocks: first, the state-level shock with the outbreak of the Bangladesh War of 1971, which resulted in Pakistan's devastating defeat and the secession of its eastern wing; and second, the system-level shock with the termination of the Cold War in the late 1980s, which brought several ongoing rivalries to an end. But paradoxically the India-Pakistan rivalry survived both shocks and did not make any headway to termination. Why the India-Pakistan rivalry absorbs such massive state- and system-level shocks and persists without showing any sign of weakness remains a puzzle that accords it, along with a few other rivalries, an outlier status in world politics.

To understand its puzzling behavior, it is important to investigate the "persisting period" of the India-Pakistan rivalry independently, that is, by splitting it from the development phase. In the post-1971 period, the two adversaries' focus was more on acquiring nuclear capability, and the subsequent nuclearization of South Asia made this pair one of the most dangerous dyads in the international system, as the two geographically contiguous rivals have not only acquired nuclear weapons but also challenged the ironclad notions attached to the stabilizing effect of nuclear weapons. Against the claims of the advocates of nuclear deterrence, this dyad indulged in a conventional war in the hilly terrain of Kargil in 1999 and, a couple of years later, it was on the verge of another war when Pakistan-supported terrorists attacked the Indian Parliament in 2001. Since the Brasstacks crisis of 1986–87, the possession of covert nuclear capabilities on both sides has taken this conflict to a different strategic plane that stabilizes the South Asian rivalry. Addition of the nuclear factor, coupled with the end of the Cold War, has brought about a fundamental change in the dynamics of the India-Pakistan rivalry in particular and the region/system in general.

To understand this dynamic and explain the continuation of this regional rivalry, consistent with the proposed model's operationalization, this study requires a division of the development phase, adding another stage in the model: the "maintenance phase." Before starting to define the final phase, "termination," it is necessary to reclassify the modified demarcation of both phases. I assign a period starting with the fourteenth militarized dispute and running to the end of the Cold War to the "development phase" (1959–89)—which covers the 1965 and 1971 wars, the Brasstacks crisis, changes in the adversaries' ruling regimes, and regional and systemic shifts— and the remaining period of the rivalry, that is, the post–Cold War period (1990 to the present day), to a new stage called the "maintenance phase."

"Termination" of the Rivalry

For rivalry termination, the punctuated equilibrium model proposes an abrupt end following a political shock and no militarized dispute for ten to fifteen years as a cooling condition—criteria, excluding shocks, also proposed by the gradualist evolutionary model. Ironically, the India-Pakistan rivalry defied these termination conditions—for instance, the Bangladesh War of 1971 and the end of the Cold War—by not adhering to the required condition of zero militarized disputes for ten to fifteen years after experiencing a shock. Having won the 1971 war, though India succeeded in converting the Cease-Fire Line (CFL) into the Line of Control (LoC), it failed to secure a formal and final peace agreement over the status of J&K, which cost the dyad immensely in later years. Despite experiencing both state- and system-level shocks, the India-Pakistan rivalry could not avoid the traps of hostile behavior and recurrent militarized disputes. Both sides' strategic maneuvers to secure an edge against one another and increased military aggression over their unresolved territorial dispute, the divided Kashmir, have assisted in resuming the traditional patterns of hostile behavior well before the rivalry could complete the cooling period required for termination. Rather than showing any sign of termination, this rivalry pursued a dangerous course after the end of the Cold War. In 1990, for example, the two adversaries were embroiled in a nuclear crisis over Kashmir and that was followed by an intensive wave of Pakistan-supported proxy war in the Indian part of Kashmir—a recent example is the 2019 Pulwama suicide attack that entangled both sides in a dangerous military standoff that increased the possibilities of nuclear engagement. The non-terminating tendency of the India-Pakistan rivalry, especially after experiencing two political shocks, the nuclearization of South Asia, changing security equations in the Asian region, and their respective positions in the regional and global hierarchy, signifies that this rivalry may require additional conditions for a stable de-escalation or termination.

Against this backdrop of difficulty in proposing a particular path to trace the trajectory of the India-Pakistan rivalry, this book explores the possibility of transformation or termination of this rivalry from the standpoint of the hub-and-spokes framework. This framework examines the current state of both sides' engagement in relation to their internal and external linkages, as well as inquiring whether there is any scope or window to de-escalate, transform, or terminate this rivalry in the near future.

CONCLUSION

After a brief introduction of three different explanations of the India-Pakistan contention, this chapter moves to outline the background conditions of the regional rivalry and then conceptualizes the case study by developing a hub-and-spokes-based complex rivalry model. This model offers an alternative understanding of the India-Pakistan rivalry by identifying and integrating the structural and temporal factors at the domestic, dyadic, regional, and extra-regional/global levels. After locating these structural and temporal factors as "hub" and "spokes," respectively, it examines their interlinkages and influence on the rival parties to show how the causal connection between the hub and spokes brought in centripetal and centrifugal stress on the rivalry by unfolding a process of change. This dynamic process, it is argued, escalates India's and Pakistan's oppressive behavior and engages them in a realpolitik mechanism which eventually gives rise to a highly competitive relationship between them, referred to as a "complex rivalry." Finally, this model lays out the conceptual foundation of the case study in four different thematic phases, over which the book's rest of chapters are built, which weave together different theoretical aspects and empirical narratives to provide an effective analytic account of the India-Pakistan rivalry from its inception to the present.

CHAPTER 4

The Shock of Partition and the Initiation of Complex Rivalry, 1947–58

INTRODUCTION: HISTORICAL ORIGINS OF THE RIVALRY

Though the shock of partition marked the beginning of a formal rivalry between India and Pakistan, the genesis of their animosity can be traced back to the divergent ideologics and state-building goals of the two principal stakeholders of the Indian national movement: the Congress and the Muslim League. To understand the background conditions that made the bifurcation of united India inevitable, it is important to briefly discuss the Congress and the League's pre-partition years' sociopolitical differences that transformed into a political-military rivalry between India and Pakistan in the years succeeding partition.

In 1885, the Congress Party was formed to launch a national movement against the British colonial rule in India. Though its primary constituents were mostly from the majority Hindu community, it had also incorporated minority ethno-religious sections in its struggle for the *swaraj*—constitutional self-rule—and independence. In the 1920s, the leadership of Mohandas Karamchand Gandhi transformed the Congress into a mass-based political organization and, more importantly, democratized it—later Jawaharlal Nehru's inclusive approach also helped in secularizing its character. All these aspects reinforced the Congress's position in favor of a unified, secular, and democratic post-independence India (Wolpert 2000: 317). In the initial years of the freedom movement, the Hindus and the Muslims together opposed the British Raj. But with the passage of time, some Muslim leaders began to identify their community as a separate nationality with different political apprehensions—particularly those who were worried about being cast in a subordinate position in the post-independence Hindu-majority India—thus they raised the demand for greater political autonomy for their community. It was against this backdrop that the Muslim League came into existence in 1906 (Cohen 2004; Jalal 1985).

In the immediate aftermath of its formation, the League began to pressure the colonial rulers to initiate measures for the protection of the minority community's rights, mainly by creating a separate electorate for the Muslims. Waiting for an opportune moment to thwart the Congress-led national movement, the colonial rulers viewed the League's demand as an opportunity to create a power struggle between the two mainstream political forces. So it recognized the League as the representative voice of the Indian Muslims and granted the Muslims a communal representation in the Government of India Act, 1909—later this safeguard paved the way for the creation of Pakistan as a separate state. Initially the Congress recognized separate electorates for Muslims in the 1916 Lucknow Pact, but later it repudiated its stand by releasing the (Motilal) Nehru Report in 1928. Basically, the Congress did not backtrack completely; it sought to limit the League's demand to the United Provinces and some Muslim-majority pockets of other provinces. Such political differences charted a course of a gradual parting of their ways, particularly when the differences disillusioned the prominent poet and philosopher Muhammad Iqbal, who later mooted the idea of a separate nationhood for the Indian Muslims (Mohiuddin 2007: 59–64).

In 1935, Muhammad Ali Jinnah took over the leadership of the Muslim League, which coincided with the Government of India Act of 1935 and the provincial election of 1937. However, the Jinnah-led League failed to receive substantial support from the Muslim-majority provinces, particularly Punjab, Sindh and the North-West Frontier Province (NWFP).[1] The Muslim electorate's lukewarm support for the League led the Congress leadership to conclude that the Indian Muslims had rejected the League's claim of their sole representation. Consequently, the Congress reneged on its pre-election intent to form a coalition government with the League in the provinces. Such a high-handed approach on the part of Congress had deepened Jinnah and other leaders' fear that the Muslims might be excluded from independent India's mainstream politics, leading the League to move a resolution— famously known as the Lahore Resolution of 1940—for the formation of a separate state for the Muslims of the Indian subcontinent. In Lahore, Jinnah argued that Muslims' political rights could not be reconciled with Hindu domination and demanded, while voicing what was eventually known as the two-nation theory, that a separate land be carved out of the united India for the Muslims of the Indian subcontinent (see Ambedkar 1946; Jinnah [1940] 2001).

The last bids to keep India united reached a dead end when the Gandhi-Jinnah talks broke down in May 1944, and the Congress-League conference of 1945 ended inconclusively in Simla, followed by the failure of the Cabinet Mission plan to reconcile the two political entities' differences in 1946. Additionally, the League's landslide victory in the 1946 legislative elections, in which it won 90 percent of the seats reserved for the Muslims, had further buttressed Jinnah's claim for a separate Muslim-nationhood and the right to choose Muslim representatives and form an interim coalition government at the center. When the Congress formed the interim government in August 1946 without considering the League's demand, Jinnah appealed to Indian Muslims to register a protest by observing August 16 as the Direct Action Day. This mass protest snowballed into wide-scale Hindu-Muslim clashes and the loss of life and property, mainly in Calcutta and Bihar (Tudor 2013: 155–58).

Against the backdrop of growing fears of a civil war, the Congress Party preferred the partition plan for "a smaller but a strong and unified Congress-dominated India," as compared to "a larger but weak, decentralized and endangered Indian Confederation" (Lieven 2011: 56). The Congress leadership, mainly Jawaharlal Nehru and Sardar Patel, were "worried that the League would make governance in united India impossible through violent, obstructive behaviour and, by continuing the struggle for separation in post-British India, encourage forces that could dismember India in the name of religion or region" (Akbar 2011: 210–11). Finally, India was partitioned in August 1947, which brought Pakistan into existence, but the legacy of the Congress and the League's divergent ideology and state-building goals did not end there. Their differences continuously shaped the policies of India and Pakistan in the years succeeding partition, which led both states to view each other with apprehensions and a sense of animosity.

This chapter is organized as follows. This section and the next briefly trace the historical origins of the India-Pakistan rivalry and present an account of major disputes that occurred between the rivals during the initiation period. This is followed by a discussion that explains how the presence of ideology, territorial salience, and geographical contiguity together evolved the Kashmir dispute as a core contention between India and Pakistan while these factors' absence/weak linkage led the challenger state, Pakistan, to give up its claim over Junagadh and Hyderabad. The fourth and fifth sections together trace the impact of international strategic factors and relative military capabilities on the embryonic conflict and how they contributed to lock both sides in a "complex rivalry." The sixth section explains how India's and Pakistan's trajectories of state-making diverged and how differences in the kinds of political regimes they evolved triggered a series of critical steps that influenced their early decisions with regard to their bilateral relationship. The concluding section sums up the key findings of the chapter.

THE ONSET OF THE RIVALRY: THE PARTITION OF INDIA AND THE ESCALATION OF MILITARIZED DISPUTES

At the stroke of midnight on August 14 and 15, 1947, the Indian subcontinent experienced a massive political shock when India and Pakistan came into existence after the partition of unified India. This historic event brought a mixed bag of memories for both dominions. On the one hand, the two-century-old British colonial rule ceased on this day and, on the other, the subcontinent recorded a bitter secession of Pakistan from the inheritor of the British Raj: India. This traumatic event marred the subcontinent with one of human history's most colossal communal riots, which resulted in massive human slaughter and migration across the hurriedly drawn borders between the two new states (see Hodson 1997; Wolpert 2006).

Under the strong currents of Hindu-Muslim violence in the months preceding partition, the retreating colonial power failed to settle the fate of 562 autonomous princely states in accordance with the Indian Independence Act of 1947, which provided only two options to the princely states: accession to either India or Pakistan (see V. Menon [1956] 2014). This decision left the leadership of the new dominions and several rulers of the princely states in a baffling situation: India and Pakistan had to persuade these scattered princely states to join one of them. Initially, several rulers refused to get absorbed in either dominion. But later Sardar Vallabhai Patel's politically astute moves—carrot and stick policies—with coercive strategies pressured almost all princely states within India to accede to the Indian Union, and likewise Muhammad Ali Jinnah succeeded in amalgamating the princely states of Kalat, Bahawalpur, Chitral, Kharan, and Swat into Pakistan's orbit (V. Menon [1956] 2014). Only three princely states had decided to not abide by the 1947 Independence Act: the Muslim-majority state of J&K ruled by a Hindu Maharaja and the two Hindu-majority states of Junagadh and Hyderabad ruled by the Muslim Nawabs. Their disagreements or contrary posi-

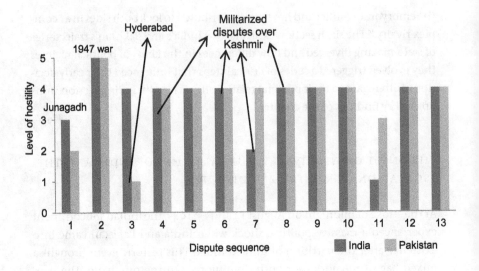

Figure 4.1. India-Pakistan hostility level (frequency and severity), 1947–58.
Source: Compiled from the COW database (2015), version 4.01 (0–5 scale); ICB database (2016), version 12.0.

tions embroiled India and Pakistan in a dispute over their status and subsequently one among them, J&K, emerged as a cause for recurrent militarized disputes and the formation of complex rivalry between India and Pakistan.

In the remaining period of the beginning phase (1949–58), the two states resorted to ten more disputes (see Table 4.1). Of the total of thirteen disputes of this phase, excluding the First Kashmir War of 1947–49, eight involved a high risk of war (see Figure 4.1). The underlying cause of militarized disputes was territory and border disagreements; however, some of them had a close association with the communal violence and persecution of minorities. For example, the Bengal dispute of 1950 and the Punjab war scare of 1951 were two such crises that forced India to amass its troops along the western border where, in the absence of mountainous terrain, Pakistan had no Kashmir-type parity against India. Though Pakistan had to back down in the end, its leadership learned the important lesson that until Pakistan attained rough parity vis-à-vis the opponent, particularly in the Punjab plains, its revisionist policy would remain on a weaker footing.

The Dispute over Junagadh, 1947–48

On August 15, 1947, the Muslim ruler of the princely state of Junagadh, Nawab Muhammad Mahabat Khan, had announced his decision to join Pakistan. A month later, on September 13, 1947, the matter became complicated when the Pakistani elites accepted Junagadh's accession by citing the ruler's absolute right to accede to either of the dominions (GoI 1947b). India, however, refused to accept the validity of Junagadh's accession to Pakistan on the basis of "geographic contiguity" and the "principles on which partition was agreed upon and effected" (GoI 1947a; GoP 2003: 269–70). Despite Pakistan's protests and threat to use force, Delhi imposed an economic and military blockade that paralyzed the administration of Junagadh (Campbell-Johnson 1951: 193). In his official communication to Lord Mountbatten, Jinnah argued that "[India's] policy and action are infringing the sovereignty of Pakistan." Delhi contested the claim and authorized an armed action against Junagadh (GoI 1947b). In the wake of increasing tensions, the Nawab fled to Karachi, leaving behind the Dewan, Sir Shah Nawaz Bhutto, to address the state's contentious issue of sovereignty and accession. The ruler's absence and India's strong foothold in Junagadh had seriously jeopardized Pakistan's claim over the state—however, Karachi steadfastly demanded the withdrawal of the Indian forces from its sovereign territory (GoP 2003: 380–81).

Facing financial collapse and lacking military might to resist the Indian squeeze, Bhutto invited the Indian government to take over the princely state's administration on November 8 (V. Menon [1956] 2014: 132–34). The Government of Pakistan questioned the Dewan's authority to negotiate a settlement with India, since the ruler had already acceded Junagadh to Pakistan, by denouncing the Indian takeover as "a clear violation of Pakistan territory and breach of International Law" (GoP 2003: 380–81). Later, Pakistan challenged India's legal claim over Junagadh by comparing it with the case of Muslim-majority Kashmir's accession to India, where India argued the ruler of the state had acceded the princely state to the Indian Union. While Holden Furber's assessment, that "the ruler of Junagadh's accession to Pakistan differ[ed] not a whit from the ruler of Kashmir's accession to India" (1951: 359), does hold merit, this argument could have consolidated Pakistan's claim to Kashmir had events occurred or taken shape in the reverse order. Karachi's acceptance of Junagadh's accession in September 1947, a step contrary to the two-nation theory, had undercut its Kashmir cause as it cre-

TABLE 4.1. India-Pakistan militarized interstate disputes (MIDs), 1947–58

S. No	Dates of Dispute	MID Initiator	Revisionist State	Cause of MID	MID Location	Fatality Level[1]	Highest Action Taken[2]	Hostility Level[3]	Regime Type
1	September 22, 1947–November 10, 1947	India	None	n.a.	Junagadh	None	I-show of force P-threat to use force	3 & 2*	Non-demo
2	September 26, 1947–January 1, 1949	India	Pakistan	Territory	Kashmir	>999	Begin interstate war	5 & 5*	Non-demo
3	August 21, 1948–September 18, 1948[4]	India	n.a.	Territory	Hyderabad	Missing[5]	I-attack and seizure P-no militarized action	4 & 1*	Non-demo
4	April 14, 1949–July 27, 1949[6]	Pakistan	Pakistan	Territory	Kashmir	None	Attack	4 & 4*	Non-demo
5	February 23, 1950–June 13, 1950	India	Pakistan	Policy	West Bengal/East Pakistan	1–25	Clash	4 & 4*	Non-demo
6	March 13, 1951–October 31, 1951[7]	India	Pakistan	Territory	Kashmir	1–25	Clash	4 & 4*	Non-demo
7	October 4, 1952–November 2, 1952	India	Pakistan	Territory	Kashmir	None	I-threat to use force P-attack	2 & 4*	Non-demo
8	May 7, 1955–July 12, 1955	Pakistan	Pakistan	Territory	Kashmir	1–25	Clash	4 & 4*	Non-demo
9	February 17, 1956–March 26, 1956	Pakistan	Pakistan	Territory	Rann of Kutch, India	1–25	Clash	4 & 4*	Non-demo

10	March 18, 1956–March 26, 1956	Pakistan	Pakistan	Territory	Punjab, India	1–25	Clash	4 & 4*	Demo
11	March 19, 1957–March 19, 1957	Pakistan	Pakistan	Policy	(New Delhi, India)	None	I-no militarized action P-border violation	1 & 3*	Demo
12	March 11, 1958–August 26, 1958	Pakistan	None	Territory	Assam, India	1–25	Clash	4 & 4*	Demo
13	November 10, 1958–August 2, 1959	Pakistan	Pakistan	Territory	Assam, India	1–25	Clash	4 & 4*	Non-demo

Source: Compiled from the COW database (2015), version 4.01; ICB database (2016), version 12.0

1. The COW database indicates fatality level of each side; the same has been retained here. Wherever both states' level of fatality varies, a separate entry has been cited against the country (that is, I or P) differently.

2. Here I stands for India and P for Pakistan.

3. The codes marked with an asterisk (*) indicate Pakistan's hostility level, and codes without it indicate India's hostility level. The COW database hostility codes are as follows: 1: no militarized action; 2: threat to use force; 3: display use of force; 4: use of force; and 5: war.

4. This dispute is missing in the COW database; hence the entry is adopted from the ICB database.

5. The ICB database does not mention the number of fatalities. However, the Sunderlal committee, which was later constituted by Nehru to assess the impact of Indian armed action, maintained that "at least 27 thousand to 40 thousand people lost their lives during and after the [armed] action" (Sunderlal Report cited in S. Raghavan 2010: 99).

6. Instead of July 19, this study extends the end date to July 27, that is, the day the cease-fire line agreement was signed between India and Pakistan in Karachi.

7. According to the COW database, this MID ended on August 14, 1951. But this study believes that it ended on October 31, 1951, when the J&K Constituent Assembly was convened for the first time.

ated grounds for India to accept Kashmir's accession in the following month. However, on November 1, after rejecting the plebiscite proposal, Jinnah told Mountbatten that "[i]f India would hand him Kashmir, he would let go of Junagadh" (S. Raghavan 2010: 61). But the Indian leadership refused such swapping.

In the meantime, to forestall India's overriding military challenge, the Dewan frantically asked for "aeroplanes," "a fully equipped battalion," and "arrangement to protect Junagadh's sea lines of communication," but Karachi "offered nothing beyond a few companies of armed police" (S. Raghavan 2010: 52, 36, 59). For Junagadh, it was a clear breach of pre-partition commitment under which Jinnah had assured Bhutto that Pakistan would not allow Junagadh to be "starved out or tyrannized and that Varavel [main port of Junagadh] was not far from Karachi" (GoP 2001: 579). In the end, the ruling elites in Karachi failed to defend Junagadh despite its accession to Pakistan. Pakistan's helplessness in the form of territorial non-contiguity and distance played a key role to not escalate the dispute militarily with its strong opponent, which ultimately paved the way for India to take control of Junagadh on November 9. Subsequently, the Indian government held the referendum in February 1948 in which more than 99 percent of the Junagadh people voted to join the Indian Union (V. Menon [1956] 2014: 136). Though the dispute over Junagadh ceased permanently, the atmosphere of mutual hatred, suspicion, and hostility spurred tensions between the newly independent states.

The First Kashmir War, 1947–49

Toward the northern tip of the subcontinent, the largest of all princely states—J&K—with its Muslim majority, was ruled by a Hindu Dogra ruler, Maharaja Hari Singh. After the partition of British India in 1947, there arose the question of accession of J&K to India or Pakistan, but the ruler ignored the principle of partition devised in the Indian Independence Act and "toyed with the idea of independence" (Stern 2008: 206). To protect the state from potential threats from both India and Pakistan, however, the Maharaja signed a standstill agreement with the government of Pakistan and proposed a similar agreement to India, which the latter rejected. A couple of months later, Pakistan backtracked from the standstill agreement and initiated invasion by deploying Pashtun tribesmen into J&K.[2] In motorized transports, Pakistan-supported raiders headed down the Domel-Baramulla road into Srinagar. The intruders' overwhelming, but undeclared, attack took the Kashmir State Forces by surprise and weakened its resistance in a couple of days, compelling the Maharaja to seek Indian help (Trumbull 1947: 1, 6; Whitehead 2007: 60–64). Though India promised to comply with the Maharaja's request, it attached a condition of formal agreement before sending its troops. Finally, the Maharaja agreed and signed the Instrument of Accession on October 26, 1947, which *arguably* made the princely state a unit of the Indian Union (Jha 1998; Lamb 1993). Pakistan disputed the legality and validity of the Instrument of Accession and consequently the two sides were embroiled in their first war over Kashmir.

To repel the raiders, India swiftly landed its armed forces in Kashmir and captured the Srinagar airport. Within two weeks, the Indian troops recaptured Baramulla by pushing raiders beyond Uri. In the beginning of 1948, Pakistan's regular forces joined invaders in a bid to annex the Muslim-majority state (Schaffer 2009: 21–22n32).[3] According to the war survivors, this undeclared war—an extension of the raiders' brutal attacks—resulted in the exodus of hundreds of thousands of rural Hindus and Muslims across the battle lines to the urban centers controlled by the rival sides, primarily on the basis of their respective religious affiliation (Devi 2021; Khajuria 2010; Mirza 2018; Payari 2020; S. Ram 2016; R. Ram 2018; Swaroop 2014). In the concluding months, the Pakistani forces lost some pockets in the southwestern and the northern sectors to the Indian forces but succeeded in holding a considerable area in the southwestern pockets of Jammu province, which Pakistani authorities later named Azad Kashmir (S. Gupta 1966; Nawaz 2008). In addition, Pakistan retained the northern part of the state, the Gilgit agency and Baltistan. To attain a strategic edge against India, Pakistan backed the Gilgit-Baltistan forces to capture important pockets of the Ladakh region. According to Asgar Ali Karbalai (2012), the former chief executive of the Ladakh Autonomous Hill Development Council (Kargil), these forces had not only captured areas extending to the north of the Khaplau region and Nubra Valley but also "attempted to seize Zansakar in the southeastern tip of the state." The Indian Army's forced opening of the Zoji-la pass, by using light tanks and armored cars, Karbalai (2012) maintained, "timely forestalled Pakistan's efforts to extend its strategic reach to the Chinese border."

By and large, the Pakistani forces withstood the Indian offensive, which convinced the Indian leadership that it had to expand the scope of war to clear the remaining territory. In hope of quick and effective steps against Pakistan's unwarranted aggression, Prime Minister Jawaharlal Nehru of

India referred the issue to the United Nations (UN) Security Council (UNSC) (Nehru 1961: 447–48). On January 1, 1949, the UN brokered a ceasefire and a fourteen-month-long war ended in a stalemate, which indecisively settled the de facto accession of J&K and divided the state into two parts (Behera 2006; Lamb 1993). From a heuristic viewpoint, what motivated the leadership of the warring states to accept the ceasefire was the existent political-strategic calculus rather than financial and societal constraints or a change in policy per se (see Jha 1998: 175–76). On the other hand, Pakistan had seized sufficient area which could ensure its territorial, strategic, and economic security. For instance, it succeeded in drawing a border line away from its vital military lines of communication and secured its agricultural economy, albeit partially, by wresting from India the Mangla Headworks—which also had an important role in the initiation of the Kashmir crisis (Akbar Khan 1975: 9–10). Later, the UNSC appointed a commission on India and Pakistan to hold a plebiscite, but its efforts to resolve the dispute faltered on Indian and Pakistani intransigence, which eventually made Kashmir a fundamental cause for repeated armed confrontation between the two states.

Hyderabad: A Low-Intensity Dispute, 1948

The Hindu-majority princely state of Hyderabad was embedded within the Indian territory and was ruled by a minority-community ruler, Mir Osman Ali Khan. Like Kashmir, Hyderabad's administrative structure was dominated by minority nobles, but unlike the former, the latter had a much stronger army, larger population, and monetary power. Therefore, in the last days of the British Raj, the Nizam and the Muslim elites "sought independent Hyderabad that would stand on equal international footing with India and Pakistan" (P. Talbot 1949: 323–24). The Indian leadership questioned the legitimacy of the Nizam's claims and argued that "Hyderabad was unquestionably a part of India." On the other hand, Pakistan was excessively eager to recognize Hyderabad as a free nation and "useful Muslim ally" within the Indian territory, so that it could continually annoy India (P. Talbot 1949: 324). Navnita Behera also notes that

Jinnah's objective, thinly veiled, was not only to keep as much territory and population away from India as possible by upholding the rulers' right to decide their people's future, but also to foment discord between the Indian union and the princely state [of Hyderabad], which would then be bound to seek a closer alliance with Pakistan. (2006: 11–12)

On November 29, 1947, Hyderabad had signed a standstill agreement with India for one year. As the integration of Indian states accelerated, a tough argumentative struggle unfolded between India and Hyderabad. Subsequently, the Nizam "broke standstill agreement in many respects, for instance by granting a secret loan to Pakistan (at a time when the conflict between India and Pakistan had come out in open) and by building up a semi-private army" (Blinkenberg 1998: 87–88). These developments, coupled with violent border raids and frequent attacks on the majority Hindu population, led India to impose an economic blockade on Hyderabad. The relationship further deteriorated when the Nizam "raised the question of arbitration on the alleged breaches of the [Standstill] Agreement; but the infringements had become relatively unimportant in the context of the increasing deterioration of law and order within the state" (Brecher & Wilkenfeld 1997: 168). The dispute intensified in August 1948 when the Nizam proclaimed Hyderabad's independence. Thereafter, he referred the contentious matter to the UN by stating that Hyderabad was subject to "violent intimidation, to threats of invasion, and to crippling economic blockade [by India] which has inflicted cruel hardship upon the people of Hyderabad and is intended to coerce it into a renunciation of its independence" (Clyde 1950: 278).

In response, the Indian leadership ordered an armed action, code-named Operation Polo, against Hyderabad on September 13. Within five days, the Indian armed forces took full control of the princely state and established a civilian administration. On September 23, the Nizam withdrew Hyderabad's request from the UNSC; however, Pakistan protested against India's iron-fist approach and excesses in Hyderabad.[4] The Indian delegates argued that the dispute over Hyderabad was India's internal issue and therefore its discussion on the international platform was irrelevant in the first place. Moreover, India had taken all possible steps to resolve the issue and resorted to arms only after exhausting all peaceful means. However, Pakistan differed and continued to demand an open discussion on Hyderabad, but the UNSC ultimately dropped the issue from the agenda. Finally, India conducted a plebiscite in Hyderabad and got overwhelming support from the people for Hyderabad to join the Indian Union.

SEEKING EXPLANATIONS: WHY DID ONLY KASHMIR EMERGE AS
A BONE OF CONTENTION?

This study argues that a combination of three structural factors—ideology/
ethno-religious linkage, territorial salience, and geographical contiguity—
produced some underlying necessary conditions that motivated Pakistan to
pursue the Kashmir dispute militarily with India in the immediate aftermath of the partition. On the other hand, the weak linkage or the absence of
one or more structural factors in the cases of Junagadh and Hyderabad had
convinced the Pakistani leadership to abandon its contention over them—
both princely states had modest Muslim population, low territorial value,
and were far from Pakistan's territorial borders. Junagadh was surrounded on
three sides by Indian territory and had access to Pakistan only through the
Arabian Sea; its main port, Varavel, lies almost 300 kilometers by sea from
Pakistan. Therefore Pakistan had no direct reach to claim Junagadh on a par
with India. Likewise, the princely state of Hyderabad was geographically surrounded by India, that is, fully landlocked, and unlike Junagadh it had not
even a direct access to the sea.

At a more sophisticated level, Pakistan's disengagement in Junagadh and
Hyderabad can be explained in terms of Kenneth Boulding's (1962) "loss-of-
strength gradient." As the strength of states decreases away from their homeland, it makes armed confrontations between the two states located far apart
from each other less likely because the state that is involved in away-from-
home disputes will be at a greater disadvantage. For Pakistan to reach and
conquer Junagadh, its forces had to sail through the Arabian Sea. Even if its
troops could have reached Junagadh, its access to or control over the princely
state would have been rendered meaningless in the absence of a stable logistic support base from home. In such an away-from-home adventure, the
Pakistani troops could have been subjected to a humiliating defeat against
the preponderant and well-entrenched Indian forces. In the other case,
reaching and conquering Hyderabad posed a nearly impossible scenario
given the combination of non-contiguity of territorial boundaries, power
disparity, and physical distance.[5] Such considerations perhaps led Pakistan
to abandon its claim over both princely states, as they were situated beyond
its geographical zone of power where its forces had no actual advantage to
enter and deter the opponent. It may be surmised therefore that Junagadh's
and Hyderabad's greater distance from Pakistan's territorial borders had
affected Karachi's capability to escalate these disputes further with India.

Alternately, had both princely states been geographically contiguous to Pakistan, the leadership in Karachi might have laid its claim over them by pursuing military means against India. In addition to distance, Junagadh's and Hyderabad's weak ethno-religious linkage and low territorial salience had further lowered Pakistan's willingness to engage India for a long time to claim these geographically detached territories.[6] As a result, once both princely states got settled in India's favor, the dyadic contention over them died out, albeit queerly.

If the cost, value, and risks attached to the acquisition of Junagadh and Hyderabad had convinced Pakistan to abandon its claim over both princely states, the very same considerations did affirm its resolve to pursue the Kashmir dispute with India. Kashmir was not only close to Pakistan from the ethno-religious angle, but was also economically and strategically salient and geographically contiguous to its borders. Its ethno-religious affinity with Pakistan, on the basis of the two-nation theory, therefore led the Pakistani elites to develop a core ideological disagreement with India. For them, the merger or accession of the Muslim-majority Kashmir into the Hindu-majority India would undermine the justification of the creation of Pakistan as an autonomous homeland for the Muslims of the Indian subcontinent. On the other hand, India disputed Pakistan's claim over Kashmir based on its secular, as well as strategic, nation-building vision. Rather than the religious parameters, it evoked the logic that the fate of Kashmir would be decided by Kashmiris through the Kashmir Valley's indisputably popular democratic force, the Sheikh Abdullah–led National Conference. This position, however, amounted to a negation of the two-nation theory; thus it was perceived by Pakistanis as the opponent's serious attempt to jeopardize Pakistan's whole state-building enterprise. Therefore, by claiming Kashmir, the Pakistani elites wanted India to acknowledge

> first, that the creation of [Pakistan] was right and proper; second, that Pakistan is a permanent addition to the map of Asia; and third, that Pakistan and India are equal successors to the Indian Empire. . . . For Pakistan, anything less than such an admission casts doubts upon the legitimacy and permanence of the national homeland. (Callard 1959, cited in Barnds 1972: 74)

Another factor that helped India and Pakistan to develop fundamental differences over Kashmir was its strategic and economic salience. The account of Major General Akbar Khan, who himself led the raiders' attack in

Kashmir while serving as a brigadier in the Pakistan Army and the head of
the weapons and equipment division at the general headquarters (GHQ),
presents Pakistan's wider security apprehensions vis-à-vis Kashmir's pivotal
importance for its security. He wrote:

> One glance at the map was enough to show that Pakistan's military security
> would be seriously jeopardized if Indian troops came to be stationed along
> Kashmir's western border. Once India got the chance, [it] could establish
> such stations anywhere within a few miles of the 180 miles long vital road
> and rail route between Lahore and Pindi. In the event of war, these stations
> would be a dangerous threat to our most important civil and military lines of
> communication. . . . This . . . could happen [not] only in the event of war, in
> peace time too the situation could be just as unacceptable because we would
> remain permanently exposed to a threat of such magnitude that our inde-
> pendence would never be a reality. Surely that was not the type of Pakistan we
> had wanted. . . . . [Similarly], from the economic point of view the position
> was equally clear. Our agricultural economy was dependent particularly
> upon the rivers coming out of Kashmir. The Mangla Headworks were actually
> in Kashmir and the Marala Headworks were within a mile or so of the border.
> What then would be our position if Kashmir was to be in Indian hands?
> . . . Thus . . . Kashmir's accession to Pakistan was not simply a matter of desir-
> ability but of absolute necessity for our separate existence. (Akbar Khan 1975:
> 9–10)

Though the contested ideology, as conventional understanding maintains, was the underlying cause of the rivalry initiation, the same could have
been an insufficient condition in the absence of Kashmir's territorial salience
and geographical proximity to Pakistan—as happened in the cases of Junagadh and Hyderabad. Once ideology and territorial salience coalesced with
geographical contiguity, it became easy for the Pakistani elites to embrace
Kashmir's ethno-religious linkage and anchor their national and territorial
claims in the two-nation theory, and the provisions of the Indian Independence Act of 1947,[7] to rationalize their political claims. In this respect, the
scholarly literature underlining the highly salient contiguous territory as a
necessary condition for competing states to confront militarily (see Hensel
1996, 2000; Hill 1945; Luard 1970; Vasquez 1993) helps to draw a parallel and
explain Pakistan's political-security behavior.

From this standpoint, it is clear that Pakistan's contiguous border with

Kashmir provided it with a necessary ability to use force closer to home, whereas the lack of the same condition in the cases of Junagadh and Hyderabad convinced its ruling elites to abandon their aggressive stance against India. Had Kashmir been situated exactly at the landlocked location of Hyderabad, Pakistan could have not claimed a non-contiguous, landlocked, and less salient Muslim-majority Kashmir solely on ideological grounds. Had that geography not been important, even the predominantly Muslim-populated Lakshadweep islands would have been part of Pakistan. This leads us to conclude that territorially salient Kashmir's geographic contiguity, rather than ideology alone, played a major role in evolving the erstwhile princely state of J&K into a core dispute between the two South Asian adversaries. In other words, when the ethno-religious affinity, territorial salience, and geographical contiguity together evolved into a stronger issue disagreement between the two antagonists, their collective impact not only intensified the challenger's (Pakistan) willingness to escalate militarily but also helped it to shape the Kashmir dispute into an issue of national honor and power struggle.

Later, when the outcome of the First Kashmir War did not favor either side, the resulting stalemate led to a puzzling division of Kashmir between the two adversaries. This division was viewed by both Indians and Pakistanis as loss of a territory of intrinsic value, which was not only the cornerstone of their respective nation-building strategies, secular and religious respectively, but also geo-economically and geo-strategically vital for their survival. "Kashmir [was] strategically so placed," as Phillips Talbot noted, "that neither Dominion felt able to yield its interests there. Whichever nation controlled Kashmir could flank the other's frontier in a military action. Furthermore, with Kashmir abutting Central Asia and looking on Soviet territory, each Dominion felt domination of the outer passes a matter essential to national security" (1949: 328).

As a consequence, Kashmir's multi-frontal geographical contiguity was considered to be integral to protect their sovereignty.[8] For this reason, both India and Pakistan wanted complete sovereign control over this salient territory, but the resulting deadlock put a question mark on the ability of either side to wield such overwhelming control. This is precisely what made Pakistan view India to be in an advantageous position and itself in a position of colossal disadvantage. As Paul Hensel argues, "when one side manages to achieve its goals over territorial issues, the other side may then have a powerful incentive to try to regain its lost territory and to overcome some of the damage to its national pride or honor, should the opportunity arise in the future" (1996: 51). From this standpoint, the Kashmir stalemate, rather than settling the dispute, contributed to increasing the sense of hostility, distrust, and reputational concerns between the sibling nation-states. Finally, this dissatisfaction turned out to be pivotal in shaping Pakistan's foreign policy, largely revisionist and dominated by the military-bureaucratic axis, which necessitated challenging the status quo at a more appropriate moment in the future.

In short, from the standpoint of the hub-and-spokes framework, India and Pakistan's ability to escalate or de-escalate their early disputes— Junagadh, Kashmir, and Hyderabad—was determined by the strong presence or weak bonding of three structural factors: ideology, territorial salience, and geographical contiguity. The outcomes of these disputes are consistent with the complex rivalry model, which posits that contiguous territorial disputes have more likelihood to recur militarily, and if that territory is salient and shares an ethno-religious population with one side, then recurrent armed confrontations increase severalfold more than those disputes where only non-contiguous territory, or non-contiguous territory involving an ethno-religious population, is in dispute.

THE ROLE OF GREAT POWERS, ALLIANCES, AND ARMS BUILDUP

The preceding discussion shows how the fusion of three structural factors comprised in the "hub" prepared the ground for India and Pakistan to escalate the Kashmir dispute. Once these factors defined and dominated the Indo-Pakistani equations, the international strategic factors and the key internal settings came into force as "spokes" and evolved a dynamic hub-and-spokes mechanism that shaped this embryonic rivalry. Major international strategic factors that impacted India-Pakistan relations and intensified their hostile competition in the early years were the great powers' interventions, rivalry linkage, alliance politics, and power capabilities. Rather than helping to negotiate their differences peacefully, these factors in fact extended Pakistan the leverage to assume a strong revisionist position and engage in repeated militarized disputes with the rival, India, that was dominant in the status quo. In the following subsections, I discuss and analyze how these factors' linkage with India's and Pakistan's early policies and actions impacted their relations, which eventually evolved into a hostile and competitive relationship.

Clash of Global Ideology: The East-West Cold War and India's Non-aligned Position

Soon after India's independence, the United States preferred India to join the Western camp to accomplish its objectives in Asia, especially in resisting the communist expansion, rather than Pakistan. "Nehru's open embrace of American foreign policy goals," calculated the Truman administration, "might prove . . . helpful to American interests in Asia and throughout the developing world" (McMahon 1994: 43). According to Robert McMahon, three main factors compelled US policy makers to look toward India: (1) the collapse of the nationalist government in China and the emergence of the Mao Zedong–led communist regime; (2) India's power potential and reputation—large resources, relative power, and political influence over other developing states—to act as a bulwark against the communist expansion in Asia; and (3) a fear of developing countries' exploitation by the communists, especially by emphasizing differences between the West and the newly decolonized Asian nations (McMahon 1994: 45).

However, the political leadership of the newly independent India did not adore the US vision and policy to shape the post-war global order. In fact, it was more concerned with adopting an independent foreign policy, guided by the non-alignment doctrine, to register its active participation in international affairs without getting entangled in the superpowers' strategic completion of stitching a large network of alliances and military bases to consolidate their position in the global struggle for supremacy (S. Mohan & Lobo 2020: 58). Apart from general disagreement with the bloc politics, India faced other defining issues that compelled it to pursue an independent foreign policy course; for instance: (1) the Western democracies' dubious practices in colonies; (2) capitalism's intricate affinity with colonialism; (3) post-war Asia's critical state of affairs; (4) fear of losing freedom to shape its foreign affairs; (5) a constructive requirement of political, economic, and social uplifting of its masses; and (6) the fact that though weak, India was strong enough to defend itself from its neighboring states, so that joining the external alliance system was not an immediate priority for its political elites (Barnds 1972: 45–46, 63).

For these reasons, coupled with India's experience of an anti-colonial movement and uncompromised stand for sovereignty in the form of the idea of non-alignment, the new political leadership of India took particular care to shape the country's foreign policy objectives so that it could maintain its strategic autonomy in international politics without taking sides with any

Cold War bloc (Nehru 1961: 24–85; S. Mohan & Lobo 2020: 58–59). In the early years of the Cold War, the main factor that derailed the possibility of formation of a political-military alliance between India and the United States was Nehru's principled stand that India would follow an independent foreign policy guided by the new-found doctrine of non-alignment. A distant second factor was Pakistan's pivotal geo-strategic positioning: it had a contiguous border with weak Afghanistan, proximity to the Arabian oil fields and the Indian Ocean, and an extended reach to the Southeast Asian region through its geographically non-contiguous eastern wing (East Pakistan) abutting the Bay of Bengal.

By refusing to line up with either bloc, Nehru had not only drawn "a pragmatic strategy" to maximize India's unquestioned leadership of a third force,[9] but also "posed a unique challenge" to the architects of the Cold War alliance politics whose definition of security was at odds with India (McMahon 1994: 38, 43). In the parliamentary proceedings, while explaining the rationale to keep distance from the bloc politics, Nehru had duly stated: "Countries get interlocked with one another, each pulls in a different direction and in a crisis they pulled away in a direction they never thought of going" (1961: 95). The Indian statesman's understanding of this, particularly when the world was entering a new phase of international politics after the collapse of Eurocentric system, had greatly disturbed the US policy makers who perceived India's third path as a potential danger to their worldwide interests. Many American analysts in fact believed that the Indian premier had "entered the arena of world politics as a champion challenging American Wisdom" (Zinkin 1987). For the US policy makers, "the global struggle that the United States was waging against communism represented nothing less than a holy war pitting good against evil." Thus in this "holy war," stressed self-righteous Americans, democratic India should align with democratic imperialist forces against the communist "evil" (McMahon 1994: 42). Nehru, on the other hand, believed that communism was in principle, akin to imperialism, in conflict with nationalism; therefore the rational policy for the Western states to contain communism would be their alignment "with the forces of nationalism in Asia and elsewhere," especially in raising their living standards (Panigrahi 2009: 153). But the Western bloc considered India's non-aligned perspective as an immoral position "because it was not stridently anti-communist" (Gould 2010: 34).

A majority of American policy makers had no firsthand knowledge of the subcontinent's complex setup. Their understanding about the region was largely based on the viewpoints of the British "Great Game"[10] exponents, such as Sir Olaf Caroe and Winston Churchill, who had little patience to understand and appreciate the Indian worldview. "Had postwar American foreign policy," says Harold Gould, "shown deeper understanding and appreciation of Nehru's determination to create a bulwark against political extremism and totalitarianism . . . , while maintaining neutrality between the two emergent global power blocs, the Cold War might well have been kept out of [several regions]" (Gould 2010: 23–24). However, as it turned out, "no U.S. official made such an effort" (McMahon 1994: 43). That left Nehru to conclude that the Americans, like their communist opponent, "have little appreciation of any attitude of neutrality and are inclined to think that those who are not with them are against them" (cited in McMahon 1994: 43). In the backdrop of bipolar settings and the rise of decolonization movements in the Afro-Asian region, the deepening superpower rivalry and its growing linkage with South Asia through economic and strategic engagement began to affect India's non-aligned foreign policy—particularly its strategic autonomy in bipolar politics—and, by extension, its nascent relations with Pakistan.

Rivalry Linkage: The Impact of Israel-Palestine Conflict and the Korean War on India-Pakistan Relations

An analysis of the India-Pakistan conflict from the vortex of the Cold War illustrates that the South Asian rivalry was significantly affected by other regional conflicts, mainly due to Cold War alliance politics and India's non-aligned doctrine. The political stand on Kashmir by the Western powers, particularly the United States and the United Kingdom, was prejudiced by their long-term security interests stretching from the Middle East to the Far East. With a declared purpose to "contain communism," they entered South Asia through the Middle Eastern conflict—the Israel-Palestine rivalry—and later the Korean War also played an important role to chart the future course of India-Pakistan rivalry (Barnds 1972: Ch. 5).

After World War II, the winning alliance legitimized the Zionist movement by evoking the logic of a Jewish "homeland" in Palestine to draw European Jews to the Middle East. On the allies' part, however, no inclusive approach was adopted to rehabilitate the Jewish Diaspora—a community which not only had made magnificent contributions in a broad range of European endeavors, but had also adopted Europe as its natural home over

two millennia—within Europe. A few years later, Israel was created forcefully
in 1947–48; the sudden shock of new development deepened the Arab-Israeli
conflict and resulted in the Arab states' attack on Israel. With Western support, Israel defeated the Arabs decisively and expelled almost 88 percent of
Palestinian Arabs from Palestine—a homeland which they had shared
together with Canaanites, Jews, and others over millennia (Shlaim 2000: 54;
C. Smith 2007: 1–2, 8–11).

The creation of Israel not only helped the Western states to shrug off Jews
from Europe, but also provided them a stable and vital strategic access "in
the oil-rich Arab lands astride the communication routes to the Far East and
Australasia" (Barnds 1972: 84). Their tactical support to the Jewish cause, at
the expense of the Palestinian community, sowed seeds of fear among the
newly decolonized Arabian states. To defend themselves from the future
Jewish-Western threats, the Arab states, mainly those bordering Israel, tilted
toward Moscow. For the Western bloc, the formation of Israel was considered
a substantial gain, but the ensuing Arabic tilt toward the Soviets was conceived as a colossal loss—mainly due to economic interests (oil) and "strategic requirements" (Gaddis 1997: 155–56). Consequently, the superpower
rivalry extended a leg to the Middle East, triggering a zero-sum and layered
contention among the key regional stakeholders and simultaneously
between the superpowers at the regional and global levels.

In order to shift the Arab states' orientation toward the Anglo-American
view, a break from the Arab-Israel conflict was needed. The British strategists
believed that "Arab opinion might be further aggravated if British policy on
Kashmir were to be seen as being unfriendly to a Muslim state" (Dasgupta
2002: 111). Therefore, instead of "aligning the whole of Islam against [the
West]" (cited in Dasgupta 2002: 111), the traditionalist Great Game faction
considered it "very necessary to place Islam between Russian Communism
and Hinduism" (Tucker 1988: 27; also see Caroe 1958). In this respect, the
Western states foiled a common strategy to block the Soviets' entry into the
Middle East by supporting a Muslim cause in South Asia: Kashmir (Mosley
1978; PRO 1948). For instance, Ernest Bevin, the British foreign secretary, saw
advantages in supporting Pakistan to further the British interest in the "middle of the planet" (Gopal 1979: 33). To use this opportunity fully to their
advantage, the Western powers began backing Pakistan's Kashmir cause
against India. On the other hand, through its regional allies, Pakistan and
Turkey, the United States continuously exerted "a constructive influence on
the Arab states" by exploiting their religious and ideological differences with

the Jews and communists (Chaudhry & Vanduzer-Snow 2008: 37). By doing so, the US-UK duo succeeded in scoring a point in the Arab world that they were not hostile to Muslims but supporters of their cause against India and the expansionist Soviet Union. Politically, it was a clever stand to cover their support to Israel by influencing the Arabs, blocking the Soviets' possible extension to the warm waters, and restraining the appeal of non-aligned India across the Afro-Asian region. With the formation of the Middle East Development Organization (MEDO), later renamed the Baghdad Pact/Central Treaty Organization (CENTO), this bond further strengthened. The newly formed regional organization helped the Western powers in three ways: first, it brought Arab states and Pakistan into their orbit; second, it helped to form an anti-communist bulwark of Muslim nations; and third, it provided the Western states a platform to spread the fear of communism among the Third World states and, at the same time, champion the cause of greater Muslim solidarity.

In a similar manner, the embryonic Indo-Pakistani rivalry had to endure a lot of diplomatic belligerence stemming from the Korean War, especially because of India's policy differences with the West and its mediatory attempts. In June 1950, the Korean civil war had broken out between the two ruling factions, Kim Il-sung's communist North Korea and Syngman Rhee's nationalist South Korea, over the right to lead unified Korea by overriding the "artificially imposed dividing line at the 38th parallel" (Gaddis 1997: 70). By initiating a series of coercive moves, "the superpowers had superimposed their rivalry upon [this] civil war," which turned the Cold War into a bitter hot war and substantially increased the possibilities of its escalation to World War III (Gaddis 1997: 71). The US global containment architects, Paul Nitze, Dean Acheson, and John Foster Dulles, perceived the Korean War as the greatest communist threat to Western interests and insisted that, if left undeterred, the loss of Korea to communists would lead to a "domino effect." The domino logic prescribed that every non-communist country must be defended against communist aggression or insurgency because if one country (domino) in a region fell to communism, it would bring down the rest (LaFeber 1991: 73). On the basis of this assumption, the American strategists "portrayed communism as a coordinated global movement" and argued that before Asia could be lost to the communists, the United States should take all necessary measures to prevent the fall of the first domino, that is, South Korea (Gaddis 1997: 76).

In this respect, the United States expected India's support, particularly to forge a collective security against the communist forces. The Western bloc was of the view that communist aggression could only be contained by aggressive military means; however, Nehru was not in favor of such belligerent options. While taking a neutral stand, he stated that the Western "security psychosis would end not in preserving the peace, but in provoking war" in the Asian region (Kux 1993: 87–88, 89). Furthermore, Nehru was worried that, on the pretext of the communist threat, the Western security model might embolden the colonial powers to delay the independence of Indo-Chinese states (Gopal 1979). These contrasting positions and worldviews widened the gap between the oldest democracy and the largest emerging democracy—the United States and India, respectively—in their very first years of policy interactions.

To achieve the peaceful resolution of the Korean conflict, India proposed three steps: (1) the UN forces should not cross the 38th parallel into North Korea, as this would provoke China to attack the UN's advance positions; (2) the communist China government should be recognized and accepted as a member of the UN; and (3) China should not be condemned as an aggressor through a UN resolution because this would lead to a stronger Sino-Soviet tie. Although the proposal appeared to be a genuine move to mitigate the crisis, its absolute zero riders against the communist stakeholders compromised India's neutral position. As a consequence, the Indian peace endeavor was perceived by the United States as "a room with only one door, 'pointing to the north'" (Kux 1993: 76). The Americans' deliberate neglect of India's repeated warnings that China would join the war if the UN forces crossed the 38th parallel ultimately brought the United States and China into a three-year-long armed confrontation (Gaddis 1997: 78). In the end, India's mediatory efforts in the Korean conflict not only failed to reconcile the two blocs' uncompromising positions but also angered the US-led Western bloc.

On the other hand, the leadership in Karachi adopted a diametrically opposite policy. They "rather adroitly played the Korean card to their maximum benefit to paint themselves as partners in the defence of the Middle East and against the communist threat worldwide" (Nawaz 2008: 96). The Pakistani policy makers not only "support[ed] the US in UN-sponsored actions against North Korea" but were also ready to commit "Pakistani troops to fight in Korea" (Nawaz 2008: 96). However, later Karachi did not oblige by citing its domestic obligations and two-front defense commitments (Jalal 1990: 111–14). Being a small state, Pakistan was not able to evoke an international uproar like India. Hence, it "spoke less moralistically" and "benefited" later when the US-UK duo rallied behind Pakistan's claims on Kashmir in the UN (Barnds 1972: 91). In short, India's differing non-aligned stance, failure in the Korean mediation, and larger political importance in the developing world together resulted in irreconcilable differences with the West which substantially affected the Kashmir issue in the succeeding years.

Tectonic Shift: Pakistan's Inclusion in the Grand Alliance and India's Compromised Non-aligned Position

Until the end of 1952, South Asia was formally outside the scope of the Cold War, though from the very beginning Pakistan's political orientation was toward the West and the latter had also prepared plans to bring the former into its fold. During the Korean War, US policy makers assessed Pakistan's importance in four fields: first, to forestall the Soviets' entry in the Middle East and Southeast Asia; second, to utilize its readily available and trained army during sudden, unforeseen crises; third, to use its air bases for air sorties in the Soviet skies to monitor the rival's territory and missile capabilities; and fourth, to counterbalance the non-aligned India (Kux 2001: 54–59; Schaffer 2009: 44–45). It was clear that the United States would compensate Pakistan for facilitating these tasks with generous military and economic aid and a possible security guarantee against India.

Once the cost-benefit analyses indicated the likelihood of favorable outcomes, the Eisenhower administration agreed to sign a military pact with Pakistan and did so in May 1954. With this fateful decision, the Cold War formally entered South Asia and baptized the Kashmir dispute. The Indian leadership viewed the militarization of Pakistan as a credible threat to the regional balance, as it would encourage revisionist Pakistan to resort to armed disputes (B. Sharma 1967: 92–93). "It adds," Nehru stressed in the parliament, "to the feeling of insecurity in Asia. It is, therefore, a wrong step from the point of view of peace and removal of tensions" (1961: 471). However, the US policy makers differed. "For Republicans like Dulles," writes historian Ramachandra Guha, "the fight against communism was paramount. Hence the tilt towards Pakistan, which he saw as a key member of a defensive ring around the Soviet Union" (2007: 159–60). Americans "did not believe that the small amount of arms aid being contemplated—perhaps $20–30 million—would upset the South Asia[n] power balance or enable Pakistan to become a credible military threat to India" (Kux 2001: 62). Interestingly, however, for the Americans the same "small amount of arms aid" was sufficient to defend an "unprotected" Pakistan and the Middle East from the communist threat.

Six months later, the US administration promised Pakistan another $171 million in aid over three to four years to re-equip and restructure its entire army and raise five new military divisions—all to a state whose military expenditure was already 71 percent of the total national expenditure (Jalal 1990: 237–40). The United States equipped Pakistan's "four infantry divisions and one-and-a-half armoured divisions" with the latest weaponry along with "twelve vessels, including destroyers and mine sweepers; as well as six air force squadrons, including three fighter bomber squadrons, one interceptor day fighter squadron, one light bomber squadron and one transport squadron" (NSC 1957: 136). Within a couple of years, the US arms commitment to Pakistan escalated to "$350 million, more than doubling the original dollar commitment," and another revision "placed those costs at over $400 million" (McMahon 1994: 205). From the US standpoint, as long as Pakistan fit well into its regional schemes, that is, acting as America's strategic counterfoil in the Asian region against the communist forces and non-aligned India, such a give-and-take relationship was a good deal.

The final step that formally dragged South Asia into the Cold War trap was the formation of two defense organizations: the Southeast Asia Treaty Organization (SEATO) and the CENTO. After the Geneva Conference on Indo-China and the French defeat at Dien Bien Phu, French power diminished drastically in its Southeast Asian colonies. Hoping to retain a considerable influence over the West-dominated Southeast Asian colonies and simultaneously offer a unified opposition to the Soviets' expansionary motives, the United States proposed the formation of a regional security organization, the SEATO. SEATO was later formed in the Manila Conference of September 1954 by the United States, the UK, France, Australia, New Zealand, Pakistan, Thailand, and the Philippines. Except for the Philippines and Thailand, the remaining states of the region did not show much interest in the Western defense arrangements, which in turn increased Pakistan's importance—as a border state of the Middle East and Southeast Asia—and its claims on US military and economic resources. In the conference, Pakistan "strongly opposed making the treaty applicable only [against] Communist aggression" and stressed that its aim in joining the SEATO went beyond countering the communist threat. This opposition brought a fundamental change in the treaty when the member states agreed to include a clause on aggression from all quarters, bringing India within the scope of the alliance's objectives (Barnds 1972: 98). Similarly, the Baghdad Pact was formed in February 1955 by Britain, Iraq, Iran, Pakistan, and Turkey (later, it was renamed CENTO when Iraq withdrew from it in 1958). Similar to the Southeast Asian states, most of the Middle Eastern states refrained from joining this regional defense organization. Once Pakistan became a key member of the US-led Grand Alliance, it "sought to use its membership in SEATO and the Baghdad Pact to put these organizations on record in support of its positions on Kashmir" (Schaffer 2009: 50).

Pakistan's blatant recruitment in the Asian security alliances brought "India involuntarily into the Cold War" (Thomas 1983: 69). Nehru's straightforward response was that "[the West] tend to encircle us" (1961: 94). To oppose India's encirclement and neutralize Washington's intervention in regional affairs, Nehru decided to seek Moscow's help. This decision charted a course to *de facto* alignment with the Soviets, consequently compromising India's non-aligned position. The Kremlin readily accepted this offer, as it hoped that a non-aligned India "would facilitate Soviet access to other members of . . . Third World" (Joshua & Gibert 1969: 55). "At a time when the West," says Denis Kux, "was seeking to contain the Soviets—vigorously trying to limit Moscow's contacts with the newly emergent nations—the chance to expand relations with the largest non-aligned country was an opportunity the Russians eagerly seized" (1993: 118). To bring Delhi closer to Moscow, the Soviet leaders, Premier Nikolai Bulganin and General Secretary Nikita Khrushchev, visited India toward the end of 1955 and proposed to their host generous military and economic aid (Malenbaum 1959: 52–53). More importantly, apart from criticizing the US-Pakistan military agreement and alliance formations, they took a clear stand on Kashmir, favoring the Indian position (B. Sharma 1967: 96–97). On December 9 in Srinagar, Khrushchev declared:

> The question of Kashmir as one of the constituent states of the Indian Union has already been decided by the people of Kashmir. . . . Facts show that [Kashmiris] do not wish that Kashmir become a toy in the hands of imperialistic forces. (cited in Lamb 1967: 88)

This unequivocal support drew India closer to the Soviets. As a result, "by arming Pakistan and checkmating neutralist India" (Gould 2010: 39), the US strategists'—who were obsessed with the communist expansion in Asia and had adamantly claimed that "the concept of neutrality is obsolete, immoral, and short sighted"—hawkish policy backfired (Crocker 1966: 114). Later, the two blocs' contrasting positions in other regional conflicts, such as the Suez Canal crisis and the anti-communist revolution in Hungary, further entangled the great powers over the Kashmir issue, which greatly affected India's non-aligned position.

Against the Soviet atrocities in Hungary, the United States and its allies proposed a resolution in the UN. This resolution was, by extension, also crucial to Pakistan's position on Kashmir as it urged speedy evacuation of the Soviet troops in Hungary followed by foreign-supervised elections under the auspices of the UN. Its adoption could have seriously undermined India's position on Kashmir (Barnds 1972: 121–22; Gopal 1984: 32–33). In Nehru's words, "Any acceptance of intervention of this type [could have] set a bad precedent which might be utilized in future for intervention in other countries" including India (1961: 556). India, therefore, voted against the resolution. The second issue that brought India and the Western powers into a collision course was the Nasser government's decision to nationalize the Suez Canal and the resulting Franco-British military campaign against Egypt. While protesting against the Suez invasion and relaying the Afro-Asian states' concerns, Nehru equated the Anglo-French military action with the revival of colonialism. Apart from Nehru's pointed attack, what disturbed Washington was the increasing resentment among the masses in Pakistan. Since the US campaign against the communist expansion was predominantly grounded on the strategic cooperation of the Asian states, siding with the Anglo-French-Israeli triad could have jeopardized its anti-communism initiatives. After analyzing the long-term risks, the United States disapproved its allies' military action and compelled them to withdraw their troops without demanding any assurances from Egypt (see Filipink 2007; Hahn 1991; Lucas 1991).

In contrast to India's ambiguous stand on the Hungarian issue and pro-Egyptian position during the Suez crisis, Pakistan's ruling elites—despite immense domestic pressure to break away from the British Commonwealth and the Western alliance system—backed the US policies. While reviewing the South Asian adversaries' political position during the twin crises, the majority opinion in Washington was that the United States must back Pakistan's Kashmir cause in the UN and, in a quid pro quo, use it to "exert a moderating influence on the extreme nationalism and anti-Western attitudes of the Arab States" (NSC 1957: 127). Thereafter the Western powers decided to reintroduce the Kashmir issue in the UN and duly raised their voices for a plebiscite in Kashmir by rejecting the J&K Constituent Assembly's reaffirmation of the state's accession to India. These moves helped Washington to accomplish its twofold objective of strengthening its relationship with the Pakistan establishment—simultaneously curtailing the growing domestic resentment in an important Muslim state against the West—and, on the other hand, sending India a strong message for assuming anti-West positions during the twin crises. The US backing of Pakistan, coupled with assurance of military assistance that included supplies of Patton tanks, howitzer artillery, F-86 jet-fighter squadrons, B-57 bombers, and modern communication and transportation equipment, won widespread approval from Pakistanis. In 1958, after the new Iraqi regime pulled out of the Baghdad Pact, the United States further beefed up its ties with Pakistan by signing a new security accord. In response, Pakistan granted US forces a ten-year lease of Badaber air base to operate U-2 spy planes against the Soviet Union and China (Kux 2001: 86–92; McMahon 1994: 254).

In sum, during Pakistan's formative years, the Western powers' consistent military-political support provided it enough means to pursue its revisionist agenda against India. By making Pakistan a key member of two separate Western-sponsored Asian defense organizations, the US-UK duo successfully made the two-wing South Asian state their strategic counterfoil to mitigate the effects of the Arab-Israeli conflict in the Middle East (which had enraged the Arabs), block the Soviets' entry in Asia's three strategic regions—the Middle East, South Asia, and Southeast Asia—and undercut India's foreign policy non-alignment. Overall, the US security alliance with Pakistan destabilized the region, entrenched India and Pakistan's immature rivalry, and forced non-aligned India to forge closer ties with the communist bloc. As a result, the two South Asian states became staunch rivals within the first decade of their independence.

INFLUENCE OF RELATIVE MILITARY CAPABILITIES

Under the terms of transfer of power, Sumit Ganguly notes, India and Pakistan inherited all movable military assets from the retreating imperial power in a ratio of 70:30, respectively (2002: 19). Similarly, Pervaiz Cheema maintains, "Of the 4,61,800 Army personnel, Pakistan's agreed total inheritance was around 1,50,000" (2002: 51).[11] But according to Shuja Nawaz, "Pakistan received six out of fourteen armoured regiments, eight of the forty artillery regiments, and eight of the fifteen infantry regiments"—an assessment that narrows the relative military gap between India and Pakistan to a ratio of 60:40, respectively (2008: 32). In addition to this asymmetry, it is argued that the Pakistan Army was facing three major issues: a shortage of army officers, slow delivery of ammunition from India, and the loss of key armament workshops, depots, and manufacturing units—more than 80 percent of which were located in India. Furthermore, it is argued that as a result of the hasty division of the united Indian armed forces and Pakistan's social, organizational, political, and economic structures being in disarray, the Pakistan Army was going through a tumultuous process of unification (see Riza [1977] 2003). Altogether, according to scholars, these logistic problems and military disparity had substantially weakened Pakistan's military capability vis-à-vis India (Cheema 2002; Ganguly 2002; Jalal 1990; Nawaz 2008).

Undoubtedly, these factors had a potential to impact the Pakistan Army in the long term, but from the standpoint of guerrilla warfare strategy their influence was minimal. During the Kashmir invasion, Pakistan had indeed deployed a guerrilla warfare requiring fewer military officers and less ammunition. In the later stage, when the dispute escalated into a war, it managed to increase the level of armed personnel and ammunition on a par with India. If the First Kashmir War had lasted for a longer time, as it was partially showing signs of doing in the middle of 1948, or turned multi-frontal along the international border, then these factors could have contributed to Pakistan's disadvantage. Of these two escalating conditions, at least one was required for these factors to play a critical role, but no such trigger occurred. Neither side perhaps had the capability to withstand such an escalation in the immediate aftermath of partition because of their poor financial resources, massive migration problem, and recurring communal violence across the new borders. Hence, within the zone of armed conflict (Kashmir), these major issues, as identified by the scholars and mentioned above, had almost *negligible* or minimal impact on Pakistan's propensity to fight a war.[12] However, on the basis of conventional understanding of India's and Pakistan's relative military power, scholars puzzled over Pakistani policy makers' decision to initiate the First Kashmir War:

> [I]t is hard to understand how any responsible Pakistani decision-maker could have believed that a war with India over Kashmir would result in Pakistani victory. More to the point, any dispassionate assessment of the relative capabilities of the two states should have made it clear to Pakistan's political-

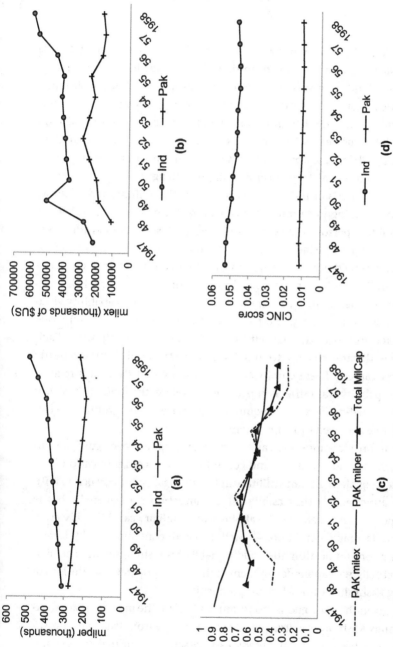

Figure 4.2. India-Pakistan relative capabilities and militarized disputes, 1947–58. (a) Military personnel (milper) ratio, (b) military expenditure (milex) ratio, (c) Pakistan's total military capability vis-à-vis India, (d) composite index of national capability (CINC) ratio. The CINC ratio comprises milper + milex + primary energy consumption (pec) ratio + iron and steel production (irst) ratio [population (total + urban) excluded]. *Source:* Compiled from the COW database (2015), National Material Capabilities, version 4.01; and, ICB database (2016), version 12.0.

military leadership that *India's military strength was substantially greater*. (Ganguly 2002: 19, emphasis added)

By evoking the logic of India's military preponderance, Ganguly (2002) argues that Pakistan's decision to initiate the war was flawed. This study, however, contends that such an assessment is misplaced, if not misleading, because the Pakistani decision-makers' choice to wage the Kashmir War was neither strategically incoherent nor irrational. The assessment of Pakistan's relative military power vis-à-vis India, as argued by Ayesha Jalal (1990), Ganguly (2002), Cheema (2002), and Nawaz (2008), has been misjudged on three counts: empirical, tactical, and willingness to fight.

Empirical analysis of India and Pakistan's relative military power shows that Pakistan had significant military capability during the Kashmir War. In 1947, its military personnel strength was roughly close to that of India's (see Figure 4.2a)—a decisive factor in the mountain warfare especially in view of the widely accepted notion in Pakistan that "man for man they were better than the Indians" (Barnds 1972: 74). In the second year of war, Pakistan's military personnel strength, expenditure, and total military capability vis-à-vis India stood at 1:1.2, 1:2.5, and 1:1.6, respectively (see Figure 4.2a–c),[13] one of a very few instances throughout the conflictual relationship when Pakistan's strength came so close to India's—an issue the book reverts to in the following chapters. These empirical findings show that Pakistan's relative military capability was rather competitive. Therefore, the kind of theatrical effects its armed actions were required to produce at the ground level in Kashmir were achieved to a large extent.

Tactical considerations, such as Kashmir's geographical contiguity, mountainous terrain, and command and control of crucial communication lines more or less equaled Pakistan's military imbalance against India.[14] Before initiating any armed action, the feasibility of such an action is considered to be the most important consideration. If Pakistan's total military capability is viewed with other favorable conditions—a well-disposed, contiguous, hilly terrain and strong communication lines; additional Pashtun strength; and the high likelihood of light weapons deployment in the military operation—the idea of annexing Kashmir became a feasible proposition.

First, given the contiguous mountainous terrain, the military maneuvering to annex Kashmir was strategically more feasible from Pakistan's northeastern border because of better roads, easy passes, and minimal grades compared with India's northwestern border, which had a single road to bring up supplies and reinforcements.[15] Additionally, the topography of Kashmir's tough terrain provided dissatisfied Pakistan an edge to inflict costs upon its opponent with relative impunity and, hence, added muscle to Pakistan's strategy. Provided with such a strategic edge, Pakistan not only troubled India by hampering its capability to fight decisively but also hindered its armed forces' rapid movements. As a result, Pakistani regular troops, initially tribesmen, took control of Kashmir's strategic peaks, which dragged the war out for a much longer time with unbearable human loss, especially those of civilians. Second, the availability of well-acclimatized Pashtun tribesmen provided Pakistan further advantage against its rival since the Indian troops were mainly from the plains as indeed was the case with the Pakistani regular troops. Finally, the high likelihood of the utilization of a selective military hardware in the hilly terrain motivated Pakistani strategists to wage the war. The logic behind this factor is well explained by Shuja Nawaz, who noted that during the partition, the armor, artillery, and infantry regiments were divided between India and Pakistan in a ratio of 58:42, 80:20, and 47:53, respectively (2008: 32). If one excludes the armor and artillery calculations, the infantry regiment ratio between the two states also stood as roughly equal. In any case, in mountainous terrain, more than the armor and artillery, infantry plays a crucial role. Based on this military logic and acquired parity at the local level, including Pashtun tribesmen and the former military personnel, the Liberation Committee, which was directly supervised by Prime Minister Liaquat Ali Khan, had anticipated vital political-military gains in the Kashmir invasion. After a careful deliberation of the "calculated risk," the prime minister-led Liberation Committee had assigned Akbar Khan, the director of weapons and equipment at the GHQ, the task to execute the covert mission by keeping it "secret from the British officers [including the British Commander-in-Chief of the Pakistan Army] and G.H.Q. Army officers"[16] (Akbar Khan 1975: 31–33). In short, Pakistan's overall advantageous position eclipsed its weaknesses and encouraged the decision-makers to assume that their country had the wherewithal to surpass its rival in Kashmir.

The element of *willingness* came into play when four factors—military parity in the local theater of the war, geographical contiguity, advantageous terrain, and accessible transportation—coalesced. Once the overall balance of power tilted in Pakistan's favor, some Pakistani strategists believed that their country now stood a chance of achieving its desired objectives (Akbar Khan 1975). In fact, the military strategists, like Akbar Khan, began to

appraise beliefs about their own country—especially about the martial prowess of their armed forces—by invoking the logic of history and religion:

> In the remotest of our villages, the humblest of our people possess a self-
> confidence and ready willingness to march forward into India—a spirit the
> equivalent of which cannot be found on the other side. It [may take] many
> generations to create such a spirit. . . . In India, in the absence of homogene-
> ity, a penetration in any direction can result in separation of differing units
> geographically as well as morally because there is no basic unity among the
> Shudras, Brahamans, Sikhs, Hindus and Muslims who will follow their own
> different interests. At present, and for a long time to come, India is in the
> same position as she was centuries ago, exposed to disintegration in emer-
> gencies. . . . The fear of the past still haunts them, because many terrible inva-
> sions have penetrated through [India] from this side [Pakistan/the Muslims
> of the West Asia], and we have ruled them for eight centuries. (Akbar Khan
> 1975: 191–92)

This shows that Akbar Khan's self-power assessment was based on the images
of Islam's glorious past and racial superiority myths—similar to that of the
German dictator Adolf Hitler's beliefs about the Aryan race—rather than the
strategic rationale. While "assessing their relative strength," as Geoffrey
Blainey suggests, states get "influenced by . . . perceptions of internal unity
and of the unity or discord of the enemy" (1973: 123). It can be argued that
Akbar Khan's perceptions about India were on a similar footing. Undoubtedly, India (read as the Indian system of states) had retained overwhelming
power since ancient times, but it had repeatedly failed to convert its greater
resources into what Joseph Nye terms "preferred outcomes" (2011: 13n5).
Likewise, India's aggregate power during the Kashmir War was severalfold
more than that of Pakistan (see Figure 4.2d), but Pakistan had formulated a
strategy that was largely based on the assessment of the target state's past
military behavior and present military capabilities rather than its aggregate
power. In other words, one may suggest that Pakistan's strategy drew heavily
on the willingness notion of power, which led it to tentatively believe that
India's overreaching capability had less to do with its willingness to defend
itself. To a sudden military challenge, Pakistan strategists might have anticipated, the modern Indian leadership might respond similarly to their
ancient counterparts. "Little if any thought," as Behera says, "had been given

to the prospect of failure or to what might happen if the Indian army fore-stalled a Pakistani [aggression]" (2006: 76).

This analysis shows that Pakistan's warring behavior during the initial years was consistent with the classical framework of the power transition theory, which emphasizes that the likelihood of war increases when a rough balance of power arises between the status quo power and its challenger. Pre-cisely what causes the challenger state to think along these lines is the power parity belief, that its net benefits will be greater than its costs. Such a reward-ing incentive motivates the challenger to use war as a means to its aims (see Organski & Kugler 1980). Vasquez (1993) supports this argument that in a dyadic conflict where adversaries' military power is consistent, one would normally expect war to occur especially when the potential initiator is the revisionist state. Similarly, Blainey argues, "Wars usually end when the fight-ing nations *agree* on their relative strength, and wars usually begin when fighting nations *disagree* on their relative strength" (1973: 122, emphasis in original). Therefore, provided with such military parity and strategic pre-ponderance, though for a brief period, any rival political-military leadership could have decided the way Pakistani leadership did in 1947. From this stand-point, it may be argued that Pakistan's decision to initiate the Kashmir War was not based on any fallacious reasoning, as some scholars have argued; rather, it was a "calculated risk" to take possession of a salient contiguous territory with a related ethno-religious population by force rather than los-ing it completely without posing any resistance to an opponent which did not agree with the two-nation theory and, by extension, the creation of a separate homeland for the Muslims of the subcontinent.

After the First Kashmir War, India and Pakistan were embroiled in several armed disputes (see Table 4.1). Empirical evidence suggests that Pakistan's increasing military capability, coupled with its confidence emanating from the stalemate in Kashmir, had serious implications for the outbreak of post-ceasefire disputes (see Figures 4.1 and 4.2).[17] Both states' aggressive military postures had not only extended the duration of these disputes but also brought them to the brink of war during the Bengal communal clashes of 1950 and the Punjab war scare of 1951 (see Table 4.1). What complicated this relationship further was precisely the territorial dispute over Kashmir and the use of force to seek its resolution. Kashmir's intrinsic value and reputa-tional concerns did not allow India and Pakistan to make vital concessions in the early years, which in turn deepened their distrust and hostility, resulting in the militarization of the region and recurrent armed confrontations between them. In the end, this pattern of conflictual interactions in their early years ensured the formation of a long-term rivalry.

IMPACT OF REGIME TYPE AND DOMESTIC POLITICAL CONDITIONS

Despite a common political history, India's and Pakistan's state-making trajectories assumed altogether divergent political paths in terms of the nature of their state structures and kinds of regime forged during their formative years. The proponents of the democratic peace theory posit that joint democracy or common democratic governance increases the chances of conflict resolution between the adversaries, as their norm-based orientation provides generous space to negotiate disagreements (Doyle 2005; Rummel 1979; Russett 1993). In light of these claims, therefore, it is important to investigate if India's and Pakistan's different political systems (or regime type) exercised any influence on their political behavior in the early years after their independence. In this respect, I inquire: Did the difficulties associated with regime type in both countries contribute to dispute recurrence and the formation of rivalry? Had India and Pakistan been stable democracies, in other words, would they have reconciled their disagreements or mended their relationship?

To address this question, I identify and examine four elements that impacted the Indo-Pakistani relationship: (1) the inability of Pakistan's founding political party, the Muslim League, to entrench itself in the political system and control the political process between the newly constructed center and the provinces which shaped Pakistan's polity in the succeeding years; (2) the prominence of the numerous landed elites, who enjoyed substantial political and social support within their own provinces as well as in the power hierarchy of the state, along with authoritarian tendencies of its bureaucracy; (3) Pakistani civilian leadership's compulsions to pursue realpolitik policies to divert domestic resentment; and (4) the evolution of different regime type and internal setups in India and Pakistan.

Right from the outset, India and Pakistan pursued divergent political processes that led to the creation of very different state structures and regimes. India's political leadership unanimously set forth a shared programmatic process to draft a constitution which laid down mechanisms and processes for power sharing among different sociopolitical groups and created a popular representative system, that is, a parliamentary democracy. Though the Congress Party was a dominant political force, it had taken particular care to ensure minority representation in the Constituent Assembly by including Muslims, Parsis, Christians, Anglo-Indians, women, and members of Scheduled Castes and Tribes. In fact, the chairman of the Drafting Committee, B.R. Ambedkar, was a non-Congress member from the Scheduled Caste community. Three major factors that laid the foundations of India as a stable democratic state include the Congress Party's organizational robustness and political will to accommodate the concerns of various political groups and sections of the society; the Constituent Assembly's ability to debate fundamental issues from different standpoints and condition them to formalize a consensual constitution; and the Indian elites'—ruling and those in opposition—political acumen and commitment to follow due political procedures to resolve intra- and inter-party disputes, political deadlocks, or other such issues (Tudor 2013: 161–69).

Unlike India's ruling elites' consensual and accommodative approach, the situation in Pakistan was the opposite. The founding father of Pakistan, Muhammad Ali Jinnah, retained his control over important political institutions and intended to build the country as a semi-authoritarian state based on British India's vice-regal system. He was not only the governor-general of Pakistan, but also the president of the Muslim League and the head of the Constituent Assembly. Jinnah's authoritative practices eventually forged a legacy of power concentration for succeeding governor-generals, which hampered the process of the constitution formation and the development of a democratic polity in Pakistan (Kukreja 2003: 8–10). Additionally, Pakistan's national leadership was extremely dependent on the provincial landlords and the civil bureaucracy; both stakeholders were least interested in the institutionalization of a genuine democratic system in the newly created state. After Jinnah's demise in 1948, three divergent factors pulled Pakistan's political institutions in different directions, especially its Constituent Assembly; these included a weak national leadership at the center and the landlord-dominated politics in major provinces; the clash of interests between the two geographically non-contiguous and divergent wings of the country: the Bengali-majority eastern wing and the Punjabi-dominated western wing; and the decisive role of the bureaucratic elites in stifling the development of democratic processes and political participation for the furtherance of their own narrow interests (Jahan 1972: 24–29).

Since the Bengalis were in the majority in the new country (Pakistan), they "desired the creation of a constitution which reflected its proportionate share of power, but the landlords of the Punjab (and to a lesser extent, Sindh) were not inclined to relinquish power and submit to a parliament which they could not control" (Tudor 2013: 173). The Muslim League's inability to control or accommodate contrary political interests of the peasantry in East Pakistan and the large landed aristocracy in West Pakistan "led to the slow, steady aggrandizement of executive authority by the civilian bureaucracy with the support of the military" (Tudor 2013: 174). This unending struggle for power and influence—mainly their deadlock over the fundamental issue of power distribution—resulted in multiple changes, revisions, and post-ponements of the draft constitution, which subverted the promise of a stable democracy. In the absence of elected civilian regimes, Pakistan's semi-political institutions promoted political instability that assisted the bureaucratic oligarchy to consolidate its hold on state authority and secure a lion's share in the power hierarchy (Braibanti 1963; Jalal 1995). By doing so, they did not allow the political leaders to expand their support base and constituencies. Frequent shuffles and hasty dismissals of leadership and institutions—for example, the sacking of the cabinet (1953); dismissal of the first constituent assembly when it tried to curb the bureaucratic oligarchy's powers through a federal democratic constitution (1954); and the installment of a series of unelected regimes (1951–58) to control the state apparatus and political process—undermined the country's prospects to emerge as a constitutional democracy (see Shah 2014: 15–17). In short, the Muslim League's inability to consolidate political power and resolve the power-sharing issues between the constituent units laid the foundation for a bureaucracy-military axis to emerge as a central source of power and stability in the country. In due course, such developments pushed Pakistan into becoming an authoritarian polity.

From a rivalry perspective, as discussed in the preceding chapters, the probability of conflict resolution is greater when adversaries are constitutional democracies and their rivalry is in the embryonic stage. The pattern of armed confrontations between India and Pakistan demonstrates that the absence of credible political institutions, coupled with Jinnah's and Liaquat's early exits from Pakistan's political landscape, certainly impacted the countries' relationship in the early years (see Figure 4.3).[18] The emergence of different political structures and the lack of a shared platform to address

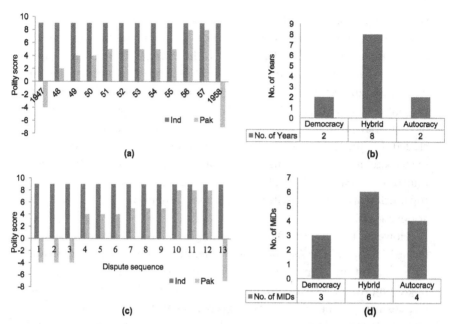

Figure 4.3. India-Pakistan regime type and recurrent militarized disputes, 1947–58. (a) Regime type, (b) regime years, (c) regime type during the initiation of MIDs, (d) no. of MIDs under particular type of regime. *Source:* Compiled from the COW database (2015), Polity IV, version 4.01. Note: In the Polity IV database, the polity score ranges from +10 (full democracy) to –10 (full autocracy) and the measure of regime is based on a combination of two scores: democracy and autocracy scores. The final regime score is calculated by simply subtracting the autocracy score from the democracy score (see Marshall & Jaggers 2002). Based on these measures, the "stable democracies" are political regimes that score above +6 (+7 to +10); "partial democracies," or "hybrids," are those that score from +1 to +6; and finally, those that score 0 to –10 are "autocratic regimes."

their contentious issues eventually led the leadership on both sides to fall in a trap called "security dilemma," under which one state's security enhancement ends up in security reduction of the other.

In due course, Pakistan's internal political discord, wherein bureaucratic oligarchy had begun controlling the political system and subverting the democratic procedures, got triangulated with Cold War politics and the Kashmir dispute that prolonged the conflict over Kashmir. There was though a very short spell of progress during 1953-1954, when Pakistan's domestic

political equations necessitated the replacement of Prime Minister Khwaja
Nazimuddin with Mohammad Ali Bogra. After a long impasse in the UN,
this shuffle brought a remarkable shift in the bilateral relations, leading to
two rounds of talks in July and August 1953. The second round in Delhi made
noticeable progress despite the dismissal and imprisonment of the head of
the J&K government, Sheikh Abdullah (Kux 2001: 65). Against the backdrop
of large-scale protests in Kashmir and Pakistan, the Nehru-Bogra talks concluded that the Kashmir dispute should be resolved peacefully without fall-
ing back to military means and the fate of the disputed state would be determined by the Kashmiri people through a free and fair plebiscite under the
supervision of a new plebiscite administrator (Ganguly 2002: 24–25; Schaffer
2009: 42–43).

However, this progress did not last long, as a result of Pakistan's signing
of the Mutual Defense Assistance Agreement with the United States in May
1954. In addition, Prime Minister Bogra's statement that Pakistan's military
upgrading would increase the prospects of the settlement of the Kashmir
dispute instead derailed the remaining chances of improvement in the bilateral relationship (Kux 2001: 65–66). From the Indian viewpoint, the US-
Pakistan military pact was counter-productive because it was against the
sanctity of the Nehru-Bogra talks, wherein the two leaders agreed on a peaceful mechanism to resolve their differences over Kashmir, and Pakistan's military upgrading would rationalize its revisionist policies against India. Consequently, Nehru backtracked from India's self-imposed commitment to
conduct a plebiscite in Kashmir, insisting that this purpose had been legiti-
mately served by the J&K Constituent Assembly in 1953 (Rostow 1960: 328).
The relationship turned grim when General Ayub Khan, the chief martial
law administrator, deposed Pakistan President Iskander Mirza in a bloodless
coup and assumed the presidency (see Wilcox 1965). After taking control of
the state apparatus, Ayub put political forces on the back foot by imposing
restrictions on political activities, abrogating the first Constitution of 1956,
and introducing a rigid institutional model that was specifically designed to
endorse the military rule. For these reasons, Nehru became wary of negotiations with a regime which came to power by means of a military coup and
did not represent the people of Pakistan.

Though the third-party strategic interventions had apparently balanced
India and Pakistan's military relationship, particularly by bringing the latter
into the SEATO and the CENTO, the same impinged on their bargaining space

and assisted them to form a highly tense political relationship in the early years. Once Pakistan started developing its offensive military capabilities—especially after aligning with the United States and joining the Western alliance system— and the Pakistan Army acquired control over the country's security and foreign policy, its authoritarian leadership began to perceive the goals of the Grand Alliance in offensive rather than defensive terms (M. Khan [1967] 2006: Ch. 9).

This critical development coupled with the growing sway of the bureaucratic-military axis cast a shadow over the feasibility and survival of parliamentary democracy in Pakistan, while India's repeated incarceration of Sheikh Abdullah had constrained Pakistan's conciliatory acts, eventually closing any early opportunity to soften the two states' antithetical national ideologies and positions on the Kashmir issue. Pakistan's inclusion in the security alliances and its political leadership's inability to craft a democratic political system had led the country's transition to a military autocracy. This not only obstructed the passage of a potential bilateral platform—pursued, albeit weakly, by Liaquat, Bogra, and Nehru—but also brought about drastic changes in the political behavior of the two sides. In other words, the great powers' interventions and the adoption of power politics practices by the two different political regimes led this embryonic rivalry into the whirlpool of a security dilemma that suspended all viable options of cooperation on Kashmir— which subsequently evolved as the single largest cause of distrust and tension between them—and escalated their hostilities to many more armed confrontations in the succeeding years.

Had Pakistan's political parties and civilian institutions been nurtured properly in the early years, probably a norm-based democratic and representative system would have evolved in the country, instead of the authoritarian centralization which materialized. Under a stable political system, the democratic forces would have easily instituted their control over the military-bureaucratic combination which later dominated the state apparatus and characterized the India-Pakistan relationship as antagonistic. It seems that democratic incompatibility and lack of reliable institutions had allowed the autocratic forces to increase their influence in domestic politics and national security policy. Once the autocratic forces had consolidated their foothold in the policy-making bodies, they prioritized militaristic security policies over moderate narratives, which could have eased Pakistan's relationship with India. On the basis of the democratic peace thesis, it may be argued that if India and Pakistan were both democracies in the first decade following their independence, the scope and range for crafting appropriate bilateral bridges would perhaps have broadened, which in turn could have created conditions for regional harmony and economic prosperity. On the other hand, however, it might be an overestimation to maintain that common democratic governance would have introduced an abrupt change in the South Asian ground reality, that is, the Kashmir dispute, or neutralized all those conditions which had engaged the two sides in a persistent rivalry in the first place.

CONCLUSION

The aim of this chapter has been to identify and understand how the structural factors encompassed in the "hub"—ideology, territorial salience, and geographical contiguity—and the temporal conditions on the periphery, which include the international strategic factors, dissimilar political regimes, and domestic politics, together brought India and Pakistan closer to the recognition of a long-term rivalry. Soon after the partition, the presence or absence of the structural factors played a fundamental role in influencing the two adversaries' decision whether to escalate or de-escalate their armed contentions over Junagadh, Kashmir, and Hyderabad. In this early phase, once the structural factors coalesced and framed India and Pakistan's relationship in a particular manner, they began to influence the peripheral temporal factors and together shaped the course of the India-Pakistan rivalry. As a result of a weaker hub, particularly non-existent geographical contiguity, Pakistan was unable to challenge India militarily over Junagadh and Hyderabad. In contrast, Kashmir's compatibility with the hub-and-spokes framework increased Pakistan's resolve to challenge India militarily and eventually made it a revisionist player. Once India and Pakistan's bilateral conflict over Kashmir consolidated, ever-increasing interaction between the "hub" and the "spokes" brought in centripetal and centrifugal stress on the embryonic rivalry by unfolding a process of change, that is, the gradual augmentation in hostility and accumulation of grievances, in a very short period from 1949 to 1958.

The outcomes and the severity levels of the past confrontations have regulated both sides' actions, especially the First Kashmir War, which did not meet India's and Pakistan's definitive aims. However, the recurrent militarized disputes also failed to resolve the Kashmir issue to either side's satisfaction, as both parties were not willing to make concessions on the territory in dispute—Kashmir—because of its intrinsic value as well as ideological-reputational concerns. The resulting stalemates after every confrontation increased distrust and hostility between the antagonists that created an atmosphere of fear and anxiety, and thereby assisted them to develop an enemy image of each other.

Additionally, the stalemated armed disputes and the development of an enemy image activated the domestic political dynamic on each side by attracting the attention and interests of important hardliners in the government, in the political opposition, and in the mass public. The domestic political opponents and the restraining forces were not ready to accept their governments' conciliatory actions toward the rival, especially a negotiated compromise on Kashmir by altering their national positions, which contributed to the adoption of hostile postures and escalation of their rivalry. On the other hand, the matrix of the Cold War started linking the Kashmir issue with other rivalries through ideological differences, security alliances, and military aid. Instead of assisting the rivals to reach a negotiated resolution, particularly by providing a more trusting environment which could have created sufficient bargaining space, the great powers' targeted support complicated the rivalry by providing Pakistan external support—especially in terms of weapons, finance, and on the political-diplomatic front—which reduced its recovery time from the previous setbacks or defeats and prepared it for future armed challenges.

In the context of the broader link between regime type and rivalry, it is clear from the literature that hybrid and autocratic regimes have a high likelihood to be involved in armed disputes, particularly when the concerned states have revisionist foreign policies. In Pakistan's case, the institutionalization of this character in its early regimes made it more conflict-prone. Beside this, Pakistan's failure to create a democratic political system contributed to the emergence of non-democratic forces whose interests lay more in furthering the militaristic policies to acquire legitimacy by exploiting people's anti-India sentiments than in building a mutual platform to negotiate differences with India. However, the Bogra-Nehru talks in July-August 1953 had created some general background conditions for conflict de-escalation, but Pakistan's signing of the mutual defense agreement with the United States in May 1954 overpowered the goal intended to be attained under the two rounds of talks: the peaceful resolution of the Kashmir dispute without resorting to military means. In short, along with disparity in strategic objectives, the divergent nature of the two regimes and reactionary domestic politics played a considerable role in shaping their ruling elites' decisions that triggered crisis after crisis rather than creating conditions for resolving the Kashmir issue. As a result, India and Pakistan increasingly adopted coercive behavior rather than diplomatic means to manage or settle the rivalry; this ensured the formation of an extreme competition, referred to as the "complex rivalry," between the two states.

CHAPTER 5

The Development of Complex Rivalry—I

Intensive Phase, 1959–72

INTRODUCTION

Chapter 4 examines how the interplay of endogenous and exogenous factors assisted India and Pakistan to form a complex rivalry. This chapter takes the discussion further and investigates the process and changing character of the rivalry in the "development phase," wherein it traversed through two phases: "intensive phase, 1959–72" and "abeyant phase, 1972–89." This chapter delves into the former, and the latter is discussed at length in the following chapter. It investigates how the great powers, including the extra-regional power, China, through their divergent policies and clashing power aspirations within the regional and systemic structures complicated India's and Pakistan's security situation, affecting their policy choices and driving them to develop a highly antagonistic relationship. In addition to third-party interventions and relative material capabilities, the two adversaries' different regime systems also contributed to shaping their ruling elites' actions and rigid thinking during the "intensive phase," driving them to fight two full-scale wars in a short span of six years. Subsequently, these factors and hostile outcomes brought in complex power shifts, albeit in small intervals, in the dyadic, regional, and systemic realms which swayed the Indo-Pakistani rivalry from the relative peace of the 1970s to the nuclear brinkmanship of the 1980s onward—an issue addressed in detail in the following chapters.

This chapter is divided into six sections. After this brief introduction, the next section begins with an account of twenty militarized disputes that occurred between India and Pakistan during the intensive phase, 1959–72. The third section explains how the major powers' intervention, mainly through Cold War security alliances and sustained arms supplies, and rivalry linkage shaped the course of the India-Pakistan rivalry. The next section traces the impact of relative military capabilities on the dyad and explains how they contributed to initiating the two major wars: the Second Kashmir War and the Bangladesh War. The focus of the fifth section is on the impact of divergent regime type and domestic politics, particularly how the two sides' decision-making process and the resulting outcomes have clustered various issues together to dominate their relationship. The last section brings together the key findings of the chapter.

MILITARIZED DISPUTES AND CONFLICT ESCALATION, 1959 TO 1972

As India and Pakistan began to accumulate a longer history of their issue differences, the most important being the Kashmir dispute, the frequency and severity of militarized disputes tended to increase over time. After engaging in thirteen militarized disputes in the initiation period (1947–58), the dyad resorted to twenty additional disputes in a short period of thirteen years from 1959 to 1972, of which nine involved a high risk of war and two escalated to full-scale wars in 1965 and 1971 (see Table 5.1). During these years, apart from severe militarized disputes, a steady recurrence of intermediate to minor disputes also contributed to maintaining the armed hostility between India and Pakistan. Some of these disputes were accompanied by the lingering after-effects of the wars they fought. For example, the twenty-fifth and thirty-third disputes, as shown in Figure 5.1, occurred in the immediate aftermath of the declaration of ceasefires of 1965 and 1971 wars, respectively. However, not every dispute in this phase was more severe than some disputes of the earlier phase.

It is not that during this phase the two adversaries were only engaged in armed hostilities and made no efforts to negotiate their differences. After the Sino-Indian War of 1962, India and Pakistan undertook six rounds of formal talks and discussed multiple proposals to resolve the Kashmir dispute that ranged from the plebiscite, to territorial adjustment, to the modification of the Cease-Fire Line (CFL) of 1949 as an international boundary. Since the proposals by Pakistan demanded almost the entire state of J&K, leaving India with a very small territory, the talks broke down (see Gundevia 1984). During the course of bilateral talks, interestingly, not a single militarized dispute erupted between the two states. However, once the talks failed, the Indo-Pakistani rivalry assumed its traditional course marred with dispute recurrence—the CFL was breached 267 times during the second half of 1963 (MEA nd: 30)—and a full-fledged war over Kashmir in a short span of two years (see Table 5.1; Figure 5.1).

It is important to note that the two rivals resorted to thirty-three armed disputes in their first twenty-five years of conflictual history, and more often than not the cause of disputes was territorial (see Tables 4.1 and 5.1). Despite the radically different nature of their ruling regimes, that many times engaged them in aggressive and violent acts, India and Pakistan did not engage in a single dispute specifically on account of regime disparity or policy until a political crisis engulfed East Pakistan in a civil war in early 1971. The Pakistan Army's Operation Searchlight against its own nationals in East Pakistan first contributed to intensifying the Bengali Muslims' secessionist demands, and then terrifying massacres caused an en masse migration to India. This embroiled India and Pakistan in a nine-month-long regime crisis that eventually concluded in a full-scale war and Pakistan's dismemberment in December 1971.

The Disappearance of Mo-e-Muqaddas and the Outbreak of Communal Tensions

In December 1963, the disappearance of *Mo-e-Muqaddas*, the Kashmiri Muslim community's most treasured relic, brought the law-and-order machinery in the Kashmir Valley to a standstill (Lyon 1967: 114). Pakistan extensively used its radio and press to unleash virulent propaganda that contributed to fueling violent demonstrations in Srinagar, followed by communal riots in East Pakistan and the expulsion of hundreds of thousands of minority Hindus to the Indian state of West Bengal (Akbar 2002: 161). In response, the West Bengal press churned "hysterical headlines" that led to another wave of brutal killings of "hundreds of minority Hindus in [East Pakistan] and hundreds of minority Muslims in Calcutta" (Sumantra Bose 2003: 79). Within days, the outbreak of mass rioting in Kashmir engulfed the two Bengals into communal tensions, triggering a large-scale crisis for India and Pakistan.

Despite persisting communal riots in Bengal and growing demonstrations demanding a plebiscite in Kashmir, India and Pakistan did not resume their inconclusive formal talks held earlier in May 1963. By the end of March 1964, according to Y. D. Gundevia, India's then foreign secretary, around 125,000 East Pakistani Hindus had sought refuge in India (1984: 396). To

TABLE 5.1. India-Pakistan militarized interstate disputes (MIDs), 1959–72

S.No	Dates of Dispute[1]	MID Initiator	Revisionist State	Cause of MID	MID Location	Fatality Level	Highest Action Taken[2]	Hostility Level[3]	Regime Type
14	April 10, 1959–April 12, 1959	India	None	n.a.	(Karachi, Pakistan)	None	I-border violation P-attack	3 & 4*	Non-demo
15	December 15, 1960–April 13, 1961	Pakistan	Pakistan	Territory	Kasur, India/ Pakistan Border	None	I-no militarized action P-border violation	1 & 3*	Non-demo
16	June 8, 1961–July 19, 1961	Pakistan	Pakistan	Territory	Kashmir	None	I-threat to use force P-no militarized action	2 & 1*	Non-demo
17	January 6, 1962–April 27, 1962	India	Pakistan	Territory	Kashmir	None	I-show of force P-threat to use force	3 & 2*	Non-demo
18	September 18, 1962–November 4, 1962	Pakistan	Pakistan	Territory	Tripura, Assam, India	1–25	Clash	4 & 4*	Non-demo
19	July (dm), 1963–August (dm), 1963	Pakistan	Pakistan	Territory	Dumabari, Lachar-Sylhet (Tripura), India	None	I-no militarized action P-occupation of territory	1 & 4*	Non-demo
20	October 16, 1963–October 16, 1963	Pakistan	Pakistan	Territory	Kashmir	None	I-no militarized action P-threat to use force	1 & 2*	Non-demo
21	March 4, 1964–September 28, 1964	Pakistan	Pakistan	Territory	Kashmir	26–100	Clash	4 & 4*	Non-demo
22	August (dm), 1964–August 5, 1965	Pakistan	Pakistan	Territory	Tripura, India	26–100	Clash	4 & 4*	Non-demo
23	January (dm), 1965–June 30, 1965	Pakistan	Pakistan	Territory	Rann of Kutch, India	101–250	Clash	4 & 4*	Non-demo
24	March 5, 1965–September 23, 1965	Pakistan	Pakistan	Territory	Jammu, India	>999	Interstate War	5 & 5*	Non-demo

#	Dates				Location	Fatalities	Action	Codes	Regime
25	September 23, 1965–January 25, 1966	Pakistan	Pakistan	Territory	Kashmir, Rajasthan	26–100	Clash	4 & 4*	Non-demo
26	April (dm), 1966–August (dm), 1966	Pakistan	Pakistan	Territory	Kashmir, Pakistan	None	I-no militarized action P-fortify border	1 & 3*	Non-demo
27	October 9, 1967–October 10, 1967	India	Pakistan	Territory	Kashmir, Pakistan	1–25	Clash	4 & 4*	Non-demo
28	March (dm), 1969–March 30, 1969	Pakistan	Pakistan	Territory	Cooch Behar, West Bengal	1–25	Clash	4 & 4*	Non-demo
29	August 12, 1969–March 17, 1970	Pakistan	None	n.a.	Air space above Northern India	None	I-show of force P-attack	3 & 4*	Non-demo
30	December 20, 1969–December 21, 1969	Pakistan	Pakistan	Territory	Malda district, West Bengal	Missing	Clash	4 & 4*	Non-demo
31	July 15, 1970–July 15 1970	India	Pakistan	Territory	Kashmir, Pakistan	None	I-threat to use force P-no militarized action	2 & 1*	Non-demo
32	April 7, 1971–December 17, 1971	Pakistan	India	Regime	East Pakistan, Kashmir	>999	Interstate War	5 & 5*	Non-demo
33	May 5, 1972–May 5, 1972	Pakistan	Pakistan	Territory	Kashmir	26–100	Clash	4 & 4*	Non-demo

Source: Compiled from the COW database (2015), version 4.01.

1. As in the COW database, missing dispute dates are marked "dm" for "date missing."
2. Here I stands for India and P for Pakistan.
3. The codes marked with an asterisk (*) indicate Pakistan's hostility level, and codes without it indicate India's hostility level. The COW database hostility codes are as follows: 1: no militarized action; 2: threat to use force; 3: display use of force; 4: use of force; and 5: war, respectively.

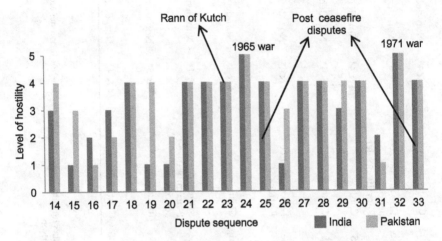

Figure 5.1. India-Pakistan hostility level (frequency and severity), 1959–72.
Source: Compiled from the COW database (2015), version 4.01 (0–5 scale)

control the deteriorating situation, the Indian government sent a memorandum to Pakistan urging President Ayub Khan to resolve the communal tensions on the basis of the Nehru-Liaquat pact of 1950 by scheduling an early meeting of the two states' home ministers. Ayub Khan agreed to the proposal, but he linked the issue of Hindu migration from East Pakistan with the eviction of Muslims from Assam and Tripura (Gundevia 1984: 396). On the other hand, despite the recovery of the holy relic in Kashmir, the newly formed Action Committee succeeded in transforming the ongoing agitation into a political campaign, demanding the release of Sheikh Abdullah and a plebiscite to determine the future of Kashmir. Pakistan's military regime supported these demands in a bid to increase pressure on New Delhi. Facing the twinned crisis on two separate borders, New Delhi reached out to the J&K government and Pakistan by devising a formula to secure compromise on Kashmir. The first step of this initiative was the withdrawal of the Kashmir Conspiracy Case against Sheikh Abdullah, Afzal Beg, and other thirteen defendants. Another step was Nehru's proposal of a confederal arrangement between India, Pakistan, and Kashmir. When Sheikh Abdullah, who went to Pakistan as Nehru's emissary, discussed the proposal with Ayub Khan, he dismissed it outrightly (M.A. Khan [1967] 2006: 149). Ayub Khan agreed, however, to have a summit meeting with Prime Minister Nehru in June, which unfortunately never took place due to Nehru's sudden death in May 1964 (Gopal 1984: 263–64).

After Nehru's exit from the political scene, Sheikh Abdullah suddenly started advocating the necessity of Pakistan's involvement "to guarantee Kashmir's rights" (Behera 2006: 42). The new development complicated Kashmir politics because Abdullah "became more intransigent, refusing to accept the existing constitutional relationship between Jammu and Kashmir and India," and foiled a plot with Bakshi Ghulam Mohammed to topple the Ghulam Mohammed Sadiq–led Congress government in the state (Behera 2006: 42). Lal Bahadur Shastri, India's new prime minister, responded by arresting Bakshi and his supporters and simultaneously assured Pakistan of the resumption of meaningful talks provided it cooperates to restore peace in the affected areas. Ayub Khan acknowledged Shastri's commitment and reciprocated by initiating steps to reduce tensions across the disturbed borders (Barnds 1972: 194). Gradually, the exodus from East Pakistan to the adjoining Indian states of West Bengal, Assam, and Tripura declined and the dispute subsided well before the beginning of the Karachi summit between Ayub and Shastri in October 1964.

The Rann of Kutch Dispute, 1965

In the beginning of 1965, a territorial dispute erupted between India and Pakistan over the Rann of Kutch—a 7,000-square-mile "tidal area on the west coast, consisting mainly of marshland and trackless waste, where the border was poorly demarcated" (Blum 2007: 60). This area was relatively of less economic value as it lay submerged in water for half of every year, that is, throughout the rainy season lasting from May to October. During the British rule, the provinces of Sindh, now in Pakistan, and Kutch, now part of Gujarat in India, had claimed the right to levy dues on the use of the Rann, but "no definitive boundary between the two had been established beyond a 40–50 mile coastal Section" (Colman 2009: 467). After the partition, India and Pakistan inherited the boundary dispute and challenged each other's ground position in the area (UNRIAA 1968).

In the wake of the 1962 war, India's deteriorating relationship with China and mounting tensions in Kashmir had emboldened Pakistan's military dictator, Ayub Khan, to embark on risky ventures by adopting a policy of "leaning on India," under which Pakistani troops were instructed to provoke their Indian counterparts by engaging in aggressive patrolling along the disputed borders (Barnds 1972: 192–95). In early 1965, Pakistan carefully planned a military action in the Rann of Kutch area to test "India's defense preparedness and commitments" (Ganguly 1997: 54). As planned, it resorted to aggressive military patrolling of the northern parts of the Rann, mainly Kanjarkot and adjacent high-ground areas, which were duly claimed by India. When India discovered that Pakistan had established posts in the area, it accused Pakistan of intrusion into its sovereign territory. Thereafter both sides laid equal claims over the area: India asserted that the boundary ran along the Rann's northern edge while Pakistan claimed almost half of the Rann on the premise that it was an inland or landlocked sea; hence the boundary should run through the center of the Rann (Colman 2009: 467; UNRIAA 1968: 22). When a series of bilateral talks seeking to reach a mutual ceasefire agreement failed, the dispute escalated to large-scale maneuvers and border skirmishes (Kux 1993: 233).

Equipped with US advanced weaponry, Pakistan not only had a military edge against India but also enjoyed positional superiority in the local theater of the conflict as its troops were dominating the highlands and holding strong communication lines (Brines 1968: 288). To deny the Indians any opportunity to recapture the highland border areas and the fort of Kanjarkot, Pakistan launched a major pre-emptive offensive deep within the disputed area against India's defensive positions and outfought the opponent in a favorable terrain (Barnds 1972: 198; Nawaz 2008: 204). Under severe domestic pressure, as the Indian leadership was not in a position to bear another territorial loss after losing a large chunk of borderland to China in 1962, the Shastri government opted to check Pakistan's advances by building international pressure against it.

Against this backdrop, New Delhi reminded Washington about its commitment not to allow Pakistan to use American armament against India (Kux 1993: 234). Interestingly, the US State Department also observed that Pakistan's military regime had "precipitated the conflict in the hope that its use of U.S. military equipment would drive a wedge between India and the United States" (McMahon 1994: 324). By adopting a middle path, however, the US disapproved the fighting and offered help in restoring peace in the subcontinent. Following this, Harold Wilson, the prime minister of Great Britain, made proposals for a ceasefire which eventually developed into a trilateral negotiation between London, New Delhi, and Rawalpindi.[1] On June 30, 1964, finally, both India and Pakistan agreed to the terms of the ceasefire, which included the withdrawal of troops, an immediate ceasefire, direct negotiations, and arbitration,[2] terminating a six-month-long dispute (GoI 1965).

The Second Kashmir War, 1965

The origin of the Second Kashmir War can be traced to Pakistan's wider strategic scheme to annex Kashmir in the backdrop of growing political unrest in the Valley. Following the mysterious disappearance of the *Mo-e-Muqaddas*, New Delhi sped up its constitutional steps to integrate J&K with the Indian Union so as to bring it "into alignment and conformity with the other states of India" (Dupree 1965: 4). Disappointed with the extension of constitutional provisions to Kashmir, Sheikh Abdullah met the Chinese Premier Zhou Enlai in Algiers and urged him to support the Kashmir cause. The Shastri government took serious note of the Pakistani hand in Abdullah's meeting with Zhou Enlai, resulting in the arrest of the Kashmiri leader in April 1965 (Barnds 1972: 194). After Abdullah's internment, notes Joseph Korbel, "the atmosphere [in the Valley] was charged with emotional and political dynamite, ready to explode at the slightest provocation" (1966: 338). Additionally, the Pakistani intelligence agencies' inputs convinced their military establishment that an indigenous Kashmiri uprising would follow soon after Pakistan's infiltration of irregulars to the Indian side of Kashmir. These circumstances, coupled with India's weak military response in the Rann of Kutch, emboldened Pakistan's long-standing ambition to annex Kashmir.

According to Lieutenant General Gul Hassan Khan, the Kashmir Cell had already planned modalities to launch a covert action in the Indian Kashmir between December 1964 and May 1965 (1994: 116). Its main objective was to "defreeze the Kashmir issue" and "think aloud" to foment uprising in Kashmir by providing training and other logistic support to infiltrators (1994: 115–16). "With a view to disrupting conditions in the Valley and eventually arming the locals and helping them rise against the Indian Army of occupation," Khan continued in the same vein, "the [Pakistan] Army was ordered to train volunteers in carrying out sabotage activities across the Ceasefire Line" (1994: 178, 114). The plan, code-named Operation Gibraltar, became operational on July 24 when the Pakistan Army troops in local attire began infiltration of the thousands of irregulars that composed the Azad Kashmir Army and mujahideens ("freedom fighters") on the Indian side of the CFL (Ganguly 1997: 55–56; Nawaz 2008: 206; Payari 2020; S. Ram 2016). According to Praveen Swami, their main objectives were "to establish bases, carry out acts of sabotage and create conditions that would be conducive to the intervention of regular Pakistani troops" (2007: 61). But the operation failed to spur revolt against the so-called Indian oppression and abuses. Having failed to secure the support of the Kashmiri people, Pakistan decided to deploy its regulars to sharpen the operation by infiltrating a battalion-size regular force from Azad Kashmir's town of Bhimbar into the Jhangar-Nowshera and Chhamb sectors of the Indian Kashmir (Khajuria 2010; R. Ram 2018; Swaroop 2014). India retaliated by dispatching a large number of troops across the CFL, mainly in the Poonch, Uri, and Tithwal areas, and captured key posts and mountain passes from the Pakistan Army (Mirza 2018).

When expectations of triggering a local rebellion were not realized, the military establishment in Pakistan terminated Operation Gibraltar, but simultaneously it sought to enhance the scope of crisis by launching Operation Grand Slam across the CFL on September 1. Within five days, Pakistan's armored columns successfully marched in the Chhamb-Akhnoor sector; they were almost at the verge of seizing India's only road link to the Kashmir Valley (Karamat 2015; Nawaz 2008: 211-12). To free itself from Pakistan's increasing military pressure in Kashmir, India launched a major offensive across the international border targeting Lahore and the border town of Sialkot (Ganguly 2002: 44). Surprised by India's large-scale offensive along and across the international border, Pakistan immediately halted its offensive in Kashmir and rushed its troops south to defend Punjab from the advancing Indian troops. Throughout the war, the Indian encirclement of Lahore forced the Pakistan Army to adopt a defensive posture (Bajwa 2005; Nawaz 2008: 230-31).

In retaliation, Pakistan launched a large-scale armored counter-offensive in the Kasur-Khem Karan sector to capture Amritsar, a border city of the Indian Punjab. In Khem Karan, a massive tank-battle occurred between Pakistan's First Armored Division and India's Fourth Mountain Division, famously known as the Battle of Asal Uttar. Pakistan used American-supplied highly sophisticated Patton tanks and India used the World War II–era slow Sherman and Centurion tanks. The Patton tanks' superior firepower helped the Pakistani armored division to penetrate the Indian defenses (Cloughley 2002: 92–110; Palit 1991: 426). When the Indian side realized that its armored units would not be able to halt the advance of lethal Patton tanks, it resorted to unconventional military rescue by opening the floodgates of irrigation works to trap the opponent's principal strike force in the mud, which ultimately ended the Pakistan Army's major counter-offensive against India (Gauhar 1996: 342; Nawaz 2008: 233; R. Ram 2018).

However, before the war drew to a close, China triggered a crisis for

India by issuing a surprise ultimatum on September 17. Beijing warned New Delhi to stop provocation on the borders of Sikkim and Tibet and dismantle all military fortifications near the Chinese border "within three-days"; otherwise it would "bear full responsibility for all the grave consequences" (Korbel 1966: 344; Yasmeen 1992: 327). To capitalize on India's fear of a two-front war, President Ayub Khan flew to Beijing for a secret meeting with the Chinese leadership. Premier Zhou Enlai "gave the Pakistani president an offer of unconditional support on the understanding that Pakistan . . . would have to be prepared for a long war in which some cities like Lahore might be lost" (Schofield 2010: 111). The Chinese strategic advice did not convince the Pakistani military dictator, however, because engaging in such a protracted conflict against a resourceful adversary was highly risky. On the other hand, apart from issuing a warning to Beijing to restrict its bellicose behavior, the superpowers sought a rapid termination of armed hostilities and increased their diplomatic efforts to secure an early ceasefire. Finally, under immense pressure from the international community, the leadership on both sides accepted the UN-brokered ceasefire on September 22, 1965, and accepted the Soviet-proposed trilateral conference at Tashkent to negotiate their differences.

Overall, Pakistan did manage to blunt the Indian advance toward Lahore and Sialkot, but in the end the Indian troops outfought their counterparts in a majority of battles—Pakistan conceded almost 710 square miles of its territory to India and managed to capture only 210 square miles of the Indian territory (Akbar 2002: 172; Hagerty 1998: 70). In military terms, the war was a draw with no decisive military victory for either side, but in political-strategic terms Pakistan was defeated because "her strategic objective remained unfulfilled" (G. Rizvi 1992: 70). On the other hand, India largely achieved its objectives by preventing the annexation of Kashmir and occupying more enemy territory. India's acceptance of a ceasefire after overpowering the adversary increased its chances to achieve more concessions during the post-war negotiations. Perhaps this led Pakistan to improve its frontline positions after the declaration of ceasefire; its seizure of large tracts of desert in Rajasthan provoked India to retaliate militarily. The renewed military hostilities lasted until the Soviet Union–moderated Tashkent Agreement was signed on January 10, 1966 (GoI 1966a). With the implementation of the Tashkent Agreement on January 25, the war ended formally; however, the basic dispute over Kashmir remained unsettled (see GoI 1966b).

The Bangladesh War of 1971

A power struggle between the two wings of Pakistan, East Pakistan and West Pakistan, had persisted since 1947 when the Muslim-majority areas of the united India were carved out as Pakistan. From the very beginning, the West Pakistanis had maintained an overwhelming control over the country's power structures and were reluctant to share it with Pakistan's eastern subjects in an equitable manner despite the fact that the latter constituted a majority community in the country. The Bengali Muslims of East Pakistan resented this disparity on the ground that Pakistan came into existence as a homeland for the Muslims of the subcontinent to exercise greater political autonomy (Jahan 1972; Islam 1972).

The year 1970, however, brought new hopes in the two wings of Pakistan as the new military dictator General Agha Muhammad Yahya Khan had announced parliamentary elections on the basis of adult franchise. For the first time since its formation a genuine democratic election had taken place in Pakistan in December 1970 that resulted in the triumph of the Sheikh Mujibur Rehman–led Awami League in East Pakistan and the Zulfikar Ali Bhutto–led Pakistan People's Party (PPP) in West Pakistan. The Awami League emerged as a majority party in the National Assembly by winning more than half of the total general seats available, and the PPP obtained a distant second position (Jahan 1972: 190; I. Talbot 2009: 200). Despite the Awami League's convincing victory, Zulfikar Ali Bhutto was not ready to accept Mujibur Rehman's right to form the next government (B. Jones 2002: 148).

Later, when the Yahya-Mujibur talks broke down on March 25, 1971, the military regime immediately launched Operation Searchlight in Dacca and banned the Awami League and all political activities in East Pakistan (B. Jones 2002: 166–67). Under Martial Law Administrator Lieutenant General Tikka Khan, the West Pakistan troops targeted the students of Dhaka University and the civilians in Dacca and its satellite towns, killing around fifteen thousand innocents in one night (Sharmila Bose 2011: 65–70, 180; Santos 2007: 29–30). Against the backdrop of these barbaric incidents, the political leadership of East Pakistan declared "the independence of Bangladesh" on March 26, 1971, which spurred mutiny in the army, and the Bengalis revolted against the state of Pakistan (Jahan 1972: 198). Archer Blood, the US consulate general in Dacca, had cabled Washington advising it to restrain the West Pakistani forces from unleashing a "wave of terror . . . against their own countrymen," but Washington appeared completely unmoved and unperturbed, which encouraged the West Pakistanis to expand on what Blood character-ized as "selective genocide" (NSA 2002a). Throughout the crisis, the US offi-cial policy was to turn a blind eye to West Pakistan's atrocities against the ethnic Bengalis in East Pakistan—which resulted in approximately ten mil-lion Bengali Muslims and Hindus fleeing across the border to India for safety (NSA 2002b; "Policy Options toward Pakistan" 1971).

The ever-increasing inflow of refugees posed multiple challenges for India, ranging from providing shelter, food, and clothing for them and maintaining law and order to dealing with demographic shifts in its already troubled northeastern states (Gundevia 1984: 397; Racioppi 1994: 76). Facing huge political and economic pressures in the domestic domain and the United States' lukewarm attitude on the diplomatic front, India responded to the East Pakistani crisis in April 1971 by granting the Awami League per-mission to run a government in exile from the adjacent state of West Bengal (Ganguly 2002: 62). With this decision, India officially stepped into an inter-national crisis which was already becoming an internal crisis for it. If the refugee influx had strained the Indian economy, it had also offered India a rare opportunity to dismember Pakistan by training refugees as guerrilla fighters against the West Pakistani forces in the eastern wing. Against this backdrop, the Indian military strategists reportedly prepared a covert plan against the West Pakistani troops. "On May 1, 1971," according to one commentator,

India's Chief of Army Staff issued a secret order initiating the war that would end with the dismemberment of Pakistan. India's objectives were remarkably similar to those attempted by Pakistan in 1965, envisaging the use of a covert army as a catalyst for insurrection and a spearhead for regular forces. . . . Oper-ation Instruction formally committed Indian forces to "assist the Provisional Government of Bangladesh to rally the people of East Bengal in support of the liberation movement," and "to raise, equip and train East Bengal cadres for guerilla operations for employment in their own native land." Eastern Command was to ensure that the guerilla forces were to work towards "tying down the Pak [Pakistan] Military forces in protective tasks in East Bengal," "sap and corrode [their] morale . . . and simultaneously to impair their logis-tic capability for undertaking any offensive against Assam and West Bengal," and, finally, be used along with regular Indian troops "in the event of Paki-stan initiating hostilities against us." (Swami 2007: 118)

Following the secret directive, the Indian Army and the Awami League officials formulated a liberation force, a group of refugees popularly known as the *Mukti Bahini*, and recruited thousands of willing Bengali refugees for military operations in East Pakistan. "On the eve of the war, at the end of November 1971," according to the log book of India's Ministry of Defence, "over 83,000 Gano Bahini fighters had been trained, 51,000 of whom were operating inside East Pakistan—a guerilla operation perhaps unrivalled in scale until that time" (Swami 2007: 119). With the Indian regulars' support, the *Mukti Bahini* conducted a series of guerrilla raids against the West Pakistani troops in East Pakistan throughout the second half of 1971. In an attempt to relieve pressure on its eastern wing, Pakistan massed its troops along the Punjab border in October; however, the move did not produce the desired results (Masood 2015; Niazi 2002: 118). In late November, according to Richard Sisson and Leo Rose, "several Indian army divisions launched simultaneous military actions on all of the key border regions of East Pakistan, and from all directions, with both armored and air support" (1990: 213).

Fearing its dismemberment, Pakistan retaliated on December 3 with air strikes on the Indian military and air bases in Kashmir and the northwestern states (C. Van Hollen 1980: 350). Already waiting for an excuse to initiate the offensive, India formally declared war on Pakistan and moved its troops toward Dacca with extraordinary speed. A day later, the Indian Air Force and Navy launched coordinated attacks on the Islamabad, Karachi, Peshawar, Lahore, and Sialkot airfields as well as on Pakistan's sole naval port at Karachi (Ganguly 2002: 67–68). This combined mission destroyed several of Pakistan's airfields and oil installations at the Karachi port, and the heavier air attacks on East Pakistan caused much destruction to Pakistan's airfields and aircraft (P. Mohan & Chopra 2013; Nanda 2007). Though this war had no direct connection with the Kashmir issue, India nevertheless launched operations against West Pakistan in Kashmir from five key locations: Samba, Chhamb, Poonch, Kargil, and Thoise (Kanwal 2016; R. Ram 2018). The logic was straightforward, as Sumit Ganguly states: to consolidate its "position along the Cease-Fire Line, seizing tactical territorial advantages, and inflicting the maximum possible damage on Pakistan's military assets, especially its armor and heavy weaponry" (1997: 59).

After managing overwhelming success in the major theater of war, India recognized East Pakistan as an independent state of Bangladesh on December 6, 1971. In the next ten days, Indians maintained superiority in all classes of war: its army wheeled around East Pakistan, the air force dominated the air warfare, and the navy succeeded in attacking and blockading Pakistan's ports by displaying an exceptional command in the Bay of Bengal and the Arabian Sea, leading to Pakistan's surrender on December 16, 1971 (B. Jones 2002: 174; Nanda 2007). A day later, East Pakistan broke away from Pakistan and became the independent state of Bangladesh. The disintegration of Pakistan had not only dealt a body blow to its two-nation theory but also undermined its long-standing claim over Kashmir on religious grounds. Later, under the terms of the Simla Agreement, India and Pakistan agreed to resolve their differences through peaceful bilateral negotiations, withdraw their armed forces from occupied territories, and change the nomenclature of the Cease-Fire Line (CFL) to the Line of Control (LoC) (GoI 1972).

THE ROLE OF GREAT POWERS, ALLIANCES, AND ARMS BUILDUP

In the early 1950s, India refused to be a party to the Western designs against the communist expansion in Asia and instead pursued a non-aligned doctrine to evolve its independent foreign policy. The members of the Western bloc, however, perceived India's non-aligned stance as a potential danger to their Cold War interests. These postures coincided with the rise of decolonization movements in developing states to join the international system as new sovereign entities. In the newly forming bipolar system, particularly the US–Soviet Union Cold War dynamics after the collapse of the Eurocentric system and the introduction of newly decolonized states' nation-building struggle, the two superpowers were employing much effort and energy to dominate the international system by exploiting the limitations of developing states. Against this setting, the leading states of the two power blocs devised different strategies to engage the developing states, and military-economic assistance was one such strategy to achieve their self-interests. To neutralize India's growing influence on the Afro-Asian states, especially those which were not interested to join the Cold War politics and preferred non-alignment as a viable middle path, the United States started intervening in the South Asian region by arming Pakistan against India.

The East-West Cold War, Non-alignment, and India-Pakistan Relations

After the US-Pakistan military pact and the formation of twin alliances, the SEATO and the CENTO, it was not difficult for India to conclude that these alliances included its non-aligned policy in their containment objectives—particularly the SEATO. To resist these moves, India initially criticized the US policy in Asia and then turned toward Moscow for help, that is, regional balancing. Once the Cold War fault lines were drawn, India and Pakistan began to witness increasing external intervention in their bilateral relations that not only exacerbated their differences but also affected the course of their individual ties with the great powers.

Since Pakistan was not able to find another source to fund its ambitious military buildup, the United States exploited that inability to accomplish its own broader Cold War objectives. In this respect, the United States' acquisition of Pakistan's Badaber air base to pursue surveillance activities against the Soviet Union (and China) proved to be a critical development. The US policy makers propagandized it as a diplomatic and strategic breakthrough against the communist bloc, but in the context of regional rivalry this lease significantly increased Pakistan's relative bargaining position to acquire qualitative military supplies from the United States, mainly state-of-the-art Sidewinder missiles and F-104 Starfighters (McMahon 1994: 267–68). However, the situation slightly changed when Pakistan emerged as a primary target of the Soviet nuclear forces after the May 1960 U-2 spy incident. This incident led Pakistan to readjust its strategic policy by roping in China, which was by then turning hostile to India over the issue of the McMahon Line, and accepting Soviet aid of $30 million for oil exploration (Barnds 1972: 162). Once again, instead of living with limited options, Pakistan's strategic rebalancing and calculated moves to forge closer ties with the forces against whom it had joined the Western alliance system consolidated its bargaining position with the United States.

On the other hand, India's December 1961 armed action against the Portuguese authorities in Goa had strained its relationship with the West (Brecher 1968: 128–33). The forced expulsion of the Portuguese from Goa provided Pakistan another opportunity to channel international pressure against India over the Kashmir issue (FRUS 1996: 185). Sensing the Western powers' humiliation, as they had shown their unwarranted inclination toward Portuguese colonialism in the past,[3] Rawalpindi indicated its "withdrawal from SEATO and CENTO . . . if the U.S. failed to live up to its commitment" to sponsor another resolution on Kashmir in the Security Council (Dobell 1964: 286). Another reason for the deterioration of Indo-US relations was New Delhi's equivocal stand over the East-West tensions in Berlin and its entering into a MiG aircraft deal with Moscow to counterbalance Pakistan's procurement of F-104 Starfighters (Thomas 1983: 75). As the largest economic aid provider, Washington was not only critical of New Delhi's compromised non-aligned stance but also made attempts to interfere with the MiG-21 deal (Galbraith 1969: 376–402). The cycle of moves and counter-moves favored India when Moscow vetoed the West's proposed resolution on Kashmir in the Security Council. However, New Delhi's communist tilt and America's unfriendly stance against India took a dramatic retreat when the Sino-India border tensions increased in late 1962 (Kavic 1967: 176–84). After the Chinese attack, the political leadership in New Delhi requested Washington to intervene directly by sending "twelve squadrons of F-104 fighters" and "two squadrons of B-57 bombers," and to extend help in operating the radar stations (Palit 1991: 342). Hoping to bring the champion of non-alignment into the Western fold, US policy makers had decided to provide India military assistance against China. Before sufficient assistance could arrive, however, Chinese troops swept into northeastern India and declared a unilateral ceasefire on November 21, 1962 (Sidhu & Yuan 2003: 15). India's humiliation in the thirty-two-day warfare opened a window of opportunity for Washington to bring India, the most important and influential developing state, into the Western fold—President John F. Kennedy dubbed it as a "fleeting . . . one time opportunity" (quoted in Schaffer 2009: 77).

After conceding defeat by its communist neighbor, India initiated fundamental changes in its existing foreign-military strategies (Brecher 1979–80: 628–30). The US-led bloc wanted to benefit most from India's compromised non-aligned stance,[4] but the triangulation of the China-India-Pakistan conflict had complicated the whole security dynamic. Nonetheless, in hope of securing India's formal or informal alignment with the West, the United States and the UK approved an emergency military assistance program. Annoyed with the Anglo-American military assistance to India, Rawalpindi perceived the allies' dualistic approach as a counter-weight to Pakistan's power capabilities; thus it accelerated the process of cultivating closer ties with Beijing (M.A. Khan 1964: 198–209). Pakistan's drastic shift toward China forced Washington to balance the situation, mainly by pressuring New Delhi to reach a compromise on Kashmir in return for its military assistance against China. In other words, since India was dependent on the West for its security fortifications, the United States considered that the time was ripe to group the two adversaries against communist China by resolving the Kashmir issue to Rawalpindi's satisfaction (see Bowles 1971: 473; Galbraith 1969: 517).

Throughout the course of the 1962–63 bilateral talks, Pakistan played its diplomatic cards adroitly. On the one hand, it successfully engaged the Western powers to pressure India to negotiate on Kashmir and, on the other, it concluded a border agreement with a common enemy of the West and India—China (Galbraith 1969: 524–25). The announcement of the border demarcation agreement with China was Pakistan's deliberate move to showcase the growing Sino-Pakistani ties to increase its bargaining leverage against India and triangulate the Sino-Indian-Pakistani security issues (Gopal 1984: 256–57). When Pakistan (and the great powers) demanded excessive concessions from India on Kashmir,[5] the prospects to reach an honorable settlement receded because reconciliation on unequal terms would have further eroded the Nehru government's domestic, regional, and international standing. Finally, the realpolitik calculus and bargaining strategies ended the six-month-long negotiations in a bitter deadlock. Instead of achieving a breakthrough to accomplish its broader Cold War objectives, Washington's efforts yielded the collapse of bilateral talks and, by extension, a strained relationship with Pakistan and without getting any leverage from India either, especially after its limited and delayed military assistance.[6]

Though the Western powers pledged military assistance of $500 million for India's $2 billion defense modernization plan, the United States refused to provide the much-required three squadrons of supersonic F-104 fighters to ease India's two-front problem (Kux 1993: 229; Thomas 1983: 75–76). Disappointed New Delhi then concluded that Washington was not willing to meet its crucial defense requirements; hence it turned to Moscow. To neutralize the immediate Chinese threat and counterbalance Pakistan's military capability, which was equipped with American Patton tanks, supersonic F-104s, and Sidewinder missiles, India signed a whopping aircraft deal with Moscow in September 1964 under which it secured collaboration to purchase 45 MiG-21s and manufacture the remaining 400 in India. This agreement further deteriorated the Indo-US relationship, which had gathered considerable momentum after China's border aggression in 1962 (Bowles 1971: 483–84; Kavic 1967: 198–200).

Around the same time, China complicated the regional security dynamics by conducting its first nuclear weapon test on October 16, 1964, at the Lop Nur test site. When the Indian leaders sought security guarantees against the Chinese nuclear threat, not a single nuclear-armed great power showed the courage to accommodate India's concern (see Perkovich 1999: 86–99). In the meantime, before the military balance could shift toward India, the Pakistani leadership made up its mind to flex its military muscle against the post-Nehru leadership in Delhi. Under such a favorable strategic environment, Ayub Khan reasoned that the "time had come to bring military pressure directly to bear on India and to settle by force the differences which had defied negotiation" (Bowles 1971: 502). Thereafter Pakistan initiated a large-scale offensive against India by employing the US-supplied military equipment, first in the Rann of Kutch[7] and later in Kashmir by launching Operation Gibraltar. The use of American weaponry was an open breach of the Eisenhower administration's written assurance to Nehru that the US armament deliveries to Pakistan would be used strictly to curtail the communist threat, and not used against India (Thomas 1983: 66). After the Rann incident, New Delhi argued that Pakistan's aggression proved its long-held fears that the American armaments would make the South Asian region vulnerable to recurrent armed hostilities.

When Washington reminded Rawalpindi that "American military equipment . . . had been provided to counter Communist aggression, not for local wars" (Schaffer 2009: 112), the Ayub-led military regime argued: How could America expect Pakistan to use motorized artillery and Patton tanks—usable only in a flat terrain—against communists in the mountainous northern terrain, while not using the same against India's flat terrain for which they had been acquired in the first place? While arguing its case, Pakistan referred to the terms of the Ankara Defense Cooperation Agreement—a bilateral agreement signed between the United States and Pakistan on March 5, 1959—which "stated that the United States would view any threat to the security, independence, and territorial integrity of Pakistan with the utmost gravity and would take effective action to assist Pakistan to suppress aggression" (Schaffer 2009: 112). From Rawalpindi's perspective, under the Ankara security agreement, Washington "was committed to assist [Pakistan] against aggression from any source, that is, India, Afghanistan, the U.S.S.R., or China" (cited in Sisson & Rose 1990: 51). However, the Johnson administration refused to accept this interpretation and declined to give Pakistan further military and diplomatic support against India, which subsequently led its defiant ally to approach China to open a second front against India. In short, as Sisson and Rose rightly observe, the United States' "*direct* military aid to Pakistan and *indirect* military aid to India" failed to deter both adversaries from engaging in a grueling war in 1965 (1990: 51).

In the wake of the 1965 war, the United States lost its interest in the South Asian region. India blamed the United States and regarded its crisis-averting

assurances and wartime even-handedness as blatantly discriminatory conduct considering that Pakistan had used the American weaponry against
India. Pakistan termed America's conduct as a betrayal. Under the circumstances, the United States made a calculated retreat from South Asia to focus
its attention on the Vietnam War and the Soviet Union emerged as an influential force in the region, especially after playing a successful mediating role
between India and Pakistan in Tashkent in 1966 (Kux 1993: 239–40). The
reshaping regional situation offered the Soviets an opportunity to engage
both rivals together; hence the communist leadership in Moscow pursued a
balanced or middle-path approach to strengthen the regional deterrence
without irking New Delhi and simultaneously engaged Pakistan's
bureaucracy-military axis to change its perception about the Soviet Union
and its security engagement in the Asian region (S. Mohan & Lobo 2020: 69–
72). With a motive to rebalance its security equations, Pakistan's bureaucracy-
military axis also responded positively by initiating key changes in the country's pro-US foreign policy, including the adoption of a "trilateral" strategy
to strengthen Pakistan's ties with the Soviet Union and China so that it could
effectively engage Beijing, Moscow, and Washington at the same time (Burke
1974: 177–82). When the Soviet Union offered Pakistan a lucrative deal of
sophisticated weaponry in exchange for closing the US surveillance base at
Badaber, Pakistan duly obliged and refused to extend the United States' lease
of the intercept facility for intelligence gathering (Barnds 1972: 216; Kux
1993: 266). By striking this deal, from the Soviet perspective, Moscow had
initiated the beginning of the end of America's Grand Alliance in Asia.

On the other hand, the Soviets' balancing act and strategic rapprochement with Pakistan irked India, as it was not dissimilar to the United States'
post-1962 integrated scheme, especially when Pakistan was also getting
extensive military assistance from China, which included T-54 tanks and
MiG-19 fighter aircraft, and crucial aircraft supplies from the United States
(Kux 2001: 172). For Moscow, however, to give priority to the Indian concerns was not possible at a juncture when it was planning to formulate the
Asian Collective Security System against the West—toward which New Delhi
was lukewarm. Additionally, addressing the Indian concerns would have
meant dislodging the growing Soviet-Pakistani ties and reinstating the pre-
1966 tilt toward New Delhi without receiving any strategic assurance in
return. Alternately, had New Delhi endorsed Moscow's Asian security proposal, the Kremlin could have readily accommodated its concerns. Given
these considerations, Moscow held back until the Indian leadership was

"prepared to sign a more ambiguous agreement that would primarily emphasize economic cooperation rather than collective security" (Sisson & Rose 1990: 198). Once the Indian leadership agreed to accept reasonably moderate terms of the Soviet proposal—which later concluded in the Treaty of Peace, Friendship, and Cooperation in August 1971—in exchange for the termination of arms sales to Pakistan, Moscow re-established its traditional policy of close ties with New Delhi (Sisson & Rose 1990: 198).

Around the same time, Richard Nixon had assumed the presidency and disbanded the Johnson administration's policy of disengagement with South Asia and re-established close ties with Pakistan (C. Van Hollen 1980: 341). The key reason for this re-alignment was that the Nixon-Kissinger duo wanted to restructure the global balance of power by using Beijing as a wedge between the two superpowers. Pakistan was expected to play an important role in this game plan, which involved approaching China with a strategic engagement proposal against the Soviet Union. The primary objective of this proposal was to materialize three long-term interests: (1) to split the Sino-Soviet communist bloc, which had been witnessing a rift since the 1969 border clashes along the Ussuri River, (2) to use Beijing as a check to counterbalance Moscow, and (3) to ease tensions with Beijing over the Vietnam War (NSA 2001).

Despite an arms embargo and the West Pakistani forces' brutal suppression of Bengalis in East Pakistan, the United States allowed Pakistan to purchase $50 million worth of military equipment and later provided secret military aid through Jordan, Turkey, Saudi Arabia, and Iran during the 1971 war (Documents 28–29, 32–36, 42, and 44 in NSA 2002b; Kux 2001: 183). The formation of a triangular alliance between Pakistan, China, and the United States, coupled with mounting tensions across the Bengal border, led New Delhi to sign a treaty of friendship with Moscow in August 1971 (R. Jackson 1975: 71). In other words, the US-China-Pakistan triad's strategic posturing compelled the Soviet Union and India, an aspirant to regional hegemony, to counterbalance the new alliance. Throughout the South Asian crisis, the United States adopted a highly provocative stance with an intention to increase the chances of a Sino-Soviet clash so that it would get "an 'opportunity to clean up Vietnam at that point' by giving an ultimatum to Hanoi and blockading Haiphong harbor" (NSA 2005). In this sense, the US leadership seems to have visualized the Indo-Pakistani conflict from the vortex of the Cold War and, if its realpolitik gamble had actually materialized, it was highly likely that the regional crisis would have engulfed other regions or at least most of the Asian region into a large-scale crisis.

When China did not intervene in the war[8] and Dacca was about to collapse, only then did the United States swing into action to protect Pakistan with an aim to secure its three long-term political objectives: first, to send a signal to the Indians and the Soviets "to give emphasis to [the US] warnings against an attack on West Pakistan" (Kissinger 1979: 905); second, to impress on China that if it formed a strategic relationship with the United States, it could count on US steadfastness in times of trouble; and finally, to "prevent a complete collapse of the world's psychological balance of power, which will be produced if a combination of the Soviet Union and the Soviet armed client state can tackle [Pakistan] without anybody doing anything" (NSA 2005). Though Henry Kissinger linked the end of the Bangladesh War to the White House's gunboat diplomacy,[9] the fact was that before the US Seventh Fleet—led by the nuclear aircraft carrier USS *Enterprise*—could have exerted "any impact on the course of the war," the war was over[10] (Racioppi 1994: 82; also S.M. Ali 2005: 236n16). It may therefore be argued that the primary objective of the US gunboat diplomacy was more to protect its global image that was torn apart by the Indo-Soviet alliance in the subcontinent—a region adjacent to Southeast Asia where the United States was toiling against Vietnam and Cambodia—rather than to assist its ally. The literature on the issue, besides the opinions of India's retired armed forces personnel, also suggests that neither Moscow nor New Delhi had any intention to act militarily and devastate Pakistan's two wings (Kak 2017; Kanwal 2016; C. Van Hollen 1980: 352–57). The Soviets' specific interest was to blow off the prestige and significance of the emerging Sino-American alliance by dismembering their interlocutor and long-standing ally—Pakistan. For America, the consequences of Pakistan's defeat were far-reaching; a majority of developing countries began to view Pakistan's unprecedented defeat and the subsequent breakaway of its eastern wing as a strategic victory of the Indo-Soviet alliance over the US-China-Pakistan triangular alliance.

In short, we notice that the great powers' military aid and alliance formations had indeed played a pivotal role in shaping India's and Pakistan's hardline policies during the intensive phase, which eventually led them to engage in two full-fledged wars in a short period of six years. The outcomes of both wars, especially Pakistan's dismemberment, further tangled this complex rivalry and ensured the defeated revisionist state would fall back on its traditional recourse of seeking revenge at a more opportune moment in the foreseeable future.

Rivalry Linkage: The Impact of Sino-Indian Border Tensions on the
Indo-Pakistani Rivalry

In the early 1950s, Pakistan entered the US alliance system to ostensibly contain communist forces in Asia; meanwhile, communist China developed a
friendly relationship with India by signing an agreement of coexistence,
popularly known as the *Panchsheel* or five-principles agreement (GoI 1958:
262). Given this background, the possibility of the formation of closer ties
between Pakistan and China was almost impossible as their diplomatic practices were entirely antithetical to each other's professed objectives. However,
soon after the *Panchsheel* agreement and the Bandung Conference, the relations between India and China began to deteriorate over the issue of border
demarcation and the future of Tibet. China repeatedly claimed vast chunks
of territory south of the McMahon Line, which India contested on the basis
of the British maps, but the Mao-led China refused to accept the legality of
the colonial demarcation as a border between the two Himalayan neighbors;
therefore the dispute persisted.

Within a couple of years, both states toughened their positions over the
border claims and resorted to aggressive patrolling along the border. Tensions escalated further when the Tibetans revolted against the Chinese bru-
talities in early 1959, which led to a mass migration, including of the Dalai
Lama, to India (Dobell 1964: 283–85; Maxwell [1970] 2010: 85–103). Since
India was dependent on US economic aid, China began to suspect its role in
the Tibetan uprising and subsequently charged it with collaborating with
the rebels and facilitating US surveillance activities against it (see Conboy &
Morrison 2002: 96–97, 117; Gopal 1984: 91, 99). In an attempt to prevent an
outburst and spread of rebellion, China rushed its troops to the border and
resorted to armed clashes with the Indian troops in Ladakh and the North-
East Frontier Agency (later known as Arunachal Pradesh) (S. Raghavan 2010:
253–61). A series of such disturbing border hostilities set the stage for India's
"forward policy" and later the Sino-Indian War of 1962 (see Palit 1991).

Until this time, Pakistan was not close to China nor did it leap quickly to
the Chinese side. In fact, Ayub Khan proposed to Nehru a joint defense of
the subcontinent against China in August 1959, but Nehru refused to accept
the offer. From the Indian perspective, accepting Pakistan's defense proposal
would imply abandoning the non-aligned doctrine and joining an arrangement designed against the communist powers, China and the Soviet Union.

Additionally, the offer was tied to a tacit bargaining on Kashmir (Dobell 1964: 284–85; Gopal 1984: 91–92). India encountered a twofold problem with regard to Kashmir: First, conceding the Kashmir Valley to Pakistan would render Ladakh indefensible as its supply line runs through it and accepting such an arrangement would mean handing over Ladakh to China by default (Gundevia 1984: 293). Second, a voluntary surrender of any part of Kashmir would have had a cataclysmic impact on the political life of the government of the day. Around the same time, when a similar proposal was initiated to resolve the issue of Aksai Chin with China, Nehru acknowledged the possibility of a similar political backlash: "If I give them [Aksai Chin] I shall no longer be Prime Minister of India—I will not do it" (Maxwell [1970] 2010: 161).

According to Sisson and Rose, India's uncompromising position toward Pakistan's proposal forced the latter to turn toward China in the early 1960s, which eventually shaped "a tacit Sino-Pakistani alliance . . . directed against their common antagonist—India" (1990: 45). Though this view holds merit, it overlooks other cooperative initiatives—for example, the Indus Water Treaty of 1960—which could have plausibly mended differences between India and Pakistan and instituted peace in the region (Indus Water Treaty 1960). Some scholars contend that the water issue was of far greater strategic importance to Pakistan than Kashmir (Iyer 2007, 2012; Miner et al. 2009; see M.A. Khan [1967] 2006: 127–33). Ever since the partition of India, the water issue was the raison d'être of recurring disputes as the water supply from East Punjab was the lifeline of agrarian West Punjab, but the conclusion of a negotiated water treaty failed to transform the two states' hostile relationship—in fact, it did not deter Pakistan from forging a strategic alliance with China against India (Gundevia 1984: 293). Furthermore, India had also proposed Pakistan a mutual "no-war pact" in 1949 and 1963, but on both occasions Pakistan rejected Nehru's peace proposal. In fact, Ayub Khan argued,

how [can] goodwill and understanding . . . develop [between Pakistan and India] when basic differences and disputes remain unresolved[?] . . . [T]he need for a "no war pact" has arisen . . . because of the existence of disputes which can lead to an armed conflict between the two countries. Now, if nothing is done to resolve these conflicts on a just and honourable basis, how does the danger of conflict disappear merely because of the existence of a "no war pact"[?] (M.A. Khan [1967] 2006: 142)

This shows how India's and Pakistan's power politics practices had complicated their relations, especially after Pakistan's membership in the SEATO and the CENTO; hence their ruling elites responded to each other's moves in accordance with the mutually adopted realpolitik practices. Once Pakistan realized that pursuing a closer relationship with China—a state which was increasingly turning hostile to India—could benefit its revisionist aims, it followed a path known in the realist literature as "bandwagoning for profit" (Schweller 1994). Another case in point is Pakistan's outspoken support of China during the Sino-Indian War of 1962. Had Pakistan taken a neutral stand or one favorable to India, arguably, the possibility of the settlement of Kashmir would have increased—after the China debacle, the Indian leadership stressed this argument (see Bowles 1971: 473). But again the realist dictum got in the way. Just six days after China's overwhelming victory over India, Zulfikar Ali Bhutto declared in a National Assembly debate that Pakistan's friendship with China "is unconditional. We will not barter or bargain it away for anything. . . . It is the fundamental principle of our foreign policy" (cited in Montagno 1965: 309–10). When Pakistan's strategic attempts to leverage India's growing tensions with China failed to yield satisfactory outcomes, it concluded a border demarcation agreement with China in March 1963 followed by trade and air travel agreements (Yasmeen 1992: 325). Pakistan's turn to China decisively transformed South Asia's bilateral conflict into a trilateral Sino-Indian-Pakistani rivalry. Robert G. Wirsing aptly recapitulates the triangulation of this conflict:

In space of four years, between the onset of the Tibetan rebellion in March 1959 and the signing of the Border Agreement between China and Pakistan in March 1963, a fundamental turnout occurred in the pattern of relations among the three neighboring states—China, India, and Pakistan. By the latter date, China had dealt a humiliating defeat to India in the border war of October-November 1962, while at the same time having entered into a multifaceted informal alliance with Pakistan. This turnabout undid the fairly straightforward bilateral contest over Kashmir between India and Pakistan that had existed at the start of the 1950s, replacing it in the early 1960s with a three-cornered, trans-Himalayan "security complex." (1998: 93)

In July 1963, in an attempt to mount strategic pressure on India, Bhutto, the then foreign minister of Pakistan, assured the Pakistan Assembly that "any attack by India on Pakistan would no longer confine the stakes to the independence and territorial integrity of Pakistan. An attack by India on Pakistan would also involve the security and territorial integrity of the largest state in Asia" (cited in Barnds 1972: 190). This declaration led New Delhi to conclude that its revisionist opponents, Pakistan and China, had planned a collective strategy against India; hence it decided to accelerate its military buildup to match the challenge (Barnds 1972: 190). Paradoxically, previously India had argued that the Western powers' military assistance to Pakistan was the cause of regional destabilization, but after the 1962 Sino-Indian War, the scenario changed diametrically and Pakistan began to argue that the US attempt to strengthen Indian military capabilities against China would prove counterproductive to Pakistan's security. In Ayub Khan's words, "[A]ny army meant for China would by the nature of things be so positioned as to be able to wheel round swiftly and attack East Pakistan" (M.A. Khan 1964: 204).

This position of Pakistan's was more stringent in many respects than its previous one specified in an aide-mémoire sent to the United States on January 3, 1962, in which it had stated that India should not be armed "until it renounces 'aggressive intentions and needs the equipment only to fight the Chinese'" (FRUS 1996: 186). Following Pakistan's strong resentment, China further complicated the South Asian rivalry by taking a clear stand against India on Kashmir and finalizing its decision to conduct a nuclear weapon test in October 1964, followed by more such tests over the next twelve years (Garver 2004: 3). These moves not only reinforced China's stand in Pakistan's favor but also intensified the triangular rivalry by introducing a nuclear dynamic into it. Further, during the Second Kashmir War, nuclear China extended Pakistan crucial support: first, by provoking Kashmiris against India by characterizing Pakistan's infiltration in Kashmir as "the Kashmiri people's" war of "self-determination" (Garver 2004: 15–16); and second, by elevating the military threat by resuming aggressive patrolling along the Sino-Indian border and assuring Pakistan of full support against India (Behera 2006: 219–20). According to Air Marshal Asghar Khan, Pakistan had prepared "a contingency plan" which "included the idea of China occupying a large tract of Indian territory in the North East Frontier . . . to siphon much of the Indian pressure off the Kashmir border and assist Pakistan in seizing Kashmir" (Yasmeen 1992: 327). However, the superpowers' "stern warnings" to Beijing averted the possibility for a two-front war (Ganguly 2002: 46).

In the wake of war, China and Pakistan jointly started the construction of the strategic Karakoram highway, a move that strengthened their collective military posture against India in Kashmir. Apart from this, China also initiated "a major and sustainable military assistance program designed to help modernize Pakistan's naval, air, and ground forces" (Wirsing 1998: 101). Such a close strategic cooperation between China and Pakistan was a clear indication to India that it was badly encircled on two fronts and must "maintain armed forces large enough to face Pakistan and China simultaneously while spending ever-increasing sums on economic development" (Barnds 1972: 221). Around the same time, the Soviet Union, the United States, and Britain formulated a cohesive platform to cap India's nuclear ambitions. Together, they shaped the Non-Proliferation Treaty (NPT) and pressured New Delhi to sign it; however, the latter refused to give up its nuclear program under the growing international pressure. The primary reason for India's dissension with the NPT was that it was viewed by New Delhi as a discriminatory agreement between the nuclear haves and have-nots, while India wanted to acquire a minimum nuclear capability to deter the nuclear threat posed by China (Perkovich 1999: 131–39). After the Indian rejection, Pakistan also refused to sign the NPT—actually the brewing nuclear issue between China and India made it hostage to India's nuclear ambition, and thereby added another knot to what Robert Wirsing has dubbed the "trans-Himalayan security complex" (1998: 93).

In response to India's support for Tibetans, China initially demanded "self-determination" for Kashmiris but later expanded its revolutionary calls to India's troubled northeast where various Naga and Mizo groups were demanding political autonomy from the Indian Union (Bhaumik 2009: 16, 97, 153–58; Raman 2007: 7–8). In a bid to exploit their political and economic grievances vis-à-vis the rest of India, China began "arming and training guerrillas so that they could erode India's already tenuous authority along these frontiers" (Barnds 1972: 220). China was prepared to foment revolution in India because it believed that India was in league with the United States and the Soviet Union to encircle it, if not detach Tibet. According to the recently declassified history of the CIA's U-2 spy plane program, China's suspicion was indeed correct—India had allowed US planes to use the Charbatia airbase in Orissa for spying missions against China from May 1964 to July 1967 (see Conboy & Morrison 2002: 184–200; Dikshit 2013; Riedel 2016: 158–60). In the late 1960s, Pakistan also joined China's campaign to cause trouble for India in the northeast by "allow[ing] the establishment of

Chinese-operated training camps in East Pakistan" (Sisson & Rose 1990: 43). In spite of strong cultural links, public support, and geographical contiguity with Tibet, New Delhi's weak China policy failed to neutralize Beijing's influence in Tibet. However, some scholars argue that it did succeed in countering Pakistan by granting "political and material (primarily financial) support to Pakhtoon dissidents" across the Durand Line (Sisson & Rose 1990: 43).

Later, when the situation in East Pakistan turned volatile in 1971, China promised full support to Pakistan. On April 11, 1971, Premier Zhou Enlai assured President General Yahya Khan, "[S]hould the Indian expansionists dare to launch aggression against Pakistan, the Chinese government and people will, as always, firmly support the Pakistan government and people in their just struggle to safeguard state sovereignty and national independence" (cited in Barnds 1972: 244). Again, a couple of months later, Zhou told Kissinger that "if India commits aggression, we will support Pakistan" (S. M. Ali 2005: 39). However, as the crisis between East and West Pakistan deepened and Delhi and Moscow concluded the treaty of friendship, China re-assessed the repercussions of its military support to Pakistan and thereafter made a calculated retreat from its previous position and promise.[11] When Bhutto led Pakistan's high-profile delegation to China to reaffirm Beijing's crucial support in November 1971, the Chinese shied away from promising any wide-ranging assistance that would "incur [them] material costs or risks" (Ganguly 2002: 67). Chi Peng-fei, the then acting foreign minister of China, suggested to the delegation that "the internal affairs of any country must be handled by its own people" (quoted in Racioppi 1994: 81).

Mainly three factors made Beijing's intervention in the war exceedingly difficult: (1) the timing of the Indian attack and geographical constraints, as most of the Himalayan passes were closed during the winter season; (2) the People's Liberation Army (PLA) of China was regrouping after the shock of Cultural Revolution; and (3) the Sino-Soviet conflict in the Ussuri region had made China's northern border vulnerable to the Soviets' pressure tactics (Lynch 2004: 188–90). Though China did not participate in the 1965 and 1971 wars, its political and material support to Pakistan had played a significant role to steer the Indo-Pakistani rivalry during the intensive phase. In the end, China and Pakistan's collective strategic front against India proved fatal for Pakistan, as it provoked India to neutralize the Sino-Pakistani collective threat—a two-front problem—by liberating East Pakistan, which in turn helped India to assert its dominance in the region.

INFLUENCE OF RELATIVE MILITARY CAPABILITIES

India's and Pakistan's aggressive military buildup to enhance their security had in fact aggravated their conflictual relationship during the intensive phase—Figure 5.2 shows how it spiraled into higher levels of insecurity and an arms race. After 1959, the Indo-Pakistani rivalry began to form a close linkage with the Sino-Indian conflict, particularly when China and Pakistan forged an informal alliance against their common enemy—India. This triangular linkage shaped a "regional security complex" that led India to adopt a policy of "two-front" buildup by directing its military capability against both Pakistan and China. As a logical corollary, drawing a comparison of India's military capability vis-à-vis Pakistan and including the part of India's military capability directed against China might be misleading. To present a reasonable assessment of India's and Pakistan's relative power, it is therefore necessary to omit India's China-specific military capability from its total or overall military capability figures. Accordingly, in Figure 5.2a and b, the curves "Ind" and "Pak" denote India's and Pakistan's overall military personnel strength and military expenditure, respectively, and the curve "I-Truncated" denotes India's actual military personnel strength and military expenditure vis-à-vis Pakistan after omitting its China-specific capabilities from its overall figures (that is, curve "Ind").[12] Figure 5.2c graphs Pakistan's relative military personnel strength, military expenditure, and total military capability vis-à-vis India on the basis of the "I-Truncated" measure.

Steps to the Second Kashmir War

After Pakistan's inclusion in the Western alliance system (1954–56), the policy makers in New Delhi initiated fundamental steps to improve India's military capability vis-à-vis the regional rival. Despite a large gap in their overall national capabilities—India held nearly a 5:1 advantage against Pakistan (see Figure 5.2d)—the two states held somewhat similar military capabilities in the early years of their conflict (see Figure 4.2a, b in Chapter 4), but the Tibetan rebellion of 1959 and the resulting Sino-Indian hostility created a baffling security situation for India which considerably affected the Indo-Pakistani military balance (see Figure 5.2a–c). From this time onward, the Sino-Indian border hostilities intensified, which mounted pressure on India to protect its vulnerable borders by devising a military upgrade policy. Con-

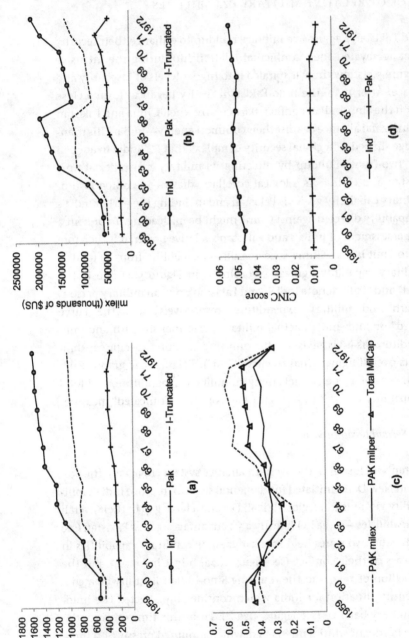

Figure 5.2. India-Pakistan relative capabilities and militarized disputes, 1959–72. (a) Military personnel (milper) ratio, (b) military expenditure (milex) ratio, (c) Pakistan's total military capability vis-à-vis India, (d) composite index of national capability (CINC) ratio. The CINC ratio comprises milper + milex + primary energy consumption (pec) ratio + iron and steel production (irst) ratio [population (total + urban) excluded]. *Source:* Compiled from the COW database (2015), National Material Capabilities, version 4.01.

sequently, India's annual military expenditure during 1959-1962 increased by 61 percent and the manpower of the armed forces increased from 535,000 to 800,000. Although this military expansion was directed toward China, it simultaneously put in motion a long-term change in India's and Pakistan's relative military capabilities which ultimately affected their political-military behavior and policies.

Influence of Windows of Opportunity and Vulnerability

Stephen Van Evera's "window theory" posits that when the perceived or actual balance of power capabilities changes or is about to change, the political leadership may see an impending "window of opportunity" during which it may be able to temporarily prevail against a rival in warfare, or it may see a looming "window of vulnerability" that undermines its prospects to prevail against the rival (1999: 73-104).[13] Windows never stay open or closed for long, argues Van Evera; therefore they "tempt declining states to launch an early war before the power shift is complete, either to avoid a later war waged under worse conditions or to avoid later being compelled to bargain from weakness" (1999: 76). Much of Van Evera's window explanation is consistent with Dale Copeland's (2000) "dynamic differentials theory" (DDT). According to it, sometimes a rival's future preponderant position convinces the overall weak state to wage war against an adversary to keep it down—as Germany did twice in 1914 and 1939 in fear of Russia's future potential, and Iraq did against Iran in the 1980s (Copeland 2000: 56-145).

In brief, both of these explanations stress that a widening gap between the rival parties' overall national capabilities compel the weaker party to opt for a risky option, that is, to wage war against the rival. In the India-Pakistan case, the two rivals' overall national capabilities did play an important role to step up their military buildup but had a limited impact on immediate strategies as their overall national capabilities more or less remained constant throughout their rivalry (see Figure 5.2d). In this case, however, what emerged as a critical factor to determine the course of the South Asian rivalry were the two sides' military capabilities.

Following India's defeat in the 1962 war, its policy makers initiated a new military expansion program that proposed the raising of sixteen military divisions (including ten mountain divisions) equipped with substantial modern weaponry, creation of a 45-squadron air force equipped with high-performance supersonics, the modernization of the Indian Navy, and improvement of infrastructure and communication facilities along the border areas (Kavic 1967: 192–93; Palit 1991: 408; Thomas 1986: 27). Within two years of India's crushing defeat at the hands of China, that is, by 1964, the drastic changes in Indian defense policy had almost doubled its annual military expenditure and increased the armed personnel strength by about 52 percent. Taken as a whole, from 1959 to 1964, India had tripled its overall military expenditure and doubled the manpower of the armed forces from 535,000 to 1,215,000 (Figure 5.2a, b).

Though much of the augmentation in India's military strength was focused on deterring the China threat, it had many unforeseen ramifications for Pakistan's traditional military balance against India as it began to plummet from 1:2 in 1961 to 1:3.6 in 1964 (see Figure 5.2c). As a consequence, the military regime in Rawalpindi began to perceive that "India's rapid militarization against China would have both short-term and long-term impact on Pakistan" (Durrani 2015). During the course of a future war, General Ayub argued, India could divert its armed divisions from its eastern border with China and deploy them against Pakistan on short notice (M.A. Khan 1964: 199–207). A second scenario worrying Pakistan would arise if India resolved its border dispute with China. Against this backdrop, the Pakistani military leadership was convinced that India's overwhelming military strength would increase Pakistani's long-term vulnerability (M.A. Khan [1967] 2006).

Given India's large resources, the overall shift in the status quo rival's military capability was comprehended by Pakistan as a grave threat to its revisionist claim on Kashmir. In other words, it can be argued that Pakistan's establishment was convinced that India's extensive investment in the military buildup would overwhelmingly undermine the country's future position by creating a huge Pakistani window of vulnerability. As the declining side in the rivalry, the Pakistani leadership was tempted to react to a perceived military shift by choosing a preventive war when it still had a chance of victory. Ayub's decision was primarily based on the logic that Pakistan still possessed considerable military might to defeat India in a limited war sooner rather than later when the capability gap would widen and make such probes questionable. Therefore, the fear due to a perceived widening military gap vis-à-vis India apparently convinced Pakistan to wage a "preventive" war against the rival at the earliest opportunity.

Offensive Capability

A second important factor was offensive capability. Though Pakistan's total military strength against India was 1:3, it had an edge against India from the viewpoint of offensive capability. Since its inclusion in the anti-communist alliance system, the United States had provided Pakistan qualitative military aid that significantly increased its offensive capability against India. By 1965, Pakistan had in its possession large quantities of modern artillery that included 200 M-47/48 Patton tanks, 12 high-performance F-104 Starfighter interceptors, 24 B-57 Canberra combat aircraft, and 168 F-86 Sabre aircraft—a large number of them equipped with sophisticated Sidewinder air-to-air missiles (Paul 1994: 115). On the other hand, the Indian Army was equipped with old British and French armory and aircraft that included one armored division each of Centurion and Sherman tanks, one regiment with AMX-13 tanks, 4 squadrons of HF Marut fighter bombers, 100 Mysteres IVs, 150 Hunters, 80 Canberra bombers, 100 Indian-manufactured Gnats, 12 squadrons of Soviet-origin MiG-21s, and several Ouragans and Vampires (*Military Balance* 1965).

Though India had a quantitative superiority over Pakistan by 3:1 in armory and 2.5:1 in aircraft and artillery, its old British and French equipment was far inferior to Pakistan's highly efficient American weapon systems. In warfare, as Raju Thomas maintains, "the principle of matching capabilities tended to be more qualitative than quantitative" (1986: 22). From this standpoint, Pakistan had better striking and maneuvering capability, and this offensive edge provided it with an incentive to penetrate the defenses of its quantitatively superior opponent in a quick short war. During April to June 1965, as discussed earlier, Pakistan had successfully tested its offensive capability in the Rann of Kutch where its troops outmaneuvered and outfought their Indian counterparts. After India's military debacle in the Rann of Kutch, Ayub Khan interpreted that Pakistan's offensive capability and soldiers had clearly outmatched the Indians. His assessment was that the Indian Army was demoralized after being defeated by the Chinese, and that this, coupled with unrest in Kashmir, left India extremely vulnerable to a vigorous foreign attack (Abbas 2005: 43–44; Feldman 1972: 135).

In the meantime, the Pakistani decision-makers were also aware that the Indian window of vulnerability was fast closing with the rival's five-year defense modernization plan (1964–69) under which it would spend $2 billion on military modernization, acquisition of offensive weaponry, and raising several military divisions. Once the Indian acquisition of large-scale qualitative armor, artillery, and aircraft—particularly forty-five squadrons of MiG-21s—was complete, it would offset Pakistan's short-term qualitative edge (Paul 1994: 115–16). Before India could close its window of vulnerability forever, the Ayub regime thought, Pakistan should reap the benefit of its current offensive edge—its window of opportunity—by waging a preventive war in Kashmir while the Indian forces were still building up rather than a couple of years later against a preponderant India. In other words, by securing the knowledge that its qualitatively superior equipment would limit Indian retaliatory action, the possession of offensive weapons had provided the revisionist Pakistan with another compelling incentive to challenge the territorial status quo in Kashmir. This underscores that Pakistan's qualitative edge against India played a decisive role in its decision and timing to initiate pre-emptive war in Kashmir in 1965.

Kashmir-Specific Tactical Advantage

A third factor was tactical advantage on account of Kashmir's mountainous terrain and communication lines that were favorable to Pakistan. From Pakistan's perspective, the combination of advantageous terrain and offensive strategy—that is, the onset of guerrilla warfare followed by a superior armored onslaught—would hinder the Indian armed forces' rapid movement and thereby hamper India's capability to fight decisively. Thus an early mobilization would increase its chances to overrun large chunks of Kashmir's territory. Once the top military leadership was convinced that Pakistan's short-term offensive strategy had a significant correlation with its tactical advantage, President Ayub Khan was sure that a quick war would not only provide Pakistan desired dividends but also keep the scope of war limited to a territory of its advantage—Kashmir.

When all these factors coalesced, further buttressed by Pakistanis' self-defined notions of Muslim soldiers' fighting prowess, the idea of annexing Kashmir became a feasible proposition. Putting all the factors together, President Ayub Khan and associates saw Pakistan's window of opportunity closing fast in 1965 with India's substantial buildup drive to enhance its military power. In a window-driven haste, the Ayub regime thought Pakistan's short-term advantage would yield it preferred dividends if it attacked while the Indian forces were still building up and unprepared to absorb a sudden offensive in Kashmir. However, Pakistan's tactics of a short, decisive war backfired when India opened a front where it had the advantage—the Punjab border—and turned the adversary's military probe into a full-fledged war. Pakistan's exposure in the plains denied it the calculated advantage it had hoped to seek; in fact, it made it vulnerable to losing its largest city—Lahore.

Steps to the Bangladesh War of 1971

After the Second Kashmir War, the ruling elites of India and Pakistan had taken additional steps to improve their respective sides' military capabilities. For instance, India had increased its armed forces manpower from 1,220,000 in 1965 to 1,550,000 in 1970 (over 27 percent)—however, its total military expenditure registered a decrease of around 17 percent of the level of 1965. On the other hand, Pakistan not only responded by stepping up its armed forces manpower from 277,000 to 390,000 but its total military expenditure had also witnessed a steep rise of around 41 percent from the level of 1965. As a result, Pakistan recorded a relative increase in its total military capability vis-à-vis India; however, from the standpoint of offensive capabilities and large military accumulation, India still had an edge over its adversary during this period (see Figure 5.2a–c).

Influence of Windows of Opportunity

If the window of opportunity had influenced the Pakistani military establishment to wage the Second Kashmir War, the same logic had played an important role to influence the Indian political leadership to intervene in Pakistan's domestic crisis and liberate East Pakistan in 1971. During this period Pakistan's total military strength against India was considerably better than in 1965, that is, 1:2, but India swiftly elevated its military capabilities in the theater of war by deploying military equipment and diverting its troops from the China border to East Pakistan—a long-held concern of the Ayub regime.

Pakistan's domestic situation further turned volatile when the military regime passed the Martial Law Ordinance in March 1971. The oppression of Bengali nationalists by the West Pakistani forces, as discussed earlier, led to a Bengali exodus to neighboring India, providing the latter a fleeting one-time opportunity to instigate rebellion in the enemy state—as Pakistan attempted unsuccessfully in Kashmir in 1965. However, the context and operationalization of Pakistan's strategy in Kashmir and India's in East Pakistan were quite different: the former had sent its armed militias to encourage the Kashmiris to start a civil war in 1965, whereas India extended its political-military support to the Bengalis of East Pakistan whose existence was under threat in 1971, and they were, unlike the Kashmiris, eager to instigate hostilities against their own state. The availability of thousands of resentful refugees, mainly youth, had not only expanded India's existential strength against Pakistan but also provided it a rare opportunity to widen Pakistan's window of vulnerability by dismembering the revisionist rival. India grabbed this opportunity; it aided, trained, and provided all necessary support to the guerrilla force, famously known as the *Mukti Bahini*, to inflict costs on the West Pakistani troops.

When the civil war broke out in East Pakistan, the Indian leadership was optimistic about its chances of victory because Pakistan's prevailing domestic turmoil had created a huge window of opportunity for India. Furthermore, India swiftly rushed its diplomatic missions to several states across the globe to bolster its political position by making them aware of West Pakistan's vindictive attitude toward fellow Bengali Muslims and the subsequent socio-economic impact on India. When the international opinion and military equations substantially turned against Pakistan, the prospects of an Indian victory seemed to be within New Delhi's reach. The Indian decision was primarily based on the logic that Pakistan's brutal treatment of its citizens had exposed and isolated it diplomatically in the world, and its isolated troops would not be able to withstand the Bengali revolutionaries and the Indian troops' collective attacks for long. Later, if the situation were to take a passive turn or the Bengali nationalists were to lose momentum in their struggle against West Pakistan—the Indira Gandhi regime appears to have thought—a war against Pakistan would become untenable as the rationale and inevitability of the need to liberate the oppressed Bengali community would wane with the passage of time. The fear of closure of the window of opportunity convinced India to wage a quick "preventive" war to cut Pakistan to size and attain the status of regional hegemon. Additionally, for New Delhi, the cost, value, and risks attached to invading East Pakistan and liberating the Bengalis were well within bearable limits compared with hosting refugees' prolonged stay in India.

Conditional Offensive Capability

A second factor that played an important role in the initiation of the 1971 war was significant improvement in India's offensive capability. Since 1962 India had substantially upgraded its military strength, which provided it capability and wherewithal to handle a two-front offensive. By 1970-71, the Indian Air Force comprised thirty-three combat squadrons, which included five squadrons of Su-7 fighter bombers, seven squadrons of MiG-21 interceptors, three squadrons of Canberra bombers, two squadrons of indigenous HF-24 Marut fighter bombers, eight squadrons of Indian-manufactured Gnats, two squadrons of Mystere fighter bombers, and six squadrons of Hunter fighter bombers (*Military Balance* 1971).[14] The Indian Navy was equipped with one aircraft carrier, three anti-aircraft frigates, two cruisers, four submarines, five anti-submarine frigates, three destroyers, and nine destroyer escorts. The Indian Army had one armored division, two independent armored brigades, thirteen infantry divisions, six independent infantry brigades, about twenty artillery units, and two parachute brigades. Apart from this, it had ten additional mountain divisions guarding the China border or the Line of Actual Control (LAC) (*Military Balance* 1971).

On the other hand, the Pakistan Army had twelve infantry divisions, two armored divisions, one air defense brigade, and one armored brigade. The Pakistan Air Force was equipped with two squadrons of B-57 bombers, one squadron of Il-28 bombers, eight squadrons of F-86 Sabre aircrafts, two squadrons of Mirage III supersonic fighter bombers, one squadron of high-performance F-104 Starfighter interceptors, and four squadrons of MiG-19 supersonics—however, in comparison to India, Pakistan's air force had more aircraft per squadron. The Pakistan Navy had four submarines, two destroyers, one light cruiser, three destroyer escorts, two frigates, and four patrol boats (*Military Balance* 1971). Unlike 1965, the Indian Air Force had attained a small qualitative edge over Pakistan by 1971 partly because it succeeded to acquire superior weaponry and technical knowhow from Moscow and out-matched Pakistan's air capability by producing MiG-21 interceptors with the Soviet technical support (Thomas 1986: 22). On the other hand, the United States had stopped all military supplies to Pakistan after the 1965 war, which attenuated its military capability (mainly air force) vis-à-vis India. Though it tried to bridge this gap by acquiring Mirage III aircraft from France, along with free Chinese arms supplies, these efforts proved to be insufficient for its obsolescing aircrafts (Yunus 2011: 129–31).

The decision-makers in New Delhi were aware that during the summer the Chinese threat would keep India from using most of its overall military capability against the two wings of Pakistan. In the winter months, on the other hand, the tactical balance would overwhelmingly turn in favor of India when its northeastern mountain passes would freeze, making the probability of China's support to Pakistan in the eastern sector almost out of the question. Additionally, in a bid to defend its western frontier from the

Indian offensive, Pakistan would mass a greater number of troops in the western wing and depute a few infantry divisions and air squadrons to its eastern wing. In such a situation, India would be free to divert some of its mountain divisions from the China border to assist its well-equipped infantry divisions in the eastern sector to beat out hapless Pakistani forces in the absence of air and sea cover—which would also by that time be internally toiling against the hostile *Mukti Bahini* revolutionaries—in the wake of West Pakistan's aerial seizure and sea blockade. From this viewpoint, it is apparent that India had carefully assessed its unprecedented superiority in the theater of war against Pakistan and then decided to reap the benefit of the situation by waging a decisive war in East Pakistan.

Tactical Advantage: Impact of Non-existent Geographical Contiguity

During the 1971 war, geographical contiguity played a critical role. Ever since its creation as an independent state, Pakistan's non-contiguous east and west wings thrived as a unit because of Pakistan's and India's mutual recognition of the partition principle as well as the latter's non-interventionist approach. For instance, during the 1965 war, India did not open a front against vulnerable East Pakistan where Pakistan had deployed "only one army division" (Jahan 1972: 166). In 1970–71, when Pakistan's two wings were embroiled in the internal conflict, the Indian decision-makers assessed that in a war situation the absence of geographical contiguity between the two wings' territorial borders would place Pakistan in a distinctly disadvantageous position. Moreover, East Pakistan was surrounded on three sides by India, and West Pakistan only had access to its eastern wing through a long sea route from the Arabian Sea to the Bay of Bengal, which was three times longer than the air route.

From the standpoint of Kenneth Boulding's (1962) "loss-of-strength-gradient," as discussed in Chapters 3 and 4, the policy makers in New Delhi knew that greater distance between Pakistan's two wings—in the form of hostile India—had accentuated Islamabad's relatively disadvantageous position, and therefore in a real war situation Pakistan's retaliatory capability would be limited in scale and scope. In addition, India's territorial proximity to East Pakistan would significantly increase its existing offensive capability, which would help confront and defeat the Pakistani forces in a quick action. In such a scenario, notwithstanding its adequate offensive capability, far-away West Pakistan would not be in position to defend East Pakistan. Non-existent geographical contiguity would make Pakistan's existing military capability ineffective, as it would not be able to extend robust air and naval support to its forces in East Pakistan, further widening the capability gap between the two adversaries. Additionally, India's contiguous border with East Pakistan would provide it with an extended ability to use force closer to home, while the lack of the same condition would make it difficult for West Pakistan to maintain its defensive posture for long.

Had the eastern wing been part of West Pakistan, like four of its other provinces, the Indian decision-makers would have seriously considered the opponent's offensive strength as a unified contiguous territory despite India's having favorable conditions to wage the war. Perhaps then the situation (and the outcome) would have been *otherwise*: Pakistan could have suppressed the Bengali resistance effectively—as it did with other national-secessionist movements in Balochistan, Sindh, and the NWFP in the 1970s and later years—or, in the worst case, could have faced a bearable secession-less defeat. It is important to note that geographical contiguity had significantly helped Pakistan withstand the Indian offensive across the Punjab plains in 1965. Had Pakistan's main military power vested in East Pakistan during that time, that is, away from the theater of war, it is highly likely that Pakistan could have suffered a massive defeat of the 1971 kind during the Second Kashmir War itself. In short, once the combination of preferential geographical contiguity, preponderant offensive capability in the theater of war, additional strength of the hostile revolutionary force (the *Mukti Bahini*), minimal external threat (China), and favorable international political conditions coalesced, India's resolve to implement an advantageous strategy in East Pakistan increased. In the end, these factors played a crucial role in India's decision to initiate a quick war against Pakistan in 1971.

IMPACT OF REGIME TYPE AND THE DOMESTIC POLITICAL CONDITIONS

In the late 1950s, when Pakistan's political class was about to complete the process of constitution-making, the military-bureaucratic axis chose to derail the whole process by imposing martial law in October 1958. Within three weeks of the onset of civilian martial law, General Ayub Khan, the chief martial law administrator, deposed President Iskander Mirza in a bloodless coup and assumed the presidency (Wilcox 1965). After taking control over the state apparatus, Ayub put political forces on the back foot by imposing restrictions on political activities, abrogating the first Constitution of 1956, and introducing a rigid institutional model that was specifically designed to endorse the military rule.

Regarding the issue, scholars have offered two alternative explanations. The first is that a fractious and incompetent political leadership at the helm of the political parties had created a power vacuum through a decade-long indecisive political process together with abortive attempts to curtail the bureaucratic-military axis. According to this explanation, the political leadership tried to reduce the powers of the governor general and impose budgetary restrictions on defense expenditure,[15] which was interpreted by the head of the state (governor general 1947-56, and president 1956-58) and the army chief as the political forces' determination to dilute their influence over the state structures and institutional interests (F.M. Khan 1963: 59; McGrath 1996: 97; H.-A. Rizvi 2000: 3-7). More specifically, the political elites' intra- and inter-party disputes and unending differences over nation-building— especially between the two geographically non-contiguous and culturally divergent wings of the country—resulted in devaluing and undermining the whole process of formalizing a consensual constitution; this decade-long deadlock, it is argued, was exacerbating political disorder that compelled the army to step into the vacuum and take charge of the state affairs (H.-A. Rizvi 2000: 68-81; Sayeed 1959: 389-401).

The second and contrasting explanation has been offered by Ayesha Jalal (1995), emphasizing that the army broke down the nascent political institutions which had almost finalized the long-awaited constitutional structures. Jalal aptly explains what caused this shift:

> [O]nce the process of constitution-making had been completed, a reference to the people was inescapable. Successful in discrediting parties and politicians, the civil bureaucracy and the army were unsure of maintaining their dominance within the state structure after the general elections scheduled for 1959. Fearing a major realignment of political forces after the elections, the army high command in combination with select civil bureaucrats decided in October 1958 to take direct control over the state apparatus and, in this way, deter all potential challenges to a position of privilege they had for long enjoyed. So it cannot be argued that the failure of the "parliamentary system" in Pakistan flowed from the "power vacuum" created by politicians at the helm of parties with no real bases of popular support. (1995: 54)

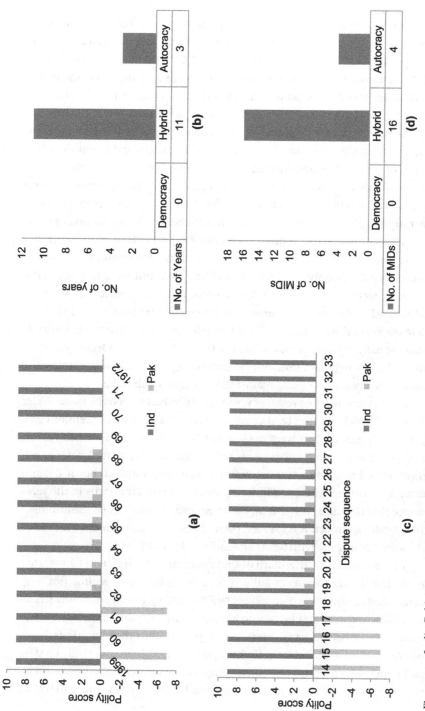

Figure 5.3. India-Pakistan regime type and recurrent militarized disputes, 1959–72. (a) Regime type, (b) regime years, (c) regime type during the initiation of MIDs; (d) no. of MIDs under particular type of regime. *Source:* Compiled from the COW database (2015), Polity IV, version 4.01

This step marked a new point of departure in India-Pakistan relations in
terms of regime disparity, a democratic regime in power in Delhi under Nehru's premiership and a military regime led by General Ayub Khan in Karachi
(later Rawalpindi). As shown in Table 5.1 and Figure 5.3, the fact of the matter
is that this was the period which shows the maximum number of bilateral
armed disputes between the two adversaries, and Pakistan was the initiator
of sixteen militarized disputes out of a total twenty, which include the two
full-scale wars in 1965 and 1971. Ayub's militaristic stand is reflected in a
series of events that unfolded in the next eleven years in the internal and
external domains. In the external domain, though it was the civilian regime
which had initiated the fundamental change in Pakistan's foreign policy by
signing a military pact with America prior to the army's assumption of political power, the "details" of this agreement were "worked out by the army, not
the foreign ministry" (Dewey 1991: 260). Primary sources duly confirm that
this pact was not only backed by Ayub Khan as commander-in-chief of the
army, in fact, it came into effect as a result of his emphatic campaigns at
home and in America for the expansion and modernization of Pakistan's
defense forces (Kux 2001: 57). Apart from this military agreement, Ayub was
also the main proponent of joining the US-sponsored Asian security pacts—
the SEATO in 1954 and the Baghdad Pact in 1955—in a bid to maximize the
country's security prospects against the principal rival: India.

After assuming the presidency, though Ayub had signed the Indus Water
Treaty with Nehru in September 1960, he rejected the Indian premier's proposal for a mutual "no war" declaration (M.A. Khan [1967] 2006: 130–33,
141–45). It was expected that the conclusion of the negotiated water agreement would transform the two states' hostile relationship, but it did not
deter Ayub from challenging India diplomatically and militarily in the years
succeeding the Indus Water Treaty. For instance, during the 1962 Sino-Indian
War, Ayub's approach was to extract benefits by pressuring America to resolve
the Kashmir dispute with terms beneficial to Pakistan.

In the immediate aftermath of India's defeat at the hands of China, that
is, during the six rounds of talks in 1962–63, his military regime not only
demanded almost the whole state of J&K but also forged an anti-India strategic alliance with China by ceding it a part of the disputed state—the Shaksham Valley (see Gundevia 1984: Ch. 12–13). Later, over the mysterious disappearance of *Mo-e-Muqaddas* in Kashmir, the Ayub regime extensively used its
radio and press to unleash virulent propaganda to fuel violent demonstrations in Srinagar that resulted in large-scale Hindu-Muslim communal riots

in geographically contiguous West Bengal and East Pakistan (Akbar 2002: 161; Sumantra Bose 2003: 79).

When these diplomatic and indirect maneuvers failed to achieve the intended objectives, Ayub pursued policies imbued with militarism to provoke India to armed hostilities. For instance, he launched an armed action in the Rann of Kutch to test India's military preparedness and the newly formed Shastri government's commitment to contest Pakistan's aggravations. After India's debacle in the marshland, Pakistan's military dictator interpreted that the Pakistani troops clearly outmatched their counterparts, an indication that the Indian Army was demoralized after its embarrassing defeat at the hands of China in 1962; therefore India was extremely vulnerable to a vigorous foreign attack (Feldman 1972: 135). Another source that confirms this was Ayub's assessment is the August 1965 directive to General Mohammad Musa, the then commander-in-chief of the Pakistan Army, to carry out sabotage activities across the CFL under Operation Gibraltar and create favorable conditions for regular Pakistani troops to intervene in Kashmir. To make his regime's undeclared operation effective, Ayub's directive advised Musa: "As a general rule Hindu morale would not stand more than a couple of hard blows delivered at the right time in right place. Such opportunities should therefore be sought and exploited" (cited in Cloughley 2002: 71).

Together with the Rann of Kutch success, Ayub's overall assessment of bilateral equations (political, military, and willingness level) had emboldened his long-standing ambition to annex Kashmir which culminated in the Second Kashmir War under the twin operations—the Gibraltar and the Grand Slam—and finally ended up in misinterpretation of the Tashkent accord. As a whole, Ayub's actions show that instead of making amends with New Delhi, he was looking for opportunities to challenge India, which entrenched the Indo-Pakistani rivalry and eventually shaped the trajectory of their future relations.

In the internal domain, Ayub needed an enemy to justify and rationalize the role of the army as a savior of the nation as well as to consolidate his position at home by building a base of support in favor of the army rule. He sought to do so by depoliticizing the society by completely banning the political activities and replacing the parliamentary system with a favorable basic democracies system. Under this military-managed political system, 80,000 local representatives (later increased to 120,000), so-called basic democrats, "were elected on the basis of adult franchise to union councils and union committees in the rural and urban areas respectively" to "elect

members to the higher level local bodies" (Jalal 1995: 56). The main purpose
of the basic democracies, Jalal argues, "was to cultivate a new rural constituency for the regime that would endorse rather than set its political and economic agendas" (1995: 56). Initially, this system effectively blocked the political parties and pressure groups, but after the setback of the 1965 war, Ayub's
control over the state apparatus plummeted—particularly after Zulfikar Ali
Bhutto's resignation from the cabinet over the Tashkent accord with India
and the religious right's and political parties' activism against his military
rule (Burki 1980: 48–55). Another drawback of the Ayub regime was that it
completely isolated East Pakistanis, especially through its constant neglect
of the majority Bengali population and the political class's due position in
the power hierarchy, which had not only increased resentment against the
basic democracies but also intensified political tussle between the two wings
of the country (see Jahan 1972). All these issues together triggered a serious
domestic crisis for Pakistan's first military dictator which eventually led to
Ayub's resignation in 1969 and the emergence of a new military regime
under General Yahya Khan.

　　At the time, India was also witnessing a democratic transition. The 1962
war with China had weakened Nehru's position at home and brought a shift
in his understanding about India's immediate neighborhood. In a bid to
arrive at a rapprochement, Nehru had sent Sheikh Abdullah and Mirza Afzal
Beg to meet Ayub in the hope of forming a confederation between India,
Pakistan, and Kashmir, but Ayub was completely dismissive of the idea. "It
was curious," Ayub later wrote in his autobiography, "that whereas we were
seeking the salvation of Kashmiris, they had been forced to mention an idea
which, if pursued, would lead to our enslavement" (M.A. Khan [1967] 2006:
149). Later Nehru was succeeded by Lal Bahadur Shastri, who was labeled a
weak prime minister, and Ayub tested his mettle through the Rann of Kutch
dispute that eventually spiraled into a major war: the Second Kashmir War.
As a revisionist power, Pakistan had tried to wrest control of Kashmir by
launching the 1965 war, and Shastri had been credited for blocking Ayub's
moves through a bold decision of opening the international front that
allowed the Indian forces to march into the Pakistani Punjab and the adjoining areas.

　　After Shastri's exit from the political scene, the Congress Party's core
group, popularly known as the Syndicate, in January 1966 selected Indira
Gandhi as the new prime minister; she continued her predecessors' policy of
constitutional integration of J&K with the Indian Union (see Behera 2000;

Chandhoke 2005). Since Indira's base and equations within the Congress Party were not strong, she focused her attention more on power consolidation than initiating any bilateral dialogue with Pakistan's military regimes. After the 1967 elections, there was a serious power tussle between the Indira Gandhi-led faction and the Syndicate that triggered multiple defections from the party. Though Indira Gandhi had acquired a certain control over the government after the Syndicate suffered a blow in 1967 elections, she could not manage a stronghold in the Congress Working Committee, which was central to policy formulation and the real powerhouse that directed the Indira-led government to implement the party program and policies. In other words, Indira's government was accountable to the party without having any say in the party affairs.

In November 1969, the Syndicate and the key regional leaders had expelled Prime Minister Indira Gandhi from the Congress Party on the pretext of indiscipline, which provoked her to set up a rival organization, known as the Congress (R), and split the party (B. Chandra et al. 2000: 236). Apart from the power tussles and party split, the Indira government was facing a series of crises on the administrative front mainly due to soaring prices, food shortages, and unemployment that eventually led to a curb on business monopolies, state control over imports and exports, and the nationalization of banks in 1969 (Denoon 1998: 49–59; Rubin 1985: 945). Another factor that contributed to the sidelining of the Kashmir issue and bilateral talks was the post-1971 war stability in Kashmir, where Sheikh Abdullah had also stopped pushing for a plebiscite. In fact, he proposed a round table conference of the representatives of India, Pakistan, and Kashmir—preferably with a third-party mediator—to work out a solution acceptable to all concerned parties (Behera 2006: 43–44). Against this backdrop, the post-1965 period was marred with social, political, and economic complexities that did not allow Indira Gandhi to focus her attention toward bilateral engagement with her counterparts in Pakistan, who were also facing a domestic political crisis after the conclusion of the Tashkent agreement.

In Pakistan, there were attempts to restore democracy after the religious right and political parties prolonged their agitation against the military rule and the Mujibur Rehman-led Awami League became vocal about the six-point autonomy agenda for East Pakistan. In a bid to control the situation, the new military dictator General Yahya Khan announced and later conducted the country's first parliamentary elections in December 1970. The East Pakistan-based Awami League emerged as a majority party in the

National Assembly by winning 160 of total 300 general seats and Zulfikar Ali Bhutto's PPP obtained a distant second position with 81 seats (Jahan 1972: 190; I. Talbot 2009: 200). According to Rounaq Jahan's account, the election results baffled Yahya as he was sure of a hung parliament, which would enable him to play the power broker's role among the political parties (1972: 191–92). But the Awami League's convincing victory dashed Yahya's chances to remain a key player in the power hierarchy, which ultimately paved the way for a triangular power tussle between Bhutto, Mujibur Rehman, and Yahya Khan.

Despite the Awami League's clear majority, Bhutto was not ready to accept a compromise on Mujib's six-point autonomy mandate (B. Jones 2002: 148). By refusing to acknowledge Mujibur Rehman's right to draft a constitution and form the next government, "Bhutto, at the behest of General Yahya Khan, drove Pakistan to a constitutional crisis" (Waseem 2015). The last-ditch effort to resolve the political crisis proved futile when the Yahya-Mujibur talks broke down in March 1971. In a bid to hold the two wings of Pakistan together, Yahya Khan immediately launched Operation Searchlight in Dacca and banned the Awami League and all political activities in East Pakistan (B. Jones 2002: 166–67). Following this, the West Pakistani troops engaged in atrocious cruelties against the Bengalis in East Pakistan, leading to the killing of thousands of civilians and forcing another ten million to flee across the border to India for safety (Sharmila Bose 2011: 65–70, 180; Gundevia 1984: 397). Facing enormous political and economic pressures on the domestic front and America's lukewarm attitude toward the issue, India responded to East Pakistan's crisis by granting permission to the Awami League to run a government in exile from the adjacent state of West Bengal (Ganguly 2002: 62). The refugee influx had strained the Indian economy, but it also provided India a rare opportunity to dismember Pakistan by training the Bengali refugees as guerrilla fighters against the West Pakistani forces in the eastern wing. This precipitated a serious political crisis between India and Pakistan which ended in a full-scale war and the dismemberment of Pakistan in 1971.

Apart from strengthening Pakistan's security alliance with the West, the absence of checks and balances in Ayub's military regime led to decisions contrary to developing peaceful relations with India or resolving the Kashmir issue through negotiations. Instead of making amends, he was all set to deal with India through Pakistan's growing military muscle and international support. This mindset motivated him and his military regime to make decisions that triggered crisis after crisis with India and developed a history of grievances on both sides that deepened their rivalry over the long run. Thereafter General Yahya also refused to give up power and reached out to the United States and China against India, relentlessly seeking their aid during the East-West Pakistan crisis of 1970–71. The 1965 and 1971 wars inscribed such deep resentment in Pakistan that successive regimes were unable to undo the damage and resentment caused after severe defeats at the hands of India. In the succeeding years, the hostile feelings brought fundamental changes in both sides' priorities that motivated them to pursue policies to acquire nuclear capability and attain strategic stability in their relations in the late 1980s.

CONCLUSION

This chapter describes how the Indo-Pakistani rivalry became more intense during the first half of the development period, that is, from 1959 to 1972. During this phase, the rival parties resorted to a large number of armed disputes, but their hostile engagement could not resolve their core dispute: Kashmir. After the 1962 Sino-Indian War, Pakistan's military regime was keen to take advantage of India's defeat before the actual balance of power would again tilt toward India and limit Pakistan's prospects to prevail against the rival in warfare. Since windows of opportunity never stay open, the military regime in Pakistan was not hesitant to employ military options to achieve its political objectives in Kashmir. To avoid later being compelled to bargain from weakness, it initiated a successful military attack against the Indian troops in the marshland of Kutch and then launched a full-scale war against India in September 1965. Later somewhat similar factors—political, military, and strategic—charted a course that extended India's civilian regime an opportunity to intervene in Pakistan's domestic crisis and dismember the enemy state in 1971. These elements underline how India and Pakistan's relative military capabilities factored into the perpetuation of a hostile interaction pattern that resulted in the onset of the 1965 and 1971 wars.

The chapter also examines how the great powers' strategic equations and power positions within the regional and systemic structures, particularly the US–Soviet Union Cold War competition and China's emergence as a regional power, increased misperceptions between militarily empowered India and Pakistan that paved their way to engage in two full-fledged wars within a short span of six years. Instead of de-escalating the rivalry, the outcomes of these wars complicated the rivalry as Pakistan's dismemberment in 1971 gripped its ruling elites with a power complex and, at the same time, provided it a compelling reason to turn to the traditional recourse of seeking revenge in the foreseeable future. However, it is important to note that the security alliances and the third-party interventions succeeded in balancing the Indo-Pakistani conflict by narrowing the two sides' military gap but, on the other hand, the same put a constraint on their conciliatory acts—particularly Pakistan's bureaucracy-military axis—and drove them to develop a highly antagonistic relationship.

In addition to the international strategic factors and ideological-territorial differences, Pakistan's failure to evolve a parliamentary democracy in the early years led the bureaucracy-military axis to control the state apparatus and frame the country's security and foreign policies from their perspective, which had no room for normative platforms to negotiate bilateral disputes with the opponent amicably. Consequently, the different regime systems within the two states—the military dictatorships in Pakistan and the parliamentary democracy in India—began to shape their leaders' key decisions and responses to domestic political pressure that triggered crisis after crisis rather than creating conducive conditions for resolving the Kashmir issue through negotiations.

CHAPTER 6

The Development of Complex Rivalry—II

Abeyant Phase, 1972–89

INTRODUCTION

Following the examination of the intensive development of Indo-Pakistani rivalry culminating in the wars of 1965 and 1971 in Chapter 5, this chapter investigates the ensuing character of the bilateral ties that initially caused the cessation of hostilities and then brought the rivals to resume their traditional conflictual course. Here the focus is on three issues. The first concerns the shift in power positions within the dyadic and regional structures, that is, how changes in the power structures have influenced and even redefined a relatively de-escalated rivalry. The second focuses on the two sides' evolving strategic actions by discussing how their past strategies' effectiveness, ever-increasing misperceptions, and nuclear programs played a key part in reshaping the course of the rivalry. The third examines how the changing nature and structure of their respective regimes affected the rivalry by analyzing how their political institutions and domestic conditions factored into the dyadic equations and impacted their ruling elites' responses to domestic political pressure.

This chapter is divided into seven sections. After briefly outlining the key issues in this section, it presents an account of eight militarized disputes that occurred between the two states during the abeyant phase, 1972–89. The third section explains how the great powers' continued intervention, mainly through sustained arms supplies, and India's and Pakistan's weapon-oriented nuclear programs brought about a turning point in their post-1971 relationship. The fourth section traces the impact of relative military capabilities on India and Pakistan's strained ties and how it pushed a comparatively de-escalated rivalry to resume the traditional course of militarized engagement. The implications of regime type and domestic politics on the dyad's decision-making and actions are discussed in the fifth section. Here it is explained how the two adversaries' combined democratic governance could not pacify their rivalry and how the differing regime structures gave a hostile drift to their ties, mainly through the eruption of secessionist attempts on the Indian side of Punjab and Kashmir. This is followed by a theoretical discussion surrounding the puzzle of why the India-Pakistan rivalry did not terminate even after experiencing a massive shock in the form of the 1971 war—which disintegrated Pakistan and established India as a dominant regional power—and an effective de-escalation in the 1970s. The concluding section sums up the key findings of the chapter.

MILITARIZED DISPUTES AND CONFLICT ESCALATION, 1972 TO 1989

Unlike the 1965 war, the Bangladesh War of 1971 ended in an overwhelming military victory for India. In the realm of conventional power asymmetry, Pakistan did not challenge the Indian supremacy in the aftermath of its shattering defeat and disintegration. More importantly, the war outcome had also undermined Pakistan's claim over Kashmir on the basis of the two-nation theory or religious affinity, as the same grounds failed to keep the Bengali Muslims of East Pakistan united with West Pakistan. However significant or path-breaking these developments were, they did not end the two adversaries' bitter rivalry over Kashmir.

Though India and Pakistan successfully negotiated their post-war differences by signing the Simla Agreement, later both parties resorted to contrary interpretations of the same accord. For India, the Simla Agreement marked an end to the UN's involvement in Kashmir as both parties duly agreed to resolve the Kashmir issue by engaging in bilateral and peaceful talks. From Pakistan's view, however, the accord did not mean a comprehensive settlement of the Kashmir dispute nor did it replace the ongoing UN efforts for its amicable resolution (Behera 2006: 221). In spite of their different understanding of the mutually negotiated agreement, which however became more drastic in later years, the two sides refrained from resorting to armed disputes until the early 1980s.

In the late 1970s, the regional situation began to witness a drastic shift with the superpowers' profound duel in Afghanistan. As a consequence, India's and Pakistan's engagement in the regional crisis increased, which inflated their strategic vulnerabilities and recurrent militarized disputes once again becoming integral to their conflictual relations—all disputes occurred in the second half of the abeyant phase under the military regime of General Zia-ul-Haq (see Figure 6.1 and Table 6.1). The data in Table 6.1 clearly show that the first half of the abeyant phase was free from dispute eruption but the second witnessed a gradual and steady increase. Of all eight militarized disputes, two serious ones—the operation Meghdoot and the exercise Brasstacks—were purposely set in motion by India against Pakistan, for reasons discussed at length in the succeeding sections. These aggressive postures, coupled with the regional security anxieties and the formation of a nuclear layer at the dyadic level, led to the renewal of armed hostilities between India and Pakistan.

Operation Meghdoot: India's Advances to Occupy the Siachen Glacier

In the early 1980s, India and Pakistan engaged in a competitive armed struggle over a no-man's-land in the Karakoram Mountains, the Siachen Glacier, which acts as a wedge between the Chinese- and Pakistani-administered parts of J&K—Aksai Chin and the Northern Areas (Gilgit-Baltistan), respectively. The glacier is around 76 kilometers long, 2–8 kilometers wide, and over 300 meters deep, covering a total area of approximately 700 square kilometers including tributaries (S. Ahmed & Sahni 1998: 9). Its vastness and high altitude make it the second largest glacier in Asia and the world's highest outside the North and South Poles (Bhola 1988: 29). In winter, the temperature of the glacier decreases sharply to minus 40–50 degrees Celsius and blizzards attain a speed of 150 knots (almost 300 kilometers per hour). Owing to its extreme altitude and remoteness, the vast glacier is commonly referred to as the "third pole" (Noorani 1994: 6).

Most observers trace the root cause of the dispute to incomplete demarcation of the Cease-Fire Line (CFL) after the First Kashmir War of 1947. The post-war agreement of July 1949 had left the status of the CFL inconclusive due to difficulties in delineating the line in the region. Samina Ahmed and Varun Sahni's account describes this point well:

The CFL ran along the international India-Pakistan border and then north and northeast until map grid-point NJ 9842, located near the Shyok river at

TABLE 6.1. India-Pakistan militarized interstate disputes (MIDs), 1972–89

S. No	Dates of Dispute[1]	MID Initiator	Revisionist State	Cause of MID	MID Location	Fatality Level[2]	Highest Action Taken[3]	Hostility Level[4]	Regime Type
34	July 7, 1981–November 3, 1981	Pakistan	Pakistan	Territory	Kashmir	1–25	Clash	4 & 4*	Non-demo
35	September 8, 1982–September 8, 1982	India	Pakistan	Territory	Kashmir	None	I-alert P-no militarized action	3 & 1*	Non-demo
36	October 20, 1983–January (dm), 1984	Pakistan	Pakistan	Territory	Kashmir	1–25	Clash	4 & 4*	Non-demo
37	April (dm), 1984–August 30, 1984[5]	Pakistan	Pakistan	Territory	Siachen Glacier (Kashmir)	101–250	Clash	4 & 4*	Non-demo
38	January 17, 1985–October 7, 1985	Pakistan	Pakistan	Territory	Siachen Glacier	1–25	I-clash P-attack	4 & 4*	Non-demo
39	October 14, 1986–November 15, 1986	India	Pakistan	Territory	Kashmir	None	I-attack P-no militarized action	4 & 1*	Non-demo
40	November (dm), 1986–February 19, 1987[6]	India	India	Territory	Along Punjab and Rajasthan border	None	Clash	4 & 4*	Non-demo

| 41 | April (dm), 1987–September (dm), 1987[7] | Pakistan | Pakistan | Territory | Siachen Glacier | 101–250 | Clash | 4 & 4* | Non-demo |

Source: Compiled from the COW database (2015), version 4.01.

1. As in the COW database, missing dispute dates are marked "dm" for "date missing."

2. The COW database indicates fatality level of each side; the same has been retained here. Wherever both states' level of fatality varies, , a separate entry has been cited against the country (i.e., I or P) differently.

3. Here I stands for India and P for Pakistan.

4. The codes marked with an asterisk (*) indicate Pakistan's hostility level, and codes without it indicate India's hostility level. The COW database hostility codes are as follows: 1: no militarized action; 2: threat to use force; 3: display use of force; 4: use of force; and 5: war.

5. According to the COW database, the Siachen Glacier dispute started on June 25, 1984. The majority of the literature, including primary sources, traces its onset from early April of the same year with a large number of fatalities. This study follows the latter.

6. The Brasstacks dispute is missing in the COW database (2015), version 4.01.

7. This dispute is missing in the COW database (2015), version 4.01.

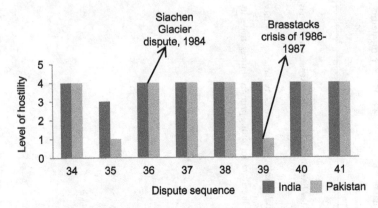

Figure 6.1. India-Pakistan hostility level (frequency and severity), 1972–89. *Source:* Compiled from the COW database (2015), version 4.01 (0–5 scale).

the base of the Saltoro mountain range. Because no Indian or Pakistani troops were present in the geographically inhospitable northeastern areas beyond NJ 9842, the CFL was not delineated as far as the Chinese border. Both sides agreed, in the vague language that lies at the root of the Siachen dispute, that the CFL extends to the terminal point, NJ 9842, and "thence north to the glaciers." (1998: 10–11)

Even after the 1965 and 1971 wars, India and Pakistan had not made any attempt to extend the CFL beyond point NJ 9842. Under the Simla Agreement, while converting the CFL into a mutually accepted Line of Control (LoC), again both sides left the glacier area un-demarcated and subsequently maintained the status quo. In the mid-1970s, however, the Pakistan government started granting permits to international mountaineering groups to scale the glacier. Islamabad's claim over the glacier was further strengthened when US mapping agencies began to show the LoC in Pakistan's favor by extending it eastward from its actual termination point NJ 9842 to the Karakoram Pass on the Chinese border (Wirsing 1998: 78–80). India strongly opposed this shift. Thereafter the two states began interpreting the statement in the Karachi Agreement, "thence north to the glaciers," in accordance with their strategic advantage and convenience. Pakistan argued that the LoC runs northeasterly beyond point NJ 9842 and terminates at the Karakoram Pass, while India maintained that the LoC extends northwesterly along the Saltaro ridgeline up to the border of the Chinese-controlled Shaksham Valley—a part of J&K ceded by Pakistan to China in the 1963 Sino-Pakistan Border Agreement—on the basis of the watershed principle. Both sides' competing interpretations placed the Siachen Glacier within their controlled territory: Pakistan considered the glacier as the eastern extremity of Baltistan, whereas India maintained that the Siachen Glacier was the western boundary of the Nubra sub-division of the Ladakh district of J&K (Bhola 1988: 39–40; Khosa 1999: 194). Some scholars believe that apart from these legal technicalities, the geo-political compulsions of India, Pakistan, and China brought the Siachen area to center stage because it was part of a region where the three states sought to assert their military control (V. Raghavan 2002: 29). A commentator has lucidly elaborated this point:

> The Siachen Glacier Complex abuts the Indo-Tibetan border along the disputed territory of Aksai Chin on one side, the Shaksgam Valley (which India regards as illegally ceded by Pakistan to China) to the north-west, and the Northern Areas controlled by Pakistan to the east. The K2-Karakoram Pass-point NJ 9842 triangle is a wedge that separates a closer Sino-Pak territorial nexus. Additionally, the strategic importance to India of its stand in the Siachen Glacier dispute is that it is in accordance with the accepted international principle of watershed. India also wants to apply this principle to its disputed Himalayan borders with China. Loss of the Siachen Glacier would have placed India in a much weaker position *vis-à-vis* China regarding negotiations on the outstanding border issues. (Khosa 1999: 199)

This shows the complexity of factors during the militarization of the glacier region. According to one view, it stems from India's military moves in 1983 when it "lifted an entire mountain battalion by helicopter onto the eastern side of the Siachen Glacier" (Margolis 2001: 132). In response, Pakistan dispatched a team from the Special Services Group (SSG) to verify the reports, which duly confirmed Indian intrusions (Musharraf 2006: 69). While acknowledging that India did deploy troops first on the Siachen Glacier in 1983, Kuldip Nayar, a veteran Indian journalist, points out that India's successful military expedition did not end in a permanent occupation of the glacier (2003: 232). Anyhow, the Indian move alarmed the Pakistan Army:

> [It] became convinced the Indians were embarked on a grand strategy to advance westward into Baltistan and occupy Skardu. Using Skardu and its

large airfield as a main operating base, the Indians, it was feared, would then drive into the Gilgit Valley, thus severing the Karakoram Highway, Pakistan's sole land link to its most important ally, China. (Margolis 2001: 132)

By December 1983, when the possibility of Indian invasion of the Siachen Glacier region increased, Pakistan's military establishment "began planning to occupy the passes on the watershed of the Saltoro Range that dominated the Siachen Glacier" (Musharraf 2006: 68). According to General Pervez Musharraf, who was deputy director of operations to the Military Operations Directorate, the General Headquarters (GHQ) had suggested early March to occupy the Siachen area, but the proposal was opposed by the general officer commanding the Northern Areas on the grounds of harsh weather; he suggested May 1 as an alternative date for troops' efficacious movement. However, this turned out to be a blunder, writes Musharraf, as Indians had already occupied the glacier's highest points by the time Pakistani troops reached there (2006: 68–69).

On the other hand, Indians claim that the crisis was triggered in early 1984 when its intelligence agencies gathered precise information that Pakistan was planning a military operation to establish its claim on the Siachen Glacier by stationing its troops there permanently (Chibber 1990: 150; Behera 2006: 67n121). Fearing the loss of these strategic heights, which could have exposed the Nubra Valley and the adjoining terrain, India launched a pre-emptive military operation code-named the Meghdoot (Cloud Messenger) in April 1984. To attain tactical advantage against Pakistan, initially it deployed fully acclimatized soldiers from the Kumaon Regiment and the Ladakh Scouts through helicopters on various strategic points on the Saltoro Ridge (Bilafond La, Sia La, and other passes) and thereafter systematically built up its forces to maintain an effective control on these peaks (Chibber 1990: 150; V. Raghavan 2002: 53–54).

Though the two sides blamed each other for initiating this dispute, there is little doubt that both were responsible as they were simultaneously planning to scale the Siachen peaks in the winter of 1983–84. The only difference on the ground was that India outmatched Pakistan in the pre-emptive race to control the Siachen. From the standpoint of the Simla Agreement, which emphasizes that neither side would take any action that might alter the ground situation, Indian military occupation of un-demarcated peaks was a clear military intrusion (Cheema 2009: 47–49; Nair 2009: 38).[1] A week after the Indian move, embarrassed Pakistan launched its own operation, code-named Abadeel (Swallow), to stall the Indians' advance. It built bases in the Khapalu Valley to support its mountain units to reoccupy and capture the remaining glacier peaks. As a result, "in a desperate effort to deny the enemy superior ground," the two states' troops clashed with machine guns and mortars, quickly transforming the unpopulated glacier into the world's highest and most difficult battleground (Margolis 2001: 132). A couple of months later, in June 1984, the Pakistani troops initiated two spirited attacks on the Indian post at Bilafond La, "each suffering losses of around one hundred dead," but its military efforts failed to wrest control of the glacier (Margolis 2001: 132). Throughout 1985, Pakistan attacked the Indian positions in an attempt to retake some critical heights, but it could not move beyond the southern Saltoro Range pass of Gyong La that overlooks the Nubra River Valley.

From the strategic perspective, according to Raspal Khosa, Operation Meghdoot conferred India a tactical advantage by extending its command over vital areas between the Pakistan-controlled Northern Areas and the Aksai Chin (1999: 196). Precisely this led the Indian decision-makers to not withdraw from the region. Apart from this, they also perceived that Islamabad might view an Indian withdrawal as a compromise on the issue "that the Line of Control, or notional line determining the jurisdiction of each country, should be drawn tangentially northeastwards to the Karakoram ranges" (Dixit 2002: 264). Additionally, vacating the Siachen region could have jeopardized India's monitoring of China-Pakistan communication through the Indira Col or the Karakoram Pass—which overlooks the Chinese-controlled Shaksham Valley—as well as India's control of Nubra Valley, its forward posts near Turtuk, and virtually the entire northern part of the state (R. Mehta 2011). Despite losing the glacier region to India, except Gyong La, Pakistan did not give up its claim and repeatedly resisted Indian control by employing military means.

The Brasstacks Crisis: From Military Exercise to Dispute Escalation

During the mid-1980s, the Sikh secessionist movement in the Indian state of Punjab was at a peak and Pakistan was providing it covert support. The political leadership in New Delhi was facing tremendous pressure to force Islamabad to cease its material assistance to the Sikh secessionists and bring normalization in the state. On the other hand, the Pakistani military establishment was not ready to concede any ground after its strategic defeat in the Siachen region. Hence, Islamabad paid no heed to New Delhi's concerns. It has been argued that Pakistan's covert support to the Sikh secessionists was one of the fundamental factors that provoked India to flex its military muscle and launch a massive military exercise, code-named Brasstacks, close to the international border (Bajpai et al. 1995: 25; Chari et al. 2008: 39–40). Devin Hagerty's study also supports this line of understanding: "Indian military movements during the Brasstacks crisis were largely an outgrowth of New Delhi's sensitivity to the instability in Punjab and its wider implications for the integrity of the Indian union" (1998: 95).

In July 1986, the Indian Army began the multi-corps Brasstacks exercise under the command of Army Chief General Krishnaswamy Sundarji, an exercise meant to be completed in four phases and continue until the end of the first quarter of 1987. The exercise was "ostensibly intended to test the readiness of the Indian army and its conventional deterrence strategy" (Blum 2007: 65). The size and scale of the exercise was unparalleled in independent India's history. Apart from the involvement of the entire western air command and other warfare logistics, it involved two armored divisions, one mechanized division, and six infantry divisions—comprising around 250,000 troops and 1,500 tanks. From this standpoint, it was comparable to the Cold War years' military exercises of the North Atlantic Treaty Organization (NATO) and the Warsaw Pact (Bajpai et al. 1995: 3, 30; Sagan 2001: 1069).

Scholars have argued that apart from pressure politics, the Indian exercise was meant to check the coordination between multi-formations and multi-services under a wartime scenario; its command, control, communications, and information mechanisms; and readiness of the newly inducted military equipment (Bajpai et al. 1995: 45n2; Chari et al. 2008: 44–45; Ganguly 2002: 85). Others, however, viewed the Brasstacks exercise as a deceptive Indian maneuver to slice Pakistan and destroy its nuclear capability (Chengappa 2000; Perkovich 1999; Wirsing 1991). According to Scott Sagan, "Sundarji advocated a preventive strike against Pakistan during the crisis. Considerations of an attack on the Pakistani nuclear facilities were debated in the highest echelons of power in New Delhi in January 1987" (2001: 1070). This was strongly endorsed by Lieutenant General P.N. Hoon, the then Indian commander-in-chief of the Western Army during the Brasstacks crisis, who claimed in his memoirs that "Brasstacks was no military exercise. It was a plan to build up a situation for a fourth war with Pakistan. And what is even more shocking is that the Prime Minister . . . was not aware of these plans for war" (Hoon

2000: 102). Later, in an interview, General Sundarji categorically denied these charges:

> Between 1972 and 1979, we had solid ground and air superiority over Pakistan. If we had wanted to exploit Pakistan's weakness, we could have done it in that seven-year period. We did not. So why should we do so now when Pakistan enjoys relative parity. (Sundarji 1988)

Though the first three phases of the exercise "did not cause much concern," the last one "triggered deep apprehensions and fears, some of them growing out of the memory of [the] 1971 [war]" (Bajpai et al. 1995: 53). The size and location of the Brasstacks exercise had caused anxiety in Pakistan, particularly when the Pakistani media began reporting on the danger of India's biggest-ever military exercise adjacent to the Indo-Pakistani border in the Rajasthan desert. Given the location of the exercise, contiguous to the troubled province of Sindh, the Pakistan Army also perceived the Indian military exercise as a design aimed at bifurcating Pakistan into two portions (Karamat 2015). To avert any possibility of Indian misadventure, it launched two parallel military exercises, code-named Flying Horse and Saf-e-Shikan, along the international borders.

The two sides' simultaneous military preparations fed the war paranoia in the subcontinent. By early December 1986, "Pakistan's intelligence agencies warned the military leadership in Rawalpindi that Exercise B[rasstacks] could be transformed into Operation B[rasstacks] and advised the deployment of armoured formations in the border areas" (B. Jones 2002: 214). Failing to get satisfactory information on the size and location of the exercise, despite the two prime ministers' impressive talk over the issue on the sidelines of the Bangalore summit of the South Asian Association for Regional Cooperation (SAARC), Pakistan's military leadership "began to view the Brasstacks as another Indian maneuver to conduct a blitzkrieg against it" (Karamat 2015). It immediately responded by putting its armed forces on high alert and extending the schedule of its own military exercises close to the Indian border. In mid-January 1987, the Indian troops noticed that after substantial military exercises, the Pakistani forces did not return to their bases and were taking forward positions against the turmoil-prone Punjab's strategic sectors (Pathankot, Bhatinda, and Ferozepur) with heavy equipment (Chari et al. 2008: 51–52; Sahni 2009: 18). Thereafter, according to Sumit Ganguly, Indian concerns began to escalate on three counts:

[F]irst, the Pakistani forces were so arrayed that they could, in a pincer movement, cut off their Indian counterparts in strategic areas; second, a demonstration of force by Pakistan along sensitive border areas in Punjab could
embolden the Khalistani terrorists, who might think they were to receive
overt military support; and third, access to Kashmir could be interdicted by
the Pakistani forces. (2002: 86)

To neutralize Pakistan's strategic moves, New Delhi responded by mass-
ing its troops along the Punjab and Kashmir borders; placing its air force on
high alert; and activating its naval units. The increasing interplay of moves
and counter-moves had almost brought the two armed forces to the verge of
collision. To control the spiraling situation, the Indian leadership asked M.
Humayun Khan, high commissioner of Pakistan to India, to convey to Islamabad that continuous deployment of Pakistani troops on the border was a
concern for New Delhi and if they were not withdrawn quickly, India would
be forced to take appropriate steps (Bajpai et al. 1995: 34). Pakistan's minister
of state for foreign affairs, Zain Noorani, also communicated President Zia-
ul-Haq's strong message to the Indian High Commissioner S.K. Singh. In the
same meeting, however, Noorani expressed Islamabad's willingness to begin
a dialogue to de-escalate the border tensions.

    Thereafter, the two sides adopted a conciliatory approach and began sev-
eral rounds of multi-level talks which resulted in an agreement that emphasized not attacking each other and withdrawing troops from the forward
positions in a fortnight. Within that time, India and Pakistan completed a
phased withdrawal from a 75-mile stretch of the border between the Ravi and
Chenab Rivers (Bajpai et al. 1995: 35-36). After the defusion of the subcontinent's large-scale military crisis, Rajiv Gandhi and Zia-ul-Haq attended a
summit-level meeting on February 21-22, 1987—famously known as the
Cricket Diplomacy—to ensure the domestic constituencies as well as the
international community that the Indo-Pakistani tensions had been completely ceased.

Militarized Clashes over the Siachen Glacier

In the winter of 1986-87, Pakistani troops managed to occupy a mountain
peak on the Saltaro ridgeline in the Siachen Glacier that dominated the Bilafond La. In early 1987, Indian troops detected their counterparts' newly
established Quaid Post at the height of 21,153 feet. Since the Quaid Post could

monitor Indian troop movements around the Bilafond La and direct accurate artillery fire, it posed a serious threat to the Indian posts maintained by helicopters—Sonam, Amar, Ashok, and U-Cut—thus seizing this post "became very critical for the Indian Army" (R. Mehta 2011; V. Raghavan 2002: 88). In May 1987, India deployed a reconnaissance mission of nine soldiers to probe the approaches to the post. This daring mission succeeded in locating it, but five Indian soldiers lost their lives when the Pakistani troops opened heavy machine-gun fire at a close range (MacDonald 2007: 154–55).

After India's first attempt, the Pakistan Army anticipated an Indian assault and therefore decided to concentrate its troops at the Quaid Post as a preventive measure (Noorani 1994: 13). In June 1987, the Indian soldiers responded by launching a series of audacious attacks. After incurring significant losses, Indians made their last desperate assault on June 26 and "overran the Pakistani post killing every Pakistani soldier left up there" (MacDonald 2007: 150). The person behind India's unlikely success was Naib Subedar Bana Singh, who dislodged the Pakistani troops from the higher position and seized control of the Quaid Post. To honor Bana Singh's bravery and leadership, the occupied post was renamed Bana Post (V. Raghavan 2002: 86–94). After the Siachen debacle, the loss of this strategic post was perceived by Pakistanis as their army's second straight surrender against the archrival, India. This failure increased the general public's suspicion over the Pakistan Army's ability to defend the nation.

The Pakistan Army earned profuse criticism for its failure to defend the post. The political parties were at the forefront in mobilizing the public against the military establishment by arguing that "the Pakistan army has become so 'flabby' that it cannot fight the Indian army and that it has lost territory which has been under Pakistan's occupation at one time" (Nayar 2003: 62). Under growing domestic pressures, the Pakistan Army hastily decided to dislodge the Indians from the Bilafond La. Within a couple of months, the military strategists in Rawalpindi brought out a costly counterattack plan, called Operation Quiadat, to be implemented by the commandos of SSG (A.A. Khan 2006). Keeping in mind the terrain's unfavorable topography, they also "developed an alternate plan to attack with battalion-size forces at three to four separate locations along the ridgeline" (F.H. Khan, Lavoy, & Clary 2009: 76–77). In the last week of September 1987, the Pakistani forces carried out the military action to reoccupy vantage positions near the Bilafond La. The surprise attack on India's two vital posts, Rana and Akbar, comprised exchange of heat-seeking and guided missiles and anti-tank rockets. Though Pakistan forces succeeded in capturing the Rana through its artillery barrage, its subsequent attack on the Akbar went awry as the Indian forces opened heavy fire that made the defense of the Rana untenable. In the end, the Pakistani military action proved to be a fatal disaster, incurring it more than a hundred fatalities (Khosa 1999: 196; MacDonald 2007: 174–80). After conceding heavy losses and realizing the unfavorable terrain's high costs, Pakistan stopped further attempts to reoccupy these vantage positions with large-scale military maneuvers.

THE ROLE OF GREAT POWERS, ALLIANCES, AND ARMS BUILDUP

After the 1971 war, the power positions within the dyadic and regional structures witnessed a drastic shift that included minimal intervention from the great powers, material capability shifts between India and Pakistan, and India's emergence as a dominant regional power. However, India's preponderant position did not last long as the superpowers got embroiled in a prolonged conflict over Afghanistan after the Soviet invasion of 1979. This decade-long armed engagement had not only renewed India and Pakistan's arms race and accelerated their weapon-oriented nuclear programs, but also overran the post-1971 subsystemic power structure by reactivating the dormant regional rivalry.

The East-West Cold War and India-Pakistan Relations

After Pakistan's breakup in 1971, India emerged as a dominant power in South Asia. The major powers also acknowledged India's regional supremacy, which was further reinforced after its successful detonation of a nuclear device in 1974 (Perkovich 1999: 184, 193). Apart from this, other factors that contributed to the post-war regional peace were the great powers' more pressing priorities elsewhere that included the 1973 Arab-Israel War, the Western states' deepening economic troubles due to the oil crisis, the United States' involvement in the Vietnam War, and an increasingly successful détente which curtailed the superpowers' arms race.

As a majority of Pakistan's military equipment was of American origin and much of that was worn out in the 1971 war, Pakistan was in dire need of arms repairs and fresh procurements. However, on the basis of the 1965 arms embargo and tougher nuclear non-proliferation conditions, the United

States had adopted a restrictive arms transfer policy toward the subcontinent. This policy affected Pakistan immensely as its armed forces were heavily dependent on American military hardware. On the other hand, India enjoyed uninterrupted military supplies from the Soviets throughout the 1970s. Apart from its bitter international isolation, Pakistan was also facing extreme political and economic problems on the domestic front (where a political struggle between the Bhutto regime and the political opposition was drawn out), an economic downturn due to the loss of East Pakistan-based export revenues, and a tense civil-military relationship which culminated in the second military takeover in July 1977 (Jalal 1995: 77–85; Nawaz 2008: 335–38). These factors compelled the Pakistani ruling elites to withdraw from the Western alliance systems, including the SEATO and the CENTO, and diversify its arms relations by turning to China and France. Under these circumstances, India enjoyed unprecedented superiority over Pakistan in the military domain.

In December 1979, the regional security environment experienced a dramatic change when the Soviet Union invaded Afghanistan to rescue Babrak Karmal's communist regime. The Soviets' sudden occupation of Afghanistan brought a drastic transformation in South Asia's security situation as it not only brought the superpowers' rivalry to the region's doorstep, which disrupted India's predominant role in the local hierarchy, but also slowly entangled India and Pakistan in the regional crisis and recurrent armed disputes. Overall, the Soviet invasion came at a juncture when the Jimmy Carter administration was in its final year and had experienced the humiliating seizure of the American embassy in Iran; the General Zia–led military regime in Pakistan was toiling against domestic political turbulence and international isolation; and the Janata government in India had lost its political mandate. The presence of the Soviet forces in such proximity posed a direct security challenge to internally fragile Pakistan, which now faced the possibility of a two-front threat (Cohen 1983: 52).

In view of India's robust relationship with the Soviets, Pakistan's military establishment and intelligence directorate were convinced that the Moscow-Delhi duo "would invade Pakistan as soon as the Afghan resistance had been crushed" (Margolis 2001: 41). After a thorough analysis of possible scenarios, Lieutenant General Khalid Mahmud Arif, then senior aide to Zia-ul-Haq, voiced the majority opinion: "[I]f we do not react to what happens in Afghanistan it will be our turn tomorrow. . . . Better to fight in Afghanistan than let it go down and fight in your own country" (cited in Kux 2001: 246–

47). Growing concerns of a two-front threat led the military establishment to conclude that Pakistan faced "a mortal danger," which in turn helped General Zia-ul-Haq to make up his mind to oppose the communist superpower in the neighborhood (Ziring 2003: 175). Eventually, this decision defined Pakistan's new role as a bulwark against the communist expansion.

New Delhi was aware that the Soviets' unexpected move had brought the superpowers' war by proxy to its doorstep and endangered the decade-long regional stability, but it was reluctant to flag its concerns to Moscow and thus assumed a middle path. What obligated India to assume such an equivocal position despite knowing that the Soviets' presence along the Afghanistan-Pakistan border would adversely impact the regional power balance? This was perhaps because of its inability to convince (or coerce) the superior ally, the Soviet Union, to withdraw from the neighborhood and simultaneously ensure protection of its vital interests in political, economic, security, and other realms. The political leadership in New Delhi realized that India's fate was not only geopolitically tied to the unfolding crisis in the neighborhood but also to its long-term strategic interests that require the invading superpower's sustained assistance and cooperation. For instance, the Indo-Soviet friendship treaty had considerably helped India to secure an emphatic victory over Pakistan in 1971 and assume a dominant power status in South Asia. Against the backdrop of the Afghanistan War, it was possible that China could use Pakistan to counterbalance India's regional hegemony or attempt to disturb the status quo in the local hierarchy to consolidate its position against the Soviet Union. In such a case, the Indo-Soviet friendship treaty would "constitute a vital strategic hedge against possible Chinese military malfeasance" (Ganguly 2002: 81).[2]

As expected, India's measured position on the Soviet invasion and subsequent abstention from the UN vote earned it global condemnation. Though India had not sacrificed its special relationship with Moscow over non-aligned Afghanistan, the growing criticism, mainly from other developing states, had naturally created room for its differences with the communist friend. Before such a rupture could take place, Moscow wooed New Delhi with a generous rice-for-oil agreement[3] and a $1.63 billion military deal that included MiG-25 and MiG-23 fighter planes, T-71 battle tanks, vessels for the Indian Navy, and other modern weapon systems (Duncan 1989: 47; Racioppi 1994: 130; Thomas 1983: 78). On the other hand, the United States also changed its arms transfer policy to contain the Soviets' splinter movement in Afghanistan. The Carter administration terminated the US arms embargo against Pakistan, which was imposed after the Bangladesh War and for engaging in a nuclear weapons program, and proposed $400 million in military and economic assistance to Islamabad. Realizing the importance of the Soviet invasion and its far-reaching impact on East-West relations, especially after the US failure in the Vietnam War, General Zia-ul-Haq declined Carter's offer by disparaging it as "peanuts" (Borders 1980; Thornton 1982: 971). This refusal was Islamabad's candid indication that Washington had not proposed the right price in return for launching covert operations against the world's most powerful military force, the Red Army.

So far both India and Pakistan had somehow refrained from jumping onto the superpowers' bandwagons, but this did not last long. The moment the East-West warring chorus intensified in Afghanistan, both adversaries' divergent objectives began to tilt them toward their respective allies. In this respect, a change in the US regime from Democrats to a Republican government led by Ronald Reagan in January 1981 brought about a tectonic shift. By shunning the Carter administration's indecisive policy, the new administration convinced Congress that the communist occupation of Afghanistan had not only threatened Pakistan's security but also posed a grave threat to America's long-term strategic interests, mainly its access to warm-water ports and oilfields in the southwest Asian region.[4] While underlining the necessity to resist the communist advance in Afghanistan and Pakistan's frontline role, the Reagan administration revised the US aid offer to $3.2 billion—a five-year proposal divided equally between economic aid and military sales (Tahir-Kheli 1997: 38–39). After years of the procurement ban, the United States' ambitious aid package provided Pakistan with a twofold opportunity: (1) to acquire sophisticated conventional weaponry in large quantity and (2) to truncate India's military capability on preferential terms. Realizing this, Zia-ul-Haq's military establishment accepted the package graciously and "ma[de] Pakistan the most allied ally of the United States all over again" (Abbas 2005: 111).

For India, the most alarming part of the package was the military component ($1.6 billion) to be used by Pakistan for procuring sophisticated weapon systems and 40 F-16 fighters (Siddiqa-Agha 2001: 93). Since the F-16s had excellent air-defense and ground-attack capability, New Delhi viewed their sale as a grave threat to regional security and argued that Islamabad was exploiting America's anti-communist sentiments to justify its requests for advanced military weapons which could eventually be used against India. Alexander Haig, the US secretary of state, a staunch Indian opponent since

the Nixon days, responded by saying: "A weak Pakistan only serves the interests of the Soviet Union. A strengthened Pakistan, in close relationship with
the USA, poses no threat to India, and indeed should contribute to the overall stability of the subcontinent" (cited in Kux 1993: 383). Despite the American's lofty arguments and Pakistan's proposed "non-aggression pact," New
Delhi suspected that the US military supplies would trigger a new phase of
the arms race in the region. To offset the F-16 threat, in late 1982 India finalized a $3.3 billion deal with France to procure 40 Mirage-2000s along with a
license to manufacture another 110 aircraft in India. In the following year,
India signed two more deals with the Soviets to purchase T-80 tanks and
MiG-29 aircraft along with a production license for MiG-27s and MiG-29s
(Racioppi 1994: 133, 136; Thomas 1983: 78).

On the other hand, apart from America's total $7.2 billion aid commit-
ment, maintained Mohammad Waseem (2015), professor of political science
at the Lahore University of Management Sciences (LUMS), "the US and Saudi
Arabia pumped billions of dollars into Pakistan for channeling weapons"
through the logistics network "to mujahideen groups in Afghanistan." As a
result, the region was transformed into an East-West battleground by the early
1980s. "Once the security relationship with the United States had been consolidated," writes Husain Haqqani, "the quantum and quality of Pakistan's
support for the mujahideen increased dramatically" along with overwhelming control over the mode and conduct of weapon supplies (2005: 188).
According to Steve Coll, "Zia sought and obtained political control over the
CIA's weapons and money. He insisted that every gun and dollar allocated for
the Mujahideen pass through Pakistani hands . . . strictly by [the] ISI officers"
(2004: 63). "This was the decision," asserts Hassan Abbas, "that led to the ISI
[Inter-Services Intelligence] becoming a large, clumsy, frequently blundering,
hydraheaded monster of great influence in the 1990s" (2005: 110). Against the
Soviet presence in Afghanistan, Washington and Riyadh's joint "covert aid
program ballooned from $60 million in 1981 to $400 million in 1984." By the
time the war approached the last phase, the United States, Saudi Arabia, and
other Islamic states were together supplying $1.2 billion worth of weapons
including deadly Stinger missiles to Pakistan (Kux 2001: 274, 282). According
to some analysts, a substantial part of weapon supplies (around 30 percent)
was stolen, sold, or stockpiled by the ISI for Pakistan's official purpose (Wirsing
1991: 56). The United States tolerated this siphoning because Pakistan was a
frontline state in the campaign to eject the Soviets from Afghanistan.

Despite knowing that the Red Army was losing ground in the covert war
and would eventually be forced to move out of Afghanistan, the Reagan

administration gave Pakistan another commitment of $4.02 billion in aid to be distributed over the 1987–92 period—the military component of this commitment was worth over $1.72 billion (Kux 2001: 282–83; Shaumian 1988: 1167). Apart from the American military commitment and China's close nuclear association with Pakistan, what heightened New Delhi's concern was Washington's decision to provide Pakistan the Advanced Warning and Control System (AWACS) as part of the new military package. The Indian policy makers argued that such a sophisticated airborne early warning system was beyond Pakistan's genuine requirement and unnecessarily provocative since it "would be of limited use against the Soviets, [was] not needed against the Afghans, but would be enormously helpful against India." Thus Pakistani acquisition of such high-end qualitative weapon systems would prompt "a 'very destabilizing' arms race in South Asia, requiring heavy Indian expenditures to match Pakistan's new capability" (Kux 1993: 408–9). Furthermore, another major concern of India was that the US arms transfers symbolized its long-term "commitment to support Pakistan and in turn postpones the day when Pakistan will accept its status of relative inferiority" (Cohen 1983: 60).

Apart from this, the consolidation of the Sino-Pakistani alliance was another critical development of the 1980s that impacted the dynamics of regional security. China institutionalized its military relationship with India's rival to a critical level; it extended cooperation to Pakistan in nuclear know-how and missile technology. To offset the US decision and China's covert nuclear support, India had to again seek Soviet collaboration. Against this backdrop, Moscow reassured New Delhi with Tu-124 Moss (their less sophisticated AWACS), long-range naval TU-142M aircraft, Kilo and Tango class submarines, and medium-range air-to-air missiles (to be used by high-altitude fighter planes to knock out the AWACS threat), as well as advancing the delivery of MiG-29s to check Pakistan's F-16s (Bobb & Badhwar 1986; Shekhar Gupta 1986). In sum, the superpowers' prolonged rivalrous meddling in Afghanistan intensified the armament competition between India and Pakistan, thereby playing a defining role in undercutting the possibility of attaining a stable de-escalation of the South Asian rivalry, for which there had been signs of hope in the 1970s.

The Nuclear Competition

After the Bangladesh War, Pakistan realized its allies' grave failure during the time of dire emergency, whereas its rival (India) had received absolute support from the Soviet Union. In the changed security environment, Islam-

abad re-assessed its security policy and decided to embark on the path of
nuclear security by building "the [atom] bomb" (Weissman & Krosney 1981:
45). Contrary to the popular perception in India, that Pakistan would abandon its revisionist policy in the wake of its colossal defeat, the political leadership in Islamabad embarked on long-term structural measures to achieve
an absolute security against India. In January 1972, Prime Minister Bhutto
convened a meeting with nuclear scientists in Multan and authorized them
to build a nuclear bomb. Munir Ahmad Khan, who became the new chairman of the Pakistan Atomic Energy Commission (PAEC), later recalled:

> On 20 January 1972, he [Bhutto] called a meeting of the scientists in Multan
> and asked them how could they contribute toward the security of the coun-
> try to meet not only a major conventional threat but also a looming nuclear
> challenge from India. At this gathering Mr. Bhutto endorsed the idea of seek-
> ing nuclear capability for Pakistan and decided to completely reorganize the
> Atomic Energy in the country. (cited in Chakma 2009: 20)

Despite its overwhelming victory and subsequent regional dominance,
New Delhi remained suspicious about Washington's intentions toward the
new regional order. The Indian leadership could not forget the Nixon administration's resort to nuclear saber rattling during the 1971 war via dispatching
the nuclear-armed Seventh Fleet to the Bay of Bengal. Furthermore, the
growing close association between the dominant United States, nuclear-
armed China, and revisionist Pakistan was perceived by New Delhi as the
renewed Washington-Beijing-Islamabad's triangular alliance to avenge their
collective humiliation of 1971. The triad's increasing strategic bonding had
apparently heightened India's sense of insecurity, which in turn compelled
it to barge into the club of the elite few nuclear states by exploding a nuclear
device in May 1974 (GoI 2000: 202–3). India's sudden leap forward into the
nuclear club brought a paradigm shift in the regional balancing that greatly
accentuated Pakistan's sense of insecurity. Reacting to the Indian test, Bhutto
said:

> Testing a nuclear device denotes that a country has acquired a nuclear
> weapon capability. But a nuclear weapon is not like conventional military
> weapons. It is primarily an instrument of pressure and coercion against non-
> nuclear powers. . . . [W]e are determined not to be intimidated by this threat.
> (cited in S. Ahmed 1979: 97)

Again in the National Assembly, he emphasized that "India has acquired nuclear weapons . . . to intimidate and blackmail Pakistan. . . . To extract political concessions, to establish domination over the sub-continent, to exercise hegemony over the neighbouring states" (cited in Pattanaik 2003: 95). He declared that Pakistanis would never accept India's nuclear dominance over the subcontinent and would "eat grass to ensure nuclear parity with India" (*Dawn*, May 20, 1974, cited in Perkovich 1999: 185).

Such vocal criticism suggests that India's show of nuclear capability had scared the Pakistani leadership, a situation analogous to the Indians' reaction to the Chinese nuclear tests in 1964 (P. Malik 2010: 52–58). China had upped its nuclear ante barely two years after India's crushing defeat, which, coupled with Beijing's threat to join the Second Kashmir War of 1965 in support of Pakistan and conducting a fourth nuclear test in May 1966, led India to initiate a weapon-oriented nuclear program (Chengappa 2000: 107–12; Mirchandani 1968: 33–35; Subrahmanyam 1998: 27). From this standpoint, the Indian nuclear test of 1974 proved to be a catalyst which accelerated Pakistan's nascent nuclear program (F.H. Khan 2013: 112–16). The Pakistani leadership largely presumed that India had nuclear bombs in its possession and that its principal target was Pakistan, not China. "They generally see it," Stephen Cohen wrote, "as enabling Indian conventional forces to seize the rest of Kashmir from Pakistan or even to dismember all of Pakistan . . . [thus the Pakistani] strategists conclude[d], a modest, limited Pakistani program is essential to deter India's nuclear forces" (1983: 53). However, some analysts argue that before India's "peaceful" nuclear test, Pakistan had already constituted a research group for developing a nuclear bomb and had secured financial assistance from the oil-rich Islamic states, particularly Saudi Arabia and Libya (see Cohen 1984: 153; Palit & Namboodiri 1979: 16; Subrahmanyam 1982: 201; Taseer 1979: 154; Weissman & Krosney 1981: 54–62). In this sense, India's nuclear test had indeed reinforced Pakistan's January 1972 decision, but it was not the underlying factor to initiate it.

However, before leaning toward a weapon-oriented nuclear program, Pakistan had sought security guarantees against India from the United States, China, and the CENTO—the latter had turned down Pakistan's request by underlining that its objective was to counter communist expansionism (Chakma 2009: 23). Thereafter, Bhutto raised the nuclear issue before the UN General Assembly in October 1974 and proposed to declare South Asia a nuclear weapon–free zone (NWFZ). India opposed the proposal on three counts: (1) it should be mooted by the members of the region rather than a multilateral forum; (2) it would clip the interests of nuclear have-nots rather than nuclear haves (mainly by not linking nuclear China with the regional NWFZ); and (3) it would shield Pakistani nuclear facilities from pre-emptive military strikes (S. Ahmed 1979: 97–99; Nizamani 2001: 58, 89). In the meantime, Pakistan had learned that the Americans were giving assurances of uninterrupted nuclear fuel supply to the Indians for Tarapur reactors (F.H. Khan 2013: 120). Perplexed with its allies' duplicitous behavior and its bitter experience of the 1965 and 1971 wars, Bhutto concluded that Pakistan was left with no other option than to continue its own nuclear program to attain a foolproof security against nuclear India.

With this objective in sight, Pakistan had taken two crucial steps: first, it initiated the construction of the Kahuta uranium-enrichment plant; and second, it signed a deal with France to purchase an advanced nuclear reprocessing unit. Additionally, it roped in China to counterbalance India's dominance in the region. Beijing provided Islamabad technological know-how and material assistance, that is, a design of one of its own atomic bombs and enough highly enriched uranium for a few bombs (Talbott 2004: 18n10). By the mid-1970s, Washington was aware that Islamabad was "trying to acquire an independent nuclear fuel cycle and the technical skills that would make the nuclear weapon explosion option feasible" (Kux 2001: 219). To block Pakistan's weapon-oriented program and stockpiling of fissionable material, the Carter administration suspended US economic and military assistance to Pakistan by invoking the 1977 Glen and Symington Amendment, which prohibits military sales to those countries that were non-signatories to the Non-Proliferation Treaty (NPT) and engaged in the development of nuclear weapons. Thereafter, Washington employed sustained pressure on Paris to withdraw from the Franco-Pakistani nuclear reactor deal, which bore results when Paris unilaterally backed out of the deal in August 1978 (S. Ahmed 1978; Kux 2001: 235–39). Though the US moves succeeded in decelerating Pakistan's nuclear program to a great extent, these measures were not sufficient to reverse the complete nuclear program, which Pakistan was determined to pursue at any cost.

After the Soviet occupation of Afghanistan, Pakistan's geo-political significance and frontline status greatly diminished the West's resolve to inhibit its nuclear program. In fact, the Reagan administration boosted it by freezing the Glen and Symington law for six years, which allowed Washington to provide Pakistan sustained economic-military aid. Throughout the 1980s, Pakistan honed its skills to engage the West and the Islamic states simultaneously against the Soviet Union while using their huge financial assistance to continue its nuclear program. A 1983 US State Department report clearly mentioned that there was "unambiguous evidence that Pakistan is actively pursuing a nuclear weapons development programme" and China had helped it "in the area of fissile material production" and "nuclear device design" (cited in Chakma 2009: 26). Apart from this report, the PAEC scientist Munir Ahmad Khan also admitted that Pakistan had "successfully conducted [its] first cold test of a working nuclear device" on March 11, 1983 (quoted in F.H. Khan 2013: 185). Similarly Dr. Samar Mubarakmand, another PAEC scientist, recalled the day the "cold test" was conducted: "We realized that 'today we have become a nuclear power.' . . . The tests, however, were not publically announced because of the international environment of stiff sanctions against countries that sought to acquire nuclear capability" (quoted in F.H. Khan 2013: 185). A year later, Dr. A.Q. Khan, the director of the Kahuta Uranium Enrichment Plant, reaffirmed these claims that Pakistan had the capacity to make nuclear bombs (Chakma 2009: 29).

Since India's first nuclear test in 1974, it had openly criticized Pakistan for carrying out a nuclear weapon program, while India concealed its own weapon-oriented nuclear program from the international community. In fact, according to the Kargil Review Committee Report, India was about to test a nuclear weapon in 1983 and pulled back only when US satellites detected the preparations at Pokhran (GoI 2000: 199, 204). Around this time, Mrs. Gandhi was seriously considering launching preventive military strikes on Pakistan's nuclear installations to destroy the opponent's nascent nuclear capabilities (Bajpai et al. 1995: 74–75; Perkovich 1999: 239–44, 258). This bold and dangerous move was primarily based on a tentative insight that

> a Pakistani bomb would provide the umbrella under which Pakistan could reopen the Kashmir issue. A Pakistani nuclear capability paralyzes not only the Indian nuclear decision but also Indian conventional forces and a brash, bold, Pakistani strike to liberate Kashmir might go unchallenged if the Indian leadership was weak or indecisive. (Cohen 1983: 54)

In the 1980s, hoping to restructure the regional strategic balance, General Zia-ul-Haq secured Pakistan's close nuclear ties with China, which assisted Beijing to proliferate the nuclear-weapon design to Islamabad and the Pakistani scientists to carry out "a cold test around January 1989" (B.

Bhutto 2004). Later both states entered into a missile collaboration which played a crucial role in Pakistan's proxy warfare in Kashmir throughout the 1990s (E. Van Hollen 1987: 152; Shaikh 2002: 33). The Sino-Pakistani nuclear ties sent a clear message to New Delhi that it must view China and Pakistan's cooperation as a collective front against its regional superiority. Despite these developments and signing the December 1985 agreement to not attack each other's nuclear facilities, the two adversaries' nuclear relationship worsened with the growing speculation that India and Israel planned a joint attack on the Kahuta nuclear plant.[5] In early 1987, Pakistan's hidden nuclear weapon ambition finally came into public view when Dr. A.Q. Khan gave a sensational interview to an Indian journalist, Kuldip Nayar. In the interview, Khan said:

> What the CIA has been saying about our possessing the bomb is correct and so is the speculation of some foreign newspapers. . . . [T]hey now know we have done it . . . nobody can undo Pakistan or take us for granted. We are here to stay and let it be clear that we shall use the bomb if our existence is threat-ened. (Nayar 1987)

Dr. Khan's candid disclosure had shaken the Indian Parliament, leading to the parliamentarians' unanimous and unrestrained expression in favor of nuclear weapons production. To assure Parliament, Defense Minister K.C. Pant said on the record: "[T]he emerging nuclear threat to us from Pakistan is forcing us to review our options. . . . I assure the House that our response will be adequate to our perception of the threat" (cited in Perkovich 1999: 284). Subsequently, Prime Minister Rajiv Gandhi galvanized the Indian nuclear program to meet any prospective threat emanating from Pakistan.

On the other hand, the Reagan administration sidelined A.Q. Khan's candid admission as well as clinching evidence against the Sino-Pakistani nuclear nexus while certifying to the US Congress that Pakistan did not possess any nuclear device. To neutralize the media reporting, particularly that Pakistan had developed an atomic bomb, the Reagan administration later attached the NPT strings to the proposed $4.02 billion aid package. However, Islamabad was assured of a favorable outcome as it knew that "if the US wanted to continue to use Pakistan as a conduit for arms supplies to the Afghan rebels and to provide them sanctuary, it would have to approve the aid package" (Bobb & Singh 1987). In the end, the United States' sustained material assistance helped Pakistan to reinforce its nuclear program that eventually produced nuclear weapons. Before General Zia-ul-Haq's plane crash in August 1988, Pakistan had already attained the know-how to assemble a deliverable nuclear weapon, which exacerbated India and Pakistan's long-standing regional conflict.

INFLUENCE OF RELATIVE MILITARY CAPABILITIES

This section examines India's and Pakistan's relative military capabilities and explains how shifts in power positions, within the dyadic and regional structures, brought changes in their respective material capabilities and how they contributed to shape the course of their relationship. India's regional dominance in the post-1971 years initially helped de-escalate the rivalry, but Pakistan's eventual progression to qualitative parity vis-à-vis India helped it reverse the strategic situation and re-activate the dormant rivalry. The following subsections explain how the matrix of power capabilities, particularly material capability shifts between the two states, has affected the Indo-Pakistani security equations in the aftermath of the 1971 war and contributed to the de-escalation and re-escalation of the rivalry.

Pakistan Turned Inward: A Phase of Relative Peace, 1972–79

As Geoffrey Blainey argues, "A decisive general war did not always lead to a long period of peace. . . . Instead a clear preponderance of power tended to promote peace" (1973: 113). Till the late 1970s, India had maintained a clear qualitative preponderance over Pakistan, but the Soviet invasion of Afghanistan provided Islamabad an opportunity to acquire modern weaponry on the pretext of resisting the communist threat and extending covert support to the mujahideen forces. Figure 6.2 shows India's and Pakistan's relative military personnel strength, military expenditures, total military capabilities, and overall national capabilities. In Figure 6.2a and b, curve Ind and curve Pak denote India's and Pakistan's overall military personnel strength and military expenditure, and curve I-Truncated denotes India's actual military personnel strength and defense expenditure vis-à-vis Pakistan after subtracting its China-specific capabilities from the overall figures in curve Ind.[6] Figure 6.2c graphs Pakistan's relative military personnel strength, military expenditure, and total military capabilities vis-à-vis India on the basis of I-Truncated measurements.

Though Pakistan's decisive defeat in the 1971 war had weakened it and compelled its decision-makers to adopt a defensive posture, it also deepened its insecurities and hostility toward India. So along with pursuing a nuclear weapons program, Pakistan also initiated a plan to expand the size of its armed forces. In contrast, after securing an edge over Pakistan by detonating a nuclear device in 1974, India had reduced its military personnel strength by almost 34 percent (1,670,000 to 1,104,000) during 1975–80 (see Figure 6.2a). India's decision bettered Pakistan's relative personnel strength; previously it had to defend East Pakistan by committing two to three divisions. After the secession of its eastern wing, Pakistan's territory decreased in size and it acquired a comparative advantage in the armed forces ratio that would be concentrated on a much shorter territorial border. Taken together, these factors significantly enhanced Pakistan's military personnel strength and, to a great extent, curtailed India's superiority in military manpower (see Figure 6.2a).

However, India's nuclear edge—which mounted tremendous pressure on Pakistan for military upgrading—a substantial increase in defense expenditure, and emphasis on the procurement of sophisticated military hardware factored into checking Pakistan's inadvertent military advantage (see Figure 6.2b). Moreover, Pakistan's American-origin weapon systems were largely worn out. In the post-1965 years, contrary to Pakistan's expectations, the United States had not only delayed weapon repairs but also refused to lift the embargo on arms procurements. Pakistan's military dependency on its patron America and the latter's continued stance of restricted arms transfers to South Asia severely affected Pakistan, while India enjoyed uninterrupted military supplies from the Soviets. In sum, India's qualitative superiority over militarily vulnerable Pakistan, which was also facing global isolation and extreme political and economic problems at home, ensured relative peace in South Asia from 1972 to 1979.

Rivalry Reinforced: Steps from De-escalation to Re-escalation, 1979–89

In dyadic contentions, generally competitors' strategic decisions have a far-reaching impact on the course of rivalry. In the India-Pakistan case, even after experiencing a decade-long post-war peace and India's substantial military prowess, the two states resorted to militarized disputes. Five factors played principal roles in reactivating the dormant rivalry: (1) India's detonation of a nuclear device in 1974 and subsequently pursuit of a weapon-oriented nuclear program; (2) Pakistan's acquisition of sophisticated military hardware after

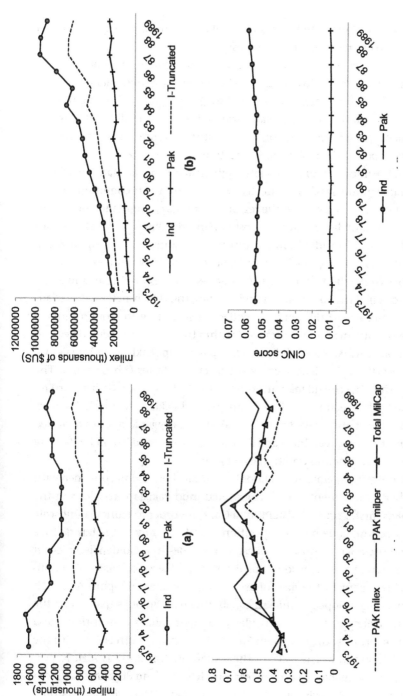

Figure 6.2. India-Pakistan relative capabilities and militarized disputes, 1973–89. (a) Military personnel (milper) ratio, (b) military expenditure (milex) ratio, (c) Pakistan's total military capability vis-à-vis India, (d) composite index of national capability (CINC) ratio. The CINC ratio comprises milper + milex + primary energy consumption (pec) ratio + iron and steel production (irst) ratio [population (total + urban) excluded]. *Source*: Compiled from the COW database (2015), National Material Capabilities, version 4.01.

the Soviet invasion of Afghanistan; (3) Pakistan's nuclear weapon program and Islamabad's repeated claims of possession of a usable atomic bomb; (4) Islamabad's covert support to the secessionist movement in Punjab; and (5) India's perceived fear of losing regional hegemony and subsequent initiation of retaliatory military measures. Once these factors gathered momentum in the region, the Indo-Pakistani rivalry again followed the traditional course of unavoidable armed confrontation and dispute recurrence in a haste driven by windows of both vulnerability and opportunity.

With the initiation of the Soviets' Afghanistan War, Pakistan started procuring large numbers of sophisticated weapons from anti-communist allies, and thereafter India's grip on the region and military preponderance began to wither. A fairly large military boost enhanced Pakistan's overall military capabilities against India from 1:2 in 1979 to 1.4:2 in 1982 (see Figure 6.2c). This shift was perceived by the decision-makers in New Delhi as a growing defensive vulnerability for India. A large section believed that under the smoke screen of the covert war in Afghanistan, the US-China-Pakistan triangular alliance might tighten their collective security grip around India, a Soviet ally, with an aim to neutralize it within the region. In order to neutralize possible threats, New Delhi preferred to pre-empt Pakistan at India's vulnerable northern borders, such as the Siachen Glacier (Khosa 1999). The Indian Army's successful maneuvering in the Siachen region helped it to create a wedge between the Chinese Xinjiang and Pakistan-controlled Gilgit-Baltistan, but it also proved to be a catalyst that triggered a series of armed confrontations between India and Pakistan thereafter and led their relatively de-escalated rivalry into traditional belligerency.

The onset of Operation Meghdoot in the Siachen region coincided with two other developments which aggravated Indo-Pakistani relations in the mid-1980s: first, Prime Minister Indira Gandhi's order to launch a full-scale military action, code-named Operation Bluestar, against the Sikh radicals who had occupied Amritsar's holiest Sikh shrine—the Golden Temple—in the Indian state of Punjab bordering Pakistan; and second, Pakistan's significant achievement in the field of assembling a nuclear weapon. Although Pakistan had developed its nuclear capabilities with an objective to alter the regional balance of power, particularly to offset India's conventional and nuclear superiority, the development also had a strong correlation with the status of Kashmir. In the wake of the Indian nuclear tests, as A.H. Nayyar (2015a), an Islamabad-based nuclear physicist and nuclear disarmament activist, points out, Pakistan's policy makers believed that without attaining nuclear parity, Pakistan would never be able to achieve effective political goals in Kashmir against the preponderant opponent. Once Pakistan's acquired qualitative strength compounded with its relatively operational nuclear capability—which it achieved after conducting "cold tests" in the mid-1980s—and its accomplished covert war experience in Afghanistan, the leadership in Islamabad began to expand on aggressive strategies to exploit India's security situation in Punjab (Hagerty 1998; F.H. Khan 2013).

From a strategic viewpoint, given its deep commitment in Afghanistan, it was in Pakistan's interest to tie down India—a close Soviet ally—to its east, where the Sikh separatist movement was at its peak. To implement this strategy, it followed India's successful covert model of 1971, under which India had trained and equipped thousands of ethnic Bengali Muslims of Pakistan's eastern wing to conduct a series of guerrilla raids against the Pakistani troops in East Pakistan, which eventually resulted in Pakistan's bifurcation. With a somewhat similar objective, Islamabad stepped up its political-military support to the Sikh secessionists for the establishment of Khalistan, a separate Sikh state, adjacent to its eastern border (Swami 2007: 137). Pakistan's sustained covert support to the Khalistan movement, coupled with its nuclear threat, had increased New Delhi's security anxiety, which consequently determined the direction of Indian military buildup. Apart from doubling its defense expenditure for qualitative procurements and a more than one-fifth increase in the armed forces manpower (Figure 6.2a–c), India launched large-scale strategic maneuvers along the international border to undermine Pakistan before its new military material could pose a serious threat.

The Indian policy makers were sure, akin to Nayyar's (2015a) observation, that Pakistan's weapon-oriented nuclear program was not limited to eliminating the Indian conventional threat, but also aimed to keep Pakistan's irredentist claim over Kashmir alive—an observation later proved correct by the prolonged proxy war in Kashmir and the Kargil War of 1999. The Indian decision-makers perhaps understood that once Pakistan attained full-fledged nuclear capability, given the Punjab insurgency experience, it might be difficult for India to resist the adversary's hostile intentions in Kashmir (Badhwar & Bobb 1987; Kanwal 2016). According to Sundarji, the then Indian Army chief, India still had considerable military might to defeat Pakistan decisively rather than postponing it to a later stage when "its nuclear capability matured and made it nearly impossible for India to wage a massive conventional battle without risking an atomic war" (Chengappa 2000: 322–23). Against this backdrop, within a couple of years of Siachen success, select political leaders and military officers had made an extraordinary decision to stage a provocative military exercise, Brasstacks, close to the international border with an intent to undercut Pakistan's military prowess (see Hoon 2000).

Another factor that contributed to India's Brasstacks decision was Pakistan's frontline role against the Soviets in Afghanistan, wherein it was deeply embroiled and therefore was not in position to open a second front or mobilize a large number of its troops against India. Thus India considered the exercise Brasstacks as a fleeting opportunity to knock down Pakistan and end its own security vulnerability for a long time. In other words, it can be argued that when the Indian decision-makers became convinced that Pakistan's nuclear capability and huge investment in modern weaponry would create a huge window of vulnerability, they were tempted to react against the adversary's qualitative overreach by staging a massive exercise to provoke it into a war when India still had a significant offensive advantage. "Had war broken out [in 1986–87] and a preventive strike been successfully executed over Kahuta," observes nuclear expert Feroz Hassan Khan, "Pakistan would have certainly been pushed back in its centrifugal program. It would have recovered eventually, but the sure consequences of war with India—once again, as in 1984—would have changed the course of the region's history" (2013: 223). This underscores the gravity of the Indian military plan (Brasstacks); it was carefully designed, as Hoon (2000) claims, to achieve long-term strategic objectives.

Though India successfully ducked Pakistan in the Siachen region and flexed muscle in the plains of Punjab by resorting to a large-scale military exercise, in the end, it could not manage to subdue its opponent as the strategists in New Delhi had originally desired. In fact, India's offensive saber-rattling produced the opposite results by raising Pakistan's security concerns. Consequently both sides began to view each other with apprehension that hastened their realpolitik policies, a long-held dyadic approach which eventually evolved into a normative practice of defensive offense, and thereby activated the dormant rivalry.

IMPACT OF REGIME TYPE AND DOMESTIC POLITICAL CONDITIONS

After experiencing authoritarian rule for nearly one and a half decades, Pakistan finally saw the light of democracy in the wake of the 1971 war. Throughout Zulfikar Ali Bhutto's tenure, Pakistan was a relatively stable civilian democracy and unlike the previous regimes it was not overshadowed by the traditional power-sharing mechanisms which awarded a veto to the army in major foreign and defense policies.[7] Ironically, when Pakistan was making important advances toward a successful democratic transition, India was going through its grimmest period of despotic civilian rule—famously known as the "emergency."[8] With the exception of the "emergency," however, India remained a robust democracy throughout the entire span of the development phase of the India-Pakistan rivalry (see Figure 6.3a).

Coincidence of Joint Democracy and the Resumption of Regime Dissimilarity:
The Slide from Relative Peace to Hostile Engagement

Consistent with the democratic peace literature, Figure 6.3 suggests that during a four-and-a-half-year joint-democratic period this dyad did not resort to any armed confrontation. Was joint democracy an underlying cause for short-term rivalry pacification? I argue that this was not the case. Though India and Pakistan shared democratic regimes from 1972 to mid-1977, their policies and actions were increasingly at variance with the established norms of democratic regimes. Despite conceding a shattering military defeat, as noted earlier, Pakistan's new democratic regime was not satisfied with the new status quo. The plan of action adopted by the Bhutto regime elucidates that it refused to make any fundamental shift from Pakistan's traditional revisionist stance and militaristic foreign policy. A quick analysis of Pakistan's civilian regime during its very first year in office illustrates this point. A month after the Bangladesh debacle and prior to the Simla Agreement (and long before the Indian detonation of a nuclear device), Bhutto had apparently instructed the nuclear scientists to build a nuclear bomb in the shortest possible time to challenge India's regional preponderance. Similarly, Bhutto's speech to Pakistan's National Assembly, just weeks after the signing of the Simla accord, may be considered as another outstanding example to judge the Pakistani leadership's mindset:

> If the people of Jammu and Kashmir want their independence, if they want to be liberated from the Hindu yoke if they want to be a free people in fraternity and friendship and comradeship with Pakistan, they will have to give the lead and we will be with them. Even if the Simla agreement is broken,

even if we jeopardise all our relations with India . . . we will be with them, no
matter what the consequences. (*Pakistan Times*, July 19, 1972, cited in Schofield 2010: 120)

These statements are glaring examples which underline how Pakistan's democratic regime resolutely pursued a course of action that focused on acquisition of nuclear weapons to challenge India over Kashmir as well as to seek to
alter the regional power structure. It may be argued that notwithstanding
the democratic nature of its regime, Pakistan under Bhutto had not substantially changed its underlying revisionist orientation and ideological differences vis-à-vis India. On a similar note, Ayesha Jalal observes that "Bhutto
never intended the Simla accord to become a prelude to a fresh chapter in
Pakistan's relations with its regional rival. . . . [H]e showed no signs of softening his government's stance towards New Delhi in the aftermath of Simla"
(1995: 81). From the standpoint of democratic peace theory, Bhutto's rigid
approach compromised the democratic regimes' inherent trait, that is, to
respect international norms and shape domestic and foreign policies accordingly. India and Pakistan's antithetical approaches and foreign policy objectives had a bearing on their respective democratic institutions.

While as a matter of fact the Bhutto regime did not resort to any military
disputes, the logic of such a course of action had more to do with the disparity
in India and Pakistan's relative capabilities rather than regime similarity.
When the post-Bangladesh military balance tilted toward India, a weakened
Pakistan had virtually no chance to defeat its rival in an early war and thus it
consciously adopted a modest posture and did not meddle with the Kashmir
issue (Burke 1973: 1037). The Bhutto regime's early actions—such as initiating
the nuclear program, organizing the Islamic Conference, and revitalizing the
Sino-Pakistani alliance—clearly reveal that Pakistan was dissatisfied with the
prevailing status quo. In other words, these actions signify that the prospect of
an intensive lock-in between India and Pakistan's democratic regimes was as
bright as it had ever been under previous non-democratic combinations. Had
Bhutto's civilian government been satisfied with the status quo, probably the
India-Pakistan rivalry could have taken a positive turn and eventually headed
toward an effective transformation, if not, termination.

On the other hand, instead of adopting an accommodative approach,
the Indian leadership sought to attain an absolute power to dominate Pakistan for a long period. The detonation of a nuclear device in 1974, apart from
demonstrating India's nuclear capability and opposition to signing the NPT,

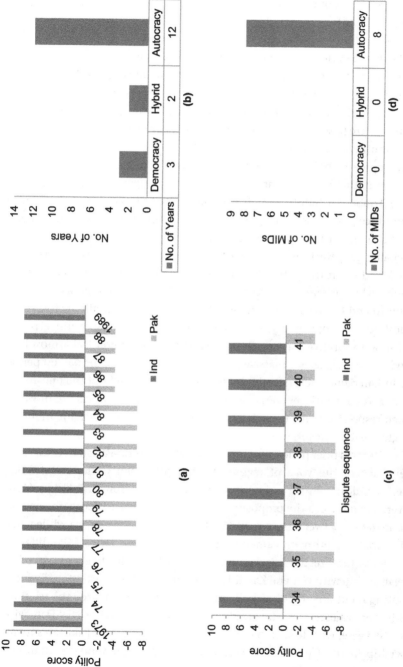

Figure 6.3. India-Pakistan regime type and recurrent militarized disputes, 1973–89. (a) Regime type, (b) regime years, (c) regime type during the initiation of MIDs, (d) no. of MIDs under particular type of regime. *Source:* Compiled from the COW database (2015, version 4.01); Polity-5 database (2018, version 5.0).

was an artifact of that thinking (Chengappa 2000: 205; P. Malik 2010: 67–70). Probably both regimes' learning from their past disputes, as Zeev Maoz and Ben Mor's (2002) evolutionary model characterizes, had induced considerable variations to the conciliatory side of their collective democratic experience. Had the Indian civilian government not adopted a coercive posture to attain an absolute status quo, which immediately intensified Pakistan's security grievances, perhaps there could have been a more suitable atmosphere to stabilize the relationship in due course.

Another factor that widened the gulf between the two democracies was their domestic political calculus. Bhutto's tenure thrived on an exaggerated populism that included anti-India rhetoric and jingoistic nationalism; Jalal (1995) dubbed it "Bhuttoism." In the name of building Pakistan anew, Bhutto introduced a set of socio-religious policies that sought to expand his popular constituency in a way that left no space for the political opposition to mount a challenge against his government's policies. Bhutto's game plan, however, backfired when the political opposition opened a collective front in resistance, which eventually resulted in yet another round of military intervention to end the persisting impasse (Jalal 1995: 77–85). Similarly, to benefit most from the 1971 victory, Mrs. Gandhi began to consolidate political power in an authoritative way which charged the domestic political atmosphere and, finally, triggered a massive political crisis resulting in the darkest period of Indian democracy, namely the "emergency." Throughout the mid-1970s, the two democratic regimes were mostly embroiled in political tug-of-war at their respective home turfs that constrained them from engaging in meaningful bilateral negotiations.

After this brief period of joint democracy, the Indo-Pakistani dyad again fell back to the yoke of regime dissimilarity when General Zia-ul-Haq dethroned the Bhutto regime and imposed military rule in Pakistan. However, in contrast to the proposition of democratic peace theory, the level of cooperation between the two dissimilar regimes increased for a while when the Janata government came into power in India. In spite of the differing nature of their regimes, India under Morarji Desai effectively improved its relationship with General Zia-ul-Haq's military regime in Pakistan. By moderating traditional hardline policies, the two sides normalized the relationship. For instance, Desai finalized the pending accord on the Salal Dam with relative ease; withdrew India's long-standing objection to Pakistan's membership in the Non-aligned Movement (NAM);[9] and similarly addressed other such issues of bilateral importance (Thornton 1999: 179). This reconciliation persisted throughout the Janata government's tenure. India-Pakistan bilateral relations began to take a hostile turn with the change of guard in New Delhi, which coincided with the Soviet invasion of Afghanistan. When Mrs. Gandhi came back to power in January 1980, a combination of regional and extra-regional pulls, the two leaders' rigid mindset and antipathy, and initiation of a domestic policy of Islamization in Pakistan had given rise to a situation that brought back hostility in the region. With superpowers' direct and indirect interventions in the subcontinent, both sides started confronting each other's policies, which eventually embroiled them in eight militarized disputes, one of which, the Brasstacks, almost escalated to a full-fledged war in early 1987 (see Figures 6.1 and 6.3c, d).

It seems that more than dissimilarity in the regime type, the hostile policies and aggressive behavior of the apex leadership provide a better understanding of why cooperation remained a non-starter between the South Asian rivals. Though the Bhutto-Gandhi era was democratic, neither side had taken any concrete step to extend the process of normalization that started with the signing of the Simla accord. On the contrary, the Zia-Desai non-democratic pair had accommodated each other's concerns to normalize the bilateral relationship. By the early 1980s, it was not only the clashing personalities of Mrs. Gandhi and General Zia-ul-Haq that made their regimes more rigid; the regional and extra-regional security apprehensions played a key role in influencing their policies. Furthermore, Pakistan's policy to covertly support the Sikh secessionist movement in Punjab in the 1980s added another point of contention in their already deteriorating bilateral ties. India's civilian regimes were profoundly suspicious of Pakistan's military regimes, which prompted them to toy with the idea of pre-emptive and coercive military adventurism during 1984–88. For instance, Operation Meghdoot and the Brasstacks exercise were launched by Indian civilian governments, while Pakistan under Zia's military rule was caught napping on both occasions. Another reason for India's aggressive posture was the Zia regime's quick accumulation of advanced weaponry, which induced a rough parity in the regional conflict. These developments had a direct impact on the domestic standing of India's civilian regimes, as the political opposition and other vocal forces' restraining impulses toward peace began to build pressure on the government to take specific measures to ensure India's regional dominance. Since India's civilian regimes risked appearing weak on national security, they started galloping down the road of military adventurism once Pakistan provided them a chance to rationalize the threat perception.

On the whole, Pakistan's aspirations to challenge the status quo and India's objective to consolidate it further brought about disparity in the two regimes' strategic interests. This eventually played a considerable role in reviving South Asia's dormant rivalry, particularly with the initiation of armed confrontations, which diminished the prospects of achieving a negotiated peace.

Dyadic Contest and Domestic Politics in Kashmir:
The Rise and Fall of Democracy

A paramount change in the character of the Srinagar-Delhi relationship and internal politics of Kashmir also affected India and Pakistan's relationship in the post-1971 period. This is especially important because Kashmir once again emerged as a key factor in precipitating escalation of armed hostilities between the two adversaries in the early 1990s. That is why developments within the Kashmir Valley merit a separate discussion, undertaken here.

Pakistan's shattering defeat and dismemberment in the 1971 war had not only altered the regional balance of power but also brought about a significant shift in the domestic political alignments within Kashmir. Sheikh Abdullah understood that Pakistan's bifurcation not only debilitated its political-military might but also left it no significant leverage which he could use to negotiate the restoration of the pre-1953 constitutional relationship between Kashmir and the Indian Union. In other words, South Asia's new reality meant that Kashmiris were left with limited political space to bargain with New Delhi. So he stopped using the Pakistan card and reconciled with the finality of Kashmir's accession to India (Behera 2006: 44). An interview with *Time* magazine reflected the changed mindset of the Kashmiri leader: "Our dispute with [the] Government of India is not about accession but it is about the quantum of autonomy" (cited in Behera 2006: 44). Though this stand was an effort to adjust to the new ground realities, it was a dramatic shift from his earlier demands for a plebiscite. In ethical terms, it was a complete surrender before New Delhi that not only stifled the Kashmiri people's political voice but also undermined Sheikh Abdullah's credibility.[10]

Prime Minister Indira Gandhi welcomed this shift and initiated long negotiations with Abdullah which concluded in the Delhi Accord in November 1974.[11] Following this, Abdullah replaced the Congress Chief Minister

Mir Qasim and managed, albeit with difficulty, the odd years of emergency. When the Janata Party came to power at the center in 1977, the state got an opportunity to function like a real democracy for the first time since 1947. Unlike the earlier three elections, the Janata regime conducted the first free and fair elections in the state and, as a result, the state witnessed relative stability and peace (see Behera 2000, 2006; Sumantra Bose 2003). Stein Widmalm noted that Amanullah Khan, the head of the Jammu and Kashmir Liberation Front (JKLF) operating in Azad Kashmir, had reportedly stated that "in 1983 conditions for launching a military campaign were not favourable. . . . With democracy functioning in a relatively peaceful way, the demand to change the political status of the region was neither raised nor supported" (1998: 153–54).

After Sheikh Abdullah's death in late 1982, however, the state's democratic stability began to wither. His eldest son, Farooq Abdullah, took over the reins of the National Conference (NC), but he lacked his father's charisma. In the 1983 election, on the other hand, Mrs. Gandhi personally campaigned in the state and stirred up regional and religious sentiments by expressing sympathy with the Hindus of Jammu region. This communal angle provoked all parties to resort to virulent campaigns that not only plagued elections with "an increased level of fraud" but also intensified religious polarization in the state (Widmalm 2002: 63). As a consequence, a new phase of deliberate subversion of democratic tradition, institutions, and organizations unfolded after the 1983 elections, in which Farooq Abdullah managed to defeat the Congress Party (Bajpai & Ganguly 1994: 404). Since Mrs. Gandhi was trying to destabilize non-Congress governments by encouraging defections in many states, several non-Congress parties, including the Farooq Abdullah–led NC, together formed an "opposition conclave" to oppose this malpractice (Varshney 1992: 219).

Farooq's resistance through the "opposition conclave" and Mrs. Gandhi's determination to strike almost all opposition leaders cost the former dearly when the newly appointed governor, Jagmohan Malhotra, sacked Farooq's government in July 1984 on flimsy grounds without giving him a chance to test the majority in the lower house (Widmalm 2002: 64; Varshney 1992: 219). Interestingly, when Farooq proposed to form a new government with outside support, the governor ruled out this proposal by dubbing it an unconstitutional and undemocratic practice (Bajpai & Ganguly 1994: 404). By violating the federal principles, akin to the post-1953 federal malpractices when New Delhi's policy regarding J&K was to install pro-center chief ministers by encouraging defections within the National Conference, Mrs. Gandhi had renewed the policy of systematically dismantling the political institutions (see Behera 2000). Most observers agree that Farooq's dismissal marked the end of the peaceful democratic era in the state.[12]

Like previous regimes, the newly formed G.M. Shah government soon became a political liability for New Delhi, which was criticized for its inability to stop the spiral of violence, eventually paving the way for another round of governor rule in March 1986. To everyone's surprise, later the same year, the National Conference hammered out a political deal with the Congress Party that defied the basic logic of Kashmiri politics. Prime Minister Rajiv Gandhi and Farooq Abdullah formed a coalition to contest the March 1987 state elections. This deal had apparently defied the rationale of democracy. When the two largest parties—the National Conference and the Congress—joined together, there was no opposition left to stand against the "tactical alliance" (Widmalm 2002: 74). Similarly, Navnita Behera has rightly noted that this political alliance

> denuded Kashmiris' secular political identity of its *raison d'être*. Kashmiris had always taken pride in standing up to political pressures from the Indian State (read central government), but Farooq's deal virtually bartered it away for the prize of power. (2000: 156)

Finally, the coming together of ideologically opposite parties forced their opponents to align firmly under a coalition of Islamic groups: the Muslim United Front (MUF). This development, however, was as unexpected as the Farooq-Rajiv alliance. Having seen considerable support for the MUF, the National Conference–Congress alliance resorted to electoral rigging for manipulating the results (Noorani 1992: 272; Varshney 1992: 220). Though this alliance managed to gain the majority, their naked opportunism robbed the Kashmiris of all their hopes in democracy. This conspiracy, notes Ganguly, "conveyed a massage that the Kashmiris of the valley simply would not be allowed or trusted to freely exercise their franchise" (1997: 92). This electoral outcome paved the way for violent insurgency in Kashmir thereafter, which in turn dramatically changed the course of India-Pakistan rivalry with the end of the Cold War.

SEEKING EXPLANATIONS: WHY DID RIVALRY DE-ESCALATION NOT LEAD TO TERMINATION?

The Bangladesh War of 1971 proved to be an immense blow for Pakistan, as it not only shattered its two-front strategic advantage but also laid the foundation for India's regional dominance. Akin to the partition of unified India in 1947, the dismemberment of Pakistan was a massive state- and regional-level shock—as Pakistan lost one-sixth of its territory and half of its population and economy. Against this background, as S. Paul Kapur notes, "Pakistan could no longer face India in a direct, large-scale conflict. If it did, Pakistan ran a serious risk of suffering catastrophic defeat" (2011: 71). Such a huge shock and drastic power shift should have compelled already subdued Pakistani elites to withdraw from the rivalry, immediately or with the passage of time. Yet this did not happen. Why? What facilitated Pakistan, the state seeking territorial revisions, to absorb a ravaging secession and continue the rivalry?

Here, I attempt to demystify this puzzle by presenting three explanations. The first explanation can be inferred from Paul Diehl and Gary Goertz's conceptualization (2000). For an effective rivalry termination, as discussed in Chapter 2, the punctuated equilibrium model sets the condition of a period of ten to fifteen years without any militarized dispute after the last armed incidence. In this sense, in the aftermath of the 1971 war India and Pakistan should have not confronted militarily until the early or mid-1980s. Although the next armed dispute between the two states occurred quite late, it was well before the expiration of the minimum time specified for rivalry termination, that is, ten years (see Table 6.1). If one takes into consideration the higher termination criterion, that is, fifteen years, by that time this dyad confronted seven times and incurred hundreds of fatalities (Table 6.1).

It is important to note that the frequency and severity of armed confrontations between the two adversaries was far beyond the specified limit of a normal rivalry. No doubt the Bangladesh War left dismembered Pakistan in a state from which its recovery was looking bleak, but the anti-communist agenda of its ally, the United States, and its billions of dollars' worth of military and economic aid over time, as discussed earlier, had significantly neutralized the devastating impact of bifurcation. Hence, before Pakistan could have withdrawn from the rivalry or abandoned its revisionist agenda against India, the key external actors' material support restored a certain degree of qualitative parity in the conflict which eventually helped Pakistan recover from the shock of secession. Within a decade, Pakistan sought to regroup and began to challenge the status quo favoring the Indian dominance in the local hierarchy of South Asia. From this perspective, it may be argued that Diehl and Goertz's (2000) criterion for rivalry termination sufficiently expounds why this rivalry persisted after experiencing a massive shock in 1971. Based on this and other key factors, the complex rivalry model comprehensively explains what facilitated Pakistan to absorb the devastating effect of its eastern wing's detachment and continue the rivalrous contention with India.

A second explanation for the continuation of the India-Pakistan rivalry may be inferred from Robert Jervis's (1976) and Russell J. Leng's (1983, 1988, 2000) "learning approaches." These approaches maintain that (1) adversaries draw lessons by evaluating their past strategies and their effects on a given outcome and then consider their future bargaining strategies accordingly (Leng 1988, 2000); and (2) mutual or one-sided misperceptions play a major role to set forth the future course of rivalries (Jervis 1976). For the most part, misperception-induced tensions are prevalent in those dyads in which the defeated sides seek territorial revisions and consistently chart plans to alter the status quo.

The road taken by the India-Pakistan dyad in the aftermath of the 1971 war apparently underscores that the logic of learning approaches was at play. By liberating Bangladesh, for the time being India succeeded in demolishing the rationale of the two-nation theory, but the territorial loss had also scarred Pakistan's national honor and prestige, deepening a sense of insecurity among its political elites.[13] For a short time, Pakistan caved in and agreed to negotiate peace with India through the Simla Agreement, but it was more of a compromised peace with a motive of revenge—its ruling elites were waiting for a more opportune moment to thwart the status quo—hence this shift brought no fundamental transformation in Pakistan's long-term strategic behavior. In fact, the Bhutto government lost no time to bring its scientists and military strategists on board to chart a future course of action that aimed to obtain nuclear weapons at any cost. This determination underlines that, despite experiencing political upheaval and economic strife, the ruling elites in Pakistan had learned contrary lessons—that is, to expand on a militarily significant scale to deter the opponent.

Furthermore, what added to Pakistan's worries was India's successful detonation of a nuclear device in 1974, which traumatized its leadership as

New Delhi chose to up its nuclear ante despite securing an overwhelming victory and carving a new nation out of Pakistan. The leadership in Islamabad perceived this development as an issue of life-and-death for their state, as it clearly indicated that even Pakistan's vivisection was not sufficient to satisfy India's hegemonic aspirations. Consequently, Pakistan sped up its ongoing nuclear-weapon program with an aim to challenge India in the foreseeable future, and the low-intensity conflict in Punjab, and later in Kashmir, was the by-product of that resolve. This way, as Ashok Kapur says, "on the strategic plane, a new layer emerged in the form of a nuclearized rivalry" (2005: 149). Finally, a mix of policy makers' rigid thinking, evolving strategic actions, and ever-increasing misperceptions on both sides kept on changing the background conditions of the India-Pakistan duel that helped sustain this rivalry to a large extent.

Maoz and Mor's (2002) evolutionary model, which further contributes to the interpretations of the "learning approaches," provides a third explanation. While agreeing with Jervis's (1976) and Leng's (1988, 2000) understanding that adversaries' strategies and learning from past crises and wars do shape the rival parties' future policies, Maoz and Mor maintain that these approaches do not sufficiently explain the complete pattern of the adversaries' conflictual behavior. According to them, inter-dispute and inter-war periods are crucial: to understand "whether they tend to stabilize the rivalries or serve as temporary breaks before the next round may well depend on what happens in the interim period" (Maoz & Mor 2002: 279). They further elaborate:

> [The] war outcomes tend to generate initial periods of stability characterized by asymmetrical satisfaction with the status quo and asymmetrical perceptions of capability. Whether these periods of stability lead to the termination of the rivalry or to the renewal of hostilities depends to a large extent on the events that tend to characterize this interim period. (2002: 279)

India's and Pakistan's post-war behaviors seem to have some consistency with Maoz and Mor's logic, which sheds light as to why the South Asian rivalry persisted even after experiencing a decisive war. No doubt the consequences of war, that is, the conclusion of the Simla Agreement and the asymmetry in power capabilities, had stabilized the two adversaries' relationship, which significantly contributed to a decade-long peace in the region. During this period, paraphrasing Maoz and Mor, Pakistan was "satisfied with the [new] status quo but its behavior [was] guided principally by capability-related calculations rather than by satisfaction-related one" (2002: 285). For Pakistan, this period actually served as a temporary break for acquiring military capabilities to continue the rivalry. Once it began to acquire a rough parity against India—mainly in the nuclear domain and conventional weapon systems—the rivalry began to pedal out of the dormant phase. Within a decade, it overran the status quo and assumed the traditional patterns of hostile behavior and reactionary policies.

In short, four factors played a major role to bring Pakistan back on the rivalry track: dissatisfaction with the post-war status quo, the unresolved territorial issue of Kashmir, the great powers' crucial material assistance and political support, and a leap forward to balance conventional military power by developing a weapon-oriented nuclear program.

CONCLUSION

This chapter describes how a combination of factors transformed a relatively de-escalated rivalry into a severe one. Some findings draw considerable support from the rivalry linkage and external shock propositions, particularly the Soviet-American rivalry in Afghanistan and its impact on the military balance of the two South Asian rivals. Re-escalation of the Indo-Pakistani rivalry is also consistent with the propositions of power transition theory. The expansion of Pakistan's conventional and nuclear capabilities to a position of appreciable parity with the superior adversary, India, proved to be a crucial condition for the rivalry resumption.

In the aftermath of the Bangladesh War, Pakistan's political leadership recognized that challenging India would be a costly and inefficient activity, which might also pose a threat to Pakistan's existence. So, while directing its energy to set its house in order, it adopted compromised peace to navigate Pakistan's way to survival with enough scope to build its power capabilities over time. In this sense, Pakistan's commitment to the peaceful bilateral relationship was purely a short-term tactical strategy of survival and was hinged upon domestic concerns and weapon acquisition compulsions. Once Pakistan began to acquire a rough parity, it was no longer hesitant to employ military options to defend its political-strategic interests. On the other hand, India was worried that the external powers' substantial qualitative assistance to Pakistan would undermine its strategic edge; thus the changing situation motivated it to react before its rival would compel it to bargain from a position of weakness. In addition to Pakistan's growing conventional military strength, which intensified the secessionist movement in Punjab, its ever-increasing nuclear capability led the Indians to adopt a more hawkish posture. The fear of future nuclear parity forced India to initiate military maneuvers to keep Pakistan down—the Brasstacks crisis of 1986–87 was part of such a strategic design. Ultimately, the mutual adoption of coercive tactics guided both adversaries to follow a trajectory of distrust and hostility which eventually reversed the post-war de-escalation progress or the course of a decade-long peace.

During their joint-democratic period, interestingly, this dyad leaned against the democratic peace thesis. Their regime similarity had an almost negligible impact on rivalry amelioration because both sides were not satisfied with the status quo—Pakistan with India's regional dominance and the latter with its temporary preponderance against the former. This disparity in strategic objectives diminished the prospects of rivalry termination. Later, however, the regime dissimilarity and domestic politics played a considerable role to shape the direction of the rivalry. The Sikh secessionist demands in Punjab provided Pakistan a chance to intervene in India's domestic sphere. Similarly, the electoral betrayal of 1987 in Kashmir added an edge to the rivalry. These developments extended Pakistan another opportunity to defreeze the Kashmir issue and continue the rivalry. With enemy images already instituted, the capture of Siachen and political turmoil in Punjab and Kashmir attracted the attention and interest of hardliners in the political opposition, thereby activating the domestic scene on both sides. The domestic opponents and the restraining forces were not ready to accept their governments' conciliatory actions over these issues; in fact, their sustained pressure considerably influenced their governments' decisions and responses, which contributed to the revival of the rivalry.

In brief, it is important to note that the magnitude and the impact of different factors on the Indo-Pakistani rivalry varied in the wake of the 1971 war. These factors jointly offer an effective explanation as to why this rivalry remained dormant during 1972–80, and why it began to escalate in the early 1980s and assumed a severe confrontational form thereafter.

CHAPTER 7

The Maintenance of Complex Rivalry, 1990–2021

INTRODUCTION

This chapter examines how a relatively de-escalated rivalry transformed into a severe one in the late 1980s when India and Pakistan acquired nuclear capabilities and the international system underwent a drastic shift with the collapse of bipolar order. It investigates how nuclear weapons, the global war against terrorism, regime type in New Delhi and Islamabad, and the regional and extra-regional power angularities have contributed to stabilize the India-Pakistan rivalry. Here the focus is mainly on three issues. The first concerns the shift in power position within the dyadic, regional, and systemic realms during the pre- and post-9/11 phases, that is, how changes in power structures—particularly in political, economic, security, and other domains—influenced and redefined the Indo-Pakistani rivalry in the post–Cold War years. The second issue pertains to the evolving strategic actions of the two adversaries, that is, in terms of understanding their past strategies' effectiveness, the increasing nuclear threat, and misperceptions, which collectively shaped their post–Cold War rivalrous course. The third issue concerns the impact of regime type and regime change on the India-Pakistan rivalry by analyzing how the two states' similar and dissimilar political institutions and domestic politics have determined the decisions of their respective political leadership. In the course of this analysis, the chapter examines the impact of subsystemic and systemic shifts, the nuclear dimension, rivalry linkage, material competition, and political regimes on India-Pakistan relations by locating how they collectively contribute to stabilize this dyadic contention.

This chapter is divided into seven sections. After this brief introduction, the second section presents an account of sixteen militarized disputes that occurred between India and Pakistan in 1990–2021, during the maintenance phase. The third section explains how the great powers' intervention, mainly through their sustained arms supplies, and India's and Pakistan's simultaneous weapon-oriented nuclear programs brought a turning point in the dyad's post–Cold War relationship. The fourth section describes how Afghanistan acts as a catalyst in this rivalry and why the US-led NATO forces' complete withdrawal from this South Asian hotspot in 2021 might affect India's security, particularly in conjunction with the deepening Sino-Pakistani strategic ties, by re-escalating the India-Pakistan hostilities. The fifth section traces how the relative military capabilities, especially nuclear weapons, brought about a stabilizing situation in the rivalry by increasing the possibility of subconventional warfare and political-military tensions between the two states. The focus of the sixth section is on the impact of regime type and domestic politics on the two states' decision making and actions. It explains how the joint-democratic periods could not normalize India and Pakistan's bilateral relations and why their varied political approaches shape their ruling regimes' policies and responses into more hostile ones. The concluding section sums up the key findings of the chapter.

MILITARIZED DISPUTES AND CONFLICT ESCALATION, 1990 TO 2021

In the late 1980s, two political shocks brought a new twist in the India-Pakistan relationship: a state-level shock in the form of the secessionist movement in Kashmir followed by a systemic shock with the termination of the Cold War. In 1987, electoral rigging during the state assembly elections had triggered public resentment in Kashmir, and later it evolved into a secessionist movement which extended Pakistan an opportunity to defreeze the Kashmir issue and challenge India by launching a proxy war in the conflict-prone state. Throughout the 1990s, the situation in Kashmir bore several similarities to the one that had prevailed in East Pakistan during 1970–71—where "ethnic kinship between the Bengalis of West Bengal in India and the Bengalis of East Pakistan led the latter to appeal to India for help" (Santos 2007: 40). Likewise, in the 1990s, the ethnic kinship between the two parts of Kashmir across the LoC led the Kashmiris of the Valley to appeal to Pakistan for political-military help. Thereafter, the formation of a strong bond between the Pakistani intelligence agencies and the Kashmiri

TABLE 7.1. India-Pakistan militarized interstate disputes (MIDs), 1990–2021

S. No	Dates of Dispute[1]	MID Initiator	Revisionist State	Cause of MID	MID Location	Fatality Level[2]	Highest Action Taken	Hostility Level[3]	Regime Type[4]
42	February 11, 1990–December 22, 1990	India	Pakistan	Territory	Kashmir	I-none P-1-25	Clash	4 & 4*	Demo
43	May 1, 1991–September 2, 1991	India	Both	Territory	Kashmir	I-1-25 P-missing	Clash	4 & 4*	Demo
44	September 17, 1993–May 10, 1998[5]	Pakistan	Pakistan	Territory	Various border areas of J&K	<999	Clash	4 & 4*	Demo
45	May 11, 1998–March 30, 1999	India	None	Territory & Policy	Pokhran (India) & Chaman (Pakistan), LoC & border	1-25	Nuclear alert & clash	4 & 4*	Demo
46	May 5, 1999–July 26, 1999[6]	Pakistan	Pakistan	Territory	Kargil sector, J&K	>999	Interstate war	5 & 5*	Demo
47	August 10, 1999–November 19, 2000[7]	India	None	Territory	Kashmir, Siachen, Rann of Kutch, IC-814 Hijacking	26-100	Clash	4 & 4*	Non-demo
48	July 13, 2001–November 22, 2003	Pakistan	Both	Territory & Policy	Indian Parliament, J&K, military standoff along the border	251-500	Clash	4 & 4*	Non-demo
49	May 18, 2004–May 18, 2004	India	None	None	Firing on Pakistani fishermen in Indian territorial waters (Gujarat)	I-none P-1-25	I-attack P-protests	4 & 1*	Non-demo
50	January 18, 2005–October 17, 2005	Pakistan	Both	Territory & Policy	Along and across LoC	1-25	I-seizure, attack P-attack	4 & 4*	Non-demo

51	May 14, 2008–December 29, 2010	Pakistan	Pakistan	Territory & Policy	LoC, Mumbai, and other parts of India	251–500	Clash	4 & 4*	Non-demo
52	January 2, 2011–December 31, 2014	Pakistan	Pakistan	Territory	Kashmir (LoC, international border), Punjab	251–500	Clash	4 & 4*	Non-demo
53	January 2, 2016–March (dm), 2016	Pakistan	Pakistan	Territory	Pathankot Airbase	1–25	Clash	4 & 4*	Demo
54	September 18, 2016–December (dm), 2016	Pakistan	Pakistan	Territory	Uri, Nagrota & surgical strike (across LoC)	26–100	Clash	4 & 4*	Demo
55	February 10, 2018–February 25, 2018	Pakistan	Pakistan	Territory	J&K (Sunjuwan attack)	1–25	Clash	4 & 4*	Demo
56	February 14, 2019–March 22, 2019	Pakistan	Pakistan	Territory	Pulwama-Balakot military standoff (LoC, international border)	26–100	Clash	4 & 4*	Demo
57	August 5, 2019–December 31, 2021 (ongoing)	India	India	Territory & Policy	J&K (abrogation of special status), LoC	26–100	Clash	4 & 4*	Demo

Source: Compiled from the COW database (2015, version 4.01), (2020, version 5.0); ICB database (2016), version 12.0; Polity-5 database (2018), version 5.0; newspaper reports 1990–2022.

1. As in the COW database, missing dispute date are marked "dm" for "date missing."

2. The COW database indicates fatality level of each side; the same has been retained here. Wherever both states' level of fatality varies, a separate entry has been cited against the country (i.e., I or P) differently.

3. The codes marked with an asterisk (*) indicate Pakistan's hostility level, and codes without it indicate India's hostility level. The COW database hostility codes are 1: no militarized action; 2: threat to use force; 3: display use of force; 4: use of force; and 5: war.

4. Regime type is recorded on the basis of regimes at the helm of affairs on both sides when the militarized dispute broke out between the rivals, except in the case of MID 47 (see note 7).

5. For methodological reasons, this study delinks the nuclear dispute of 1998 and the Kargil War from the COW database single MID entry (dispute 4007) and considers all of them as three separate MIDs (i.e., MIDs 44, 45, and 46).

6. This dispute started on May 5, 1999, when Indians got their first information about the intrusion, and it ended with India's ceasefire declaration on July 26, 1999.

7. Though this dispute started on January 2, 2016, when Pakistan was under democratic government, it was largely carried forward by the military regime from October 13, 1999 onward. For this reason, the dyad's regime type is identified as "Non-demo."

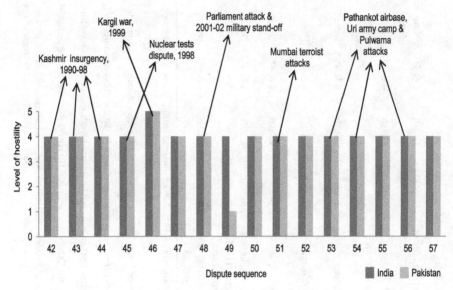

Figure 7.1. India-Pakistan hostility level (frequency and severity), 1990–2021.
Source: Compiled from the COW database (2015, version 4.01; 2020, version
5.0); ICB database (2016, version 12.0); newspaper reports 1990–2022.

secessionist leadership aggravated India and Pakistan's security competition
that marked the beginning of a prolonged low-intensity conflict or subconventional warfare in Kashmir.

Within a few years, a full-blown, Pakistan-supported insurgency movement was under way in Kashmir. Mainly it began with the Muslim United
Front (MUF) members' decision to cross the LoC and get training and weapons from the Pakistan Army. Though the Jammu and Kashmir Liberation
Front (JKLF) first spearheaded the secessionist movement in Kashmir, it was
soon followed by the Islamic militant organization Hizb-ul-Mujahideen
(HuM). Advocating an Islamic ideology, the HuM demanded that the state
join Pakistan, while the JKLF propounded the idea of a democratic, secular,
unified, and sovereign state of J&K. These groups not only encouraged young
Kashmiris to cross the LoC to join the extremist groups supported by Pakistan's Inter-Services Intelligence (ISI) for armed training, but also started
operations inside the Valley which caused large-scale political violence and
exodus of the minority Pandit community (see Evans 2002; Rashid 2008).

In addition to the internal political discord in Kashmir, a massive external political shock—the termination of the Cold War—also played a signifi-

cant role in shaping the trajectory of the India-Pakistan relationship. The Soviets' destructive defeat in Afghanistan encouraged Pakistan to test India in Kashmir by employing a similar covert strategy under the protective shield of nuclear weapons. The nuclear factor in particular played a key role in the conflict transformation. It brought to the fore new dynamics of conflict escalation and covert aggression that favored Pakistan despite India's conventional superiority and overly strong power-hold in the region. Since the nuclearization of South Asia, the nuclear weapons and missile systems have not only increased the frequency of militarized disputes to a dangerous level but also the rival parties' tendency to engage in nuclear brinkmanship. A few examples in this respect are the Kargil War of 1999, the twin crises of 2001–2, the 2008 Mumbai terrorist attacks, the 2016 Pathankot airbase attack, and the Pulwama-Balakot military crisis of 2019 (see Table 7.1 and Figure 7.1). At present, a full-scale war under the nuclear threshold seems impossible, but the possibility of a "limited war" cannot be ruled out. The "limited war" strategy—mainly the "Cold Start"—has been envisaged more by Indian analysts as an attempt to counter terror strikes unleashed from Pakistani soil; meanwhile, Pakistan has also inducted tactical nuclear weapons to neutralize India's punitive strategy. Such aggressive measures have the potential to break into risky conflict spirals which might give rise to a situation or compel both sides to advance their respective border units to escalate the conflict and end up in a dangerous short or full-blown conventional or nuclear war— the 2019 Pulwama-Balakot military crisis is a case in point that almost pushed the rivals in that direction.

The Kashmir Crisis of 1990: South Asia under the Shadow of Nuclear Clouds

Three years after the Brasstacks dispute, India and Pakistan were again at loggerheads over Kashmir in 1990. This dispute persisted throughout the year and later got compounded by a near-nuclear confrontation. A more immediate cause of this dispute can be traced back to the rigged state assembly election of 1987 followed by New Delhi's coercive policies against the dissenting Kashmiri youth. The turning point came when some members of the JKLF kidnapped Rubiya Sayeed, daughter of India's then home minister, Mufti Mohammad Sayeed, on December 8, 1989, and demanded the release of five jailed militants in ransom. The new Janata Dal government under V.P. Singh's premiership lacked a coherent strategy to respond to the crisis and conceded to the militants' demand (Dulat 2015: 47–53). Thereafter, in a bid to pressure

New Delhi over the Kashmir issue, Pakistan initiated its largest-ever military exercise, code-named Zarb-e-Momin, which involved around 200,000 troops, seven infantry divisions, four army corps, and one armored division along the international border in Punjab. The Pakistan Air Force also started a separate exercise, code-named Highmark, involving several squadrons of offensive and defensive units, which were later added to the Zarb-e-Momin to demonstrate the country's military prowess (Salamat Ali 1989). The sheer size of Pakistan's exercise was a fitting reply to India's Brasstacks exercise of 1986–87. According to General V.N. Sharma, then India's chief of the army staff (COAS), India got worried when it found that Pakistani "troops were not going back to their peace stations, but they were staying on in the exercise area . . . quite close to the international border and the [LoC] . . . [to] take full advantage of terrorist successes to support military intervention" (V. Sharma 1993).

By mid-January 1990, the situation in Kashmir became volatile and New Delhi responded by deploying thousands of troops to control the situation. The scale and the magnitude of uprising in Srinagar and other Valley towns led the Indian state to unleash its military might, and hundreds of pro-independence demonstrators were killed. The Indian security forces' high-handed approach toward the pro-freedom demonstrations and large-scale repression provided Pakistan an opportunity to extend full political and diplomatic support for the Kashmiris' demand for the right to "self-determination" (Behera 2000; Viswam & Ali 1990). Islamabad's increasing interference in Kashmir affairs pressured New Delhi to up its military ante by deploying striking units along the LoC and international border. Soon both sides locked in a retaliatory cycle that triggered escalatory spirals of violence and thereby changed the dynamics of the Kashmir conflict. To relay Islamabad's concern over the increasing level of tensions in Kashmir, Prime Minister Benazir Bhutto had sent Foreign Minister General Sahibzada Yaqub Khan to New Delhi. In a meeting with his Indian counterpart, I.K. Gujral, Yaqub Khan warned that "war clouds would hover over the subcontinent if timely action was not taken" (Dixit 2002: 267). Gujral understood the gravity of the "war clouds" message and firmly told Yaqub Khan, after consulting Prime Minister V.P. Singh, that Pakistan's forewarning and conduct were unacceptable to India and the escalation of the conflict "would only evoke a firm and decisive response from India" (Dixit 2002: 268).

Tensions escalated further when the key personalities on both sides embarked on inflammatory war rhetoric. On January 30, 1990, for instance,

General Sharma declared that the Indian troops were prepared to protect Kashmir "at any cost" (ICB 2016). On the other side, General Mirza Aslam Beg, Pakistan's COAS, claimed that the Iranian government had assured "support that would enable Pakistan to win if war erupted over Kashmir" (Perkovich 1999: 307). In the meantime, the US journalist Seymour Hersh (1990) claimed in a sensational *New Yorker* article, titled "On the Nuclear Edge," that the US administration had received intelligence reports that India and Pakistan were on the verge of nuclear war. According to him, General Beg had authorized technicians at the Kahuta nuclear facility "to put together nuclear weapons" (Hersh 1990: 64). In the face of a growing risk of a nuclear war arising out of miscalculation, and fearing the worst, the Bush administration decided to send a mission led by Robert M. Gates, the deputy national security adviser, to the subcontinent to address India and Pakistan's differences.

The Gates mission reached Islamabad on May 20, 1999, and stressed that Washington had war-gamed the Indo-Pakistani confrontations exhaustively and found that Pakistan would suffer a grave defeat in a potential war with India; hence it should refrain from war-mongering behavior (Ganguly 2002: 94). In New Delhi, the mission stressed that war would not serve the purpose of either side as the long-term costs would be unbearable for both states. It advised the Indian leadership to exercise great restraint in its military posture, and especially cautioned against a Bangladesh-like blitzkrieg operation to sever Sindh from Pakistan, because desperate Pakistanis might resort to a nuclear strike (Hagerty 1995–96: 100–101). After the US intervention, Islamabad assured that it would close the training camps for Kashmiri militants and New Delhi announced the withdrawal of its armored regiments from Rajasthan's Mahajan ranges (ICB 2016; Swami 2007: 173–74). As a result, by the end of June 1990 the intensity of the dispute was reduced to a remarkably low level and the strained bilateral relationship began to witness slow, albeit effective, recovery.

The Kashmir Insurgency and Nuclear Tests Dispute, 1991–98

Despite the outbreak of a serious nuclear crisis in 1990, Pakistan's enduring support to the Kashmiri secessionists did not wane, thereby deeply straining India-Pakistan relations. In the early 1990s, the JKLF, Kashmir's most prominent insurgent group, "attracted a new generation of radicalized young men" and "emerged as the vanguard and spearhead of an uprising centered on the Kashmir Valley" (Sumantra Bose 2007: 180). Once thousands of Kashmiri youth picked up guns to fight the Indian rule, the state's administrative system crumbled. Though New Delhi's timely deployment of security forces had warded off the early threat of secession, its massive military response failed to quell the Kashmiri secessionist movement. In the name of combating insurgency, the Indian security forces inflicted grave injuries on the Kashmiri people, especially by resorting to midnight warrantless searches, intimidation, widespread torture, rape, arbitrary detention, and shootings at non-violent public processions, which further spread the armed struggle to other parts of the Valley (Behera 2006: 48–49; Noorani 1992: 273).

In mid-1992, the Indian security forces launched "catch-and-kill" drives to execute captured militants under Operation Tiger and Shiva; in doing so, they failed to make a distinction between civilians and militants (Asia Watch and Physicians for Human Rights 1993). As a result, several outrageous cases of human rights violations occurred which resulted in the killing of several "unarmed and innocent persons without any provocation—verbal or physical" (Puri 2008: 79; Gossman 1995: 67). Around the same time, the JKLF employed "rally-around-the-flag" tactics and emerged as the sole and effective representative of the Kashmir cause. This development raised alarm bells not only for the Indian Army but also the rank and file of the ISI as the JKLF's objectives began to collide with Pakistan's long-standing ambition to bring Kashmir into its domain. The ISI adopted a two-pronged strategy to divert the Kashmiri movement from being pro-independence to becoming pro-Pakistan: first, it began to mastermind feuds within the JKLF's ranks; and second, it started nurturing parallel militant groups to replace the JKLF with the HuM and the Harqat-ul-Ansar (HuA). By 1993–94, the JKLF suffered heavy losses at the hands of the Pakistani militant groups, whose members were mainly Pakistani Punjabis and the Afghan mujahideen, and simultaneously at the hands of the Indian security forces (Behera 2006: 81–82; Z. Hussain 2007: 124–25).

Sandwiched between the pro-Pakistani groups and the Indian troops' onslaught, the JKLF soon lost its sheen and was eventually reduced to the margins of the armed struggle. Thereafter the pro-Pakistani groups beefed up their position in Kashmir by killing religious, social, and political figures who opposed their pro-Pakistan stance (Sumantra Bose 2007: 181). Against this backdrop, the local support for the insurgency began to decline. In 1993, the situation took a dramatic turnaround with the formation of the All Party Hurriyat Conference (APHC)—an umbrella organization of several separatist Kashmiri political parties descended from the Plebiscite Front and the

MUF—however, the APHC could not succeed in arriving at any markedly acceptable agreement with New Delhi (see Behera 2000: Ch. 7). Though New Delhi succeeded in consolidating its position in the mid-1990s, the military success did not result in a safer life for ordinary people as the death toll increased consistently (see Swami 2007: 175). Gradually, New Delhi realized that its coercive approach could hold the ground in Kashmir but it might not lead to normalcy in the state. So it prepared the ground for the general election to revive the stalled democratic process in the state that concluded with the parliamentary and state assembly elections of 1996. Despite pro-independence and pro-Pakistan groups' boycott, New Delhi widely publicized these elections as a demonstration of the Kashmiris' rejection of violence and of the Pakistan-supported insurgent movement (Sumantra Bose 2003: 138; Koithara 2004: 64).

Despite successful elections and a strong military hold over Kashmir, the insurgency did not wane; instead it "moved out of population centers into remote rural areas that afforded the cover of forested and mountainous terrain" within the Valley and spread to mountainous areas of the Jammu region—especially the Muslim-populated Doda, Poonch, and Rajouri districts—to exploit its multi-religious composition (Sumantra Bose 2007: 182; Koithara 2004: 64). To minimize the insurgents' targeted killings, mainly security personnel and members of the minority Hindu community, the Indian security forces resorted to a punishing counter-strategy without understanding the nature of the militants' objectives, the region's social fabric, and the grounds for several processions. For instance, in May 1990, the people were angry with militants who were responsible for the murder of Mirwaiz Maulvi Farooq, but their anger was diverted against India when the security forces fired on the funeral procession; sixty mourners were killed and hundreds injured (Puri 2008: 79–80). Whenever the Indian security forces engaged in retaliatory assaults against the Kashmiri Muslims, Islamabad exploited such incidences to internationalize the Kashmir issue by giving *bandh* calls (that is, calling for general strikes) in Pakistan and the state of J&K (see HRW 1994, 1996).

Around mid-1997, however, India and Pakistan's relationship improved when the two newly elected prime ministers, I.K. Gujral of India and Nawaz Sharif of Pakistan, met at the SAARC Summit at Male and agreed to initiate foreign secretary–level talks. A month later, Prime Minister Gujral visited Kashmir and extended an unconditional offer of talks to militants (*Kashmir Times* 1997a). The Pakistan Army reacted to Gujral's offer by resorting to a large-scale shelling along the LoC in the Kargil, Siachen, Uri, Kupwara, and R.S. Pura sectors (Joshi 1997: 40; *Kashmir Times* 1997b, 1997c, 1997d, 1997e, 1997f). Later when the Bhartiya Janata Party (BJP)-led National Democratic Alliance (NDA) formed a coalition Indian government in March 1998, Pakistan reacted to the Hindu nationalist party's anti-Pakistan stand by testing the Ghauri ballistic missile, which embroiled both sides in heavy artillery fire along the LoC. In response, India conducted a series of nuclear tests on May 11 and 13, 1998, at Pokhran that triggered a nuclear crisis in the region. Under unprecedented domestic pressure, the Nawaz Sharif–led Pakistan Muslim League (PML) government responded in haste by detonating six nuclear devices in the Chagai Hills of Balochistan in the end of May (S. Ahmed 1999: 178; Perkovich 1999: 433). To deter any imminent Indian attack, as there were reports that New Delhi had already inducted Prithvi missiles into the Indian Army, Pakistan also readied its Ghauri missiles with nuclear warheads to target India's major cities, which further intensified tensions in the region (Yasmeen 1999: 46). Since both sides were prone to misinterpret each other's moves, a scenario that could have resulted in monumental destruction for the subcontinent, the gravity of tensions certainly signified that the region's nuclearization had brought a remarkable change in the Indo-Pakistani rivalry. On June 11, 1998, however, under intense international pressure, Pakistan announced a unilateral moratorium on nuclear tests and agreed to formalize a nuclear arrangement with India and other countries (ICB 2016). With this decision, the two sides calmed their belligerent postures and terminated their nuclear dispute; however, the Kashmir conflict continued to fester.

The Kargil War of 1999

Following the nuclear crisis of 1998, the political leaders of India and Pakistan were facing severe international criticism that pressured them to explore the possibilities of rapprochement (Swami 1998b). To de-escalate the bilateral tensions, Indian Prime Minister Atal Bihari Vajpayee made a symbolic bus journey to Pakistan in February 1999 for a two-day summit with his counterpart Nawaz Sharif. On February 21, the two leaders signed the Lahore Declaration to foster peace and stability in South Asia (GoI 1999a). It is interesting to note that when the Lahore peace process was under way, the Pakistan Army had set in motion a "dramatic anticlimax": a dangerous covert military operation atop the Kargil ridges on the Indian side of the LoC (Qadir 2002).

In early 1999, around one to two thousand Pakistani soldiers and Islamist insurgents crossed the LoC and occupied over 40 square miles of high-altitude Indian territory in the Kargil sector that spread from Chorbat La in the east to the Mushkoh Valley in the west. Armed with heavy machine guns, land mines, mortars, and portable surface-to-air missiles, the intruders had occupied dominating peaks which overlooked India's most significant road link between Srinagar and Leh, National Highway 1A—wherein a stretch from Dras to Kargil was particularly vulnerable to interdiction at a number of locations as it was fairly close to the occupied heights (Kanwal 1999: 145–46). Initially Pakistan denied the involvement of its regular armed forces in the intrusion; however, later it was proved that the invaders mainly consisted of its Northern Light Infantry (NLI) soldiers (Rikhye 2001) and that "the Islamic militants probably accounted for no more than 10 percent of the total force and were given only portering duties" (B. Jones 2002: 90). An unofficial account of a retired Pakistan Army brigadier, Shaukat Qadir, confirmed these claims. He maintained that the

> total number of troops occupying these posts never exceeded 1000 all ranks,
> [while] four times this number provided the logistical backup to undertake
> the operation. While the occupants were essentially soldiers of the Northern
> Light Infantry (NLI), there were some local *Mujahideen* assisting as labour to
> carry logistical requirements. (Qadir 2002: 26)

The Pakistani troops and irregulars together occupied around 130 Indian outposts before the intrusion was first detected by local shepherds in early May 1999. Caught unprepared by an intelligence failure, the 121st Infantry Brigade of the Indian Army dispatched four patrols between May 4 and May 10 to investigate the presence of intruders along the LoC in Kargil. Though the patrol parties succeeded in discovering that their posts, vacated for the winter, had been occupied by the Pakistani troops, this probing resulted in several casualties and injuries (Bakshi 2009: 44; Musharraf 2006: 90–91). In the meantime, the Indian Air Force (IAF) also carried out surveillance sorties along the Tololing ridge and confirmed that hundreds of "heavily armed infiltrators had occupied at least 35 well-fortified positions atop the ridges facing Dras, Kargil, Batalik, and the Mushko valley" (Vinayak 1999). The conflict intensified on May 9 when the intruders launched a rocket attack on the 121st Brigade's ammunition dump near the town of Kargil, causing a loss of roughly 50,000 artillery rounds (Lancaster 1999).

The Indian Army's top brass had severely underestimated the scope of intrusions.[1] Such misjudgments led to poor strategy, chaotic management, and glib pronouncements, altogether giving rise to a grave crisis[2] (Bedi 1999: 31; V. Malik 2006: 105–9; Tipnis 2006: 8–10). When the Indian surveillance drives fully assessed the scale and the scope of the intrusion, India's Cabinet Committee on Security (CCS) met under the chairmanship of Prime Minister Vajpayee on May 25 and ordered the armed forces to take any necessary action against the intruders' fortified positions within the Indian side of the LoC (Tipnis 2006: 12). The following day, India's air and armed forces launched a joint counter-offensive, code-named Operation Vijay (Victory). India's sustained air and ground bombardment was a combination of tactical maneuvering and balanced firepower, mainly involving Bofors guns, jet fighters, and helicopter gunships. Pakistan had not anticipated such a massive retaliation in a limited war scenario.[3]

On May 27–28, Pakistani troops responded with a counter-attack and shot down two Indian fighter jets (MiG-21 and MiG-27) and one helicopter (Mi-17). The intruders' demonstration of air-defense capability led the IAF to deploy the supersonic Mirage-2000, which successfully bombarded the occupied bunkers and shattered the opponent's command and control structures (Lambeth 2012: 16). Though the war was mostly fought in the Kargil region, the Indian Navy was keen to join the Indian Army and Air Force. To signal its readiness and resolve, the navy rescheduled its large-scale summer training exercises, Summerex, from the Bay of Bengal to the North Arabian Sea—closer to Pakistan's Makaran Coast. In mid-June, along with its Vishakhapatnam-based eastern naval fleet, it also diverted its lone amphibious brigade from the Andaman and Nicobar Islands to the west coast and launched Operation Talwar (Sword) to check any Pakistani naval misadventure in the event of escalation of the war (Gill 2009: 110).

By late June, the war tide had begun to turn toward India in the vital Tololing ridgeline, which overlooked the main Indian supply line to the Siachen. India's steady gains in the theater of war, without crossing the LoC, began to mount pressure on Islamabad to up its security ante by expanding on the nuclear scourge (Riedel 2002). Thereafter, both sides consolidated their strategic postures by advancing mechanized and artillery divisions along the border, raising fears of a wider horizontal escalation (Chengappa 1999). When Pakistan's Kargil adventurism, a campaign to internationalize the Kashmir dispute, began to turn counterproductive, Prime Minister Sharif requested US assistance to cease the hostilities. On July 4, he touched down

in Washington with "one principal objective . . . to seek international mediation over Kashmir as a quid-pro-quo for withdrawing forces from the LoC"
(Bidwai 1999). However, President Bill Clinton declined to support Islamabad's stand and backed New Delhi's position, that is, to initiate an unconditional ceasefire and withdrawal from the Kargil peaks (Riedel 2002). At the
end of a three-hour-long meeting, the joint Clinton-Sharif communiqué
stated that "concrete steps will be taken for the restoration of the Line of
Control in accordance with the Simla Agreement" ("Text of Joint Clinton-
Sharif Statement" 1999). It also maintained that "the bilateral dialogue
begun in Lahore in February provides the best forum for resolving all issues
dividing India and Pakistan, including Kashmir" ("Text of Joint Clinton-
Sharif Statement 1999"). In the meantime, the Indian forces recaptured the
strategic peak Tiger Hill and thereby secured control over the crucial Srinagar-
Leh Highway (CNN 1999).

On July 11, the directors general of military operations (DGMOs) of both
sides met to plug the gaps in the Washington communiqué, which was silent
on the time frame of the ceasefire and the withdrawal of the intruders.
Besides agreeing to end hostilities along the LoC, the DGMOs also framed
the pullout timetable for the Pakistani troops. A day later in a televised
address, Nawaz Sharif announced that Pakistan recognized the sanctity of
the LoC in Kashmir and would withdraw all troops to its side of the LoC
(Sharif 1999). After the intruders' complete withdrawal from the Kargil
region, India called off all offensive operations and the war came to an end
(GoI 1999b).

*The 2001–2 Compound Crisis: Terrorist Attack on the Indian Parliament and the
Initiation of Operation Parakaram*

Pakistan sought to revitalize its decade-old proxy war by adopting a new
strategy of *fidayeen* (suicide) attacks and expanding its scope to new theaters
outside Kashmir. The main objective of this strategy was "to maximize the
frightening psychological impact on the enemy by inflicting death and
destruction on their targets" (Sumantra Bose 2003: 142). Interestingly, when
terrorism was expanding globally, Pakistan unhesitatingly employed the ISI-
backed jihadi fighters to target India to achieve its political aims in Kashmir.
In fact, Pakistan stepped up militant attacks in Kashmir during the July 2001
Agra summit itself in which "eighty-six militants, soldiers, and civilians . . .
were killed" (Rashid 2008: 115). The Indian government alleged that the mil-

itant groups involved in these attacks were actively supported, funded, and trained by Pakistan. However, Islamabad downplayed New Delhi's claims and in turn contended that these attacks were part of Kashmiris' long-standing struggle for *azadi* (freedom) (*Hindu* 2001a).

Amid a new round of war of words, the terrorists attacked the J&K Legislative Assembly on October 1, 2001, killing around forty people (*BBC* 2001; *Tribune* 2001). New Delhi again blamed Pakistan for the attack and issued a strong statement that "India cannot accept such manifestations of hate and terror from across its borders" (*CNN* 2001). Prime Minister Vajpayee hinted to the Bush administration that if it could not convince Pakistan to control terrorist groups, India would be forced to take punitive action against the militant camps in Azad Kashmir (Sood & Sawhney 2003: 9). Since the United States desperately needed Pakistan to cooperate in its anti-terrorism operations against the Al Qaida in Afghanistan, the decision-makers in Islamabad apparently paid no heed to New Delhi's repeated warnings. As a result, India escalated the scale of firing along the LoC to check the terrorists' bid to infiltrate into the Indian side of Kashmir (*Hindu* 2001b). In the meantime, Hafiz Muhammad Saeed, the Lashkar-e-Taiba (LeT) chief, announced that his organization's jihadi suicide squads would conduct similar attacks against India with unflagging resolve (Swami 2009: 148–49). Probably the Indian inaction against the Pakistan-based terrorist outfits, even after the *fidayeen* attack on the J&K state assembly, had given encouragement to Hafiz Saeed to pose such a daring challenge to India.

Despite Saeed's forewarning, the Indian security forces failed to avert a chain of suicide attacks that eventually resulted in a fateful assault on the Indian Parliament on December 13, 2001, triggering a severe military dispute between the two states (J. Singh 2006: 63–67). New Delhi charged the ISI-backed terrorist organizations, the LeT and the Jaish-e-Mohammad (JeM), for the attack and accused Islamabad of sponsoring a sustained terrorist campaign against India (*Hindu* 2001c, 2001d, 2001h). Islamabad refused to take responsibility for the attack as it contended that the terrorists involved in the attack were neither Pakistani nationals nor raised, nurtured, assisted, and trained by "Pakistan's military and intelligence services" (Nayak & Krepon 2011: 146). Additionally, it rejected New Delhi's demand to take action against the terrorist organizations in light of inadequate proof and evoked the possibility of "stage-managed" and/or "designed operation" to divert attention from "internal problems" and defame the "freedom struggle" in Kashmir (*Hindu* 2001e, 2001f).

A day after the terrorists' flagrant assault on the seat and symbol of India's democracy, Prime Minister Vajpayee publicly declared that India had accepted Pakistan's challenge and it was ready for a decisive battle (*Hindu* 2001g). On December 15, India galvanized its armed forces with offensive and defensive formations on its western border—much like the United States did after the 9/11 attacks—under the code name Operation Parakaram to pressure Pakistan to dismantle its jihadi infrastructure. According to India's former COAS, General V.P. Malik, Operation Parakaram was "the largest deployment of the forces on the borders since the 1971 Indo-Pak[istani] war" and was launched without a requisite "warning phase"[4] (V. Malik 2006: 374). Threatened with the possibility of war, Pakistan also escalated troop mobilization along the LoC and the international border (*Hindu* 2001i).

By December 25, the bilateral situation turned grim when India put its air force on alert and Pakistan moved its Hatf-I and Hatf-II missiles into eastern Punjab (*Hindu* 2001j). In response to the redeployment of Hatf missiles, India moved its Prithvi missiles to northern Punjab (Moles 2012). As the possibility of a horrific nuclear exchange increased, the international community exerted pressure on President Pervez Musharraf to take concrete action against the terrorist organizations operating from Pakistan against India (*Hindu* 2001g, 2001h, 2001k). The Musharraf regime could no longer underestimate the US pressure as well as ignore the growing nuclear threat; it announced the arrest of Hafiz Muhammad Saeed and the founder of JeM, Maulana Masood Azhar, on the pretext of taking action against their inflammatory and extremist rhetoric (*Hindu* 2002a, 2002b).

On January 11, 2002, a day before Musharraf's televised national address, the Indian Army chief, General S. Padmanabhan, announced that India's nuclear weapons were ready and its armed forces were only awaiting the final nod from the political leadership to punish the enemy (*Hindu* 2002c; Nayak & Krepon 2011: 147). Facing both India's rapid military buildup and increasing external pressure, President Musharraf became more responsive to Indian demands. In his televised speech on January 12, he declared that his government's highest priority was eradication of terrorism and that it would not allow any "organization . . . to perpetuate terror behind the garb of the Kashmir cause" (*New York Times* 2002). While announcing a ban on the terrorist outfits, he promised that the government of Pakistan would duly stem the flow of militants into India by cracking down on terrorist organizations and dismantling their infrastructures. Though New Delhi approved Musharraf's promise for the time being, it remained skeptical for weeks as it wanted "to look for progress in terms of the rate of terrorist attacks and infil-tration" (Bajpai 2009a: 166). The televised assurance had shown consider-able results by the end of February, and tensions visibly eased thereafter. Three major factors helped de-escalate tensions: (1) extensive international diplomatic efforts, as the Indo-Pakistani military standoff increasingly made the US war on terror in Afghanistan vulnerable; (2) the assembly elections in Punjab and Uttar Pradesh; and (3) the eruption of communal riots in Godhra, which resulted in the diversion of troops from the border to assist the civil-ian government to maintain law and order in Gujarat (V. Malik 2006: 376–77).

When the dispute had almost subsided, another terrorist attack occurred in J&K. On May 14, 2002, Pakistan-based terrorists targeted a civilian bus and the Indian Army base in Kaluchak near Jammu, killing around thirty-four civilians including the gruesome killing of children and women (*Hindu* 2002d). This attack enraged public sentiment across India, thereby increas-ing the possibility of India's retaliatory actions against Pakistan. On May 17, the Indian Cabinet Committee on Security (CCS) met under Vajpayee's chairmanship and considered all options ranging from a diplomatic path, to the use of force, such as launching military strikes on the militant camps in Azad Kashmir, to the "breaking of relations with Pakistan and the abroga-tion of the Indus Rivers Treaty" (Bajpai 2009a: 167). Finally, the CCS con-cluded that diplomatic options would be explored before resorting to a retal-iatory military response, leading New Delhi to announce the expulsion of Pakistan's High Commissioner Ashraf Jehangir Qazi (Bajpai 2009a: 167; *Hindu* 2002e). Thereafter, a war of words ensued on both sides and culmi-nated in the re-mobilization of troops along the LoC (S. Shukla 2002). How-ever, President Musharraf convened a cabinet meeting and informed the group that "the international community was firmly on India's side and that the distinction that Pakistan had made between freedom fighters and terror-ists was not finding acceptance" (Bajpai 2009a: 168).[5] In such a scenario, he emphasized, "the only way to avoid war with India was to stop terrorists from going into Kashmir" (Bajpai 2009a: 167–68). To defuse the crisis, Islam-abad then decided to shut down terrorist camps and appealed to New Delhi for talks (Zaidi 2002). India, however, refused to negotiate with Pakistan until the Musharraf regime carried out concrete steps against the terrorist organizations.

In a bid to pressure Pakistan, India moved its warships from the east coast to the west, but Islamabad responded by test-firing several nuclear-capable missiles (*CNN* 2002; *Economic Times* 2002). The fast-escalating tensions once again forced the US administration to urge President Musharraf to prevent militants' infiltration into Kashmir and, on the other hand, assured New Delhi about substantial actions against the Pakistan-based terrorist outfits (Zaidi & Weir 2002). Musharraf once again made a nationwide address on May 28 and assured India that Pakistan would not allow terrorists to infiltrate into Kashmir (*Hindu* 2002f). India responded by lifting "the overflight ban on Pakistan and ordered its naval flotilla to return to Mumbai" (Bajpai 2009a: 169). Though the US pressure succeeded in reducing tensions, India did not pull back its troops from the forward areas until the completion of the J&K state assembly election in October.

Finally, on October 17, both sides announced a mutual demobilization of troops, which set the course of dispute termination (*Hindu* 2002g, 2002h). Though Washington brokered de-escalation of the twin crises, the terrorist attacks from Pakistani soil continued throughout 2002–3 and decelerated only when the Vajpayee government proposed a dozen significant non-military confidence-building measures (CBMs) in October 2003 that included cross-LoC road travel (*BBC* 2002; *Hindu* 2003a, 2003b, 2003c, 2003d). In response, Pakistan offered a unilateral ceasefire on November 23 and India reciprocated by implementing the ceasefire along the LoC (*Hindu* 2003e).

Terrorist Strikes across India and the 2008 Mumbai Attacks

After the implementation of the ceasefire agreement in November 2003, followed by the peace process, the scale of infiltration and militant violence effectively declined in Kashmir. Despite such a favorable situation on the ground, the leadership on both sides failed to resolve their differences over Kashmir in a timely manner. In fact, Islamabad was increasingly frustrated that New Delhi was not willing to take the Kashmir issue to any logical conclusion. Thereafter, it seems, Islamabad adopted a "new terror strategy" to pressure New Delhi. On the one hand, it continued its gesture of goodwill and flexibility and, on the other, it frequently relied on the jihadi groups—particularly the banned LeT and its various splinters, allies, and ideological affiliates—to launch terror strikes in the Indian heartland and major cities. Steve Coll, a senior *New Yorker* writer, now the dean of the Graduate School of Journalism at Columbia University, has aptly noted a significant shift in Pakistan's terror strategy in relation to India's fast-changing polity and social landscape:

Pakistani strategy in this clandestine war has recently emphasized attempts to "indigenize" the Islamist militants operating in India. To some extent this has involved dialing back direct military, tactical supervision of Kashmiri fighters; instead, the fighters are equipped and trained to operate on their own, and even to choose their own targets. This strategy has also involved attempts to recruit from India's large non-Kashmiri Muslim population, a small minority of which has been radicalized by the country's longstanding religious conflict between Muslims and a Hindu majority that has produced its own fringe, radical Hindu vigilantes. (Coll 2008)

Against this backdrop, India faced over two dozen terrorist attacks between 2005 and 2007, including several Delhi markets in October 2005, the Hindu holy city of Varanasi in March 2006, a series of carefully orchestrated horrific blasts in Mumbai in July 2006, and the Samjhauta Express bombing in February 2007 (*BBC* 2006; *Hindustan Times* 2006; Raju 2011; *Tribune* 2006). The year 2008 proved a watershed in Indo-Pakistani relations, as India was rocked by terrorist bombings masterminded by the Pakistan-based jihadi groups. A series of nine bomb blasts took place in Jaipur in May 2008, and another nine bombs exploded in Bangalore and over twenty in Ahmadabad on July 25 and 26, 2008, respectively. In September 2008, Delhi was again attacked twice. On November 26 of the same year, Pakistan-based terrorists attacked Mumbai causing immense casualties: 164 people lost life and over 300 were wounded in ten locations. The terrorists' daring sea assault from Karachi on India's financial capital seized the city for almost three days and left the country bruised and nearly broken (Rabasa et al. 2009: 1–6; Riedel 2010: 156–57). India claimed that these attacks were planned and executed by the LeT with the support of Pakistan's official agencies, mainly the ISI (Kronstadt 2008: 5; Varadarajan 2009). Nonetheless, New Delhi's reaction was relatively balanced in the aftermath of the Mumbai attacks, as no panic buttons were pressed to escalate the conflict.

Though India did not amass troops along the western border, External Affairs Minister Pranab Mukherjee indicated that India might initiate military strikes against terror camps in Pakistan to protect its territorial integrity (*CNN* 2008; *Hindu* 2009). However, in order to avert any possibility of an Indian attack, Pakistan moved its troops to the international border and put its air force on high alert. Until mid-December 2008, the new PPP-led civilian government was not willing to accept that there had been any Pakistani involvement in the attack and, therefore, was reluctant to ban the LeT and its charitable foundation Jamaat ul-Dawa (JuD) (*BBC* 2008). However, the situation changed when the UN Security Council (UNSC) listed the JuD (and its four key leaders) as a Pakistan-based terrorist group in December 2008; Islamabad thereafter arrested the perpetrators of attacks—notably the LeT chief Hafeez Saeed and the LeT's chief military commander Zaki-ur-Rahman Lakhvi (Roggio 2008). But Hafeez Saeed's subsequent release in July 2009 led to the suspension of the track-II process and the composite dialogue at the bilateral level (Lakhvi was also released on bail in December 2014). With this, all the progress to resolve the Kashmir issue in the years succeeding the 2003 ceasefire was reversed.

Cross-Border Tensions and High-Magnitude Terrorist Attacks:
Pathankot, Uri, and Pulwama

After Nawaz Sharif's return to power in May 2013, the scale and frequency of ceasefire violations along the LoC and the international border in J&K (which Pakistan maintains is the working boundary)[6] and terrorist attacks on Indian armed bases have witnessed a sharp rise. Between 2013 and 2018, the India-Pakistan dyad encountered over 200 militant attacks/encounters, 300 civil-military casualties, and over 5,500 ceasefire violations—the figure is even more dramatic for 2018, with 2,936 ceasefire violations from the Pakistani side alone—that led thousands of civilian to vacate the areas adjoining the LoC and the international border (see *BBC* 2015; *Hindu BusinessLine* 2019; *Hindu* 2018; *Hindustan Times* 2013; *Indian Express* 2013a, 2019a; *NDTV* 2013; SATP 2018).

Tensions between India and Pakistan began to increase once the Narendra Modi–led NDA government assumed power in New Delhi in May 2014. After a brief thaw following the oath ceremony of Narendra Modi, the two sides began to face a downturn as the new Indian government called off foreign secretary–level talks in August 2014 to register its protest against the Pakistan High Commissioner Abdul Basit's meeting with the Kashmiri separatists (*Indian Express* 2014a). Thereafter, a series of ceasefire violations and exchange of fire along the LoC locked India and Pakistan into a retaliatory cycle that spiraled into heightened attacks in October 2014, triggering a serious militarized dispute for both sides (ICB 2016; *Kashmir Times* 2014a, 2014b). As the crisis escalated and resulted in heavy shelling along the LoC, India resorted to a major response by retaliating with heavy mortar fire. Though hostilities subsided without any bilateral resolution or international mediation sometime in the early part of November 2014, the shelling and firing continued across the LoC and the international border into 2015. Later, the two sides held additional meetings and renewed their commitment to restore peace along the border by entering into a ceasefire agreement in September 2015 (ICB 2016; SATP 2018).

Unfortunately, this understanding did not last long, as the Pakistan-based terrorist outfits attacked the Pathankot airbase, which is part of the Western Air Command of the Indian Air Force, in January 2016 followed by another major attack on the Uri army brigade headquarters in September of the same year (*BBC* 2016a; *Indian Express* 2016a; *Reuters* 2016). Both incidents brought India and Pakistan at loggerheads, triggering high-magnitude escalatory spirals of dueling that completely debilitated Narendra Modi's unscheduled goodwill meeting with his counterpart Nawaz Sharif at Lahore on Christmas Day 2015. The Pathankot attack was conducted by a heavily armed *fidayeen* group—terrorists were carrying 52 mm mortars, grenade launchers, AK rifles, and a GPS device—that resulted in the death of three security personnel and six attackers during the three-day seizure of the air base. The primary objective of this *fidayeen* mission was to damage the "high-value assets" installed and parked at the airbase located near the international border (*Reuters* 2016). Though the Indian security forces neutralized all the intruders before they could have posed any serious damage to the airbase, this attack exposed several procedural lapses in the security of the Indian airbase that had aided the intruders to breach it and conduct a high-magnitude attack.

New Delhi blamed the Pakistan-based terrorist outfits for the Pathankot and the Uri attacks by stressing the ISI's concealed role to exploit the Kashmir unrest through proxies—particularly after the death of a twenty-two-year old local militant, Burhan Wani, in July 2016 that sparked mass protests and prolonged violence in the Valley (*BBC* 2016b; *Indian Express* 2016f; *NDTV* 2016a). Since India incurred high causalities in the Uri attack, the key decision-makers in New Delhi then decided to beef up security in Kashmir and areas along the LoC after a high-profile ministerial meeting with the country's top security brass (*Indian Express* 2016e). India's "full alert" triggered a crisis for Pakistan, as it had to take precautionary steps to match the opponent's move (*Daily Excelsior* 2016; *Express Tribune* 2016b, 2016c). The high alert on the LoC and sharp diplomatic maneuvering on both sides caused the postponement of the 19th SAARC summit scheduled to be held in Islamabad in November 2016. After India canceled its participation, Afghanistan, Bangladesh, and Bhutan also withdrew from the summit in a show of solidarity with New Delhi (*Indian Express* 2016g; *NDTV* 2016b).

Meanwhile, against the backdrop of political-diplomatic maneuvering, the Indian Army strategized and responded to terrorist attacks by conducting retaliatory raids, popularly known as "surgical strikes," on "several" militant "launch-pads" along the LoC in Azad Kashmir (*BBC* 2016c; *Express Tribune* 2016b). Though the Indian response was retaliatory in nature, the Indian director general of military operations (DGMO), Lieutenant General Ranbir Singh, justified it by presenting it as a pre-emptive strike against "terrorist teams" preparing to "carry out infiltration and conduct terrorist strikes inside Jammu and Kashmir and in various metros in other states" (*BBC* 2016c). Pakistan downplayed India's claims of "surgical strikes" on its side of the LoC—however, media reports establish that Indian soldiers did cross the LoC and attacked Pakistan's bunkers at several locations, but they could not confirm the Indian DGMO's claim about strikes on militant hideouts (*Al Jazeera* 2016; *BBC* 2016d). After a couple of months of sharp diplomatic exchanges and political rhetoric on both sides, the dispute faded sometime in late 2016, but it ensured a prolonged deadlock over the possibility of peace negotiations between the two states.

The political-military relations remain tense throughout 2017–18, and the two states again engaged in a major and dangerous military confrontation in early 2019 when a young Kashmiri terrorist affiliated with the JeM carried out a deadly suicide attack on February 14 by ramming an explosives-packed car into an Indian paramilitary convoy in Pulwama, killing forty security personnel on the spot (*BBC* 2019). The Modi government blamed Pakistan for the suicide attack and promised "a befitting reply"; Pakistan, however, denied any involvement in the bombing by labeling the Indian allegations a "knee-jerk reaction" (*Dawn* 2019; *Guardian* 2019). On February 26, the conflict heightened when India made an unprecedented decision to carry out retaliatory airstrikes inside Pakistan by hitting the terrorist training camp in Balakot in the Khyber Pakhtoonkhwa province (*NDTV* 2019). In response, a day later, Pakistani fighter planes also crossed the LoC and dropped bombs outside the "target military installations" in Rajouri district—India, however, claimed that it "successfully foiled" the opponent's attempt to "target military installations" (*India Today* 2019; *Times of India* 2019b). The conflict was almost escalated to the nuclear level, particularly when the Pakistani retaliatory airstrikes resulted in a serious dogfight of warplanes over the LoC area and an Indian MiG-21 Bison fighter jet was shot

down and its pilot, Wing Commander Abhinandan Varthaman, was taken
into custody—later Pakistan released him on March 1 (*India Today* 2019;
Nation 2019a). Throughout the crisis, amid a major military standoff and
escalation of tensions across the Kashmir frontier, India and Pakistan were
almost on a knife edge awash with rumors of large-scale escalation of hostilities. Finally, the dispute subsided on March 22 when the prime ministers of
the two states agreed to engage in peace negotiations to terminate hostilities
and fight against terrorism.

In spite of the apex leadership's vow to normalize bilateral relations,
another dispute erupted between India and Pakistan on August 5, 2019,
when the Modi government took a controversial, but widely popular, decision to revoke J&K's special status and bifurcated the state into two separate
union territories—J&K and Ladakh (*Indian Express* 2019b). This decision
heightened the armed confrontations and the exchange of fire along the
LoC. Furthermore, coupled with an unprecedented clampdown on communication and restrictions on movement, New Delhi had simultaneously
imposed a security lockdown in J&K and arrested thousands of youth and
detained key political leaders that included three former chief ministers of
the state—however, between March and October 2020, it freed the mainstream political leaders from protective detention. The issue of the abrogation of Article 370 persists as this book goes to press (in early 2022), as the
Modi government has not reversed its decision. In fact, New Delhi moved
ahead with the implementation of the Jammu and Kashmir Reorganisation
Bill 2019 and introduced a new domicile rule in March-April 2020, which
added another layer of complication to J&K's political situation and strained
India-Pakistan relations amid the pandemic outbreak of the novel coronavi-
rus (COVID-19) and strict lockdown. Throughout the COVID-19 pandemic
(as of early 2022), India and Pakistan remained at loggerheads over the political status of Kashmir—however, peace returned to the LoC as the two sides
agreed to respect the 2003 cease fire by adhering to it from midnight of February 25, 2021—without any major breakthrough to initiate intrastate and
interstate dialogues to resolve the political deadlock.

THE ROLE OF GREAT POWERS, ALLIANCES, AND ARMS BUILDUP

Soon after the end of the Cold War, the subcontinental rivalry underwent a
radical transformation. Mainly three broad issues—the separatist insurgency

in Kashmir, nuclear non-proliferation, and the regional balance of power—and their correlation defined the United States' and China's policies toward the India-Pakistan dyad. In the pre-1998 phase, the United States had adopted a "dual containment" policy with respect to India and Pakistan, whereas China systematically assisted Pakistan to act as a regional balancer against India. In the post-1998 phase, particularly after the Kargil War and the 9/11 terrorist attacks, the United States again reframed its policy and forged strategic ties with India to counterbalance China and restrain Pakistan from sponsoring and hosting terrorist groups. To strike a balance in South Asia, Beijing also committed significant resources to build Pakistan's conventional and nuclear capabilities and, simultaneously, deployed its "string of pearls" strategy to encircle India so that it could not step out of the region and challenge China's primacy in Asia and beyond.

Even after the Soviet Union's disintegration, the United States continued to regard Pakistan as a crucial non-NATO ally for providing strategic support to accomplish its most important foreign policy objective of the time, that is, defeating the Soviet Union in Afghanistan. On the other hand, as Stephen Cohen notes, "India was widely regarded as pro-Soviet, anti-American, and having betrayed its own lofty Nehruvian-Gandhian standards on nuclear issues" (1999: 195). With the sole superpower on its side and India's fragile international standing, particularly in the absence of the Soviet Union, the leadership in Islamabad was confident of exploring the possibilities of Kashmir's secession from India to form a "greater Pakistan" (Siddiqa 2015). To turn the regional tide in its favor, Pakistan replicated the successful Afghanistan model—under which the CIA-ISI axis had used Islamic mujahideen against the Soviets to achieve its political and strategic objectives—in Kashmir. The ISI had already developed a large network of jihadi organizations with the US-Saudi money that flowed into Pakistan for the Afghanistan War; therefore without much trouble it waged a cost-effective proxy war against India that effectively bogged down the Indian Army in Kashmir (Hoodbhoy 2015; Waseem 2015).

Pakistan's strategy, however, backfired when it used a nuclear threat against India during the Kashmir crisis of 1990. The Gates mission, which played a crucial role in diffusing the crisis, as discussed earlier, had further toned up the White House's understanding with regard to the dangers associated with the regional nuclear saber rattling (see Hersh 1990; Meyer 1993). Following this crisis, the Bush administration backed off from its obligation to certify to Congress that Pakistan did not possess an explosive device and thereafter tightened the nuclear noose around both regional adversaries with a motive of, as Cohen puts, "capping, freezing, and rolling back" their nuclear programs (1999: 199). To achieve this objective, the White House dramatically tilted the balance of America's regional policy toward the single issue of nuclear non-proliferation (Cohen 1999: 199).

In the meantime, the Kashmir conflict began to act like a double-edged sword for India. On the one hand, Pakistan's proxy war successfully internationalized the Kashmir issue, and on the other hand, the US-led nuclear restraint regime started characterizing Kashmir as a potential threat to the existing nuclear order. While testifying before a congressional committee on July 28, 1993, CIA director R. James Woolsey warned that the continuing tension in South Asia "poses perhaps the most probable prospects for future use of weapons of mass destruction, including nuclear weapons" (quoted in Meyer 1993: F3). It is important to note that the great powers' non-proliferation agenda of the time also required political instability in Kashmir to justify their restraint efforts and simultaneously squeeze both India's and Pakistan's nuclear aspirations. In other words, with the pretext of maintaining balance in the region, the United States continued its military and diplomatic support to Pakistan to keep the Kashmir pot boiling at the right temperature (Kanwal 2016; Siddiqa 2015). Another objective of bolstering Pakistan militarily was to contain Pakistan's nuclear program by giving its policy makers a sense of security vis-à-vis India (Durrani 2015; Ziauddin 2015). The resumption of sales to Pakistan of F-16s, which were capable of delivering nuclear weapons, was such a move (Z. Hussain 1998: 41–43). Given the fact that insurgent violence in Kashmir was at its peak, New Delhi reasoned that in the absence of functional missile systems on both sides, these aircraft could be used by Pakistan as a primary delivery mechanism against India in the event of crisis or war (Kux 2001: 327, 331). Since New Delhi's argument was against the United States' "dual containment" policy, it failed to find any takers in Washington.

For the permanent members of the UNSC, strengthening the international arms control and nuclear restraint regime was a reasonable enough pretext to prevent the South Asian adversaries from going overtly nuclear; hence the Clinton administration intensified its non-proliferation efforts and successfully lobbied for indefinite extension of the Non-Proliferation Treaty (NPT) (F.H. Khan 2013: 262–65; Talbott 2004: 34–36). However, before it could have drawn both India and Pakistan into the ambit of the NPT and a global Comprehensive Test Ban Treaty (CTBT), its non-proliferation drive received a severe jolt on the home turf when the Republican-majority Congress refused to ratify the CTBT in 1996. Nonetheless, the Clinton administration continued its non-proliferation efforts by employing a stick-and-carrot policy to make the South Asian nuclear tests virtually impossible (Masood 2015; Ziauddin 2015).[7]

Even after the fall of the Soviet Union, China's strategic relationship with Pakistan did not change, on account of its geo-strategic location, size, and enmity with India—for these reasons, Beijing was particularly keen to slowly bring Pakistan out of the US camp and counterbalance India's regional dominance. So it assisted Pakistan's nuclear program by providing important nuclear weapon parts and transferring the M-11 missile technology and components via North Korea—all in violation of the Missile Technology Control Regime (MTCR) (Corera 2006: 88–90; Mann 1999: 250–52; Sawhney 2000: 35). According to Ashraf Jehangir Qazi (2015), Pakistan's former ambassador to India and the United States, Washington viewed the tacit Sino-Pakistani missile cooperation as a strategic misstep which could have provoked India to test nuclear weapons; perhaps that is why it "rearranged its policy priorities in South Asia in the second half of the 1990s."[8] Another reason for this policy shift was the rising tide of terrorism which also began to affect US assets and interests across the globe—for instance, the bombing of the World Trade Center in 1993, attacks on the American embassies in Kenya and Tanzania in 1998, and an attempt to sink the American destroyer USS *Cole* in 2000 (Rashid 2008: 16–18; Riedel 2010: 3–6, 60). Furthermore, US policy makers were not ready to disregard politically vibrant India because it not only liberalized and integrated its messy socialist economy with the international market, but was also an impressive market with significant military might to offset China's influence in the Asian region.

However, the US non-proliferation drive reached a dead end when India and Pakistan conducted a series of nuclear tests in May 1998. Within a year, Pakistan mounted a large-scale intrusion in the Kargil sector which "provided the impetus for dramatic changes that got the stalemated nonproliferation dialogue off dead centre" (Gould 2010: 96). After the Kargil War, a series of dramatic events came to the fore—the fall and the exile of Prime Minister Nawaz Sharif, the military coup by General Pervez Musharraf and the resurgence of military dictatorship, the ISI-Taliban's joint role in the IC-814 hijacking, and a sharp rise in *fidayeen* attacks across India—that compelled Washington "to tailor US policy to the ugly reality of a failing Pakistani state and a contrasting politically viable Indian state" (Gould 2010: 97).

In the wake of these events, the United States tilted its South Asia policy toward India, particularly over the issues of regional balancing, the Kashmir insurgency, and the nuclear relationship. Several rounds of high-profile strategic dialogue between Strobe Talbott, the former US undersecretary of state, and Jaswant Singh, India's former finance and foreign minister, followed to rework the bilateral relationship between the two democracies. This engagement brought a paramount shift in the Indo-US equations that resulted in President Clinton's five-day visit to India and a symbolic five-hour stopover in Pakistan to underline the burgeoning US-India relationship and increasing differences between Washington and Islamabad (Talbott 2004: 196–205). By reversing its priorities, the White House had set forth a new course of America's South Asia policy which was, to a great extent, tilted toward India's regional and extra-regional power position and aspirations.

However, this extraordinary tilt did not last long, on account of the fateful terrorist attacks on US soil in September 2001. While strategizing to wage a global war against terrorism, US policy makers realized they could not ignore Pakistan's geo-strategic importance to contain Al Qaida's and the Taliban's terrorist networks in Afghanistan. Hence, the United States changed its post-Kargil disengagement from Pakistan and adopted an ambiguous two-pronged policy of dual engagement with India and Pakistan to take the global war on terrorism to a logical conclusion while simultaneously forging a long-term strategic collaboration with India, and to some extent with Pakistan, against China—which may be termed a "dual containment" policy. By employing this strategy, the United States hoped to reap significant military and economic payoffs not only from the management of the India-Pakistan conflict[9] but also from the growing Sino-Indian competition in the Asian region, which could further increase the significance of America's strategic ties with India. It was important because the United States faces a prospect of an emerging power transition in the coming decades vis-à-vis China. Perhaps that is why it sought to reconfigure its pre-1998 dual containment policy vis-à-vis India and Pakistan by delinking India from it and subsequently incorporating it in its larger scheme of regional and extra-regional balancing (Dominguez 2015).

In the post-9/11 period, therefore, both India and the United States consolidated their endeavors to limit Pakistan and China through a long-term strategic policy. Despite loosely following this framework, the two democracies prioritize and pursue their different interests. For instance, Washington's emphasis (which continued as of mid-2021) is more on China's containment and seeking a working engagement with Pakistan to remain strong in the Af-Pak region to keep the terrorist networks in check. On the other hand, New Delhi's foremost priority is revisionist Pakistan, which is steadily expanding its nuclear capabilities to exert pressure on India, rather than initiating an undesirable confrontation with China, with whom it has established strong economic ties over the last two decades—bilateral trade rose to a record high of $95.54 billion in 2018–19 (World Bank 2019). Despite such differences in their policy priorities and separate economic relations with China, India and the United States have much in common, so they are keen to work together to check the Sino-Pakistani strategic alliance.

From the Sino-Pakistani perspective, the Indo-US civil nuclear deal and the ever-increasing strategic partnership between the two democracies is not only strengthening India's position in the subcontinent but also in the Indo-Pacific region. In the long term, this will help India to institute its hegemony in South Asia and eventually pull out of the regional security complex to become an influential Asian or Indo-Pacific power.[10] A case in point is the ten-year defense pact between India and the United States, called the 2015 Framework for the India-US Defense Relationship, signed in June 2015, under which the two sides have reviewed their existing and emerging regional security challenges and "reaffirmed their commitment to expand and deepen the bilateral defence relationship" (GoI 2015). Prior to this, in the May 2015 meeting in Singapore, US Defense Secretary Ashton Carter had confirmed that this framework "will open up [the Indo-US] relationship on everything, from maritime security to aircraft carrier and jet engine technology cooperation" (quoted in Dominguez 2015). With regard to this development, Ijaz Khan (2015), professor of South Asian Security and International Relations at Peshawar University, lucidly presents Pakistan's concern: "[T]he Indo-US strategic partnership implies rejection of strategic balance in South Asia by widening [the] capability gap between India and Pakistan," thereby "reducing [Pakistan's] status to a meager regional power."

For China, India remains a competitor in the Asian region. India's growing economic strength and hard power capabilities with conventional and nuclear deterrence not only upset the existing regional and extra-regional balance but also undercut China's influence in Asia and beyond. That is why China is keen to encourage security competition within and around South Asia to check India's growing power. Scholars have pointed to China's long-standing strategy, termed the string of pearls, to counter India by investing in key port facilities or strategic locations that surround India—for instance, the Hambantota and Colombo ports in Sri Lanka, the Coco Islands and the Kyaukpyu port in Myanmar, the Gwadar deep-sea port in Pakistan, Marao Atoll in the Maldives, Bangladesh's Payra deep-sea port (after the Chittagong port did not materialize), and drawing Nepal into its larger framework of the Trans-Himalayan Multi-Dimensional Connectivity Network (see Krupakar 2017: 210; Mamun 2016; C. Mohan 2012: 124–30; S. Mohan & Abraham 2020: 84; Pehrson 2006). Apart from this, in a bid to undercut India's growing role in the region and presence in Afghanistan and Central Asia, China has also signed a $62 billion dual-purpose agreement with Pakistan for developing a mega strategic-economic corridor between Pakistan's southern Gwadar port on the Arabian Sea and China's western Xinjiang region (*CPEC Portal* 2018; *Straits Times* 2015).

Overall, the United States' and China's competitive policies are not only making South Asia more insecure but also indirectly helping Pakistan to maintain the regional rivalry despite a stark power asymmetry vis-à-vis India. For instance, China's policy of cultivating economic ties with India while simultaneously building Pakistan's and other South Asian states' economic and military capabilities, which are much more open to external influence, keep India under strategic pressure (S. Mohan & Abraham 2020: 84–85). Likewise the United States' ambiguous dual engagement of India and Pakistan exacerbates their conflictual relationship. On the one hand, the United States has signed a civil nuclear deal and defense-cum-technology-sharing pacts with India to develop a long-term strategic partnership. On the other hand, it provided Pakistan over $34.1 billion of economic and military aid in a recent 16-year period (2002–2018)—which significantly beefed up Pakistan's air and naval capabilities against India—and kept its options open for signing a civil nuclear deal in the future (see Congressional Research Service 2019; *Indian Express* 2015b). From the regional standpoint, it is safe to say that the structural factors' constant stress on the Indo-Pakistani rivalry is exerting pressure on the peripheral temporal factors and vice versa, thereby influencing the external powers' policies.

In sum, in the wake of the Kargil War and the 9/11 terrorist attacks, despite Pakistan's frontline role to contain the terrorist networks in Afghanistan, the great powers have started tilting toward India and its position against Pakistan-sponsored terrorism. Since 2001, India has used this opportunity and beefed up its global standing by developing closer ties with the West and, at the same time, consolidated its economic and military capabilities to enhance its regional and international influence. Yet despite such a favorable shift, the ground situation at the dyadic level has not witnessed a significant change. The India-Pakistan rivalry is still far from experiencing a stable de-escalation or transformation because Pakistan is not willing to change its revisionist policy nor has it exhausted its resources and support from key states—mainly from China and the key Muslim states—to concede on terms that demand significant concessions on Kashmir. Under the circumstances, especially in the backdrop of China's Belt and Road Initiative (BRI) and the emerging Quadrilateral Security Dialogue (QSD or the Quad) in the Indo-Pacific that loosely aligns Australia, India, Japan, and the United States, it is highly unlikely that the key players in the international system would completely dismiss Pakistan's geo-strategic relevance and extend New Delhi overwhelming support to coerce Islamabad at will. In other words, the great powers' increasing involvement in the Indo-Pacific and India's and Pakistan's important, but clashing, roles in the reshaping regional security architecture indicate that their power angularities have high likelihood to gravitate them toward intense competition rather than cooperation.

RIVALRY LINKAGE: THE INDIA-PAKISTAN RIVALRY OVER AFGHANISTAN

With the Soviets' final and complete withdrawal from Afghanistan by early 1989, in the words of Ayesha Siddiqa (2012), "the US achieved its goals [and] stopped funding Islamic jihadis, but the ISI did not close its shop there." Americans' hasty exit with the end of the Cold War created a power vacuum in the regional hotspot which, coupled with fragile socio-political conditions inside Afghanistan, intensified India and Pakistan's power competition in the neighborhood. India backed the Ahmad Shah Massoud-led Northern Alliance to neutralize the Pakistan-sponsored Taliban's stronghold in Afghanistan. On the other side, the Pakistan Army envisioned the Taliban regime as a close ally which would help it to use Afghanistan as a sanctuary to groom anti-India Islamic terrorists and fight its proxy war in Kashmir (Coll 2004; Hoodbhoy 2015; Z. Hussain 2007; Rashid 2008: 110–11).

A second logic that motivated Pakistan to support the Taliban was grounded in the concept of "strategic depth." Many scholars maintain that during the tenure of General Zia-ul-Haq the Pakistan military planners had projected the strategic-depth doctrine to forestall any future Indian blitzkrieg design against Pakistan with a retreat option. According to this doctrine, if India were to invade Pakistan in a future war and establish control over the Pakistani territory—as it did in East Pakistan in 1971—the Pakistani establishment, along with its military troops and weapon systems, would retreat to Afghanistan and challenge India from there (Rashid 2000: 186–87; Rubin & Siddique 2006: 6). In close agreement with this narrative, retired Lieutenant General Asad Durrani, former chief of the ISI, puts the strategic-depth doctrine in broader perspective by locating its origin even prior to Zia-ul-Haq's period:

> Strategic depth is not only a concept, but an undeniable reality . . . and life-line of Pakistan. You can call it anything, "strategic depth," "flank protec-tion," or "forward depth." For us, it is like the Monroe Doctrine or Indira Doc-trine.[11] It has always provided us depth. In fact, during the 1965 and 1971 wars, Kabul had sent us a message: "Since you have a problem on the eastern borders, please move all your forces from the western. We [Kabul] will ensure that the (Af-Pak) border remains quiet." [In other words, this] means opera-tionalize the strategic depth doctrine. . . . [It] is a very valid and accepted con-cept in [international affairs]. Even *Startfor* says that Ukraine creates a forward depth for Russia. Similarly, geographically contiguous Afghanistan—as a "strategic depth"—is very natural [for Pakistan's endurance] . . . and we have an inbuilt role in the country as we share a long border and population over-lap. That is why we have [a] problem with foreign interventions in Afghani-stan. (Durrani 2015)

Since the operationalization of strategic depth was exclusively grounded on Afghanistan, it was important for Pakistan to exercise a controlling influ-ence over its northwestern neighbor—either by developing friendly rela-tions or installing a puppet regime there—so that it could access a secure refuge in the event of an Indian invasion (Nasr 2005: 187–89). For Pakistan, managing such a tilt from Kabul, despite its preponderant position in post-1989 Afghan affairs, was out of question until Indian influence was com-pletely uprooted from the Afghan soil. In this respect, an outstanding change occurred when the Pakistan-backed Taliban captured Kabul in 1996. The Taliban victory was a decisive security achievement for Pakistan, as it pro-vided Islamabad a rare opportunity to mold its long-envisaged strategic-depth doctrine into a pragmatic policy against India (Rashid 2015).

Despite such a drastic shift in Afghanistan's political-strategic landscape, India continuously backed the Northern Alliance and refused to recognize

the Taliban regime, which resulted in the closure of its embassy and two consulates and later culminated in the IC-814 hostage crisis in December 1999
(see Z. Hussain 2007: 61–63). In contrast, Pakistan enjoyed unprecedented
influence over the Taliban-ruled Afghanistan until the Al Qaida radicals
launched massive terror strikes against the United States in September 2001.
Throughout the entire period of the Taliban rule, Pakistan had enjoyed operational "strategic depth" in Afghanistan which turned out to be a "strategic
strangulation" for India—because the ISI-Taliban cartel successfully chan-
neled terrorist violence into Kashmir that heightened India's security
vulnerability.

In the wake of the 9/11 attacks, the situation underwent a drastic turnaround when the US-led global war against terrorism ousted the Taliban
regime, and the India-friendly Hamid Karzai–led regime, which had its origins in the Northern Alliance, presided over the war-torn country. With the
fall of the Taliban regime, which had provided Pakistan strategic depth and a
safe haven to groom Islamic jihadis, Islamabad suffered a setback in Afghanistan that ultimately set up a strategic competition between India and Pakistan and gradually reshaped their power positions in the region. Apart from
this transition, Pakistan became the victim of its own dreadful investment
when its terror harvesting backfired and endangered its own internal security
and strategic relationship with the United States (Gul 2015). In other words,
as Mani Shankar Aiyar (2012) puts it, the Pakistan Army's quest for strategic
depth in Afghanistan ended up "providing strategic depth to the Taliban [and
Al Qaida] in their own country" that eventually allowed the United States to
breach Pakistan's sovereignty by extending drone attacks to the porous borderlands of Pakistan and Afghanistan, famously known as the Af-Pak region
(see Johnston & Sarbhai 2016: 203–18).

India also seized this opportunity to increase its influence in Afghanistan
by adopting a long-term strategy of political engagement and reconstruction
assistance—its five major pillars of development partnership with Afghanistan till August 2021 were humanitarian assistance, economic development,
capacity building, infrastructure, and connectivity (GoI 2019). India re-
opened its embassy in Kabul and consulates in Kandahar and Jalalabad, later
established two new consulates in Herat and Mazar-i-Sharif, and provided
over $3 billion of aid to create social infrastructure in the war-ravaged
country—including the completion of the $290 million Afghan-India Friend-
ship Dam, the Afghan highway network to Iran, the Afghan parliament complex, and the 202-kilometer-long Phul-e-Khumri transmission line (which

provides electricity to the city of Kabul), and it signed an agreement for the construction of the Shatoot Dam to provide drinking water to the city of Kabul (GoI 2010, 2012, 2019, 2020a; *Times of India* 2019a).

From the context of regional rivalry, it is apparent that New Delhi's coordinated political-economic program for Afghanistan has been prepared and carried out to achieve its intended objectives, that is, to curtail Pakistan's influence over the Afghan government. Vivek Katju (2016), India's former ambassador to Afghanistan, deliberates on India's major concerns with regard to Afghanistan:

> India considers Afghanistan as a country of strategic significance and does not want a government in Kabul which is hostile to [its] interests. Any such government in Kabul will allow Pakistan a degree of influence that would be utilized against India, especially through the use of reactionary forces and religiously motivated people or groups. So India's posture in Afghanistan is not offensive, it is essentially defensive . . . and we have taken steps in accordance to this understanding.

While conducting field study in Lahore and Islamabad in October 2015, however, I found a majority of Pakistani observers—mainly researchers and academics, opinion-makers, journalists, and retired armed forces personnel and diplomats—tend to view India's Afghan engagement from the strategic prism. For instance, retired Lieutenant General Talat Masood (2015) opined that "India's overall policy in Afghanistan," including economic aid, "is grounded on [a] 'tit-for-tat' dynamic which . . . [has potential] to destabilize the region, particularly Pakistan." "If Indians say that [their] economic engagement in Afghanistan is not dual [or two-pronged]," argues Imtiaz Gul (2015), a journalist and executive director of the Islamabad-based Centre for Regional and Security Studies (CRSS), "then it would be extremely naïve and blatant misrepresentation of the ground realities. Indians have, I think, made 'no secret' about this[12] . . . [in fact] Sushma Swaraj has on record said that we need to counter Pakistan's policies in Afghanistan." With certainty in his voice, he further added:

> If Indians are suggesting that they are just [there] for economic reasons and that economic reason could stabilize Afghanistan, [in that case my point is]: if Americans could not stabilize Afghanistan with nearly a trillion dollars— all together with the NATO members—how can a couple of or few billion dol-

lars from India . . . stabilize [Afghanistan]. So certainly it is a strategic intervention as well as economic intervention and this is anchored primarily in
the mistrust between India and Pakistan and it flows from Kashmir. The core
of all policies that India and Pakistan are framing vis-à-vis each other is Kashmir. (Gul 2015)

Likewise, Akmal Hussain (2015), professor of political economy in Forman Christian University Lahore, says that "our policy makers think that
India's economic assistance [to Afghanistan] is far from development purpose and [is] designed to harm Pakistan's interests." Hussain (2015) also
argued that "for the greater good of the region . . . [and] to restore peace in
Pakistan, Islamabad needs to have more influence over its northwestern
neighbor than distant India." However, Pervez Hoodbhoy (2015) sees it differently. In a personal interview with the author, he outrightly said that the
"Pakistani side is over-reacting to Indian economic assistance." "Of course,"
he says, "the element of strategy is implicit [in the Indian aid program] but
there is no way out for Pakistan. It has to compete with India to win the
Afghan hearts, particularly by increasing its humanitarian aid and engagement in other social sectors" (Hoodbhoy 2015). In strategic terms, Ijaz Khan
(2015), professor of South Asian Security and International Relations at
Peshawar University, takes a more nuanced position on the issue. According
to him, "[Islamabad] has no objection to the Indian economic assistance to
Afghanistan, but if money trickles down to anti-Pakistan elements then it is
really a matter of great concern for Pakistan" (I. Khan 2015). But Aziz Ahmed
Khan (2015), Pakistan's former ambassador to India and Afghanistan, differs
in starkly realist terms with Pervez Hoodbhoy and Ijaz Khan's viewpoint:

Look, Pakistan has [a] 2,640-kilometre-long border with Afghanistan, called
the Durand Line. Around three million Afghans (that is, 10 percent of the
total Afghan population) live in Pakistan and every day around 50,000
Afghans come to Pakistan through open border without any visa. This underlines how closely Afghanistan is knitted with Pakistan and its society; hence
Pakistan has [a more] important role in this part of the world than distant
India.

This implies that "distant India" has no *locus standi* in Afghanistan. Or, put
differently, India should take a back seat and allow geographically contiguous Pakistan to deal with the Afghan problem and its socio-economic issues.

Interestingly, Barnett R. Rubin and Abubakar Siddique's argument nearly a decade earlier counterpoints Ambassador Aziz Ahmed Khan's rationale. "In practice," according to them,

> Pakistan has . . . undermine[d] the status of the Durand Line as an international border. Successive governments in Islamabad have exploited the porosity of the threefold frontier to use covert asymmetrical warfare as a tool of national security policy. While the Pakistani military's deliberate fashioning of the Afghan resistance on an Islamist model gave Pakistan strategic depth and neutralized Afghan nationalism, it also relied on transnational networks that ignored the Durand Line as consistently as any border tribe. Pakistan is now paying the price for this policy by losing control of much of the frontier area to groups it has supported, groups that exploit their ties in Afghanistan just as the Taliban exploit their ties in Pakistan. (Rubin & Siddique 2006: 14)

Security experts in New Delhi, on the other hand, maintain that India's involvement in infrastructure projects in Afghanistan is largely directed at ensuring that the economy of the landlocked country would grow rapidly and contribute to regional progress and stability (Kanwal 2016; Katju 2016; Parthasarathy 2016). According to Ambassador Katju (2016),

> India would like to use Afghanistan for natural resources and transit goods and energy in the long term. Pakistan is aware that India's reconstruction assistance will not only help Afghanistan to create social infrastructure but also lead to a formidable economic cooperation between India and Afghanistan (extendable to Central Asia), a situation against Islamabad's longstanding strategy to control the policy levers in Kabul; thus it wants to block India's economic initiatives in Afghanistan.

But speaking from a zero-sum perspective, India's development initiatives also act as a strategic loss for Pakistan as these projects have potential for dual civil-military use. New Delhi–steered stability in the neighborhood, believe a majority interviewed in Pakistan, will eventually result in Kabul's over-dependence on New Delhi and undermine Islamabad's traditional influence over its neighbor. For Islamabad, this implies, the new situation jeopardizes its longtime quest for strategic depth and might augment tensions with Kabul over the Durand Line—which the latter has never recognized as an international border—in the medium to long term. For these reasons, Pakistanis believe that India's reconstruction engagement in Afghanistan is imbued with strategic objectives which not only undercut Pakistan's vital interests and capabilities but also increase its domestic and two-front vulnerability.

In support of this argument, the area experts and opinion-makers in Pakistan point toward the Indian attempts to "contain and encircle" Pakistan strategically by building up a network of roads along the Durand Line, such as the Zaranj-Delaram Highway through the Iranian port of Chabahar—which India and Iran have developed jointly—on the pretext of facilitating the movement of goods and services to Afghanistan and Central Asia (Durrani 2015; Gul 2015; A. Hussain 2015; I. Khan 2015). In this context, Ijaz Khan (2015) poses a counter-question: "How would New Delhi react if Islamabad could adopt a similar strategy in India's neighborhood, as for example, Nepal or Bhutan?" While stressing "a propitious environment" as a pre-condition, Iqbal Ahmad Khan (2015), Pakistan's former ambassador to Bangladesh and Iran, asserts, "[W]herever possible and in the interest of regional cooperation and connectivity the two countries should give transit rights to each other. India can go to Central Asia and Afghanistan, and Pakistan to Nepal and Bangladesh." India's security managers, on the other hand, argue that since Pakistan denied India overland trading access to Afghanistan, so New Delhi was left with no other alternative than building a supplementary access route to overcome Pakistan's virtual blockade (Katju 2016; Parthasarathy 2016).

During the 2015 Heart of Asia conference in Islamabad, the Indian External Affairs Minister Sushma Swaraj and Ashraf Ghani, the president of Afghanistan, raised the issue of transportation of Indian goods to Afghanistan via the Wagha-Attari border. While raising this issue, Sushma Swaraj said: "The 'Heart' of Asia [Afghanistan] cannot function if arteries are clogged." She reminded Islamabad that if the situation remained unchanged, India will access the landlocked state via the Chabahar port to "augment its connectivity with Afghanistan and beyond" (quoted in Ajai Shukla 2015). In December 2018, as expected, India managed to neutralize Pakistan's obstructive policy by formally taking over operations at Chabahar port to support the war-ravaged Afghanistan and expand its trade connectivity with the Central Asian states (*Hindustan Times* 2018). Despite deteriorating Iran-US relations, India managed an exemption from the US sanctions on Iran to continue its development works on Chabahar port and doubled its allocation to $13.98 million for 2020–21 fiscal year (*Financial Tribune* 2020).

Increasingly wary of Indian activities in Afghanistan, Pakistan has long held Indian diplomatic missions responsible for its deteriorating internal security, particularly in Balochistan and the Federally Administered Tribal Areas (FATA). For instance, Senator Mushahid Hussain Sayed categorically claimed that "[the] Indian diplomatic missions [in Afghanistan] serve as launching pads for undertaking covert operations against Pakistan. . . . Particularly, the Indian consulates in Kandahar and Jalalabad and their embassy in Kabul are used for clandestine activities inside Pakistan in general and . . . the FATA and Balochistan in particular" (quoted in Baabar 2006). Later, in June 2015, Raheel Sharif, the Pakistan chief of army staff (COAS), also affirmed the Indian hostile intent behind the "bloodletting" in Balochistan, the FATA, and Karachi (ISPR 2015b).[13]

The Pakistani area experts and opinion-makers also contend, in line with the official or army version, that the Indian consulates close to Pakistan's porous northwestern border are serving as network bases for aiding anti-Pakistan elements and armed insurgency in Balochistan and the FATA (Durrani 2015; Gul 2015; A. Hussain 2015; I. Khan 2015; Ziauddin 2015). "We have credible information and evidence," maintained Shahid Malik (2015), former high commissioner of Pakistan to India, "that the Indian consulates are supporting elements against Pakistan in FATA and Balochistan. They are not only channeling money to the militants but also providing weapons and political support to foment crises in the tribal belts."[14] Likewise, Professor Akmal Hussain (2015) argued that "India has invested in Afghanistan to destabilize the FATA and Balochistan. Over a period of time, it is possible that [New Delhi] might turn Afghanistan . . . [into] an instrument to destabilize Pakistan." However, Ahmed Rashid (2015), a renowned Pakistani author and expert on Afghan-Pakistan affairs, downplayed the magnitude of the Indian involvement in violent nationalist insurgency in Balochistan. Brushing aside Pakistan's inflated charges, Rashid (2015) said:

> In my opinion, up to some extent, it might be the case—limited to monetary or political support—but not beyond that. To claim that India is behind all this [that is, directing secessionist movement(s)], and systematically promoting nationalist insurgency in Balochistan, is not correct. Given the fact [that] India has close relationship with Balochis—as Pakistan has with Kashmiris and, in the past, it had with Nagas and Punjabis—against this [backdrop], these types of narratives are being constructed and over-used in Pakistan.

Pakistan's concerns may hold some rationality but the core issue that disturbs its policy makers is that, as Rubin and Siddique rightly noted a decade and half ago, they see "the Indian presence [in Afghanistan] as a major strategic defeat and a loss of years of investments that established an Islamist regime that kept all things Indian away from Pakistan's western borders" (2006: 14). On the basis of their competitive policies, it can be argued that India's and Pakistan's interests in Afghanistan are placed in such a way that both sides view the entire situation in a zero-sum perspective: one party's gain becomes the other's loss. In the post-9/11 environment, India's presence and influence in Afghanistan has neutralized Pakistan's "strategic depth"—a reverse situation to the 1989–2001 period—and aggravated Islamabad's strategic anxiety. For instance, India and Afghanistan have expanded their relationship to the geo-strategic domain by signing the Strategic Partnership Agreement (SPA) in 2011 which evolved into a joint Indo-Afghan "hedging triad"—political, economic, and strategic—to check Pakistan's influence in Afghanistan so that it would not manage any strategic depth inside the war-ravaged country and use its geo-strategic advantage against the growing India-Iran-Afghanistan partnership (GoI 2011, 2018).

To neutralize Pakistan and promote its vital interests in the region and beyond, India signed a trilateral connectivity deal with Iran and Afghanistan in May 2016 that provides it connectivity to Afghanistan by strategically outflanking Pakistan through the Chabahar port via a 240-kilometer road corridor (Kutty 2016). Under this agreement, India committed to invest $20 billion for the expansion and modernization of the Chabahar port, the Chabahar Special Economic Zone (SEZ), and the Chabahar-Hajigak rail corridor connecting Iranian ports with the India-promoted $11 billion Hajigak iron mining and steel project in central Afghanistan (P. Bose 2016). For India, the Chabahar port will be a game changer as it will not only neutralize intransigent Pakistan and the China-Pakistan Economic Corridor (CPEC) but also increase its potential for many-fold more trade with Central Asia, Europe, and Russia through a 7,200-kilometer-long multi-mode International North–South Transport Corridor (INSTC) (see GoI 2017, 2020b).

To counter the Indian squeeze, particularly when the US-led global war against terrorism and the reshaping Asian security architecture is favoring India, Pakistan has taken steps to undercut New Delhi's presence in Afghanistan through proxy means. For instance, the ISI has used the Haqqani network and other Taliban offshoots, which have established themselves in Balochistan and Khyber Pakhtoonkhwa, to target Indian diplomatic missions in Afghanistan. Repeated incidents of suicide bombings and gun attacks on the Indian embassy and consulates are prime examples of this strategy (see *BBC* 2009; *Economic Times* 2018a; *Indian Express* 2009, 2016b, 2017). Particularly after the US decision to completely withdraw from Afghanistan, Pakistan has adopted a twofold strategy to counter the Indo-Afghan strategic partnership and India's reinforced Connect Central Asia Policy, which broadens New Delhi's economic-security role in the region. First, Pakistan signed an extensive Gwadar-Xinjiang corridor deal with China, widely known as the CPEC, which will provide China permanent access to the Indian Ocean through the Gwadar deep-sea port to neutralize India's influence and economic-strategic reach in Afghanistan and Central Asia (*CPEC Portal* 2018; see Manish 2021). Second, it has reactivated its terror strategies, particularly through the Quetta-based Taliban offshoots and its own terror machinery, to target India's and Afghanistan's security forces, diplomatic missions, and vital military assets and bases (see *BBC* 2016a; *Economic Times* 2018a; *Indian Express* 2016a, 2017; *Week* 2019).

The United States' conclusion of a peace deal with the Taliban, dubbed the Doha agreement (*BBC* 2020a), to end its longest war made India anxious and vulnerable as the agreement's ambiguous nature had the potential to jeopardize the security situation of South Asia. The Doha agreement had not only opened the avenue for the Taliban's return to power, which could increase risk to India's $3 billion in progressive investments in the country, it also provided Islamabad an edge to re-establish its power hold in Kabul by ensuring a significant role for the Taliban in key regions of Afghanistan or in the Afghan government. The Indian fears became a reality with the complete withdrawal of US troops from Afghanistan in mid-August 2021, particularly when the fast-changing political landscape and power-sharing equations in the war-ravaged country led to the fall of Ashraf Ghani's democratic government and the return of Taliban militants to power. This turn of events in Afghanistan, in political-strategic terms, appears to be an action replay of the 1990s when Pakistan managed strategic depth in Afghanistan by installing and controlling a puppet Taliban regime there. The Taliban's surprising and resistance-less takeover of Afghanistan has once again posed a serious challenge to regional security, as now Pakistan and the fundamentalist Islamic militia of Taliban may not hesitate to pursue anti-India policies to maximize their power and influence in the war-ravaged country and its neighboring territories. If this happens, and power equations tilt in favor of the Taliban and Pakistan with China's lethal aid and political support, South

Asia will certainly witness another spell of instability and the return of violence in Afghanistan and Kashmir.

In sum, Afghanistan acted as a catalyst in the Indo-Pakistani rivalry over Kashmir prior to the 9/11 terror attacks. Afterward, till mid-August 2021, it acted as an insulator by arduously engaging Pakistan in unstable border areas, forcing its attention away from Kashmir and denying it any strategic depth on Afghan soil, and assisting India to strengthen its position in the South Asian region and beyond. With the withdrawal of US troops and the return of a Taliban regime in Kabul, another transition is possible whereby India's regional stronghold may again be challenged by Pakistan with China's aggressive support and Afghanistan's re-emergence as a potential zone of strategic depth, which might intensify the ISI-directed terrorist operations in Kashmir. Under such circumstances, there is a higher likelihood that the India-Pakistan dyad might again entangle in an intense action-reaction conundrum and end up injecting another wave of insecurity and uncertainty in the region and Kashmir in particular.

INFLUENCE OF RELATIVE MILITARY CAPABILITIES AND THE LOGIC OF "NUCLEAR SHIELD": PAKISTAN'S COVERT AGGRESSION IN KASHMIR AND RIVALRY STABILIZATION

After securing the knowledge that a handful of nuclear bombs may be enough to deter India, Pakistan started using its opaque nuclear capability as a shield to promote proxy war in Kashmir. In this respect, Pakistan's former COAS Mirza Aslam Beg's noteworthy declaration of the early 1990s shows how the logic of a "nuclear shield" was perceived in Pakistan: "[Our country] has acquired the minimum deterrent level. . . . Despite having a massive strength in conventional arms, India cannot dare attack Pakistan because of the fear of a nuclear strike which will render a vast portion of [its] conventional army ineffective" (cited in *Dawn* 1994). This line of thinking, particularly in the 1990s, motivated the Pakistani policy makers to "raise the threshold for nuclear use and ma[ke] their opaque nuclear deterrent credible for defensive purposes" (Hoyt 2009: 153). The Kashmir crisis of 1990 is a classic example of its operationalization in doctrinal fashion, which brought the subcontinent close to a cataclysmic nuclear war. In this crisis, believes Pervez Hoodbhoy (2015), the Lahore-based nuclear physicist and anti-nuclear activist, Pakistan had not only "deliberately upped nuclear ante against

India" but in fact "[its] leaders—who had a dim understanding that many people would die—were desperate to use nuclear capability to wrest Kashmir from India." Though never officially articulated, this doctrine emboldened Pakistan to annoy India continually in Kashmir during the 1990s and simultaneously pressure the international community to give precedence to its demands, as for example to compel New Delhi to resolve the Kashmir conflict on preferential terms.

Although the size and extent of Pakistan's nuclear arsenal was not known during the opaque period, as no official reports were available, some scholars claimed that Pakistan had "as many as twenty-five quickly deployable nuclear weapons with a capacity to produce a limited number of additional weapons annually" (S. Ahmed & Cortright 1998: 92). Since Pakistan had acquired sufficient means to deliver nuclear weapons—including thirty-four F-16s and fifty-six French Mirage-5s, and its short- and medium-range ballistic missile projects (*Hatf-I*, *Hatf-II*, and *Ghauri*) that were also close to completion—its proxy war in Kashmir and unabated nuclear threats had greatly aggravated India's strategic anxiety (see *Military Balance* 1996–97: 66). The *Kargil Review Committee Report* also underlined this fact:

> It would not be unreasonable for Pakistan to have concluded by 1990 that it had achieved the nuclear deterrence it had set out to establish in 1980. Otherwise, it is inconceivable that it could sustain its proxy war against India, inflicting thousands of casualties, without being unduly concerned about India's "conventional superiority." (GoI 2000: 241)

In the midst of the Kashmir insurgency, Pakistan's widely successful proxy campaign coincided with another critical development: the formation of the BJP-led National Democratic Alliance (NDA) government in India, whose election manifesto had clearly stated that it would "re-evaluate the country's nuclear policy and exercise the option to develop nuclear weapons" (BJP 1998). Soon after assuming power in 1998, the BJP adopted aggressive policies to achieve an operational nuclear arsenal on the pretext of India's ambiguous stand on the nuclear issue and the growing security threat (see Bajpai 2009b). This development brought a critical shift in India's and Pakistan's strategic policies. Perhaps Islamabad had taken the BJP's election-time dramatic claims seriously—particularly its prime ministerial candidate Atal Bihari Vajpayee's statement that India would forcibly take back Azad Kashmir from Pakistan—or intended to know more about the new Indian government's real plans; in any case, it test-fired its first nuclear-capable missile, Ghauri (Hatf-5) (Baruah 1998; Perkovich 1999: 410–11).

Since the Ghauri had demonstrated Pakistan's capability to strike India's large cities and New Delhi had no arsenal in its military system to match the rival, the Vajpayee government encountered a serious policy-cum-military crisis. In other words, as George Perkovich has noted, "The Ghauri test spoke for itself . . . India could not meaningfully 'improve upon' its capacity to destroy/deter Pakistan. But Pakistan did have room for 'improving' its capacity to threaten and deter India" (1999: 410). The new situation not only posed an immense threat to India but also engaged it in a pattern of one-upmanship in strategic capability that required a matching response to ensure credible deterrence (S. Khan 2009: 78).

The Vajpayee-led NDA government used the crisis situation to rational-ize its decision to acquire credible nuclear deterrence to (1) attain security, (2) accomplish its political goals or interests, and (3) reap symbolic reward and prestige, that is, great power status or regional hegemony. Though these conditions played a crucial role to shape New Delhi's decision, albeit of varied degree,[15] the principal condition that compelled India to go nuclear was "security" (see Ganguly & Hagerty 2005; C. Mohan 2004; Sagan 1996–97).

Under the fast-changing regional security environment and the looming threat of the Comprehensive Test Ban Treaty (CTBT), it was increasingly dif-ficult for India to effectively deter both Pakistan and China—whose close nuclear cooperation posed a greater potential threat—without having the "absolute" weapon in its stockpile. Left with limited options to roll back the Pakistan-steered proxy war in Kashmir at the one extreme and the US-led non-proliferation squeeze and the Chinese threat at the other, India chose to carry out nuclear tests in the summer of 1998 (see C. Mohan 2004; Tellis 2001). The official Indian version also supports this explanation (see GoI 1998). For instance, Naresh Chandra, then India's ambassador to the United States, had accepted in an interview that the underlying cause for nuclear tests was India's security concerns. He said:

> [W]e have been thinking for some time that our national defense effort requires certain deterrent capability. . . . We have a neighbor to our North, which has a very substantial nuclear arsenal. We also have a neighbor to our West, and they have a very deep kind of relationship. (N. Chandra 1998)

Given the fact India had then limited delivery capability to deter China, these tests intimidated none other than the weaker side in the conflict: Pakistan.[16] To ward off the Indian threat, Pakistan hurriedly conducted its own nuclear tests in a tit-for-tat response to consolidate its position in the regional rivalry.[17] Rather than reducing hostilities and halting the nuclear competition, the two adversaries' open nuclear tests had triggered new strategic developments ranging from nuclear brinkmanship to a sophisticated missile race. Barely a year after these tests, against the realist notion that nuclear weapons deter states from war engagement, the two adversaries not only fought an intense war in the Kargil sector of J&K but also signaled their readiness to cross the nuclear "red lines."[18]

Some scholars, however, argue that the Kargil War stemmed from the Indian occupation of the Siachen way back in 1984 which, apart from domestic criticism, shattered the Pakistan Army's morale (S. Kapur 2008). To reclaim its lost honor, writes S. Paul Kapur, the Pakistan Army was planning an operation to oust the Indians from the glacial region. In support of his argument, Kapur quotes Benazir Bhutto, the former prime minister of Pakistan, and Jalil Jilani, a former director-general for South Asia in Pakistan's ministry of foreign affairs, claiming that the Siachen was the core factor for the Kargil intrusion (S. Kapur 2008: 125). However, Hassan Abbas does not mention the Siachen when recounting Pakistan's Military Operations Directorate discussion of this plan with President General Zia-ul-Haq, who rejected it twice on the grounds that it could "lead us [Pakistan] into a full scale war with India" (Abbas 2005: 170, 168–72). Inconsistency in the two accounts does not make it clear whether the Siachen was the underlying cause for the Kargil intrusion or the possession of nuclear capabilities had encouraged the Pakistani decision-makers to take a calculated risk. In this context, Pakistani General Asad Durrani's version, which emphasizes strategic compulsions, gives a crucial lead that has potential—if tied together with Abbas's and Kapur's versions into a whole—to offer a credible explanation. According to Durrani (2015),

> The seizure of the Siachen Glacier [in 1984] was India's "strategic extension." Prior to this, in 1965 and 1971, India did manage effective "forward depth" in the Kargil sector—which was located very close to [the CFL/LoC]. . . . Pakistan's Kargil venture of 1999 was to undo the Indian gains in that sector.

From Durrani's (2015) viewpoint, what seems obvious is that the Kargil intrusion was Pakistan's compound strategy to manage forward depth/territorial extension under a protective nuclear shield. Prior to the 1998 nuclear tests, the single most important reason that made Pakistan's planned intrusion a "non-starter" was the lack of credible means to control possible escalation or deter the Indian retaliation. Precisely for this reason, the Pakistani decision-makers, particularly General Zia-ul-Haq and Benazir Bhutto, were not convinced that the planned intrusion to reverse the Indian gains (in Kargil and the Siachen) would be of significant advantage in the absence of credible deterrence. In this respect, South Asia's overt nuclearization proved to be a turning point. The new situation opened a window of opportunity for the Pakistani military planners to conflate historical and strategic conditions—entwined with a strong urge to reclaim lost honor—to justify a large-scale intrusion against the superior adversary.[19] As a consequence, Pakistan deployed a dangerous strategy, "fait accompli," to wrest Kargil from India—under which "it tried a 'quick, decisive' military operation" without doubting "India's commitment to defend its territory along the LoC"[20] (Lavoy 2009a: 5). Reliance on a fait accompli clearly shows that the planners of the Kargil invasion believed that the occupation of strategic peaks across the LoC would not be reversed because of a favorable terrain and the newly established nuclear balance in the region (Lavoy 2009a, 2009b).

A couple of years later, during the compound crisis of 2001–2, again both sides seemed to be on the verge of yet another full-scale war when they upped their nuclear ante by testing ballistic missiles (see F.H. Khan 2004; Sood & Sawhney 2003). Washington's timely interventions on both occasions brought India and Pakistan back from the brink, but the point that warrants attention here is that the nuclear weapons, coupled with an increasing missile race to give credence to delivery capabilities, instituted a fundamental change in the regional rivalry. Though the nuclear weapons' massive destructive capacity had prevented India and Pakistan from entering into all-out wars, as nuclear optimists have argued,[21] it neither stabilized the region nor established a robust nuclear deterrence between the two states. In fact, far from inducing stability in the region, the nuclear factor has provided revisionist Pakistan a compelling incentive to provoke India (Hoodbhoy 2015; S. Kapur 2008). Knowing that the possession of nuclear weapons would limit India's retaliatory options, Pakistan placed the nuclear threat as its foremost option against the superior adversary. A.H. Nayyar

(2015b), Pakistan's renowned nuclear physicist, also agrees with this understanding. According to him:

> When India did not escalate hostilities after the 2001–2 crisis, Pakistanis
> began to believe that nuclear deterrence works. The fear of nuclear escalation
> [further went] down when the Mumbai attacks replicated the same; [these]
> experiences strengthened this thought. (Nayyar 2015b)

Besides making the dyad vulnerable to smaller wars, the post–nuclear
tests experience—the Kargil War, the compound crises of 2001–2, the 26/11
Mumbai terrorist attacks, and the 2019 Pulwama-Balakot near-nuclear
standoff—underlines that the nuclear weapons have played a fundamental
role in stabilizing the India-Pakistan rivalry. However, after Operation Parakaram in 2002, India was determined to come out of the nuclear logjam by
framing a new policy which could provide it sufficient room to respond to
Pakistan's high-intensity provocations or subconventional attacks under the
nuclear threshold. Against this backdrop, the Indian Army brought out a
limited war doctrine, called Cold Start, in 2004. The main objective of this
doctrine, which is not yet formally adopted by the Indian government as
"policy," is

> to establish the capacity to launch a retaliatory conventional strike against
> Pakistan that would inflict significant harm on the Pakistan Army before the
> international community could intercede, and at the same time, pursue nar-
> row enough aims to deny Islamabad a justification to escalate the clash to the
> nuclear level. (Ladwig 2007–8: 164)

In addition to the Cold Start, India's growing strategic partnership with
the United States has added a new dimension to Pakistan's security equations, especially after the conclusion of the nuclear deal in 2005–6. Some
Pakistani analysts argue that the Indo-US defense relationship "directly
impinges" on Pakistan's strategic security (I. Khan 2015; Ziauddin 2015). A
comparison of India's and Pakistan's post-Kargil military expenditure gives
adequate ground for these concerns, as India has quadrupled its defense
budget over the last twenty years to $65.1 billion (see Figure 7.2b)—making it
the world's fourth largest military spender (*Military Balance* 2022: 9).

A general opinion is that India's extensive military procurement and
qualitative enhancement has heavily tilted the region's strategic balance

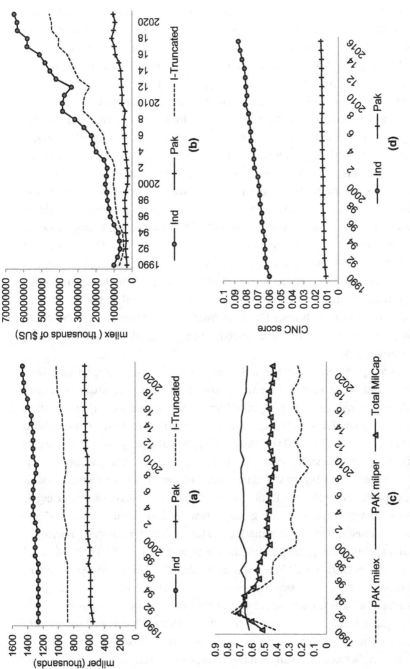

Figure 7.2. India-Pakistan relative capabilities and militarized disputes, 1990–2021. (a) Military personnel (milper) ratio, (b) military expenditure (milex) ratio, (c) Pakistan's total military capability vis-à-vis India, (d) composite index of national capability (CINC) ratio. The CINC ratio comprises = milper + milex + primary energy consumption (pec) ratio + iron and steel production (irst) ratio [population (total + urban) excluded]. *CINC data available till 2016. *Source:* Compiled from the COW database (2021, version 6.0); National Material Capabilities Data (2021, version 6.0); *Military Balance* 2010–22.

toward India. Prime examples that give credence to India's increasing military clout are the acquisition of ten Lockheed Martin C-130J Hercules, ten Boeing C-17A Globemaster military transport, three Il-76TD Phalcon, and one EMB-145 AEW&C aircraft; an $8.7 billion deal for thirty-six French multi-role combat aircraft Rafale (equipped with the latest weapons); an agreement to purchase two hundred Russian Ka-226T light helicopters; a $3.1 billion deal with the US aviation giant Boeing for twenty-two AH-64E Apache Longbow attack helicopters and fifteen Chinook heavy-lift helicopters; a defense deal worth $6.5 billion for the purchase of eighty-three LCA MK1A Tejas fighter jets; and the induction of the aircraft carrier INS *Vikramaditya* (another locally built aircraft carrier, which will be called INS *Vikrant*, also began sea trials and is scheduled to enter service in August 2022), Kolkata-class guided-missile destroyers (equipped with the navalized Brahmos supersonic cruise missiles), and the nuclear-powered submarines INS *Chakra* and INS *Arihant* in the naval service; and finalization of a whopping $5.43 billion deal to purchase five Russian S-400 Triumf air-defense missile systems and a $2.5 billion contract with Israel for a joint Indo-Israeli Barak 8/MR-SAM surface-to-air missile system (*Business Insider* 2021; *Economic Times* 2018b, 2018c; *JNS* 2017; *Indian Express* 2016d, 2018, 2022; *Military Balance* 2018, 2019, 2020, 2021).

From these procurements and upgrades, one can comprehend how India's substantial quantitative and qualitative military expansion has consolidated its position in the regional hierarchy. It is noteworthy that India's post-Kargil growth is much more significant and has left Pakistan far behind (see Figure 7.2b, c), but still the strategic balance at the dyadic level is not in its favor. From the standpoint of a real war scenario, one can argue that India's noticeable military strength is not sufficient to choke Pakistan's strategic capability in a short or limited war. For instance, the two adversaries' air balance heavily favors technologically advanced India, but it is still not sufficient to alter the strategic situation. Pakistan has dramatically narrowed the air capabilities gap over the last decade by acquiring several sophisticated fighter planes and ten AEW&C aircrafts from the United States, Sweden, France, and China, and simultaneously managed to induct over 120 JF-17 Thunders, built as a joint Sino-Pakistani venture, as well as offering to sell additional Thunders to the Afro-Asian states (*Express Tribune* 2020; *Military Balance* 2016, 2018, 2020, 2021, 2022; Roblin 2020). Like the army and the air force, India has a far stronger navy. It has one aircraft carrier, one amphibious warfare ship, and ten destroyers where Pakistan has none; eight corvettes with anti-ship missiles to Pakistan's one; seventeen frigates to Pakistan's eight; and one nuclear-powered, one nuclear ballistic missile–equipped, and fifteen diesel-electric tactical submarines compared to Pakistan's conventional eight[22] (*Military Balance* 2021: 261–63, 291). India's larger fleet size extends it a clear advantage against the opponent in the sea-based domain. It will further expand, as India's chief of the naval staff Admiral Karambir Singh (2020) claimed in an interview, once the Indian Navy completes the acquisition of forty-three ships and submarines, a second aircraft carrier (INS *Vikrant*), four destroyers, and seven frigates between 2021 and 2024.

But the real question is, as Christopher Clary (2012) asked a decade ago, whether the Indian naval and air forces could defeat their Pakistani counterparts effectively and quickly so that the Indian Army could attain its objectives on land in a limited war. Pakistan has taken significant initiatives over the last decade to resist an Indian blockade by opening up two new ports close to the Gulf of Oman, Ormara and Gwadar, and constructing a dual-purpose road from both ports to the country's heartland and on to Xinjiang under the CPEC project (see *Aaj News* 2016; *CPEC Portal* 2018). In addition, as some report by quoting US and Pakistani officials and nuclear experts, Pakistan is advancing toward sea-based nuclear weapons to offset India's fast-expanding naval capabilities or second strike capability (see Kristensen, Norris, & Diamond 2018: 355–56; Kristensen & Korda 2018: 365). Tom Hundley (2018) reports that Pakistan has developed a nuclear-capable submarine-launched cruise missile (SLCM), the Babur-3, which has an estimated range of about 450 kilometers:

> The Pakistan navy is likely to soon place nuclear-tipped cruise missiles on up to three of its five French-built diesel-electric submarines. . . . Even more disturbing, Pakistani military authorities say they are considering the possibility of putting nuclear-tipped cruise missiles on surface vessels like the Zulfiqar. Pakistan says its decision to add nuclear weapons to its navy is a direct response to India's August 2016 deployment of its first nuclear submarine, the Arihant.

This step is Pakistan's counter-move to neutralize India's possible pre-emptive maneuvers, that is, sea versions of the Cold Start, and the new inclusions in the naval service—the aircraft carrier INS *Vikramaditya*, Kolkata-class guided-missile destroyers, and the nuclear-powered submarine INS *Arihant*—which are part of New Delhi's ambitious long-term plan to attain a "blue-water navy" capability and dominate the Indian Ocean region. In fact, during the 2015 Carnegie International Nuclear Policy Conference, General Khalid Kidwai, former head of Pakistan's Strategic Plans Division (SPD), confirmed Pakistan's next step:

> [A]t some point in time Pakistan should be looking at a second strike capability [that is, a sea-based nuclear deterrent capability], particularly in a scenario where India is already well on its way. So we can't allow balances . . . to be disturbed. Balances must be maintained. (2015: 15)

Pakistan's steps limit India's options to pose a decisive challenge to it in a quick and limited war, which means the Indian capabilities are still not sufficient to undo Pakistan's strengths in the region. Additionally, Pakistan has adopted a two-prong strategic approach to offset India's growing offensive capabilities and the Cold Start doctrine. First, it has increased the rate of fissile material production, which gives it one of the fastest-growing nuclear weapons stockpiles (Hoodbhoy 2015; Kanwal 2016; Toon et al. 2019). A combined report by the Carnegie Endowment for International Peace and the Stimson Center concludes that Pakistan is rapidly expanding its nuclear arsenal, may be building around twenty nuclear warheads annually, and could overtake Britain, France, and China within a decade to become the world's third-largest nuclear weapon power after the United States and Russia (Dalton & Krepon 2015; see Kristensen, Norris, & Diamond 2018). Second, it has produced around twenty-four highly accurate short-range (60–70 kilometers) nuclear-tipped missiles of unknown yield—the Nasr (Hatf-IX) and Abdali—for use on battlefields against invading Indian troops and tanks (see ISPR 2017a, 2017b, 2019a, 2019b; Toon et al. 2019: 2). However, General Kidwai claims that "[Nasr is] a Pakistani defensive, deterrence response to an offensive doctrine [of India]." "I strongly believe," he continued, "by introducing the variety of tactical nuclear weapons in Pakistan's inventory . . . we have blocked the avenues for serious military operations by the other side" (Kidwai 2015: 4, 5). Put differently, he claims, "Nasr" is a weapon of peace whose "main purpose . . . is to ensure that war will not break out" in South Asia (Kidwai 2015: 10).

On the whole, Pakistan's expanding nuclear capabilities and lowering threshold for nuclear use at the subconventional level clearly indicates that it intends to give credence to its "aggressive-defense" capabilities (via tactical nuclear weapons) to counterbalance India's punitive schemes like the Cold

Start. In other words, Islamabad's tactical strategy signifies that New Delhi must re-examine its uncertain and limited Cold Start–style military operations before undertaking any risky maneuver against Pakistan as it now possess credible deterrence—that is, "full spectrum deterrence" (strategic, operational, tactical)—to neutralize India at all levels of threat (see GoP 2022; ISPR 2017a, 2019a).

There is much debate about why India did not put the Cold Start into effect in 2008 despite knowing that the Mumbai terrorist attacks were planned in and executed from Pakistani soil—it restricted its action to some precautionary military measures (see *Hindu* 2009). If tactical nuclear weapons factored in New Delhi's post-Mumbai response, though at the time Pakistan had yet to completely develop low-yield battlefield nuclear weapons, as Adil Sultan, former director of the SPD for Arms Control and Disarmament Affairs (ACDA) later said, this implies that Pakistan has successfully plugged "the operational and tactical level [gaps] . . . to deny India the space to launch limited military operations in the form of [Cold Start]" (Sultan 2011–12: 159). Likewise, nuclear physicist A.H. Nayyar (2015b) believes that

> [t]he Pakistani policy makers think that their countermeasure to the Cold Start, in the form of short-range Nasr tactical missiles, worked to Pakistan's advantage. They [see] the Indian political leadership's disowning of the Cold Start doctrine as a reflection of Pakistan's tactical nuclear [capability].

After the flight test of the Nasr in February 2013, General Khalid Kidwai, former head of the SPD, told US officials and academic visitors that through the Nasr short-range system Pakistan has not only attained strategic parity at the tactical level but also succeeded to "pour cold water on Cold Start" (cited in D. Smith 2013: 80). In July 2017, when Pakistan inducted the Nasr missile into its strategic arsenal and its first training launch was held, the COAS Qamar Bajwa had again repeated Kidwai's words: "Nasr has put cold water on Cold Start" (*Dawn* 2017a). Given the contentious history of India and Pakistan, apart from large nuclear buildup, the acquisition and deployment of tactical nuclear weapons has increased the possibility of an inadvertent or unauthorized launch of short-range systems close to the forward positions, which could create tit-for-tat dynamics leading to a conventional or nuclear escalation (Hoodbhoy 2015; Kanwal 2016; also see Toon et al. 2019).[23] "This scenario is alien to classical Western deterrence theory," write Toby Dalton and Michael Krepon, "which holds that nuclear weapons are meant to deter nuclear exchanges and existential conventional military threats, but not lesser contingencies sparked by subconventional warfare" (2015: 11). However, General Jehangir Karamat, Pakistan's former COAS, disagrees with arguments emphasizing the possibilities of nuclear escalation or the danger of nuclear war in the region. In defense of Pakistan's nuclear expansion, he asserts:

> Now the lines of conflict or war escalation have been blurred, [hence] subconventional nuclear escalation is not possible. Look at nuclear weapon states' equations since 1945, despite all hawkish posturing and having tactical systems in their arsenal; they have not gone beyond a limit. This shows that nuclear deterrence works and is equally relevant [to the South Asian conditions]. (Karamat 2015)

Some Pakistani analysts, on the other hand, give sympathetic consideration to such a serious situation by maintaining that "Pakistan is merely responding to the threat environment being constructed around it as it did by conducting its nuclear tests in 1998" (Naqvi 2015). However, Maria Sultan, the chairperson of the Islamabad-based South Asian Strategic Stability Institute, an organization with close links to the Pakistan Army, strikes off defensive portrayals and flatly asserts: "Before, we only had big weapons, so there was a gap in our deterrence, which is why we have gone for tactical nuclear weapons and cruise missiles." She warned: "We are saying, 'We have target acquisition for very small targets as well, so it's really not a great idea to come attack us'" (quoted in Craig & DeYoung 2014).

In contrast, Professor Ijaz Khan (2015) candidly accepts that "Pakistan is following a risky strategy which might spark the greatest uncontrolled escalation leading to a war with India." He, however, does not really elaborate what makes Pakistan adopt an aggressive posture and which factors could provoke the two adversaries to war. Dalton and Krepon, on the other hand, provide a straightforward argument that "Pakistan's nuclear posture with *the apparent continued toleration of some extremist groups* [might] trigger a war with India" (2015: 11, emphasis added). "Under the circumstances," Ijaz Khan (2015) suggests,

> to ward off impending danger, there is only one precautionary measure: India should reverse the Cold Start doctrine by taking credible [and verifiable] measures and, in reciprocity, Pakistan should pull out from threatening

tactical nuclear [schemes] which might compel India to [abandon its] "no first use" policy.

But the possibility of accommodation of such suggestions in practice is questionable because, as General Durrani (2015) meaningfully puts it, "Pakistan has no incentive to abandon its [aggressive] posture and [adopt an] unfavorable 'no-first-use' policy; the nuclear overhang in the region provides [it a perpetual] edge against India."[24] The underlying logic is that, as General Kidwai reasserts, "[nuclear] weapons will continue to form the bedrock, and the cornerstone of Pakistan's security policy, and provide security in a certain threat spectrum, in a certain threat environment that prevails in South Asia" (2015: 14).

Time and again, the Pakistani policy makers have pointed out that they might be forced to use nuclear weapons should India ever invade Pakistan or hinder its interests in Kashmir by introducing radical changes through large-scale military maneuvers. "If India initiates Cold Start," for instance, reminds retired diplomat Aziz Ahmed Khan (2015), "Pakistan will react strongly by attacking India." A glaring example of provocative intent or extreme mindset was shown by the former ISI chief Hamid Gul's reaction to the arrest of a Pakistan-based terrorist, Usman Khan, in J&K in 2015: "India should mend its ways else we [nuclear Pakistan] will not hesitate to make Delhi and Mumbai as today's Hiroshima and Nagasaki" (News Nation 2015). Likewise, soon after the cancellation of talks at the national security advisor (NSA) level in August 2015, Pakistan's NSA Sartaz Aziz said: "Modi's India acts as if they are a regional superpower, but we are also a nuclear-armed country and we know how to defend ourselves" (Indian Express 2015a). In January 2018, a couple of years later, India's then COAS Bipin Rawat had also raised the provocative bar from the Indian side:

If we will have to really confront the Pakistanis, and a task is given to us, we are not going to say we cannot cross the border because they have nuclear weapons. We will have to call their nuclear bluff. (Economic Times 2018d)

Again in January 2019, exactly a year later, while addressing the army personnel on the occasion of Army Day, General Bipin Rawat warned Pakistan: "I am warning our enemy [Pakistan] that we will not hesitate in carrying out strong action against any inimical action" (Rediff 2019). Barely a month later, on February 14, 2019, a young Kashmiri terrorist associated with the JeM carried out a deadly suicide attack by slamming his car into a convoy of India's paramilitary forces in Pulwama, an incident that almost escalated the Indo-Pakistani tensions to the point of nuclear exchange.

According to informed media reports that claimed to be based on information provided by a source from the office of the US national security advisor, a key member of India's Cabinet Committee of Security (CCS), and diplomats and intelligence officials in New Delhi and Islamabad, "India and Pakistan came perilously close to firing missiles at each other on February 27" (*Hindustan Times* 2019a; *Reuters* 2019). "The Pakistani civilian and military leadership believed," reports *Hindustan Times* (2019a), "India was planning to launch at least nine missiles at Pakistani targets on the evening of February 27." On the other side, precautions and retaliation were readied: "[T]he Pakistani military ordered a blackout in several areas of cities such as Islamabad, Lahore and Karachi with defence installations and military residential colonies" and "had made preparations to retaliate by firing at least 13 missiles at Indian targets" (*Reuters* 2019; *Hindustan Times* 2019a). Had any side shown a decisive instinct with intentions to secure an edge over the other on February 26–27, it is not difficult to say that the two nuclear adversaries could have crossed the nuclear red lines in a fraction of a moment and fought an unwanted nuclear war.[25]

Before the military tensions could be fully de-escalated, Prime Minister Imran Khan threatened to use the country's ultimate firepower (read as nuclear weapons) against India and the superpower United States—which took India's side during the crisis and condemned Pakistan in the UN debates—in a public rally in a village close to the border with India. Imran Khan said:

> If someone, if it is India or any superpower, wishes to enslave the Pakistani nation, I want to make it clear that my nation and I will fight until the last breath to save our independence. . . . [And] keep in mind; you will receive a befitting response from here. (*CNN* 2019)

From such reactionary statements one can infer that the Pakistani policy makers are aware that the deterrent power of nuclear weapons has brought a fundamental change in the character of the dyadic relationship which, despite India's dominant status in the local hierarchy, favors Pakistan to continue its revisionist policy and covert aggression against India. Though it is correct that nuclear weapons' destructive power and their catastrophic impact on human civilization have compelled the nuclear states to preserve the tradition of nuclear non-use (see Tannenwald 2007; Paul 2009), that tradition's sustenance in the subcontinent seems doubtful in light of India's and Pakistan's contentious political behavior and threatening nuclear postures, which includes the former's punitive Cold Start strategy and the latter's responsive countermeasure in the form of "full spectrum deterrence." During the Pulwama-Balakot crisis, the eruption of aerial battle between the two nuclear powers and downing of an Indian MiG-21 jet fighter in a dogfight with Pakistani fighter planes further casts doubt on whether New Delhi and Islamabad would be able to honor the tradition of nuclear non-use without dropping nuclear red lines in a future crisis or war.

In short, the South Asian nuclear experience shows that nuclear deterrence works differently in the context of the India-Pakistan dyad and plays a key part in giving rise to certain conditions which drift them toward security maximization obsession, thereby prolonging the regional rivalry. Given the circumstances, notwithstanding the bargaining moves of the two sides and apart from achieving an impossible condition of rolling back Pakistan's nuclear capabilities, it is highly likely that the India-Pakistan nuclear logjam—or "strategic stability," as Pakistanis prefer to refer to it—will persist and keep the Kashmir conflict intact in the foreseeable future.

IMPACT OF REGIME TYPE AND DOMESTIC POLITICAL CONDITIONS

Soon after the end of the Cold War, the systemic shift and chaotic political situation in J&K had encouraged the Pakistani decision-makers to employ militaristic means to wrest control of Kashmir from the opponent. Thereafter Islamabad actively pursued the revisionist policy, as discussed in the previous sections, and engaged India in a direct armed confrontation along the LoC and a sustained proxy war inside Kashmir. The most perplexing aspect of the situation was that the two states' relationship worsened at a time when they were together governed by democratic regimes (see Figure 7.3c and Table 7.1). This situation was opposite to the notions of the democratic peace theory, which posits that states sharing democratic values generally witness conflict reduction and form peaceful ties. So a few questions emerge: What led India and Pakistan to engage in aggressive behavior despite being ruled by democratic governments in the 1990s? Why did the civilian regimes on both sides ignore peaceful and diplomatic avenues to address the Kashmir issue or resolve their differences? Why did the Pakistani political leadership pursue policies which were not in conformity with the democratic norms?

In the 1990s, mainly three issues affected the India-Pakistan relationship: (1) the Pakistan Army's extensive control over the country's foreign and defense policies; (2) the Pakistani civilian regimes' weakness and domestic compulsions, the latter of which was also applicable to India; and (3) India's mishandling of the secessionist upsurge in Kashmir and Pakistan's unabated political-material support to the Kashmiri people for armed resistance.

Regarding the first issue, after the demise of General Zia-ul-Haq in 1988, the military establishment in Pakistan came under enormous pressure from internal and external quarters to restore the stalled democratic process. However, the successive civilian governments proved ineffective as they failed to carry out key changes to limit or end the military's intervention in state politics. Against the oligarchy of bureaucracy and military establishment, which had traditionally exercised the state's real power, the alternating governments of Benazir Bhutto's PPP and Nawaz Sharif's PML struggled to consolidate their position. A tripartite division of power among overlapping hierarchies, which include the prime minister, the pro-army president, and the COAS, eventually evolved into a chaotic state of affairs in Pakistan (H.-A. Rizvi 2000: 1–2; see B. Bhutto 2004). Though the army was only one element of the triad, it had maintained its control, if not supremacy, over the functioning of the elected governments, which institutionalized asymmetry between the civilian and the military arm of the respective regimes (Waseem 2015; Ziauddin 2015). For instance, before assuming office in December 1988, Benazir Bhutto was forced to accept the army's scheme of power arrangement by retaining General Sahibzada Yaqub Khan as her foreign minister and accepting Ghulam Ishaq Khan as the new president (N. Ahmed 2010: 326).

Even after accommodating the military general headquarters' (GHQ's) demands, the Bhutto government could not manage to gain the upper hand because, as Veena Kukreja notes, the "state structure dominated by the nonrepresentative institutions . . . was not inclined to a transformation that readily asserts the ascendancy of the elected institutions" (2003: xv). The military dominance was not restricted to checking the influence of democratic institutions; its outreach was so deep and extensive that it often caused dismissal of the elected government.[26] Constantly facing the threat of military takeover, Pakistan's civilian governments could not manage to function normally—or as democratic regimes are supposed to function.

Pakistani observers agree that Pakistan's defense policy was exclusively under the army's control rather than that of the elected representatives (Rashid 2015; Siddiqa 2015; Waseem 2015; Ziauddin 2015). On major security issues, particularly vis-à-vis India (read Kashmir) and Afghanistan, Pakistan's democratic governments were mostly kept in the dark or compelled to toe a line dictated by the army (Cohen 2004; Waseem 2015). During the Kashmir crisis of 1990, for instance, Iqbal Akhund, Benazir Bhutto's advisor on national security and foreign affairs, learned from a Pentagon official that the Pakistan Army and its spy agency ISI were conducting a covert operation in Kashmir behind the prime minister's back (Akhund 2000: 222). Likewise, the army torpedoed the Lahore Process in 1999 by launching a highly risky military venture in the Kargil sector without informing the elected government of the day in detail (see Lavoy 2009a; Qadir 2002).

Apart from framing national security policies unilaterally, the army's closely guarded approach to running militant training camps through civilian contractors to sustain the proxy war in Kashmir "led to an element of deniability and ambiguity with regard to controlling the activities of these groups" (Mukherjee 2009: 421). These covert actions substantiate that Pakistan's sustained armed support for insurgency in Kashmir has more to do with the army's revisionist design than the civilian regimes' systematic plan to promote conflict in the state (Haqqani 2005; Siddiqa 2015; Waseem 2015; Ziauddin 2015). In other words, it may be surmised that the civilian leadership's failure to resist the pressure tactics of the interventionist military—which exercises complete control over the Kashmir policy but shares no responsibility—rendered it powerless on crucial decisions that not only embroiled Pakistan in a prolonged armed confrontation with India but also incurred thousands of civilian and military fatalities on both sides (see Table 7.1).

Second, in the tug-of-war for power and influence, Pakistan's civilian stakeholders faced tremendous credibility pressure from their domestic constituencies in the 1990s. Since they risked appearing weak on the issues of national security, they resorted to rhetorical campaigns and war-mongering behavior against India that eventually escalated the violence and proxy war in Kashmir. For instance, while delivering an inflammatory speech in Muzzafarabad during the Kashmir crisis of 1990, Benazir Bhutto had echoed a "thousand-year war" in support of the armed insurgency in Kashmir (Chari

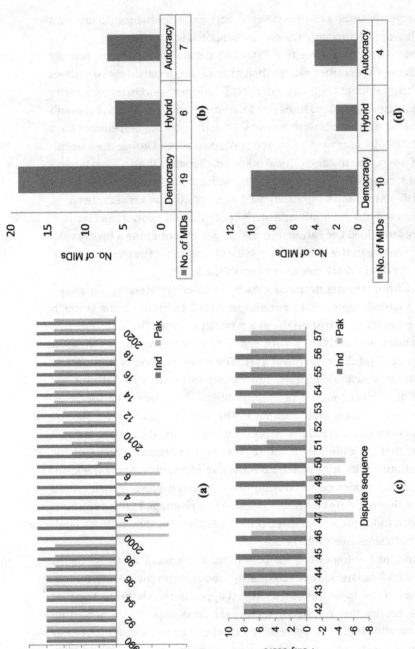

Figure 7.3. India-Pakistan regime type and recurrent militarized disputes, 1990–2021. (a) Regime type, (b) regime years, (c) regime type during the initiation of MIDs, (d) no. of MIDs under particular type of regime. *Source:* Compiled from the COW database (2015, version 4.01; 2020, version 5.0); Polity-5 database (2018, version 5.0); newspaper reports 1990–2022. India's and Pakistan's polity scores for 2019, 2020 and 2021 are assessments based on their current state of democracy and the previous few years' polity scores.

et al. 2003: 74). This was important partly because her foreign minister was a retired army general, Sahibzada Yaqub Khan, and the GHQ was manipulating the Kashmir policy through him. From another point of view, one can draw a parallel between Benazir Bhutto's hawkish postures and her father's post–Bangladesh War hostile attitude. Instead of learning a lesson from Pakistan's several failed attempts to seize Kashmir and the loss of East Pakistan, Zulfikar Ali Bhutto desisted from normalizing relations with India. In fact, as discussed earlier, he was keen to take revenge and thereby set in motion a complicated nuclear policy to challenge India at the cost of common Pakistanis' survival. Benazir Bhutto's hostile approach, like her father's democratic and previous autocratic regimes, elucidates that she was also not interested in bringing about any fundamental change in the country's traditional security and revisionist policies.

The Indian leadership responded to Benazir Bhutto's rhetorical posturing in kind. "[T]hose who talk about 1000 years of war," said Prime Minister V.P. Singh, "should examine whether they will last 1000 hours of war" (cited in Hagerty 1995–96: 99). Such excessive use of political rhetoric snowballed and the successive civilian regimes on both sides began to propagate and promote violent acts, as many chauvinist nationalist parties and the pressure groups then gripped with the war paranoia desired, that escalated the Kashmir dispute in the 1990s. For instance, the Indian leadership from the ruling nationalist party, the BJP, resorted to war rhetoric after conducting the nuclear tests in 1998, which compelled the Sharif regime to respond in kind.[27] Undoubtedly, both elected regimes' aggressive postures and strategic decisions were devised to portray a nationalist image to their respective domestic constituencies, but these steps greatly undermined the prospect of achieving normalization in the fast-deteriorating bilateral relationship. Once the nuclear component became part of the rivalry, unabated pressure from the reactionary domestic groups and the Pakistan Army—which was determined to reverse the Indian gains in the Kargil/Siachen region (Durrani 2015)—began to coerce the political leadership to step up its efforts to wrest Kashmir from India. Eventually, this state of affairs had extended the Pakistan Army an opportunity to push aside the spirit of Lahore and resort to intrusion in Kargil. This fateful move undermined the democratic peace thesis that elected civilian regimes are less conflict-prone and have a tendency to be satisfied with the status quo.

Third, in comparison to the previous decades, the political conditions were remarkably different in Kashmir during the 1990s. In the aftermath of the 1987 state assembly elections, which were largely rigged, the Kashmiri youth completely lost faith in the political system and picked up guns to fight the Indian state. In order to bring the situation under control, New Delhi mishandled the pro-freedom demonstrations, which provided Pakistan (and the international community) an opportunity to intervene in the crisis and support the Kashmiris' right to self-determination (see Behera 2006; Sumantra Bose 2003; Gossman 1995). The unending political turmoil in Kashmir had strengthened the nuclear component in the rivalry, as discussed earlier, which played a key part to prolong the Kashmir conflict in the 1990s. In addition, a favorable combination of circumstances in Kashmir, especially after the Soviet Union's humiliating defeat in Afghanistan and its subsequent disintegration, had activated Pakistan's domestic political scene that extended the religious right and hardliners extensive space to argue for and build momentum against India over the Kashmir issue. Such a state of affairs had not only assisted the domestic hardliners to keep their ruling regimes under stress, but also denied the regimes the required space to negotiate and compromise on their respective national positions on Kashmir. This way the restraining forces on both sides succeeded in fueling the Kashmir dispute and remaining relevant in shaping the nature and direction of the India-Pakistan rivalry.

Conflict De-escalation and Peace Process under Dissimilar Regimes, 1999–2008

After a decade-long unfruitful democratic experience, the India-Pakistan dyad once again returned to the yoke of regime dissimilarity when the Pakistan Army triggered a bloodless coup in October 1999 and dismissed Nawaz Sharif's elected government. Soon after the Kargil War, India was hardly prepared for such a sudden regime change in Islamabad, as its past experience with the military-ruled Pakistan was more hostile and frustrating. Given that states pursuing revisionist or militaristic foreign policies have a high likelihood to become involved in armed disputes, the prevalence of this tendency in Pakistan's autocratic and hybrid regimes has over the years evolved them into more conflict-prone entities. For this reason, General Pervez Musharraf's military regime was not hesitant to use terrorism as a foreign policy tool to achieve the country's political goals in Kashmir. The bilateral situation turned so grim, said Ashraf Jehangir Qazi (2015), then high commissioner of Pakistan to India, that "even an attempt like the Agra Summit failed to normalize the relationship." This summit meeting in fact proved counter-productive, he maintains: "the 'letdown effect' of terrible failure" had stepped up domestic pressure on the military regime to pursue aggressive strategies to compel India to negotiate Kashmir (Qazi 2015). From that time on, as noted in the preceding sections, the military regime decided to intensify shelling along the LoC and expand terrorist strikes across India that included a fateful attack on the Indian Parliament in December 2001.

However, it is important to note that the India-Pakistan relationship did witness a significant change due to the global rise and spread of terrorism and the Musharraf regime's credibility-cum-legitimacy crisis at home. The worldwide upsurge in terrorist attacks, beginning with the spectacular Al Qaida strikes demolishing the World Trade Center in New York in September 2001, had compelled the United States and its allies to launch a global war against terrorism to uproot the jihadi networks in Afghanistan and elsewhere. This anti-terrorism drive had also extended India a long-awaited opportunity to mount sustained pressure on Pakistan. Consequently, New Delhi argued that the global terrorism was closely linked with Pakistan's policy of harboring armed extremists and using the terrorist groups against India, Afghanistan, and the West to secure its objectives (Chellaney 2001-2: 97–99). Such pressure on Pakistan from different international quarters, coupled with the increasing two-front vulnerability after its military engagement in the Af-Pak region, effectively coerced the already intimidated Musharraf regime to soften its aggressive policy against India. With the beginning of the US-led NATO strikes on the Taliban in Afghanistan, the Musharraf regime came under pressure from two quarters: (1) domestic political opponents started "questioning the legitimacy of his unelected and unconstitutional regime" (Hoodbhoy 2015); and (2) the previous civilian governments' better diplomatic record—for instance, the 1972 Simla Agreement and the 1999 Lahore Declaration—that earned them political legitimacy at home and endorsement from the regional and international bodies.

Faced with such a grim situation, General Musharraf was in dire need of a face-saving negotiation on Kashmir so that his regime would again tilt the institutional balance in its favor and against the domestic political opponents and unruly jihadi groups.[28] Another incentive for such negotiations or getting an opening to start a peace process with India was perhaps to show the mass public that "the military regime could engage New Delhi effectively and more meaningfully than the elected regimes" (Waseem 2015). With an objective to bring about a dynamic change in the bilateral relations, Musharraf broke new ground in proposing what is famously known as the "four-point formula" for resolving the Kashmir issue that envisaged (1) softening of the LoC without altering the demarcation, (2) self-governance, (3) phased withdrawal of troops from the entire state of J&K, and (4) joint supervision of the state by India and Pakistan (Aziz Ahmed Khan 2015; Baru 2014; Kasuri 2015).

Apart from consolidating Musharraf's position at home, this proposal had potential to earn currency in India too because, in pragmatic terms, New Delhi could see an incentive to consider a proposal that was prepared by a stable and powerful regime.[29] General Musharraf's four-point formula was certainly the most far-reaching proposal with regard to Kashmir and progressed almost to the point of signing a landmark agreement in 2006-7[30] (Baru 2014; Kasuri 2015; S. Malik 2015). The key shortcoming of the whole exercise was that it was advanced by a regime whose constitutional standing was questionable and any succeeding civilian government could have distanced itself from it for political reasons. In June 2010, for instance, a fortnight before the first foreign minister–level meeting over the issue of the Mumbai attacks, Pakistan's Foreign Minister Shah Mahmood Qureshi distanced his government from General Musharraf's four-point formula by dubbing it "his thinking" which was "neither discussed by the cabinet nor endorsed by the parliament" (quoted in *Times of India* 2010). He further elaborated:

> [Pakistan is] a democracy, Parliament has to own [peace formulas], Parliament has to endorse them, Cabinet has to discuss them . . . [but proposals like the four-point formula were] neither discussed by Cabinet, nor endorsed by Parliament. So, as democrats, there are certain Parliamentary procedures that we have to fulfill. (quoted in *Times of India* 2010)

Before the four-point plan there were doubts about the Musharraf regime's credentials over credibility and legitimacy issues, but such a remarkable breakthrough on Kashmir during his regime underlines that non-democratic regimes and dyads can also overcome the limitations that the democratic peace thesis calls attention to. Perhaps the 2001–2 military stand-off acted as a catalyst that made New Delhi and Islamabad better understand the dangers of dispute escalation in a nuclear environment. After this near-nuclear crisis, a more rational view prevailed, opined Aziz Ahmed Khan (2015), then high commissioner of Pakistan to India, that sped up the two dissimilar regimes' efforts to find a common ground on Kashmir.

Beginning with the ceasefire along the LoC in November 2003, Musharraf's military regime succeeded in improving Pakistan's strained relations with the BJP-led and the Congress-led coalition governments in New Delhi. Thereupon the two sides had shown a remarkable maturity, particularly by prioritizing their peoples' interests over their long-standing differences, and they initiated a series of historic steps related to Kashmir that concluded in a formal ceasefire in Kashmir in December 2003, the opening of five points along the LoC to facilitate meetings between divided families in the aftermath of the October 2005 earthquake, and a set of confidence-building measures (CBMs) such as the cross-LoC bus service on the Srinagar-Muzaffarabad and the Poonch-Rawalakot routes and much-awaited cross-border trade (Aziz Ahmed Khan 2015). Similarly, the reopening of the Wagah-Attari checkpoint, resumption of the air and train links, and the composite dialogue at the bilateral level had considerably altered the traditional security narratives across the border (S. Malik 2015).

Even after Musharraf's exit in 2008, successive regimes in both India and Pakistan have ensured the continuation of the cross-border/LoC movement of people and goods. Overall, these progressive steps brought a better sense of normalcy in the bilateral relationship. Substantial success of the Indo-Pakistani peace negotiations under dissimilar regimes during the 2003-7 phase underlines that even a conflict-prone non-democratic dyad can also promote peace or de-escalate a conflict marred by historical complexities and intangible issues provided that the ruling elites on both sides are willing to make and implement risky decisions.

Regime Similarity and the Limitation of Democratic Conditions

It may be argued that the political stakeholders in India and Pakistan, despite having strong differences on domestic issues, tend to share a consensus over the established national policy: Pakistan follows the policy of persistent revisionism toward India and the latter relentlessly seeks to maintain the status quo. The successive regimes in New Delhi and Islamabad have more or less followed this stance for decades. For instance, the PPP government, under Asif Ali Zardari and Yusuf Raza Gilani, had continued General Musharraf's peace process to find a common ground with India over the Kashmir issue. In fact, weeks before the Mumbai terrorist attacks, "Zardari offered to drop Pakistan's stated nuclear-weapons policy, under which it retains the right to launch a nuclear strike against India in the event of an Indian invasion, in return for a comprehensive peace agreement" (T. Hussain 2013).

But the military again stepped in steadfastly and effectively torpedoed the elected government's proposed plans by launching audacious and unprecedented terrorist attacks across Mumbai through its proxy networks. Desynchronization of actions between the civilian and the military arms of the government indicates that either there had been no civil-military agreement on the PPP's proposed policy shift or the post-Musharraf military establishment in the GHQ wanted to signal the new civilian government that it must not presumptuously overstep the country's established policies. Here one can draw a parallel between Zardari's proposed shift with that of Sharif's Lahore rapprochement of 1999 and how on both occasions the Pakistan Army had undermined, if not practically invalidated, the elected governments' reconciliation initiatives by staging high-magnitude offensives against India: the Kargil intrusion and the Mumbai attacks. This clearly underscores that despite following a common revisionist policy vis-à-vis India, Pakistan's civilian and military stakeholders differ on its implementation.

In India, on the other hand, Pakistan is broadly not a partisan issue as the approach of both mainstream parties, the BJP and the Congress, toward Pakistan allows them adequate room to accommodate and advance each other's policies. However, in the context of a broader link between party ideology and foreign policy, the two mainstream political parties' contrasting ideologies bring a wide variation in the trajectory of India's foreign policy that affects India-Pakistan relations to a large extent. People having close or firsthand knowledge about the finalization of the four-point formula, for instance, claim that the Manmohan Singh–led UPA regime lacked the willpower to move toward entente with Pakistan even when conditions for achieving a breakthrough were ripe—partly this happened as a result of the BJP's hardline position[31] and varied pressures from the coalition partners in the United Progressive Alliance (UPA) (Baru 2014: 191–97; see Kasuri 2015; *New Indian Express* 2014). At present, though the BJP's staunch nationalist reputation imparts it leverage to assure its constituents of the acceptability of a peace agreement, it would suffer blowback from its own hardline position (and staunch nationalist stand) while negotiating a peace agreement with Islamabad. The reason is straightforward: the same undercuts the Pakistani ruling elites' leverage to reach an agreement, or make effective concessions, for an honorable political solution with the BJP. For instance, the BJP General Secretary Ram Madhav's interview with the Doha-based news channel *Al Jazeera* reflects the party's nationalist position and the long-term goal:

The RSS [*Rashtriya Swayamsevak Sangh*] still believes that one day these parts [India, Pakistan and Bangladesh], which have for historical reasons separated only 60 years [*sic*] ago, will again, through popular goodwill, come together and *Akhand Bharat* [an undivided India] will be created. (Madhav 2015)

This position, in practice, not only jeopardizes Pakistan's whole state-building enterprise by negating the two-nation theory, but also amounts to reversing the former Prime Minister Atal Bihari Vajpayee's famous commitment to the people of Pakistan at the Minar-e-Pakistan—a monument that commemorates the call for Pakistan's creation—that India acknowledges the legitimacy of Pakistan as a separate and permanent sovereign state in the comity of nations. Another paradox of this idea, mainly from a religious viewpoint, is that the more Pakistani and Bangladeshi territories would integrate with India, the more Muslim population the country would acquire. So it not only undermines the RSS's political ideology of Hindu nationalism but also negates its majoritarian and nationalist state-building endeavor in which the religious minorities have limited role and space (see Ambekar 2019; Chatterjee & Das 2021; Jaffrelot 2009). In real terms, instead of solving the problem, the proposed idea of integration seems to make the ground realities more grim and complex; it is also possible that some right-wing entities may even confront this population-inclusive idea or perceive it as a prescription of India's religious enslavement.

In other words, the limitation of the BJP's staunch nationalist position is that it makes it altogether difficult for the BJP to find "genuine" takers in Islamabad. This is because no Pakistani regime, democratic or non-democratic, can afford to negotiate a peace agreement which would project it as undermining the national interest as well as its own position with a terrible feeling of defeat. From this standpoint, the BJP's objective to achieve a negotiated agreement from a position of strength might remain a non-starter, particularly in times of peace, given that India's option to hand Pakistan a conclusive defeat under the nuclear conditions is practically ruled out—the post-Pulwama military tensions are the best example of the situation. This underlines that the BJP's nationalist position, particularly with excessive *hindutva* emphasis, limits its ability to compel Pakistan to concede on Indian terms.

Against this backdrop, and from the broader context of the linkage between stable democratic order and rivalry, it seems that the prospects for transformation or termination of the India-Pakistan rivalry are somewhat limited. This situation might not change even if a civilian regime in Islamabad were to exclusively shape the country's foreign and domestic policies, as Christine Fair has argued, because it "does not obviously follow that the civilians would abandon the policy of persistent revisionism with respect to India" (2014: 265). But Rasul Baksh Rais (2015), professor of political science at the LUMS, disagrees with this understanding and stresses the ground reality of the whole issue is that "there is no political will to resolve the Kashmir issue and the political leadership [on both sides] has no vision to look into and digest the peace building proposals."

Another factor that makes it difficult for both states to negotiate a mutually acceptable political compromise over Kashmir is their respective complex domestic settings. The ruling regimes on both sides are vulnerable to powerful domestic hardliners, as Rajesh Basrur notes, who are "prone to 'outbid' each other" to expand their influence or manipulate national security issues in collaboration with extended stakeholders to oppose any reconciliation between India and Pakistan (2010: 22). Interestingly, apart from the domestic pressure groups, one can draw relative similarities between the BJP *in opposition* in India and the Pakistan Army when not directly at the helm of affairs. Their somewhat similar approaches toward the long-standing conflict undercuts the prospect for peace, as "they assume hawkish foreign and security positions to pressure the governments at the helm of affairs" to ensure that the ruling regimes on both sides would not be able to strike a reconciling deal to resolve the Kashmir issue (Waseem 2015).

For instance, the PPP government's serious endeavor to improve relations with India was forestalled by the military through terrorist strikes on Mumbai in 2008. Through its conspicuous intervention, the GHQ succeeded in demonstrating that (1) it does not endorse and is not ready to seek a testing reconciliation with the archrival; (2) the civilian regimes in Islamabad are (and will remain) ineffective to make use of their constitutional position and legitimacy to shape the country's foreign and security policies; and (3) the army is the foremost power in Pakistan and it will continuously call shots to shape the country's foreign and security policies despite any elected regime being at the helm of power. On the other side, the BJP sought to blame the Congress government's soft policies for the Mumbai attacks, thereby managing to pressure it to suspend the track-II process and composite dialogue until Pakistan brought the perpetrators of the Mumbai attacks to justice—notably the LeT chief Hafeez Saeed and his chief military commander Zaki-ur-Rahman Lakhvi. Had the Mumbai attacks not occurred, believe many Pakistani observers, continuity in negotiations in a democratic environment would have certainly sped up the peace process and prepared better ground conditions to address the Kashmir issue (I. Khan 2015; Masood 2015). Though later New Delhi and Islamabad took some bold initiatives to resume the peace process, like the July 2009 meeting between Prime Minister Manmohan Singh and his Pakistani counterpart Yousaf Raza Gilani in Sharm-el-Sheikh, progress remained impaired by domestic criticism in India and political uncertainty in Pakistan.[32]

The smooth democratic transitions of 2013 and 2018 signify a substantial improvement in Pakistan's polity (see Figure 7.3a), but its democratic system, as Reeta Chowdhari Tremblay and Julian Schofield correctly noted years ago, remains constrained by the army's "structural and normative distortions in decisionmaking" (2005: 226). In other words, Pakistan's civil order is still fragile; it lacks capacity to withstand pressure from the military-bureaucratic axis and the intra- and inter-party rivalries that considerably affect Pakistan's relationship with India. For instance, there was a political stir in Pakistan to destabilize the PML government after the Modi-Sharif goodwill meeting on the sidelines of Narendra Modi's swearing-in ceremony in May 2014. A couple of months later, the political opponents in Pakistan had activated the domestic scene by raising a demand for Prime Minister Nawaz Sharif's resignation for alleged electoral malpractices. The primary motive of his political opponents, mainly the Imran Khan–led Pakistan Tahreek-i-Insaf (PTI)—which later won election in August 2018 and assumed power in Islamabad—and Islamic cleric Mahammad Tahir-ul Qadri's Pakistan Awami Tehreek (PAT), was to destabilize the elected government by running it into a political logjam (*Indian Express* 2014b, 2014c, 2014d). Such demands and political movements are not a new trend in Pakistan—for instance, both Benazir Bhutto and Nawaz Sharif had conspired to overthrow each other's regimes in the 1990s, which eventually factored into ushering in an era of elected governments' dismissals at the hands of the military-bureaucratic axis. But the disturbing side of the August–December 2014 protests was that the army, which was responsible for several coups and political disorder in the country, was mediating to defuse the political crisis.

By accepting the military's arbitration to resolve the political crisis, the political leadership in Pakistan, particularly those in opposition, had shown that they not only lack necessary skills to resolve their differences but were also politically immature—as they could not understand that the military had no *locus standi* to interfere in the political domain and assume the mediation responsibility to resolve the political crisis. Since mid-1970s, such invitations have promoted and justified the army's unique role in Pakistan's political affairs which posed a serious challenge to the political institutions and elected regimes in the succeeding years. Keeping in mind the army and the political opposition's tumultuous record of cooperation with the elected regimes, particularly the army's uneasy relationship with Nawaz Sharif after the Kargil debacle, it is safe to say that the army might have collaborated with the strong political opponents—particularly the PTI—against Prime Minister Nawaz Sharif during the political crisis.[33] This crisis reaffirmed that all political stakeholders, across party lines, could have made collective efforts to resolve their political disputes by adhering to the constitutional norms. In the absence of any political mechanism or tradition to resolve their differences, Pakistan's two consecutive democratic transitions and relatively stable democracy run a risk of being subverted from within, which might adversely affect the country's relations with India.

On the other side, the Modi government's hard handling of the Kashmir issue, especially its decision to cancel the August 2014 foreign secretary-level talks after Pakistan High Commissioner Abdul Basit's meeting with the Kashmiri separatists, also contributed to undermining Nawaz Sharif's domestic standing and political will to improve the bilateral relationship (*Indian Express* 2014a). Mohammad Ziauddin (2015), Pakistan's veteran journalist and the former editor-in-chief of the *Dawn* and the *Express Tribune*, while referring to the August 2014 and August 2015 developments, opined that "Modi's rhetoric, tough posturing, and inflexible policies have potential to disturb the India-Pakistan relations [rather] than stabilizing [them]." Indeed, there is merit in Ziauddin's (2015) observation as the Modi government's tough posturing did help the Pakistan Army to score a point in its tussle for power against a civilian prime minister who had categorically stated that "the Prime Minister would be the army chief's 'boss'"[34] (*Zee News* 2013). Even during his election campaign in May 2013, Nawaz Sharif had candidly expressed his willingness to end the terrorist activities against India from Pakistani soil and publicized his commitment to improve bilateral relations by picking up the threads of the Lahore Declaration (see *India Today* 2013; *Indian Express* 2013b). Because of strained relations with Nawaz Sharif's civilian government, the Pakistan Army resorted to excessive firing toward the Indian side of the LoC in 2014–15, the severest clash since the 1971 War, resulting in the forced migration of thousands of civilians from the adjoining areas (see *Kashmir Times* 2014a, 2014b).

Similarly, the cancellation of the NSA-level talks in August 2015 had heightened tensions along the LoC and the international border; this was followed by the Pakistan-based terrorist outfits' attacks on the Pathankot airbase and the Uri army headquarters (see *Huffington Post* 2015; *Indian Express* 2015a). The Modi government's tough diplomatic stand, as security expert Ayesha Siddiqa (2015) anticipated, had yielded a militaristic response from the Pakistan Army and its terrorist networks. Such policy steps from the Indian side assist the GHQ to secure its desired objective of stalling the Pakistani civilian government's every progressive step toward peace negotiations by creating a wedge between the democratic regimes at the helm of power in New Delhi and Islamabad.

On this front, Pakistan's political system has not witnessed much difference even after the departure of the army-unfriendly Nawaz Sharif regime and the formation of the army-friendly new civilian government of Imran Khan in August 2018. Unabated firing along the LoC and the terrorist strikes on the Indian military bases and convoys are prime examples of the Pakistan Army's unflagging resolve—the deadly suicide attack on the Indian security convoy in February 2019 is a case in point that almost escalated the military tensions between the two nuclear states. By employing such risky strategies and exploiting all possible security gaps on the Indian side of the LoC, such as the civil unrest in Kashmir, the GHQ had not only undermined the Pakistani civilian regimes' legitimacy and reconciliation efforts with New Delhi but also kept India under political-strategic stress.

In the recent past, from the viewpoint of power angularities, the Pakistan Army's calculated schemes and continued intervention in the civil domain indicate that the country's prospects to evolve as a stable democracy, despite its second successful democratic transition and third consecutive elected government, are not so bright and this state of affairs might not allow India and Pakistan to de-escalate the rivalry under common democratic conditions anytime soon. This is because the prevalent power setting within Pakistan does *not* permit a comprehensive transformation of the country's polity in a way which could vest democratic institutions with the supremacy and authority to make decisions freely. From this viewpoint, if any elected government tries to tamper with the established foreign and security policies, the GHQ perceives such a shift as an infringement on its principal domain; therefore it checkmates the particular civilian regime either by destabilizing it or targeting India through the proxy networks to undermine its credibility. A few examples are the Pathankot airbase attack in January 2016, which took place a week after Prime Minister Modi's unscheduled visit to his counterpart Nawaz Sharif's home in Lahore; the Uri army base attack in September 2016; and the February 2019 attack on an Indian paramilitary convoy in Pulwama, which was another stark reminder to the new Imran Khan–led civilian government that it has limits and it must not cross the established red lines.

In the backdrop of the civil-military discord in Pakistan, where the two power centers are poles apart in their approach to pursuing the revisionist policy vis-à-vis India, coupled with their unending struggle for supremacy and their tactics to undercut each other's reconciliation efforts, it is safe to say that the prospects of peace between India and Pakistan are not promising under either democratic or non-democratic conditions in the near to medium term.

CONCLUSION

This chapter describes how in the early post–Cold War years the systemic shift and favorable political conditions in Kashmir, coupled with ever-expanding nuclear stress, have emboldened the Pakistani decision-makers to pursue aggressive armed strategies to wrest Kashmir from India. Some findings here draw considerable support from the propositions regarding internal and external shocks and rivalry linkage—particularly in the cases of the global war against terrorism, India and Pakistan's strategic competition in Afghanistan, and the impact of military capabilities on the India-Pakistan rivalry. Likewise the periodic escalation and de-escalation of the subcontinental rivalry, that is, before and after the 9/11 attacks, is partly consistent with the power transition theory. It is obvious that the expansion of Pakistan's qualitative capabilities in conventional and nuclear weaponry to a position of relative parity with that of India is playing a defining role in rivalry stabilization.

From the standpoint of the hub-and-spokes framework, it is safe to say that the structural and the temporal factors' synchronous interactions in the early post–Cold War years had tilted the dyadic balance in Pakistan's favor. However, the situation took a drastic turnaround after the Kargil War when the peripheral temporal factors started exerting stress on the structural factors. Major developments that contributed to this shift were the global expansion of terrorism and the US-led reactive war against it in Afghanistan, which collided with Pakistan's militaristic interests, and India's stable polity and increasing economic integration with the objectives of globalization. These developments significantly influenced the great powers' opinions about the India-Pakistan conflict, particularly in the backdrop of changing regional security and order, which resulted in recognition and accommodation of New Delhi's concerns.

It is correct that India's fast-growing capabilities and increasing international clout has pressured Pakistan to desist from launching sustained armed hostilities in Kashmir, particularly the 1990s-type secessionist movement, but unabated terrorist attacks on the Indian armed forces and military underline that the prospects of conflict transformation or termination seem unlikely in the South Asian case. Additionally, Afghanistan's increasing security vulnerability, particularly after the withdrawal of US troops and the return of Taliban militants to power, has increased the likelihood of the escalation of India-Pakistan conflict in the near future. The last few years' heightened tensions between India and Pakistan along the LoC, increased militant activities in the Kashmir Valley, and the abrogation of Article 370 and downgrading of J&K's status are disturbing facts to this light.

Since the nuclearization of South Asia, the nuclear factor has taken this dyadic contention to a different strategic plane which has brought a dramatic transformation in the rivalry context and that might keep the Kashmir problem persisting for years. At present, the changing regional power equations, particularly with the Taliban's power consolidation in Afghanistan and Kashmir's unending political instability, have once again provided Pakistan another opening against India and, it seems, this time Islamabad might take steps to turn the new situation to its favor. So, it is certain that the nuclear factor will continuously play an underlying role to assist Pakistan in maintaining its revisionist position against India and prolong the regional rivalry. In other words, despite India's preponderant position in the region and recognition as an emerging power, one can safely assume that the power of nuclear weapons will consistently act as a rivalry stabilizer between the subcontinental adversaries and might not allow them to de-escalate their long-standing contention easily in the near to medium term.

In the context of the broader link between regime type and rivalry, it is clear that the autocratic and hybrid regimes have a high likelihood to become involved in militarized disputes, particularly when one or both parties have revisionist foreign policies. Internalization of this trait in Pakistan's political system tends to make its ruling regimes more conflict-prone. Since the early

1990s, the similarity in India's and Pakistan's regime types has created some general background conditions for rivalry de-escalation, but the Pakistani civilian regimes' and the GHQ's repetition of counter-productive policies overpowered the goals that might otherwise be attained under joint-democratic conditions, that is, a negotiated resolution of the conflictual issues. In short, the established and rivalry-steering interactions between the structural and temporal factors are not allowing India and Pakistan to reframe their clashing foreign and security policies; hence the two state are prone to continue the Kashmir conflict under both democratic and non-democratic conditions. Despite favorable democratic conditions in the present day, it is highly unlikely that the Pakistani civilian regime could afford to reverse the country's traditional revisionist policy. So the prevalent situation in the subcontinent indicates that the prospects of a peaceful change in the Indo-Pakistani rivalry are weak in the near to medium term.

CHAPTER 8

Prospects for Rivalry Termination

INTRODUCTION

As the preceding chapters make evident, India and Pakistan's competition has become enduring as a result of the formation of an interactive mechanism between the structural and temporal factors. As long as the association of these factors remains dynamic and intact, particularly in the form of "hub" and "spokes," India and Pakistan's relations may fluctuate around the basic rivalry level. In other words, until the feuding states do away with the established hegemonic structure, the trajectory of their policies and the prospects of rivalry transformation may remain bleak. To mitigate the interplay of hub and spokes, this dyad requires some essential conditions—such as some kind of shocks, accommodation, or reconciliation—so that the structural factors' bonding within the hub and the latter's interactions with the temporal factors on the periphery (spokes) can be effectively neutralized. Here, it is important to note that mere mitigation of the structural factors might not prove a sufficient condition to bring about the preferred changes or transformation in the rivalry; the mitigation of the temporal factors is also essential to achieve such objectives.

In the succeeding sections, I discuss the relative position and the current interplay of structural and temporal factors to examine whether any change in their internal and external dynamics is possible. And, if change is possible, how could a new situation potentially impact the India-Pakistan rivalry positively and assist their ruling elites to transform one of the most intractable conflicts of the present times peacefully?

RECASTING THE HUB: CHALLENGES AND PROSPECTS

India's and Pakistan's divergent national ideologies, which rest on the disputed status of Kashmir, shape their foundational principles and state-building strategies. For India, Kashmir, its only Muslim-majority state,[1] is important because it not only keeps India's secular identity intact but also counterbalances the secessionist demands in other parts of the country. On the other hand, the leadership in Islamabad is also obsessed with the Muslim-majority Kashmir, but on religious grounds, and believes that Pakistan will remain an incomplete Islamic Republic till this part unites with it. Precisely for this reason, even the secession of East Pakistan could not dent the Pakistani elites' faith in the two-nation theory; hence they repeatedly employed varied strategies to change the territorial status of Kashmir. For this reason, coupled with other conditions, the endogenous shock of the Bangladesh War and the exogenous shock of the end of the Cold War failed to dislodge this rivalry. Over the last decade or so, the proxy war in Kashmir has witnessed a relative decline due to Pakistan's deepening economic troubles, engagement in the Af-Pak region, and sustained pressure from the international community, but it has not lost its relevance in the Kashmir dispute—the post-Pulwama military standoff and the eruption of a policy dispute with India after the abrogation of J&K's special status in August 2019 are recent examples. This underlines how India's and Pakistan's divergent nation-building strategies and political objectives have exacerbated their differences that cast doubt about the possibility of rivalry transformation or peaceful coexistence between them in the near term.

In addition to India's and Pakistan's mutually invalidating claims of what constitutes nationhood, coupled with Kashmir's geographical contiguity and territorial salience, now the fast-emerging climate change threat to economic development is adding another layer to their security interests and rivalrous relationship. Against this backdrop, the Pakistani policy makers and intelligentsia are now more conscious and concerned about water as it is the mainstay of Pakistan's economic survival—around 40 percent of its population is engaged in agriculture and allied sectors—and all of its major rivers either originate in or flow through Kashmir. Pakistan's dependency on Kashmir's water system—particularly in light of future needs for more water and electricity for its growing population, agriculture, and industry—has made the Indian part of Kashmir a perceived economic disadvantage/vulnerability for Pakistan because the superior rival's upstream riparian status vests it with a natural advantage to regulate and manipulate the flow of waters in the Indus River system and, by extension, monitor resource-stressed Pakistan's agricultural economy.

For this reason, despite the Indus Water Treaty that allotted to Pakistan exclusive rights over the three western rivers of the Indus River system (Chenab, Jhelum, and Indus), Pakistanis voice their concern that their country's increasing water stress and/or resource dependency will certainly influence its bilateral policies vis-à-vis India in due course (A. Hussain 2015; I. Khan 2015; S. Malik 2015). Therefore, in their opinion, until Pakistan is vested with complete control over Kashmir, or the upper reaches of its river system, its overall economic development will remain in a hostage situation or rooted in questions of resource dependence which might aggravate tensions and escalate armed hostilities between the two adversaries. Over the last few years, Pakistan's insecurity dilemma has compounded to a more advanced stage as the Indian prime minister, Narendra Modi, has taken a tough stand against cross-border terrorism by linking the terrorist acts with the Indus Water Treaty. While chairing a post–Uri attack meeting with the officials of India's Water Ministry, with an aim to mount pressure on Pakistan and increase its sense of strategic vulnerability through resource supply control, Modi said that "blood and water cannot flow together at the same time" (*Indian Express* 2016h).

As an upstream riparian state, India's status quo posture not only gives it operational control over Kashmir's three rivers but also facilitates its harnessing of their water for electricity generation and irrigation—India's proposal to construct more dams on the Chenab River and use its share of water from the Kashmir river system substantiates this (see *DNA* 2019; *Hindustan Times* 2019b; *Indian Express* 2016h). Though India's hydropower projects do not prevent or reduce the flow of water into Pakistan, Islamabad is concerned about New Delhi's extensive plans to develop water infrastructure over Kashmir's river system and perceives these projects as the rival's ploy to create livelihood insecurity for Pakistan (A. Hussain 2015; I. Khan 2015; S. Malik 2015; see *Dawn* 2017b, 2018). Due to India and Pakistan's increasing agricultural and industrial dependency on water and the centrality of Kashmir in a three-cornered geostrategic contest between India, Pakistan, and China, it is highly likely that the political-economic value of retaining salient Kashmir or gaining control over its geographically contiguous areas might increase among contestants in the near future. These issues, coupled with the increasing climate change threat and water insecurity,[2] have compounded Pakistan's long-term security concerns despite the CPEC project having provided it an immediate relief and space to limit India's strategic squeeze.

From a Pakistani viewpoint, India's status quo position over Kashmir undermines Pakistan's strategic interests. As long as India retains its control over Kashmir, Pakistan's geo-strategic alignment with China will remain on India's security scanner as Kashmir acts as a geographical wedge between both anti-India allies. This is especially true from the standpoint of the Sino-Pakistani strategic alliance against India, their common adversary, which also has a collective purpose to maximize territorial gains in the adjacent hilly terrains of Kashmir and Ladakh so that India's strategic advantage in the local and regional spheres can be effectively neutralized. For instance, amid the pandemic spread of COVID-19, Islamabad intensified firing along the India-Pakistan Line of Control (LoC) and Beijing activated its armed troops to overstep the status quo by escalating hostilities at multiple locations along the India-China Line of Actual Control (LAC) in eastern Ladakh to secure an advantageous position against India—as of this writing in early 2022, this militarized territorial dispute is inconclusive despite fifteen rounds of Corps Commander–level meetings between the Indian and the Chinese militaries since May 2020 (see *Hindu* 2020a, 2020b, 2020c, 2020d, 2021, 2022). On the whole, from a Pakistani viewpoint, solutions grounded in the status quo unduly favor India and undermine Pakistan's vital interests (see *Dawn* 2017b; GoP 2022). Such a position constitutes an overall and long-term disadvantage for Pakistan; thus pressure mounts on its ruling elites to make "repeated attempts to alter the status quo in Kashmir or replace it with an advantageous one" (Durrani 2015). The same rationale compels India to strive hard to uphold the status quo position to maintain its territorial integrity—particularly in the wake of the US-led NATO forces' withdrawal from Afghanistan and the Taliban's return to power, the conclusion of a comprehensive deal between Iran and China (which has potential to jeopardize the Indo-Iranian joint Chabahar project), and the sharpening Sino-Pakistani collective challenge in the form of a multi-purpose connectivity project: the CPEC.

Putting it differently, Pakistan's ideological differences, resource-based insecurity, and strategic weakness together shape its revisionist position that compels as well as provides an incentive to its ruling elites to make irredentist claims with an objective to upset the status quo opponent, India, until it agrees to give sufficient concessions on Kashmir. In this sense, Kashmir acts almost like an Alsace-Lorraine that intertwines identity and salient territory in such a manner that the two countries' respective positions and interests end up charting a zero-sum equation. For instance, if India concedes on either of these two factors, identity and salient territory (the third factor, geographical contiguity, acts as a constant) the emerging situation would result in giving up its complete control over Kashmir as both factors are intertwined in such a way that conceding either one leads to an involuntary loss of the other too. In such a situation, India's loss would be an absolute gain for Pakistan. This underscores how the placement and interplay of the structural factors forming the "hub" make it difficult for India and Pakistan to retreat from their principal positions, status quo and revisionist, respectively, thereby shaping Kashmir as a more toilsome dispute to resolve. Against this backdrop, the question remains: What is the way forward from this impasse?

India and Pakistan's record of hostile policy making and aggressive security postures suggest that their hegemonic relations will not allow them to transform their rivalrous equations so easily. Since the partition, India has failed to compel Pakistan to accept the status quo and, on the other hand, all of Pakistan's attempts to seize control of Kashmir or redraw favorable boundaries could not help it to secure the desired objectives. Given the circumstances, if both sides keep on strategizing to counterbalance each other, then the possibility for an amicable resolution of the conflict or transformation of the rivalry will remain dim in the near to medium term.

To seek a peaceful resolution of Kashmir, New Delhi and Islamabad have to acknowledge that a drastic policy shift away from their existing realpolitik engagement is essential, particularly by adopting and adhering to alternative approaches, even if that means making unpopular and risky decisions. In this direction, transformation of the LoC may possibly be one such nontraditional step that has potential to provide their divergent positions a middle ground. Sometimes contentious issues between rivals emerge as a source of cooperation, provided they are handled patiently and differently by their ruling elites. For instance, Alsace-Lorraine was a high-magnitude territorial/nationalism dispute between France and Germany from 1870 to 1945. After World War II, it emerged as a torchbearer of the new Europe when Franco-German cooperation created the European Coal and Steel Community (ECSC) with Belgium, Luxembourg, Italy, and the Netherlands, which later evolved into a highly progressive multi-state organization: the EU.

Whether such an initiative could work in the India-Pakistan case is not clear as of now because unlike Europe, where the Franco-German hostile equations underwent a drastic change in the post-war years, the South Asian dyad has not experienced much change despite fighting four wars and engaging in a prolonged and unfruitful armed duel at the subconventional level. Having said that, some bilateral initiatives have potential to transform India and Pakistan's frozen relations—for instance, a shift in their focus from military acquisitions to meeting the imperatives of a globalizing world or from territorial acquisitions to addressing the question of economic development and people's rights in the case of Kashmir—provided the policy makers on both sides approach the dispute differently and show the will to implement politically risky decisions. *Only* then may the factors constituting the "hub" be effectively recast. In the following subsections, I discuss some of these elements with an objective to see whether they have potential to steer such a change in the India-Pakistan case.

Reframing the Bilateral Context: From Realpolitik to Alternative Paradigm

In interstate conflicts, geographical contiguity by and large favors the state pursuing irredentism and revisionism—even if it is a weak military power—against the superior status quo opponent, as it augments the concerned state's capability to use force closer to home. Since geographical contiguity cannot be changed and, in addition, if the contiguous territory in dispute constitutes hilly terrain and an ethno-religious population with political differences with the parent state, the possibility of conflict protraction increases as "distance," "hilly terrain," and "ethno-religious population" together inflate the revisionist state's actual advantages which more or less undercut the superior opponent's offensive capabilities.

In the Indo-Pakistani case, Kashmir's mountainous terrain and resentful ethno-religious population allow Pakistan to consolidate its strategic position and inflict cost on the stronger opponent, India, by continuing the agenda of territorial revisionism against it. After the Modi government's decision to abrogate the state's special status and statehood in August 2019, the probability is now greater that the resentful Kashmiris might turn to Pakistan or form reactionary platforms to increase New Delhi's political-security anxiety. India and Pakistan's historical record shows that neither side has been able to prevail over the other despite engaging in interstate wars and prolonged armed hostilities in Kashmir. However, the experience of the Kargil War underlines that the control of strategic heights can also be reversed if the security interests and national honor of the status quo power are at stake. During the crisis, for instance, the policy makers in New Delhi felt that the loss of the Indian territory had dented the country's pride; this led them to respond by deploying all possible means to recapture the lost territory from the Pakistani intruders. This shows that though the advantageous terrain favored the revisionist Pakistan to inflict damage on the status quo opponent, Pakistan could not materialize its advantage to change or redraw borders as its decision-makers had originally strategized. This substantiates that the revisionist state does hold an advantage against the status quo opponent in a salient contiguous territory comprising an affiliated ethno-religious population, but more often than not, this works favorably while deploying low- or medium-range proxy strategies to prolong the conflict—not in high-magnitude intrusions or conventional warfare.

Along with territorial borders or favorable terrain, the political complexities of the border areas also count as an important factor in the India-Pakistan case—for instance, right from the outset of the conflict the Cease-Fire Line (CFL; later the LoC) had a political rationale. In the years preceding accession, Kashmir's two mainstream political parties—the Muslim Conference and the National Conference—had their political base in different parts of the state. The Muslim Conference was the ideological protégé of the Muslim League with a strong political base in the Muslim-majority border areas of Jammu region, and the National Conference was secular in its outlook—like the Indian National Congress—and an indisputably popular political force in the Kashmir Valley. During the First Kashmir War, their support bases factored in India's and Pakistan's war strategies, territorial control, and the timing of the ceasefire declaration, which eventually resulted in a de facto border—the CFL/LoC—between the warring states. For instance, Prime Minister Nehru was not keen to bring the Muslim Conference-dominated parts of the state, mainly "Azad Kashmir" and the northern territories of Hunza, Baltistan, and Gilgit, against their wishes into the Indian Union. For this reason, the Indian political-military planners focused their attention on seizing specific territorial pockets to consolidate the country's strategic position as well as Sheikh Abdullah's political hold in J&K (Jha 1998: 175–76).

Even now the territorial compulsions and political complexities play a relatively larger role in J&K's domestic politics and India and Pakistan's bilateral ties. For example, the divided state's three distinct regions—Kashmir, Jammu, and Ladakh[3]—have been carved along the lines of religious, ethnic, lingual, and political affiliations; the Muslim-majority districts of Rajouri, Poonch, Muzaffarabad, Mirpur, and Kotli hold different political positions;

and, on the basis of its religious differences with the Sunni-majority Kashmir Valley and Pakistan, the Shia Muslim population of Kargil extends its support to India and that of Gilgit-Baltistan remains indifferent to Pakistan (see Behera 2000; Sumantra Bose 1999; Snedden 2013). Of late, the Modi government has bifurcated the J&K state into two union territories, but again the whole task was carried out more or less by keeping the logic of these equations in mind and striking a strategic balance to incur minimal operational loss both at the intrastate and interstate level.

All elements of the entire spectrum of violence, from full-fledged conventional wars to proxy war to nuclear blackmail, have not changed the fundamental equations between India and Pakistan, including any territorial changes except those negotiated at Tashkent and Simla in 1966 and 1972, respectively. Over the decades, India's and Pakistan's steady military buildups have instituted deterrence by scaling up the war threat, but to retain it, both sides have to continuously balance each other's capabilities. Such an instituted security dilemma does not allow the weaker side, Pakistan, to give up any sooner than it otherwise might have done. This is because the phenomenon of balancing capabilities immunizes the contesting parties by preparing them to absorb more damage before they can be forced to give up.

In essence, this deadlock remains a defining feature of the India-Pakistan rivalry even after it experienced a long period of no-war-no-peace from 1972 to the early 1980s and the Pakistan-steered intensive wave of militant violence against India since the end of the Cold War. In the near to medium term, the situation might again turn volatile in the Kashmir Valley as the Modi government has abrogated J&K's special status and downgraded its statehood without consulting Kashmiris. In the absence of political dialogue, as some senior journalists, intellectuals, and retired security officers have time and again flagged, the Modi government—unlike the Vajpayee and Manmohan Singh regimes—has not shown much interest in reviving the stalled political dialogue with the Kashmiri separatists and other stakeholders in the state (see Behera 2019; Kak 2017; P. Mehta 2019; Padgaonkar 2016; Sen 2016). With the backdrop of growing external security stress, particularly Afghanistan, coupled with the abrogation of Articles 370 and 35A, the possibility of another political-security transition in Kashmir cannot be ruled out wherein India might be again challenged by Pakistan with China's active support to undermine their common rival's regional status and growing global clout. Such a transition, if it occurs, may again evolve Kashmir as a catalyst to reshape the regional security order and the India-Pakistan rivalry.

As their bilateral record shows, India's and Pakistan's power politics practices, particularly in the shadow of nuclear weapons, have a high likelihood to continue their hegemonic relationship. Such a stabilized instability at the strategic level encourages them to inflict losses upon each other, or acquire superior military position along the LoC without engaging in a large-scale warfare, and continuation of such aggressive postures at the subconventional level undermines the prospects of rivalry transformation. So far, policies imbued with militarism have failed to engage the two sides in meaningful dialogues and overcome their differences. Against this backdrop, what appears to be more reasonable for India and Pakistan is to look into other conflict resolution approaches, or adopt alternative policies, which could assist them to negotiate their differences and transform the long-standing rivalry. By focusing on this theme, the next section discusses the basic propositions of making borders irrelevant, supporting bilateral trade and dialogues, and promoting people-to-people contacts to assess whether they have potential to extend any leverage to the rival parties to bring about a peaceful change in their relationship.

Sustaining the Peace Process and Making Borders Irrelevant

While delivering his convocation address at the University of Jammu in July 2007, Prime Minister Manmohan Singh outlined his ideas to transform the India-Pakistan relations: "[B]orders cannot be changed, but they can be made irrelevant. There can be no question of divisions or partitions, but the Line of Control can become a line of peace with a freer flow of ideas, goods, services and people" (GoI 2007). Similarly, the local stakeholders have also endorsed the idea of transformation of the LoC. For instance, the Mehbooba Mufti–led People's Democratic Party's (PDP) "self-rule" framework comprises such elements, which also form its pro-Kashmir political program. Beside seeking demilitarization and certain amendments in the Indian Constitution, the party's primary focus is on making the borders irrelevant, increasing the India-Pakistan joint coordination mechanism for development projects, and political restructuring and economic integration between the divided parts of J&K (PDP 2008).

Likewise Sajad Lone, chairman of the Jammu Kashmir People's Conference (PC), has also proposed a peace plan—famously known as the "achievable nationhood"—that envisages the unification of both Kashmirs with an autonomous status, unhindered and tax-free movement of goods between them, and the formation of a single Jammu and Kashmir Economic Union (Lone 2006). Within the larger framework of their vision documents, the PDP and the PC's proposals envision an economic union of the two parts of Kashmir and a system of shared sovereignty with India and Pakistan. In the immediate context, the possibility of the formation of an economic union by diluting territorial boundaries, or political sovereignty, is out of reach given the intensity of political discord India and Pakistan have. However, demands comprising the economic aspects and social connectivity—as Dr. Manmohan Singh clearly spelled out in his July 2007 address—are of an accommodative nature, albeit in part or in abridged form, as they have potential to foster a layered socio-economic interdependency and relative normalcy in Kashmir.

From the economic standpoint, the opening of the land routes holds enormous economic potential for Kashmir in particular and the India-Pakistan bilateral trade in general. In this direction, the two sides already laid the foundation between 2003 and 2008 that resulted in the opening of the cross-LoC bus services and trade routes.[4] However, despite initial success, these initiatives could not flourish on a par with New Delhi and Islamabad's expectations, particularly after General Musharraf's downfall in Pakistan and the 2008 Mumbai terrorist attacks that debilitated the two sides' four years of substantive progress.

Since both parts of Kashmir are landlocked and are underdeveloped as a result of limited exposure to industrialization, the barter trade is important for locals residing near the trade junctions—mainly small traders, suppliers, transporters, and laborers—who rely on it for commercial enterprise and job support (Anand 2016). According to Pawan Anand (2016, 2019), president of the Chamber of cross-LoC Traders (J&K) and president of Poonch cross-LoC Traders Council, the cross-LoC trade is limited in scope and localized in nature as the annual barter trade on both routes—the Uri-Muzaffarabad and the Poonch-Rawalakot—from the Indian side is around INR 700 crores (i.e., $93.3 million); this implies the total import-export or intra-Kashmir trade is worth around INR 1,400 crores (i.e., $186.6 million)—which is very small in comparison to India and Pakistan's overall trade of $2.55 billion (see DGFT 2019). From Anand's (2016) viewpoint, major issues that contribute to the low trade volume are, for instance, the barter-based trading system, limita-tions on trade volume, restrictions on goods (out of 21 approved items, only 5 to 6, such as dry fruits, herbs, fruits, spices, and embroidery items, have a trade or economic rationale for traders and consumers), inadequate communication facilities, and strict security and inspection regimes. He believes that the potential of intra-Kashmir trade is worth INR 3,500 crores (i.e., $466.6 million), or more, provided that the ruling elites on both sides address the trading community's concerns like the continuation of trade and maintenance of the supply chain during armed hostilities or political deadlocks at the bilateral level (Anand 2016, 2019). Additionally, he suggests, the two sides must take crucial steps to promote cross-LoC trade: (1) replace the barter-based trading system with the banking system to avoid financial difficulties and disturbed payment cycles; (2) equip the check-posts with full-body scanners to inspect vehicles; and (3) allow traders to commute across the LoC, at least once in a quarter, for business negotiations and market assessment (Anand 2016, 2019). Apart from the promotion of intra-Kashmir trade, accommodation of these concerns may also increase the locals' stakes in the peace process through sustained socio-economic cohesion.

Research shows that comparative advantage in bilateral trade increases the probability of conflict de-escalation by evolving economic interdependency between the disputants (see Doyle 1986; Hegre, Oneal, & Russett 2010; Oneal & Russett 1997, 1999; Polachek 1980). Over the last four to five decades, for instance, the intra-regional bilateral trade in Europe, Southeast Asia, and South America has not only registered a substantial increase but also brought down tensions in the major regional rivalries such as France-Germany, Indonesia-Malaysia, and Argentina-Brazil (see Hegre, Oneal, & Russett 2010; Polachek 1980). This indicates that the movement of goods, people, and ideas also has potential to increase the prospects for economic growth, employment, and socio-economic interdependency in the case of India and Pakistan as they are also liberal market economies. For instance, the potential of bilateral trade between India and Pakistan is estimated to be around $37 billion as compared to their current trade of $2.55 billion—which is also less than 1 percent of their total global trade (DGFT 2019; Kathuria 2018). Such a huge economic opportunity cannot be properly tapped without a shift from the two adversaries' informal trading via longer routes and third-country ports (mainly Dubai) to the cost-efficient formal channels, establishing robust financial mechanisms (mainly bank branches), and diversifying the only land link—the Wagah-Attari route—for rail and road transport of goods.

To improve their weak trade relations and nominal economic interdependency, the opening of more land routes across the LoC and the international border—like the Munabhao-Khokhrapar and the Hussainiwala-

Ferozepur—may prove significant initiatives in the long run as they have
potential to connect the border economy of India and Pakistan (mainly
Gujarat, Sindh, Rajasthan, and the two Punjabs).[5] From the regional perspective, given that India and Pakistan have large markets and economic clout in
South Asia, as both states together own around a 90 percent share of the
SAARC's GDP, their bilateral trade has potential to evolve economic interdependency and act as a unifying force for the region (see World Bank 2018). In
the context of two Kashmirs, even if the nominal cross-LoC trade and social
contacts are no match to the scale of India-Pakistan trade initiatives and outcomes (which are also not on a par with their bilateral potential), their continuation has enough potential to emerge as a meaningful channel or platform to enhance New Delhi's and Islamabad's political leverage over local
issues, raise their concerns effectively during militarized disputes, and scale
down their violent engagement in Kashmir.

To increase the prospects of normalization in bilateral relations, Professor Rasul Baksh Rais (2015) and Ambassador Aziz Ahmed Khan (2015), who
played a significant role in promoting cross-border initiatives during his tenure as high commissioner of Pakistan to India from 2003 to 2006, stress that
New Delhi and Islamabad must take concrete steps to expand socio-economic
ties by relaxing the post-Mumbai administrative hurdles—like visa restrictions, difficult travel procedures, frequent trade suspensions, and other such
issues—because they have immense potential to neutralize the civil and
military orthodoxies on both sides. This view also substantiates the belief of
Shashi Tharoor (2012), the former Indian minister of state for external affairs,
that such "risks are worth taking [in the social, cultural, and economic
spheres], since the advantages of enhancing opportunities for Pakistanis in
India outweigh the dangers; after all, the Mumbai terrorists did not apply for
Indian visas before sneaking ashore with their guns and bombs."

On a similar note, while agreeing with the viewpoints of Shashi Tharoor,
Rasul Baksh Rais, and Aziz Ahmed Khan, the policy makers in New Delhi and
Islamabad must recognize that they need to think about alternative arrangements which could extend them room to open borders for the people's
movement and trade to evolve socio-economic bonding or interdependency
between the two sides. Though it is a long, gradual process, it is attainable
provided that the leadership of the rival parties patiently and proactively
continue the positive initiatives without resorting to periodic disrup-
tions—as Monmohan Singh and General Musharraf managed to a certain
extent through the peace process.

These perspectives, apart from promoting trade and socio-economic interdependency, also emphasize that the resumption of composite dialogue—which was suspended after the 2008 Mumbai attacks—has huge potential to negotiate bilateral issues ranging from their core dispute over Kashmir to the Siachen Glacier, the Wullar Barrage Project/Tulbul Navigation Project, Sir Creek, terrorism and drug trafficking, economic and commercial cooperation, and promotion of friendly exchanges in various fields.[6] In short, continuity in the peace process, expansion of the cross-LoC and bilateral trade, and the softening of borders has potential to tie together the two states' collective interests and reduce tensions. Once engagements like trade, travel, and cultural exchanges gain momentum and consolidate different stakeholders' interests on both sides, the new situation might provide India and Pakistan the required space to evolve a conducive environment to limit the influence of territorial nationalism and orthodox practices on their policy making and scale down their mutual animosity with an objective to prepare a ground for rivalry transformation.

THE POSITION AND INTERPLAY OF SPOKES: CHALLENGES AND PROSPECTS

The preceding discussion of this chapter shows how the structural factors comprised in the hub have shaped the India-Pakistan relations right from the onset of the rivalry and how their recasting may prepare a ground for conflict mitigation between the two states. Continuing this theme, this section inquires whether the temporal factors' relative position and interplay in the changing domestic, dyadic, and regional/global environments offer India and Pakistan any ground or opportunity to break their long-standing deadlock; or if they will remain engaged in an unending duel with little prospect of peaceful change in the near future. To begin this exercise, let us first consider the linkage of the India-Pakistan rivalry with other regional issues and rivalries in the backdrop of reshaping Asian security architecture.

The Asian Security Architecture and the Rivalry Linkage

From the geo-political and geo-economic perspectives, as discussed in Chapter 7, the United States and China are the two key external powers whose regional and global strategies as well as individual equations with India and

Pakistan play a crucial role in shaping the latter two states' relations. Since the end of the Cold War, in broader terms, the United States' and China's strategic equations and competing policies have given rise to an aggressive competition in the Asian region which has consolidated the US-dominated network of alliances[7] at one extreme and aggravated China's security anxiety and determination to resist the US strangulation by charting competitive strategies, such as the Belt and Road Initiative, at the other. To understand the present state of the India-Pakistan rivalry and look into the prospects of its possible transformation, it is important to examine how the reshaping Asian security architecture (ASA) may affect the subcontinental rivalry in the near term.

In the post-9/11 years, the United States compromised on its long-standing non-proliferation policies and negotiated India's entry into the nuclear group through a privileged civil-nuclear deal. From the two states' growing strategic equations, now it is apparent that the United States' unusual support to confer India an ad hoc nuclear power status was hinged to its long-term strategic objectives—particularly to counterbalance China's growing military power and influence in the Asian and the Indian Ocean regions. So far, the United States has succeeded in engaging India in its bilateral security activities and multilateral arrangements, such as the emerging Quadrilateral Security Dialogue (QSD or the Quad) in the Indo-Pacific, to offset China's influence and uphold its hegemonic status in this part of the world (see Lobo 2021; S. Mohan & Abraham 2020; Rajagopalan 2020). For Pakistan, on the other hand, India's increasing strategic proximity with the sole superpower implies the superior adversary's slow-motion, but wider, security enhancement in terms of modern weapon systems that impinge on its security. For instance, the conclusion of a ten-year defense pact between New Delhi and Washington has added another knot to the Asian security dynamic, as it expands India's security ties with the United States beyond South Asia to the Indo-Pacific region, which has potential to disturb China's and Pakistan's security interests and equations (see GoI 2015; US Department of Defense 2019: 33–34).

In a bid to neutralize the Indo-US strategic expansion and change the geo-politics of the Indian Ocean region, China and Pakistan have reinforced their strategic ties—often termed an "all-weather friendship"—by engaging in dual-purpose agreements and activities. For instance, they have signed a $62 billion CPEC deal, which is likely to balloon beyond $100 billion by 2030, and sped up work at the Gwadar port to make it a hub for the Maritime

Silk Route and a permanent base for the Chinese fleet to support the PLA Navy's presence in the Indian Ocean (*CPEC Portal* 2018). This alternative route and the port of Gwadar will also permit China to escape the US-led squeeze of its eastern seaside by getting direct access to the Arabian Sea and simultaneously allow it to open a western naval front against India (see V. Malik 2016; R. Menon 2016; S. Mohan & Abraham 2020). On the basis of these competing moves, Pratap Bhanu Mehta, the former president of Delhi-based Centre for Policy Research, flags the possibility of collision between India and China. "There is reason to worry," argues Mehta (2016), "the escalating nature of our defence agreements with the US will put us on a slippery slope where we may not be able to manage our own geopolitical positioning in the world's major conflicts."

From the US perspective, on the other hand, despite an impressive transformation in the Indo-US relations, Pakistan has not lost its geo-strategic relevance. Given the range and variance that US foreign policy has in multipolar Asia, it is noticeable that it requires working ties with Pakistan to maintain its influence in West and Central Asia and, on the other extreme, needs India to neutralize Pakistan in both regions and consolidate its position against China in the newly shaping Indo-Pacific subsystemic order. To achieve these foreign policy goals, though clashing in nature, the United States strikes a delicate balance in its ties with India and Pakistan. For instance, its growing strategic ties with India have raised Pakistan's security vulnerabilities; hence it provides Pakistan relatively smaller, but very potent, perks—that is, sustained economic and military aid and keeping options open for signing a civil nuclear deal at a more opportune time in the future—on the pretext of beefing up its security against the Taliban and other jihadi outfits in the region (Congressional Research Service 2019; *Indian Express* 2015b).

At the same time, as indicated by a ten-page sensitive document titled "US Strategic Framework for the Indo-Pacific," which was declassified in the Trump administration's last days, the US security moves are drawing India deep into its larger schemes for Asia through a series of strategic and defense agreements which have potential to pitch India against China (see White House 2021). The best examples of agreements that effectively nudge India toward the "Asian NATO" or the quadrilateral grouping (the Quad), along with Australia and Japan, are the conclusion of the "2015 Framework for the India-US Defense Relationship" and the signing of three key foundational agreements to become a strategic defense ally of the United States—the "Logistics Exchange Memorandum of Agreement" (LEMOA) in 2016; the

"Communications Compatibility and Security Agreement" (COMCASA) in 2018; and the "Basic Exchange and Cooperation Agreement for Geo-spatial Cooperation" (BECA) signed during the annual "2+2" high-level talks held in New Delhi in October 2020 (*BBC* 2020b). "These steps," as Achin Vanaik (2016) opined a few years ago, "are part of America's extension of the NATO-type arrangement to Asia whose primary purpose is to better control the Indo-Pacific waters and as part of a containment policy for China and Russia over the next decades." On a similar note, Mehta (2016) questions India's "unthinking embrace of the US" which "poses considerable risks" to its vital immediate and long-term interests:

> The US is making no secret of the fact that it wants to position India in its plans for China. But it is not in India's interests to become a frontline state in that emerging faultline. Its interests have always been to do business with both countries so that both take it seriously. . . . But an open declaration of a political and defence alignment with the US forecloses those options. We will come to be unwittingly identified with American rhetoric and designs for Asia. And the overblown rhetoric emanating from Washington about positioning India in its pushback of China will reduce our options.

In this respect, the former US Defense Secretary Ashton Carter's April 2016 statement before the Senate Appropriations Committee (Defense) clears the air. According to him, Washington's strategic agenda with respect to the Indo-Pacific includes India, a key Asian power, which is committed to prevent the domination of the region by any one power and balance their collective immediate and long-term security concern: China. During the hearing, Carter told the Senate Armed Service Committee: "[W]e're entering a new strategic era. Today's security environment is dramatically different from the last 25 years, requiring new ways of investing and operating. Five evolving strategic challenges—namely Russia, China, North Korea, Iran, and terrorism—are now driving DoD's [the Department of Defense] planning and budgeting as reflected in this budget" (US Department of Defense 2016). He further said that China is behaving aggressively in the Indo-Pacific, and so

> [t]here, we're continuing our rebalance to the region to maintain the stability we've underwritten for the past 70 years, enabling so many nations to rise and prosper in this, the single most consequential region for America's future. And, as I saw in India and the Philippines at the beginning of my trip,

our engagement in the [Indo-Pacific] is deeply appreciated and in high demand—by enduring allies and new friends alike. (US Department of Defense 2016)

Carter further stressed that the United States requires new investments, strategic postures, and advanced capabilities to not only address all the "five evolving strategic challenges" but also maintain its supremacy in the Indo-Pacific. "For example," he said,

we know we must deal with these challenges across all domains—and not just the usual air, land, and sea, but also especially in cyber, electronic warfare, and space, where our reliance on technology has given us great strengths and great opportunities, but also led to vulnerabilities that adversaries are eager to exploit. Key to our approach is being able to deter our most advanced competitors. We must have—and be seen to have—the ability to ensure that anyone who starts a conflict with us will regret doing so. In our budget, our capabilities, our readiness, and our actions, we must and will be prepared for a high-end enemy—what we call full spectrum. (US Department of Defense 2016)

From the US standpoint, such policy initiatives are vital to safeguard its regional and global interests, which include maintaining the post–Cold War *systemic primacy*; hence its "interest largely lies in encouraging India to offset China's influence . . . so that it could prevent [the opponent's] potential domination of the [Asian] region when no other Asian power has capability to balance China alone" (S. Mohan & Abraham 2020: 87; cf. White House 2021). In broader terms, from another viewpoint, it is also worthwhile to mention that America's interventionist foreign policy, military assistance, and presence in Asia plays a central role in stirring crises and rivalries among the regional players which impinge on their interests, create security tensions, and often play them against each other (see Ling 2013; Ross 2012). Being entangled in a complex web of balancing, the Asian states' security equations often end up charting contrary courses which limit their ability to manage bilateral and multilateral relationships and, by extension, create space for America to knit a favorable security alliance with key Asian partners and play a predominant role in the ASA. In this sense, the fundamental problem of the whole security issue in Asia revolves around the United States' dominant presence (with a clear motive to undercut China) which is contingent on continuing competitive, if not conflictual, relationships among the Asian states to justify its role and "strategic primacy" in this part of the world.

According to Vanaik (2016), the US role in ASA cannot be justified. However, this does not inversely imply that if the Asian states were given an opportunity to be part of the Western Hemisphere's security architecture then the US involvement in the ASA would be rational or justified. With the increasing profile of Asian states, it is possible that the key regional players may raise this issue. This is especially true for China, which is increasingly asserting itself in shaping the structures of global governance in military as well as economic domains with its stakes being the highest as they impinge on its backyard, that is, Asia. It is entirely possible that Japan and India may also seek a similar role in the Western Hemisphere in the near future, which is in consonance with their aspirations to become global powers or to have a say in global affairs. Vanaik (2016) believes that the United States would never tolerate such an arrangement because any such move would be perceived as an intervention in its domain; however, when it comes to the US presence and prominence in the ASA, "the same becomes a matter of its right." Hence, given the emerging competitive setting in the Indo-Pacific region, the larger question remains: Is any fundamental transformation in the existing ASA possible to attain peace in the Asian region, particularly in the context of India-Pakistan and India-China relations?

Against this backdrop, it seems that until China and India, the two major competing Asian powers, mutually transform their relationship by delinking from the ASA, the existing security structure might continuously exert pressure on the India-Pakistan and the India-China rivalries and shape their future course accordingly. Based on these background conditions, it is safe to assess that any transformation in India-Pakistan, India-China, and Pakistan-China relationships is unlikely to materialize till the concerned states remain part of the US-dominated ASA or they challenge the ASA by forming an alternate security forum which could unite them as NATO has united the North Atlantic states by coalescing their major policies and common interests. In this respect, Mani Shankar Aiyar's interstate oil and gas pipeline proposal, mainly the Iran-Pakistan-India (IPI) gas pipeline extendable to China (which has been shelved since 2006), has potential to normalize India and Pakistan's bilateral relationship as well as bring a geopolitical change in the ASA by forming a collective "Asian Energy Grid" (Jha 2006; Rais 2015; World Bank 2007: 16). But India's slow-motion engagement with the United States, particularly after the conclusion of the civil nuclear deal, has not only foreclosed the IPI pipeline project but also diminished the prospects of a collective Asian Energy Grid.

With regard to New Delhi's newfound tilt toward the American position and policies, a small section of scholars' criticism of India's foreign policy does hold some merit. But in the present context, particularly when the Indo-US, Sino-Indian, and Sino-Pakistani security ties are simultaneously assuming contrary positions on the Indo-Pacific strategic plane, it is not feasible for India to freeze its evolving ties with the United States and pursue an equidistant strategic policy in the emerging regional order. For instance, India's growing strategic ties with the United States render Pakistan insecure and offset China's power calculus in the Asian hierarchy and ambition to become a maritime power in the far seas. Other key developments of the last few years which might play an important role in shaping the concerned states' future interactions or policies vis-à-vis each other are Pakistan's indifferent approach to cease terrorist activities against India from its soil—the Pathankot, the Uri, and the Pulwama attacks are fresh examples to this effect; Afghanistan's emergence as a critical extension of the India-Pakistan rivalry, which has potential to further consolidate against the backdrop of the Taliban militia's return to power and India's and China's increasing involvement in competitive connectivity projects to neutralize each other's influence in the West, South, and Central Asian regions; China's opposition to India's bid to include the JeM chief and the Pathankot and the Pulwama attacks' mastermind Masood Azar in the UN sanction list; and the India-China military standoff in eastern Ladakh since May 2020.[8]

In other words, if China would continuously abet Pakistan as a hostile force against India, coupled with its objection to New Delhi's bid for permanent membership in the Nuclear Suppliers Group (NSG) and the UNSC, then the deepening Sino-Pakistani strategic ties have potential to further strain India's relations with both neighbors as they share political and terrestrial border disputes with it. Under such circumstances, the "tilted" India might completely turn toward the US-led camp to neutralize Pakistan's nuclear and terror belligerence and China's regional and global aspirations, which collectively undercut its interests to attain the status of strong Indian Ocean or Indo-Pacific power. At present, it seems, the formation of the Quad and India's participation as a core member of the quadrilateral grouping is a step in that direction.

Given the circumstances, India's expanding security ties in the Indo-Pacific and its weak political relations and non-existent economic interdependence with Pakistan limit its options to distance itself from the United States and forge closer political-security ties with China. Against this background, especially when the Indo-US and the Sino-Pakistani strategic equations are juxtaposing their vital national and security interests, it may be an overestimation to expect that India, Pakistan, and China would take extraordinary steps to exploit vacuums in the Asian alliance system and form a comprehensive trilateral relationship, which could tie together their interests into a whole and gradually cease their association with the US-dominated ASA. In fact, in the immediate context, a reverse scenario seems to be more imminent wherein India, as a "swing state," may prefer to consolidate the US position in Asia in return for strong economic ties, technological and military assistance, and strategic alignment to become a venerable and leading Indo-Pacific power. On the other hand, China and Pakistan have a deep mistrust of the United States and India's strategic ambitions; thus they are consolidating their military-economic ties through the CPEC-based projects and other collective security ventures to neutralize the opponents in the key Asian regions and the northern theater of the Indian Ocean. Hence, under the shadow of emerging power alignments and reshaping security equations in Asia and its adjoining waters, it seems that the United States and China's growing clash in this part of the world and India and Pakistan's opposing political-security interests might not allow the Indo-Pakistani dyad to delink from the US-dominated ASA and explore possible avenues for rivalry transformation in the near future.

Strategic Balance and the Rivalry Transformation

With India's steady economic rise and increasing competition with China, it is likely that the Indian defense budget will witness a considerable hike over the years and thereby constrain economically weak Pakistan from sustaining the arms competition at the bilateral level. Such capability buildup efforts will certainly help India to enhance its conventional power and consolidate its position in the regional hierarchy; however, the same might not suffice to prevent nuclear Pakistan from challenging the superior rival. It is also possible that India's extensive capability-building initiatives might increase risks at the strategic level as Pakistan is steadily expanding its nuclear weapons stockpile and delivery systems to offset India's military superiority and limited war strategy—the Cold Start doctrine. Pakistan's acquisition of "full spectrum deterrence" capability—strategic, operational, and tactical—and the deployment of short-range missiles in forward locations to make India's Cold Start non-operational, as discussed in Chapter 7, have lowered the threshold of nuclear use at the subconventional level. Against this backdrop, it might be an overestimation to generalize that nuclear weapons will continuously limit the possibility of escalation of conventional conflicts into nuclear war by replicating the Western experience, where this logic prevented American-Soviet nuclear confrontation during the Cold War and kept the world *safe*, in South Asia's complex settings.[9]

Despite being aware of this limitation, the contemporary debates on the Indo-Pakistani nuclear conflict are either tilted toward or based on the optimist school's position—whose leading proponent is Kenneth Waltz—or the Western experience, as a principal condition for maintaining peace in the subcontinent (see Basrur 2006; Ganguly 2008; Karnad 2002, 2008; Kidwai 2015; Krepon 2004, 2005; Rajagopalan 2005, 2016). For instance, the nuclear optimists contend that the nuclear factor has made India and Pakistan more cautious in their interactions and therefore nuclear war between them is unlikely. In other words, nuclear weapons' unimaginable destructive power prevents the two states from entering into an all-out war; therefore the nuclear factor stabilizes the region and makes nuclear deterrence robust in South Asia (Ganguly 2008). "There is no more ironclad law in international relations theory than this," as Devin Hagerty has argued, "nuclear states do not fight wars with each other" (1998: 184). However, what happened during the Kargil War, when Pakistan elevated the conflict to internationalize the Kashmir issue under the cover of nuclear weapons, baffles the nuclear optimists. In Kargil, the two adversaries not only were engaged in severe conventional warfare after acquiring nuclear capability, but were also on the verge of a nuclear exchange (see Chengappa 2000: 437; Riedel 2002: 8). In other words, contrary to the nuclear optimists' thesis, the Kargil War of 1999 had brought the world close to a cataclysmic situation.

At present, the regional situation is again grim as the nuclear race has taken a dangerous turn, particularly as a result of India and Pakistan's competitive missile race and the latter's induction of tactical nuclear weapons to neutralize the former's retaliatory Cold Start doctrine and superior nuclear weapons (see ISPR 2017a, 2017b, 2019a, 2019b, 2020a, 2020b), and there is no mutually acceptable framework in place to subdue the recurrent militarized tensions at the bilateral level. A recent case in point is the two nuclear-armed adversaries' unprecedented decision to carry out retaliatory air strikes inside each other's territories following the deadly suicide attack on the convoy of Indian security forces in Pulwama on February 14, 2019 (*India Today* 2019; *NDTV* 2019). The Pulwama-Balakot military tensions almost spiraled out of control and edged India and Pakistan closer to nuclear exchange (see *Reuters* 2019; *Hindustan Times* 2019a). Though a larger military clash was averted, the two nuclear-armed states' baffling decision to engage in retaliatory aerial battle heightened the international community's concerns as their risky strikes against each other could have escalated and embroiled them in a bigger and dangerous nuclear conflict. The tense cross-border situation, lasting over a month, and continued unrest within Kashmir, which has always been a flashpoint for tensions and become a more toilsome political-security issue after the Modi-led NDA government annulled its special status and statehood in August 2019, indicate that nuclear deterrence-induced stability has limitations of its own in this part of the world where it largely acts as rivalry stabilizer.

Given these concerns and dangers of escalation of a miscalculated war in South Asia, it seems that the nuclear pessimists' observations deserve closer attention: that nuclear weapons have strengthened Pakistan's resolve by providing it a compelling incentive to challenge India at the subconventional level without fearing major retaliatory action from the adversary (Hoodbhoy 2015; S. Kapur 2009; Sagan 2009). This view derives strength from Pakistan's continued support to terrorist outfits which have repeatedly triggered high-magnitude crises by targeting India, a few examples of which are the 2001–2 twin attacks, the 2008 Mumbai attacks, the 2016 Pathankot airbase attack, and the 2019 Pulwama suicide attack. So, as a whole, the deadly combination of nuclear power and unending terrorist acts have made the South Asian dyad more vulnerable to subconventional attacks with the possibility of an uncontrolled escalation leading to a cataclysmic war.

Apart from these concerns, some other aspects also underline why the replication of Western experience in the subcontinent is problematic. First, the case of India-Pakistan nuclear rivalry is contrary to "Cold War stability/ instability logic," according to which a superior conventional power had directed its nuclear power against the nuclear first-use doctrine of a conventionally weaker rival (S. Kapur 2009: 186). In the South Asian case, in contrast to the Cold War experience, the revisionist but weaker conventional power, Pakistan, is maintaining a nuclear threat against its conventionally superior opponent, India (S. Kapur 2009: 186). The leadership in Islamabad believes that by placing nuclear use as its foremost option, even during minor crises, it can deter India from overrunning Pakistan. Second, the nuclear deterrence in the Indo-Pakistani case is not as mature as the US-Soviet deterrence was during the Cold War, where both superpowers had mutually taken several initiatives and measures to limit the dangers of nuclear mishaps and escalations (S. Kapur 2009; Krepon 2004).

In contrast, what makes the India-Pakistan rivalry more dangerous in comparison to the US-Soviet one is its ethno-territorial character and symbolic linkage with the core dispute (Kashmir), which was absent in the superpower rivalry and thus favored the stability/instability paradox to hold correct or survive in the Atlantic region. Another intrinsic character of this rivalry lies in its weak command and control structure, which carries a threat of nuclear mishap. Over the last decade, for instance, Pakistan's increasing radicalization and domestic instability have increased the international community's concerns, especially after the 2009 terrorist attack on the GHQ complex from where Strategic Forces Command "runs the nuclear program on a day-to-day basis"; the May 2011 attack on the Karachi naval base, which was "only a few miles from the Masroor air base where nukes [were] stored"; and the August 2012 attack on the Minhas Air Force Base at Kamra, which potentially houses nuclear warheads (Rashid 2012: 62). Given the delicate state of Pakistan's internal security (including a dismal record of its authorities in thwarting insider threats), external threats from rogue or radicalized elements (like the Taliban and the ISIS), and its political-military leadership's decision to expand nuclear facilities to produce tactical nuclear weapons on a large scale, the chances of fearsome attacks on its nuclear facilities or inadvertent and unauthorized use of tactical nuclear systems deployed in forward positions cannot be ruled out.

In addition to operational lacunas, the nuclear dimension confronts certain limitations in the South Asian context. First, while the relative nuclear equality between India and Pakistan has facilitated deterrence by increasing the costs and risks of large-scale wars, on the other hand, the same phenomenon has also promoted an enduring competition between them by stabilizing their strategic policies and postures. This has increased the possibilities of conflict persistency at a lower level which, in turn, makes Kashmir a fertile ground for consistent fighting and thus inhibits the prospects of rivalry de-escalation or termination in the near future. Second, even if nuclear deterrence helps in attaining a temporary state of peace, particularly by mounting pressure on the two sides to remain ready for offensive actions, it fails to avoid the threat of war, dispute recurrence, and subconventional (terrorist) attacks. The post-1998 experience underlines how nuclear stability has increased Pakistan's urge to challenge India by employing lower-level maneuvers, which include a mixed strategy of war threat, dispute recurrence, and terrorist attacks, to pursue territorial revisionism in Kashmir and consolidate its strategic position against the superior rival. Third, the nuclear weapons–steered strategic stability has not opened a window of peace or conflict resolution by averting major war; therefore, it seems, the solutions proposed on the basis of nuclear notions are incompatible with attenuating the India-Pakistan conflict. And finally, confining the nuclear dimension to the concept of deterrence in the war aversion paradigm to explore the conditions of peace is open to debate because this approach ignores the impact of nuclear deterrence on the process and sustenance of rivalry. By combining all aspects together, it is clear that the existing nuclear debate has limitations to grasp the overall impact of nuclear weapons on the state and the future path of the India-Pakistan rivalry.

To conclude, against the backdrop of Pakistan being in the driver's seat to steer the South Asian strategic balance and India's limitations to undercut Pakistan's revisionist policy, the prospects of rivalry termination are not looking promising at the moment, and this pattern is likely to persist particularly in the shadow of their nuclear strategies. Over time, even if other variables change or create conditions for rivalry de-escalation or transformation, it is highly likely that the Indo-Pakistani nuclear deadlock will act a sort of catalyst to continue the rivalry because, as Achin Vanaik notes, "once [nuclear weapons] emerge they tend to remain in existence even if the initial conditions which provoke [rivals to acquire these weapons] disappears" (2015: 57). The US-Russia rivalry substantiates this point as it still exists despite the collapse of the Soviet Union and the US domination of the international system, albeit the magnitude of this conflict in the present times is not as severe as it used to be during the Cold War years. On a similar note, it is possible that the nuclear weapons could or would help Pakistan to stand its ground against India, even when the latter would acquire a dominant regional or Indian Ocean power status with a strong economic clout and influence in the international system, and prolong the course of the rivalry for many more years.

Domestic Politics, Regime Type, and Foreign Policy Restructuring

Democratic peace scholars argue that when a rival pair of states collectively experience democratic governance and remain in that state for a long period, such pairs have a strong propensity to end the rivalry (Bennett 1997a; Diehl & Goertz 2000; Hensel 1999; Rummel 1979, 1995; Russett & Oneal 2001). Though the literature establishes a significant relationship between liberal democracy and rivalry termination, the India-Pakistan dyad has shown minimal variance despite some short spells of collective democratic periods in the past. Since the late 2000s, the two states are again governed by parliamentary democracies, but their deep political-security discord is not allowing their leadership to change the course of the rivalry or bring about a preferred outcome in their rivalrous relationship. It is correct that democratic inconsistency between India and Pakistan (largely due to the latter's hybrid and autocratic regimes) has affected their political behavior and policies, but the mere acquisition of democratic parity is not sufficient to bind the rivals by an obligation to pull out of their prolonged security dilemma and animosity.

Critically, we need to acknowledge that democracies have a weak side of their own that comes to light when power-maximizing leaders/forces with strong rhetoric come into power. From this standpoint, the negative aspect of the parliamentary democracy is that the political leaders and regimes are under constant pressure to secure power, so they turn rhetorical and ultra-nationalist during election time. Moreover, the situation backfires when territorial-religious nationalism builds up a narrow narrative and a hostile environment that keeps leaders under constant pressure to not appear politically weak, and this undermines the possibility of initiating meaningful and outcome-oriented negotiations over the issues of difference. In the India-Pakistan case, apart from joint democracy, what is required is that the civilian regimes tone down their nationalistic rhetoric and refrain from projecting their policies as security issues to secure political advantage against their domestic competitors. For instance, the Imran Khan–led PTI government has continued Pakistan's revisionist agenda against India by retaining terrorism as a foreign policy tool and, on the other hand, the Modi-led NDA government has adopted populist policies which have potential to trigger political disagreements or unrest—an example is the withdrawal of J&K's special status and downgrading the state's status by splitting it into two union territories. Until such centralized, populist, and personalistic approaches[10] in the decision-making process are moderated, it is difficult to see any room for, or acceptance of, alternative viewpoints in their policies even if civilian regimes remain at the helm of power in New Delhi and Islamabad.

Pakistan's political history shows that it often experiences unstable democratic phases, and its military (and their protégés in power) either controls the state power or undercuts the constitutional authority of the civilian regimes. Mohammad Waseem (2015), professor of political science at the LUMS, agrees with this understanding. "The political system in Pakistan is not stable," he maintains, because "the military intervention in the civil domain has adversely affected the [country's] political fabric and the development of democratic institutions. . . . That is why we failed to frame better and conducive national policies over the last several decades" (Waseem (2015). To legitimize its control over the state system, the military-bureaucracy axis generally resorts to three strategies: (1) it exaggerates the security threat from India and identifies the army's interests with Pakistan's survival; (2) it systematically promotes national radicalization; and (3) it draws policies that favor a hybridized form of governance.

Having limited room to function like a real democratic government, the civilian regimes in Pakistan either engage in political rhetoric against India to consolidate their position, which also carries domestic symbolic value, or remain content with their limited political power and role. In both situations, they end up creating space for authoritarian stakeholders who monitor the elected regimes' actions and policies. Maintenance of such a political structure helps the GHQ to coerce the elected governments and compel them to function like hybrid regimes; this practice affects not only Pakistan's political institutions but also its bilateral ties with India.

To bring about an effective change in Pakistan's polity, what is needed is a mechanism to stabilize its political system by initiating key political reforms so that the army's role can be confined to its primary responsibility of defending the country from external threats and the orthodox groups' interference is minimized in the political domain. Until these goals are achieved, it is difficult to see a stable political order in Pakistan which could offer its political elites, as Anit Mukherjee points out, a desirable space and autonomy to "accept and implement politically risky decisions vis-à-vis India" (2009: 422). Some scholars express their reservations about such a transition as they believe "Pakistan has miles to cross before calling itself a true democracy and it may never become one" (Paul 2014: 67). Though this observation is worthy and deserves attention, Pakistan of late has shown some signs of democratic consistency, political consolidation, and maturity—perhaps that underscores its two consecutive democratic transitions in 2013 and 2018.

On this aspect, Rasul Baksh Rais (2015), professor of political science at the LUMS, takes a leap forward and expresses his reservations to "apply the developed democracies concept in the case of India and Pakistan [as] both countries have not attained [the required democratic] level." "If we consider the level of corruption," he says while building his case against the state of Indian polity, the "Indian democracy is more corrupt and in no ways a progressive democracy, particularly from [a] procedural and sustainable viewpoint. In my opinion, India is a better democracy than Pakistan but this comparative edge does not make it a real democracy" (Rais 2015). Undoubtedly, India and Pakistan have a lot more to do before calling themselves true procedural democracies, but given their long conflictual history and political limitations, the two sides still have sufficient room to carry on the present political structures, gradually shape their polities into robust democracies, and, simultaneously, make their bilateral ties amicable. The research shows that democratic consistency for a long duration at the dyadic level can create conditions to evolve cooperative policies and fractionate the rivals' principal issues for amicable resolution, as shared political values and norms help democracies to employ peaceful conflict management tools to improve their relations.

Other possibilities of change in the India-Pakistan rivalry may emerge if one or both rivals experience a collective failure in domestic and foreign policies, which may prompt changes in their established environments and political preferences. This may compel their leadership to modify national policies to adjust to the new situation or bring into power new political groups committed to changing the state of affairs (see Cox 2010; Checkel 1997; Legro 2005; Rosati 1994). Fundamental change in an enduring competition is possible when a hawkish leader is replaced with a dovish leader who is more willing to make concessions and reach compromise with rivals, not otherwise. This underlines that, apart from a combined failure in domestic and foreign policies, the direction and functioning of the domestic regime are important to seek a successful transformation in interstate relations (see Cox 2010).

It is important to note that in spite of changes in domestic politics and foreign policy transformation, the two states may show reluctance for a formal peace agreement in the absence of popular consensus at home or genuine commitment to end the rivalry—which is precisely what India and Pakistan have done repeatedly ever since the onset of the rivalry. In the subcontinental context, chances of conflict transformation may further increase if Islamabad and New Delhi take a series of small unilateral or bilateral steps over their core dispute—Kashmir—to demonstrate a commitment to achieve normalization without pressuring one another for extensive concessions in the early stage of negotiations. During the 2003–8 period, the leadership in New Delhi and Islamabad had partly tried this while negotiating the "four-point formula." This engagement signifies that the rival parties are capable of fractionating their core issues of dispute and negotiating at the most senior governmental level without much publicity to achieve a breakthrough in their frozen relationship.

It is correct that economic ties and joint democracy are important for India and Pakistan to reduce their mutual mistrust and form economic interdependency to create conditions for rivalry transformation. But their historical record substantiates that attaining democratic-economic coherence to transform their relationship is not so easy, as the Pakistan Army and its supported proxy entities' interests are placed diametrically opposite to norm-based interdependency. Under such circumstances, Charles Kupchan's (2010) "deft diplomacy" proposal offers an alternative window to rivals like India and Pakistan, which does not prioritize or make liberal democracy and economic interdependency inevitable conditions to engage in de-escalatory measures. By building on this insight, the two sides can ignore the necessity of "democratic peace," which emphasizes democratic parity and trade interdependency for rivalry transformation, and focus more on rapprochement initiatives by taking clues from the successful examples of East and West Germany; the United States and China under Nixon and Mao, respectively; Begin's Israel and Sadat's Egypt; and Brazil and Argentina under authoritarian military regimes.

In the South Asian context, some of these scenarios offer ideas for India and Pakistan to approach each other on a regular basis by taking unilateral or bilateral steps, engaging in appeasement and reciprocity initiatives, and continuing the government-level and societal interactions until, as Kupchan (2010) suggests, peace "breaks out" between them or they become friends. From this view, the lesson for today's regimes is before them: the exemplary rapprochement between General Musharraf's military regime and the Manmohan Singh–led multi-party coalition can be replicated to bring the two states close and negotiate the Kashmir issue. Though the Musharraf–Manmohan Singh rapprochement could not succeed to achieve the desired goals, their four-year engagement in a peace process signifies that even a non-democratic Indo-Pakistani dyad with weak economic ties has potential to transform the rivalry provided the policy makers on both sides adopt rapprochement and appeasement as approaches to engage in meaningful negotiations.

STEPS TO PEACE: THE WAY FORWARD

If the ruling elites and society continuously support policies to preserve the rivalry or resist peaceful change, then there is no end to the conflict. At some point, the political communities and the informed societies have to break away from the pessimistic depiction of bilateral relations and pursue a progressive path of peace-building and conflict resolution so that a new beginning in their relationship can materialize. To bring such a fundamental shift in their relationship, the rival parties need to have *peace strategists*. By "peace strategists," I mean a layered and diversified community of visionaries comprising the two sides' mainstream political leaders, key policy makers, experts from varied and associated fields, and informed members of the civil society, who can devise mechanisms to weave together the rival parties' long-range interests and simultaneously downgrade the dyadic hostility to make a meaningful transformation possible. In other words, the peace strategists are the mainstay of the rivalry transformation process because they are willing to learn from the past crises, conceive and re-assess the common plans, and transform the two sides' orientation to the rivalry by not replicating and relying on decades-old divisive beliefs that support and justify one side's image and reflect a negative image or perpetuate erroneous perceptions of the other (see Bar-Tal 2000; Burns 1978; Levy 1994; Premashekhara 2008; Russett & Starr 1992).

By building on this view, I seek to propose a gradual and progressive path of conflict transformation that concludes with the termination of the rivalry. It emphasizes, from the standpoint of the hub-and-spokes framework, that the foremost condition required to break the cycle of India-Pakistan rivalry is to do away with the closed-mindedness and de-institutionalize the practices of power politics in a phased manner. To achieve such a reorientation in bilateral relations, the political establishments on both sides, irrespective of the nature of their polity (i.e., democratic or authoritarian), have to pursue a long and multi-dimensional peace process covering several elements of their issues and differences. Once the decision-makers are motivated to initiate the peace-building process, the two sides must show genuine commitment to the "do not harm" principle by refraining from vindictive intentions and simultaneously employ a hybrid of short- to long-term political, cultural, economic, and military measures to create conducive conditions for rivalry transformation (Anderson 1999; Bercovitch & Jackson 2009). In other words, as Jacob Bercovitch and Richard Jackson have suggested, "peacebuilding entails a combination of top-down and bottom-up processes . . . guided by a carefully conceived political strategy that defines a clear hierarchy of priorities. These priorities need to be responsive to the specific needs of the situation and flexible enough to adapt to changing political dynamics" (2009: 173).

Since the India-Pakistan dyad has often been characterized as resistant to change, particularly due to its unique capability to absorb shocks, how this rivalry might possibly proceed to termination partly depends on the two sides' key actions and objectives to support rivalry-defusing structures and partly on the situation arising out of a range of leverage, concession, and accommodation measures taken by them to target the source of the rivalry. Against this backdrop, the complex rivalry model presents a "staggering forward" approach—a nonlinear and prolonged transformation process— guided by reframing the dyad's principal issues under conditions of risk to achieve stable and peaceful change in three different sequential phases. This heuristic approach provides an analytical tool for examining the situations in which the structural factors' rearrangement can impact the temporal ones in predictable ways and, in doing so, potentially impact the outcome of the rivalry positively.

This rivalry transformation approach encompasses three different phases: "de-escalation," "de-rivalization," and "termination" (as illustrated by Figure 8.1). The first phase, de-escalation, begins when the rivalry is still going on and the two states are engaged in power politics practices and armed hostilities. Despite such an unfavorable atmosphere, some political elites or individuals on both sides devote themselves to the ambitious mission of bringing peace or a peaceful change in the drawn-out conflict. They take risks to initiate ideas for the transformation of the hostile environment by stressing policy changes and negotiations on select issues or sectors which have potential to give momentum to the peace process and create conditions for rivalry de-escalation. The decision-makers frame a method and the order of the issues to be considered at this stage (and also which ones are not) according to the potential of a method or issue to alter the long-standing logjam and produce desired outcomes for de-escalation so that the transformation process will be effective with minimal differences.

Following the measured compromises and successful de-escalation, the dyad enters the second phase, de-rivalization, wherein the peace strategists aspire for a fundamental change in the bilateral relationship that, more than the cessation of hostilities, paves the way for a new situation of political

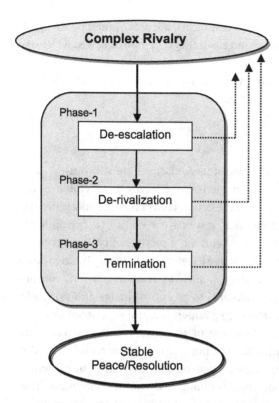

Figure 8.1. Steps to peace: The process of rivalry transformation

compatibility. The success of this phase relies more on the decision-makers' assessment about shaping new standards of behavior, their negotiation ability, and their courage to take risky, but progressive, decisions to create favorable conditions for de-rivalization. Since the peace process is gradual and nonlinear, the first two phases may take about five to seven years each to mature and accomplish the prioritized objectives before advancing to the next phase. After the successful completion of the first two phases, the dyad enters the third and the final phase of rivalry transformation: termination. In this crucial phase, the two sides adhere to the agreed norms of the peace process and systematically employ advanced accommodative strategies to transform their strained relationship into a peaceful one without engaging in any militarized or policy dispute for ten to fifteen years. Once this phase is effectively completed, particularly by institutionalizing peace, the rivalry may be considered fully transformed with a peaceful settlement of protracted contestation or deemed as terminated. Here, it is important to note that the duration of each phase is suggestive or provisional. Actual durations of these phases and their paths, in real terms, are determined by the rivals' political will, negotiating skills, and capability to remain engaged while navigating the political-security waters.

A detailed description of the process of rivalry transformation is outlined next as three different sequential phases.

De-escalation

De-escalation begins when the two states' relations are still hostile, often punctuated with institutionalized victimhood and armed violence, and their different political aims situate them on contradictory trajectories that draw consistent support from their respective societies to continue the rivalry. Despite such a hostile environment, a section of political community and informed society remain active to reframe the rivalry by advocating effective conflict resolution strategies, such as accommodation, compromise, concession, and rapprochement, to promote change and normalize bilateral relations (see Armstrong 1993; Kupchan 2010; Rock 1989).

To break the hegemonic structure of the rivalry and proceed to de-escalation, the ruling regimes have to build trust and common ground so that the reconciliation steps signal their seriousness and political will to embark on the risky road of peace-building and conflict resolution. They need to construct a new ethos of peace that "consist[s] of societal beliefs about the utility of cooperative relationship mechanisms that maintain peaceful relations, a vision of peace and the necessity of providing the conditions for trustful and empathic relations with yesterday's enemy" (Rouhana & Bar-Tal 1998: 768). To move in this direction, the rival parties have to take a series of small unilateral or bilateral steps over their core issues to demonstrate a commitment to achieve normalization. At this early stage, they must not pressure one another for extraordinary concessions or a comprehensive settlement. Additionally, they have to show the will to "adopt ambiguous formulations allowing differing interpretations to be used to overcome disputes over matters of central principle" (Armstrong 1993: 134). Once the two sides make positive stride toward the viability of the transformation process, they need to downgrade their political differences as well as armed hostilities and, simultaneously, develop interdependent goals to manage a successful progression toward de-escalation. For instance, as New Delhi and Islamabad made progressive and peacemaking efforts during a short span of five years (2003-8)—mainly through cross-border trade and movement, multi-level political dialogues, and significant control over armed violence—that reflected their seriousness toward de-escalation and progressed almost to the point of framing a compromise agreement popularly known as the "four-point formula."

However, the major drawback of the 2003–8 peace process was that the political leadership had adopted a back-channel approach that induced an element of obscurity in the peace process and that, with the passage of time, baffled, irked, and polarized some segments of their societies. Another limitation was its excessive focus on the end result—that is, the conclusion of the agreement—rather than on de-institutionalizing the culture of conflict by deepening the peace process and coping with the polarization and terrorist acts. With the turn of events, particularly after the Mumbai terrorist attacks and drastic change in the regional and global equations, the Indian decision-makers could not cope with the domestic criticism nor did they withstand the political forces and conflicting entities that objected to the peace process. Unable to wade through troubled waters, the Manmohan Singh government discontinued the peace process to cool down the charged political climate. Later, its interest in the stalled process waned and with that a reasonable peace initiative came to a grinding halt, along with the two sides' collective objective to de-escalate the rivalry.

At present, despite the two sides' deep-seated differences, the stalled peace process can be resumed if the policy makers in New Delhi and Islamabad show extraordinary courage and political will to work out modalities to negotiate their differences. By reframing their beliefs, perceptions, policies, and priorities, they can design a desired variation in the structural and temporal factors' interplay—which shapes the India-Pakistan rivalry—to transform the dyad's hegemonic relations. However, the reversion of the structural factors from their perpetual state of fusion to a neutral or normal one is a challenging task, particularly with the gradual augmentation of hostility and accumulation of grievances, as their unification into a whole has significantly complicated the trajectory of the India-Pakistan rivalry (see Figure 8.2 in conjunction with Figures 3.1 and 3.2). To dislodge the structural factors' strong bonding within the hub and gravitate them toward normalization, the policy makers have to deploy a hybrid of alternative and accommodative strategies so that these factors' hegemonic alignment can be reversed to a reasonable extent without generating a security dilemma—as illustrated in Figure 8.2 by parts 1a →2a. In doing so, the established centripetal and centrifugal stress between the hub and the spokes can be reduced to initiate a

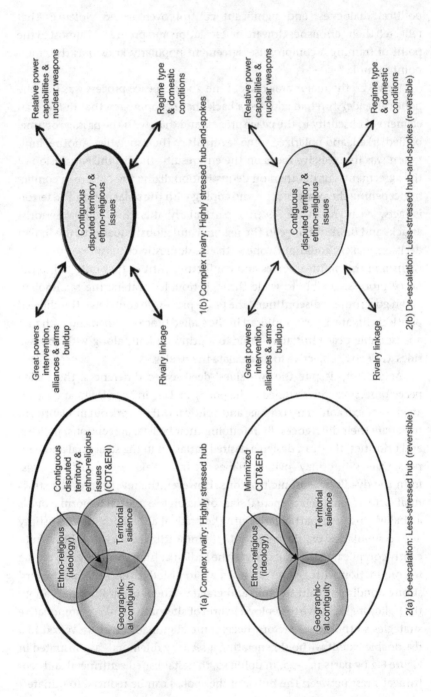

Relative power capabilities & nuclear weapons

Regime type & domestic conditions

Contiguous disputed territory & ethno-religious issues

Great powers intervention, alliances & arms buildup

Rivalry linkage

1(b) Complex rivalry: Highly stressed hub-and-spokes

Relative power capabilities & nuclear weapons

Regime type & domestic conditions

Contiguous disputed territory & ethno-religious issues

Great powers intervention, alliances & arms buildup

Rivalry linkage

2(b) De-escalation: Less-stressed hub-and-spokes (reversible)

Ethno-religious (ideology)

Contiguous disputed territory & ethno-religious issues (CDT&ERI)

Territorial salience

Geographical contiguity

1(a) Complex rivalry: Highly stressed hub (reversible)

Ethno-religious (ideology)

Minimized CDT&ERI

Territorial salience

Geographical contiguity

2(a) De-escalation: Less-stressed hub (reversible)

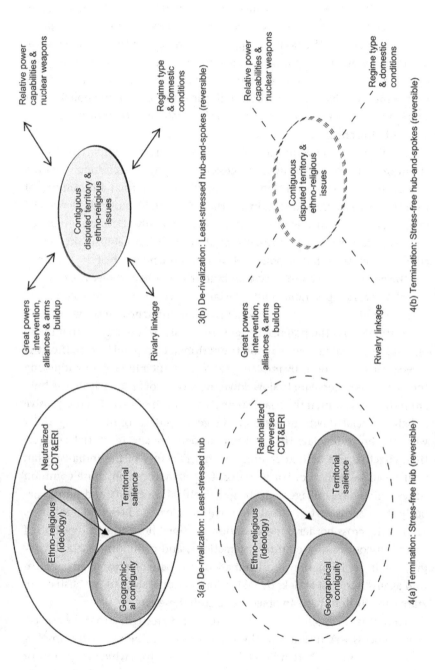

Figure 8.2. Steps to peace: A gradual process of rivalry transformation reversible 3(a) De-rivalization: Least-stressed hub, like 2(a) and 4(a)

change in the context of the rivalry (as illustrated by parts 1b→2b in Figure 8.2). Indeed, such a transition requires extraordinary policy efforts and political adjustments as the political opponents on both sides may show resistance to any dialogue with the adversary from the outset. More than this, they might make all possible attempts to derail the reformative initiatives by portraying the adversary as diabolical in the hope of retaining policies that support and justify the continuation of the rivalry and their own existence as conflicting entities.

To initiate a change in India-Pakistan relations, it is important to pay attention to a particular structural factor, the geographical contiguity, which frames an antecedent condition that magnifies the interplay and bonding of the other two structural factors inside the hub. Both ideology and territorial salience, as discussed at length in Chapter 3, are highly active structural factors in the case of the subcontinental contest, and what stabilizes their interaction and expansion (i.e., policy relevance) is the presence of the third factor, the geographical contiguity, that binds them into a whole. The ensuing causal process shapes India's and Pakistan's respective positions—status quo and revisionist—against each other. It is important to note, if the geographical contiguity has the potential to govern the size of the impact that ideology and territorial salience have on the peripheral temporal factors, then the reverse can also be done by inducing variance in their interplay or adjusting their patterns of behavior to slow down the process of fusion within the hub. From this viewpoint, if the peace strategists on both sides design progressive policies associated with or based on the geographical contiguity, especially with an aim to regulate the interplay of ideology and territorial salience, then effective and desired changes in the trajectory of the India-Pakistan rivalry can be achieved. For instance, they may focus on those common issues which have linkage with the geographical contiguity and simultaneously share some sort of association with ideology and territorial salience, such as the cross-border trade, cessation of armed hostilities, promotion of shared discourses and cultural interactions, and common transboundary projects. In addition, they must embark on the path of a sustained cooperation against terrorist attacks by taking foundational steps to establish cooperative institutions with an objective to curb these acts.

From this viewpoint, it is not inappropriate to recognize that the 2003–8 peace process was heading in the right direction. The leadership in New Delhi and Islamabad had indeed taken select initiatives, which were more or less associated with the geographical contiguity, to create conducive conditions to slow down the impact of ideology and territorial salience on the rivalry. This change therefore widened the window of opportunity and encouraged the ruling regimes on both sides to expand the peace process, which relatively reduced stress on the hub and weakened its interaction with the temporal factors on the periphery. In other words, the success of geographical contiguity–based initiatives in reducing the centripetal and centrifugal stress on the rivalry significantly aided the regimes of Manmohan Singh and General Pervez Musharraf to continue the peace process.

The relative success of the 2003–8 peace process provides us crucial leads that the geographical contiguity–based initiatives have potential to extend New Delhi and Islamabad sufficient space to control or downgrade the impact of ideology and territorial salience on their national security policies. This underlines that such initiatives have potential to hinder or inhibit the unwavering interplay between the hub and the spokes. Continuation of such policies for a considerable period may increase the prospects of normalization of bilateral relations, or in other words, open new avenues for the political regimes to embark on the path of peace and de-escalation. Against this backdrop, the phase of de-escalation is a crucial one to advance the process of rivalry transformation to a more promising level. However, the peace strategists of each side have to ensure that change in their state's behavior, coupled with other essential dimensions (identity, territory, and security), toward the opponent is not fast and extreme, but gradual and measured. If this phase steadily develops and succeeds in sustaining the peace process, the peace strategists will certainly have confidence in their alternative ideas/policies and more leverage from the society to make risky, but productive, decisions to negotiate a peaceful settlement of the rivalry in the subsequent phases.

De-rivalization

The next phase in the process of rivalry transformation is de-rivalization, defined as *a political process of neutralizing the magnitude of interstate conflict by revising, de-institutionalizing, and reversing policies supporting the continuation of the rivalry*. It comes to life once the rival parties successfully lay the foundation of the peace-building process in the de-escalation phase, which propagates alternative ideas for a qualitative change in the hegemonic relationship, and the parties mobilize the public to support the peace process. Once the two sides develop significant pro-peace initiatives and institutionalize them as norms and means for rivalry transformation, the new situation encourages the leadership—irrespective of the regime type—to take promising or course-corrective steps and set the ball rolling by deepening their mutual vision of peace to carry out key changes in the bilateral relationship.

In this phase, the peace strategists' focus remains on limiting, revising, and de-institutionalizing the static policies so that the culture of conflict can be de-legitimized and the course of the rivalry shifted to a different, but mutually cooperative, plane. To sustain this process, the rival parties need to engage in a more promising policy reorganization drive so that the structural factors' bonding and their interactions with the peripheral temporal factors, and vice versa, can be significantly altered or adjusted to advance the transformation process to the desired stage of "neutralization" from the "minimization" one accomplished in the first phase—as illustrated by parts $2 \rightarrow 3$ in Figure 8.2. In other words, India and Pakistan's hegemonic relations may witness transformation if the ruling regimes reframe their policies to induce a variation in the structural factors' behavior so that their causal interactions neutralize the hub and hinder its interplay with the spokes to make both parties' respective positions—status quo and revisionist—politically neutral and thus inoffensive. This stage can be attained if the rival parties reshape their foreign and security policies, particularly by restraining the use of extraordinary measures and the practices of power politics; revise their national priorities to repose confidence in peaceful transformation techniques; and abandon their hostile approaches (military or non-military) intended to harm each other.

In the de-rivalization phase, the peace strategists have to withstand the restraining forces channeling grievances in the society and posing "resistance to change" (see Watson 1971). These forces may resort to excessive pressure tactics, such as organizing political agitations and engaging in socio-religious polarization or violent expressions, to exert and expand their influence to validate the old societal beliefs about the rivalry (Bar-Tal 2013: 354–58). In this course-corrective phase, more often than not, the peace strategists engaged in the formulation of alternative policies may be viewed or judged by some segments of the society and political opponents as "naïve" (as they are detached from reality), "traitors" (as their attitude-reframing initiative is "an act of treason" that signals weakness and undermines the country's status), and "illusionists" (as their conciliatory moves are perceived to support the opponent) rather recognizing them as resolution-seeking visionaries toiling for a peaceful settlement of the rivalry (Bar-Tal 2013: 350–

51). The resolution seekers and the promoters of rivalry transformation have to withstand such stinging criticism and de-legitimizing portrayal till their minority, but persistent, ideas about a peaceful change may gain their society's support as reformative policies that have merit and potential to change the course of the ongoing rivalry.

During the de-rivalization process, however, the dyad may not witness tension-free relations, as hostilities may continue to exist with violence and political rhetoric, such as militarized disputes, armed proxies, or aggressive mass agitations. Against this backdrop, if terrorist attacks on civilians continue to exist and non-compliant political groups oppose the continuation of the transformation process, then the leaders on both sides have to make all possible efforts to reassure the public how they will address the issue without undermining their commitment to peace. Attentively, they have to acknowledge that such intended challenges are an inevitable part of the transition process which they are ready to face to bring peace and change with yesterday's enemy. The political leadership must lead the society by continuing their alternative initiatives, that is, the revision and reversal of hostile national policies, and simultaneously carve new progressive norms and an ethos of peace to set an example for the succeeding regimes to not succumb to undue pressure from any quarter, particularly in haste, to discontinue the transformation process.

In the immediate aftermath of the Mumbai attacks, for instance, the leadership in New Delhi indeed succumbed to such domestic pressures and discontinued a fairly developed peace process which had potential to reframe the bilateral relationship at that juncture, if not lead to an imminent new beginning. Alternatively, the situation could also have been different had the new PPP government in Islamabad framed policies against the terrorist acts and taken promising and verifiable steps to bring the perpetrators of the Mumbai attacks to justice. Such cooperative and sincere moves on Pakistan's part could have extended the Indian leadership much-needed political leverage, and assured Indian society about the opponent's commitment to peace, to continue its efforts to save the peace process.

From this discontinued peace process come two lessons for today. First, New Delhi's and Islamabad's normative efforts were less extensive or comprehensive than necessary, if not hollow, so now they need to institutionalize norms to such a degree that any future peace process would possess the wherewithal to absorb such shocks. Second, while building a normative base and addressing the high-magnitude issues of security and reputation, the political regimes shall not hesitate to open a parallel channel with the relevant domestic stakeholders and the restraining forces—which in a way works to contain their negative feeling, instills a sense of hope, and partially legitimizes them in a quid pro quo for their advocacy of peacemaking—to address the political rhetoric and deactivate the socio-religious polarization. By taking these conflicting entities' fear and concern into account, the ruling elites will have a fair chance to handle the domestic forces manifesting resistance to peaceful change at one extreme and keep the peace process afloat by breaking through the policy regression at the other.

Since the rivalry transformation is not a linear process, it may even stop at a certain level without making any progression toward the intended goal(s); therefore the peace strategists need to be mindful of a hurried leap forward to the next phase—termination. Before heading to the final phase of the rivalry transformation, the political regimes on both sides must ensure that they have (1) acquired considerable maturity on select issues or sectors to support the rivalry-defusing structures and (2) achieved the desired objective of rivalry neutralization by revising, reversing, and de-institutionalizing their key national policies as mutually planned by them before stepping into the de-rivalization phase. Once the rival parties successfully implement the alternative policies and bring about a qualitative change in their hegemonic relationship, particularly after reducing the level of armed violence and societal polarization, the situation may be ripe to accommodate and make compromise on "hard" issues and concurrently seek support from the international community to mobilize resources to evolve "stable peace" in the final phase.[11]

Termination

Transition from the de-rivalization phase to the phase of termination requires a significant refinement in the two states' beliefs, attitudes, goals, and actions so that the new situation, in congruence with the process of change, helps the former adversaries to target key domains—mainly political, economic, and cultural—with concrete programs to foster interdependent relations. In this phase, the former adversaries have to create a common framework by building on the agreed standards of behavior and norms they have mutually set, recognized, and accomplished in the preceding phases. Once they have entered the termination phase, the major challenge for both parties is to (1) fractionate their principal issues (that is, separate them and reduce their scope) and advance their accommodative strategies without engaging in any military or policy dispute; (2) construct mechanisms that create favorable conditions to reduce the perception of threat; and (3) implement the risky decisions to transform their hostile relationship into a peaceful one.

To seek a formal termination of the rivalry, the political regimes have to design their policies to induce a qualitative change in the interactive behavior of the structural factors so that the altered environment may facilitate their transition from the stage of "neutralization" to the "rationalization" stage, as illustrated by parts 3→4 in Figure 8.2. This transition may be accomplished under a variety of conditions, involving the rationalization of structural factors to manage a fusion-free state within the hub, so that the two sides would effectively adjust their actions to minimize the stress (centripetal and centrifugal) between structural and temporal factors and attain a formal termination of the rivalry. Such changes offer clues as to how a shift in the rivals' position from mutual antagonism to mutual coexistence/acceptance can be attained and which options shall be pursued to expand the scope of bargaining for the resolution of a drawn-out conflict.

While in the termination phase, the mainstream leaders of India and Pakistan have to recognize that realities of the contemporary world are far different from those that led to or shaped their states' conflicting origins. To face future challenges, and remain relevant in the fast-emerging knowledge-based economic system, they need to set an advanced standard of behavior which would increase their prospects to expand their development goals on a par with the advanced or developed states. If the leaders on both sides genuinely embark on this path, then there is a high possibility that the former adversaries may take effective measures to break out of the cycle of animosity and negotiate a compromise agreement to settle the rivalry peacefully. With such a favorable alteration, coupled with the pressure of progress, it is highly likely that their leaders cannot afford to defend the status quo anymore and will gradually change or modify their policies to adjust to the new situation. The formal process of rivalry termination, however, may comprise a series of agreements that set the conditions to restructure their policies and abandon violent means or armed hostilities before reaching the final settlement (Bar-Tal 2013: 364).

At this juncture, the two sides have to take utmost care to avoid aggressive and violent acts, particularly terrorist attacks. It is not easy for the political regimes to wield complete control over the terrorist organizations, but if terrorist acts remain unchecked, they have a high potential to disrupt or even derail the fairly developed peace process as they provide the restraining forces with the required fuel "to inflame animosity, fear, and hatred" in the society (Bar-Tal 2013: 362). At this point, if the former adversaries distract from their mutual transformation mission or succumb to opponents' pressure, then the whole transformation process may collapse with the least possibility to return to it anytime soon. The political leaders at the helm of power must be cautious and take all possible steps in advance to avoid such a situation.

Upon the completion of this phase, with a degree of qualitative change in the dyad's behavior and hostile environment, the rivalry may be considered fully transformed with a peaceful settlement of protracted contestation or deemed as terminated. However, before formally recognizing the termination of the rivalry, the former adversaries have to effectively eliminate incompatibility between their goals and neutralize the restraining forces that obstruct the institutionalization of stable peace, or the stabilization of peace, crucial for settling differences and lasting peaceful relations in the post-termination period. To take steps in this direction, the former adversaries have to deepen their mutual understanding by softening their intransigent and polarized positions so that "an adequate degree of reconciliation occurs between [them]" to address the issue differences and facilitate them to develop "sustainable and self-correcting" solutions to maintain peaceful relations (Fisher 2005: 189).

Over the last seven decades or so, we have seen that the most striking attribute of the Indo-Pakistani dyad is its resistance to change or tendency to absorb political shocks to continue the rivalry. For the stabilization of peace in the post-termination years, there have to be forward-looking leaders at the helm of power who can ably manage minimal overlap in the two sides' political goals, despite having disagreement between the governments and pluralistic societies, and effectively cluster issues together to create a more favorable environment for cooperation. Their control over the state apparatus and the political process can facilitate similarity in the socio-political attributes to limit ideological differences and, with a clear hierarchy of priorities, allow linkages among issues to continue the bilateral interactions at different levels—that include the top-down and the bottom-up processes—and domains to attain cooperative outcomes. Such policy efforts support the former adversaries to shape ideas about conflict resolution and gradually develop social learning that contributes to the onset and maintenance of stable peace in the post-termination years.

Notes

Chapter 1

1. The divided state's official name is Jammu and Kashmir (J&K); however, the literature on its disputed status widely changes its nomenclature to Kashmir. This study uses both terms interchangeably and addresses the two parts of J&K administered by Pakistan as Azad Kashmir and the Northern Areas as Gilgit-Baltistan. Since August 2019, from the Indian side, the situation has taken a drastic turn with the abrogation of Article 370—which conferred on J&K a special status within the Indian Union—and the downgrading of the state's status by splitting it into two union territories: J&K and Ladakh. Additionally, after the Sino-Indian War of 1962, a part of J&K—Aksai Chin—is controlled and administered by China. Since then, India and China have maintained the status quo, but their policy-cum-territorial differences with regard to this part of the state remain unresolved.

2. The nine major armed crises are the Punjab War Scare (1951), the Rann of Kutch (1965), the Brasstacks crisis (1986–87), the Kashmir nuclear crisis (1990), the India-Pakistan nuclear tests crisis (1998), the Parliament attack crisis (2001), the Kaluchak attack crisis (2002), the Mumbai terrorist attacks (2008), and the Pulwama-Balakot military crisis (2019) (see COW 2020; ICB 2016; *Week* 2019).

3. To understand how the acquisition of nuclear weapons changes the foreign policies of states, see Bell (2015).

4. Realism is not a single theory; instead it is a group that accumulates all those theories that share a common set of assumptions but also include some distinctive elements. Here, the focus is more on structural and offensive realism than classical and neoclassical variants of realism. Additionally, other realist variants, such as power transition and deterrence, are discussed separately.

5. Valeriano's (2009) empirical study shows the shortcomings of Mearsheimer's (2001) "offensive realism." He argues that the norm-based and the issue-based theories, that is, the two opposite sets of theories, perform far better than offensive realism to explain the major powers' actions. According to him, the uniform acceptance of normative rules and states' reduced indulgence in territorial conflicts, rather than the realist power projections, ensure peace in the system.

6. In IR, for instance, Vasquez maintains that realism "works as an intellectual guide, because its dominance has created a kind of self-fulfilling prophecy. It can provide accurate predictions about how actors will respond both cognitively and behaviorally to certain war-threatening situations, but it is able to do this because power politics theory itself and the structures it has created have 'taught' leaders to respond this way" (1993: 87).

7. According to Popper (2002), the validity of inductive reasoning is always uncertain because of the n+1 problem: just because x is true in n cases does not guarantee that it will be true in the n+1th case.

8. For a hypothetical Indo-Pakistani nuclear conflict and consequences, see Batcher (2004) and Toon et al. (2019).

9. He places the Bangladesh War in the cluster of high-severity crises (7.00–10.00) with a severity score of 7.00 and concludes that the overall impact score for Bangladesh places it in the highest-impact group of international conflicts since the end of World War I (Brecher 2008: 194).

10. For a detailed interpretation, see Brecher (2008: ch. 9) and Buzan and Waever (2003). For small states' impact on the system, see Bueno de Mesquita (1990a, 1990b).

11. In Brecher's words, "the polarity findings suggest that . . . unipolycentrism [i.e., power unipolarity and decisional multipolarity] [is] the least stable and bipolycentrism—power bipolarity and decisional multipolarity—the least unstable (most stable) structure since the end of World War I" (2008: 269, emphasis removed).

12. Levy and Thompson (2010) maintain that there are ample possibilities for both theories to hold correct in their own sphere; however, Vasquez differs. According to him, the "logical contradiction" between these two theories "make[s] it likely that neither would prove to be correct" (1993: 55).

13. If we consider only relative military capability then it seems the power transition theory has relevance to explain some aspects of the India-Pakistan rivalry. For example, the First Kashmir War is consistent with the power transition hypothesis that parity leads to war. Similarly, the Indo-Pakistani periodic peace, after the Bangladesh War, is consistent with its hypothesis that preponderance results in no war (for a detailed account, see Chapters 4, 5, and 6).

14. The definition of "power" is again disputable from the standpoint of power transition theory. According to it, power comprises "population," "area of state," "industrial potential," and "military capability." For 1998, India and Pakistan's capability ratio, the Composite Index of National Capability (CINC), portrays a contrary picture as India's CINC score was fivefold more than Pakistan's. From the standpoint of "power," which is thus defined as overall capability, the empirical data question the claims that Pakistan had attained parity vis-à-vis India during the Kargil War. And, if "nuclear weapons" alone is a factor sufficient to bring parity in this case, then the power transition theory requires a substantial change in its criteria for "power."

15. In the 1971 war, India had initiated a full-scale war against Pakistan soon

after the latter had launched pre-emptive strikes against its air force stations in northwestern India.

16. To understand more about how and when deterrence works, under what conditions deterrent threats become successful, and under what conditions deterrent threats fail, see Levy's (1988) detailed and comprehensive review of various approaches of deterrence theory.

17. However, Huth and Russett's (1993) study presents the applicability of the deterrence model in a new way by finding its correlation with rivalry relationship: the deterrence model is successful for those years in which rivals do not resort to dispute or war.

18. On February 27, 2019, India and Pakistan "came perilously close to firing missiles at each other" (*Hindustan Times* 2019a; see also *Reuters* 2019).

Chapter 2

1. This dataset (version RIV5.01) replaced the COW's previous MID dataset (1816–1992) (D. Jones, Bremer, & Singer 1996) with an extension (1816–2001) (Ghosn, Palmer, & Bremer 2004) to re-cast the original dataset of rivalries.

2. This implies that rivalry termination cannot take place in the first twenty years. If a rivalry terminates within this period, according to Bennett's identification, then a particular dyad cannot be considered to have entered into a rivalry at all. For example, the India-Pakistan rivalry experienced its first MID in 1947, and most of the rivalry literature marks its beginning date as 1947, but Bennett's (1997b) conceptualization requires twenty years for rivalry maturation. By this measure, the Indo-Pakistani rivalry marks its beginning from 1967 onward and was not a rivalry until then (see Table 2.1 for a comparison of all conceptualizations).

3. Diehl's (1985: 1204–5) early study also affirms that territorial rivalries have a shorter life, but he attributed it to "resource constraints" rather than the spatial stakes' resolvable characteristic, later proposed by Thompson (1995).

Chapter 3

1. By "international strategic factors," I mean factors related to the external strategic situation—such as great powers/third-party intervention, alliances, arms buildups, power capability, and the dynamics of regional and global settings—which aggravate the rivals' relationship by gravitating them to more militarized and policy disputes, hostility, and issue differences.

2. By "key internal settings," I mean the rival parties' different regime systems, domestic politics, leadership ideology, and the like.

3. With regard to the India-Pakistan conflict, Benjamin Miller notes that the great powers' involvement, especially through arms buildups and alliances, has considerably contributed in the formation and persistency of this conflict which evolved South Asia into a "high war prone" region "in comparison with other, more peaceful regions" (Miller 2007: 13n35).

4. The robustness of this argument is fairly established in the literature, although there is considerable opposition to the universality of this understanding (see Desch 2002; Gibler 2007; Henderson 2008; Layne 1995; Rosato 2003).

Chapter 4

1. The League won only one of eighty-six seats in Punjab and, more shockingly, failed to even open an account in Sindh and the NWFP.

2. For a direct account of Pakistan's involvement in the Kashmir invasion, see Akbar Khan (1975).

3. However, Nawaz (2008: Ch. 3) maintains that throughout the war only the Azad Forces and raiders were toiling against the Indian armed forces. What makes Nawaz's analysis questionable is the raiders' preferred war strategy, vast control over mountainous terrain, and impressive early resistance to the Indian offensive. Any strategist would question how untrained and out-of-supply irregular forces—as portrayed by Nawaz—could control and retain the world's highest battle peaks, the Ladakh region, without any logistic support from Pakistani regulars. What dynamics was at play is, however, missing in his study.

4. Later Nehru constituted a committee to assess the impact of Indian armed action. The committee reported that the Indian troops had not only "encouraged, persuaded [or] . . . compelled the Hindu mob to loot Muslim shops and houses," but also taken active part in the butchery: "At a number of places," the Sunderlal Report underlines, "members of the armed forces brought out Muslim adult males from villages and towns and massacred them in cold blood" (cited in Thomson 2013). The report maintained that "at least 27 thousand to 40 thousand people lost their lives during and after the [armed] action" (Sunderlal Report, cited in S. Raghavan 2010: 99). This report clearly validated Pakistan's charges of Indian excesses in Hyderabad; probably for this reason the report was never published by the Indian government.

5. However, to overcome this limitation to some extent, the Pakistan government provided "modest quantities of weapons to Hyderabad" and helped it by allowing Sydney Cotton, an Australian aviator who owned the Aeronautical and Industrial Research Corporation and had a history of smuggling arms, "to use Karachi as a staging area" to "fly into Hyderabad" (S. Raghavan 2010: 94). "[C]ommenced on June 4, [1948]," writes Srinath Raghavan, "Cotton carried out 39 sorties ferrying 400 tons of small arms, mortars, 20 mm cannons, grenades, assorted ammunition, and communication equipment" (2010: 94).

6. In a personal interview with the author, Talat Masood (2015), a retired Pakistan Army general and defense analyst, has also shared this assessment. General Masood, who migrated to Pakistan from Hyderabad after the partition of India, maintained that "territorial distance and ethno-religious factors did play a considerable role in shaping the Pakistani policy makers' early years' decisions," which include military engagement or disengagement with India.

7. The Indian Independence Act necessitated Muslim majority areas to join

Pakistan and non-Muslim majority areas to remain with India, provided they were geographically contiguous with the respective countries (see Mountbatten 2003).

8. The South Asian history of the last two millennia demonstrates that India's sovereignty was repeatedly breached by aggression from across the northwestern frontier (see Thapar 2002: 425–41). During the British rule, the subcontinent once again came under the Russian threat that eventually evolved into an extreme strategic competition between Britain and Russia famously known as the "Great Game."

9. In the immediate aftermath of World War II, former US Secretary of State Henry Kissinger acknowledges, the United States wanted to accredit a similar role to itself in the international politics: its "secret dream in the first postwar years was to play the role that India's Prime Minister Nehru later arrogated to himself" (1979: 114). However, according to Brecher, the hidden objective of Nehru's non-alignment policy was to avoid the alienation of China and the Soviet Union (1959: 213).

10. In the early nineteenth century, a political-diplomatic tension erupted between the British Empire and the Russian Empire over the control of key territories of Central and South Asia to expand their spheres of influence. To defend their most prized possession, the Indian empire, the leading British geo-strategists charted a containment strategy to expand Britain's influence northward (Afghanistan and its neighboring territories) and hinder czarist Russia's southward expansion in Central Asia. Between the two empires, this struggle for supremacy and protection of interests continued beyond their borders till the first half of the twentieth century and was known as the "Great Game." Some scholarly accounts claim that Sir Olaf Caroe's close attention to the regional affairs, mainly as the last British governor on the Afghan frontier, had predicted the scope of the Great Game in South Asia's borderlands even after the end of the British rule in India. (For a deeper understanding, see Ingram 1980; Johnson 2003; Rezun 1986).

11. However, the COW (2015) dataset negates the validity of this claim. It records India's and Pakistan's military personnel strength as 311,000 and 275,000, respectively (see Figure 4.2a).

12. Akbar Khan's (1975) firsthand account demonstrates this fact in detail.

13. Pakistan's military expenditure entry for 1947 is missing in the COW dataset (2015, version 4.01). Therefore, the total military capability has been not calculated for this year.

14. Kashmir not only was geographically contiguous to Pakistan but its crucial transport links, major and minor, were also through Pakistan.

15. Kashmir had only four major motorable roads from its main cities to the united Punjab: (1) Sialkot–Jammu–Banihal pass–Srinagar; (2) Rawalpindi–Murree–Kohala–Domel–Srinagar; (3) Rawalpindi–Abbottabad–Mansehra–Muzaffarabad–Srinagar; and (4) Gurdaspur–Kathua–Jammu–Banihal pass–Srinagar. The shock of partition had brought a paramount shift in the taxonomy of Kashmir's security, as its main communication lines were suddenly shifted toward Pakistan.

328   NOTES TO PAGES 107-40

16. By keeping this mission secret from the Pakistan Army, the Liberation Committee, which comprised a select group of political leaders, civil bureaucrats, and military strategists, circumvented the military chain of command—which might have disapproved the planned attack in view of the Pakistan Army's transformation from an ex-British Indian Army to a national army.

17. Figure 4.2a–c provides clear evidence that between 1949 and 1952 Pakistan's military expenditure swung up almost three times its 1948 outlay. However, its military personnel strength shows a gradual decrease in comparison to its counterpart, but this did not affect its total military capability until the mid-1950s because of the steady increase in the military expenditure.

18. On the basis of the Polity IV dataset (Marshall & Jaggers 2002), Figure 4.3 plots the regime type of the India-Pakistan dyad and its correlation with dispute recurrence from 1947 to 1958.

Chapter 5

1. While Islamabad was being built, Rawalpindi served as the capital of Pakistan from 1959 to 1969. Prior to that, Karachi served as the national capital from 1947 to 1959.

2. Later, in February 1968, the ad hoc Indo-Pakistani Western Boundary Tribunal awarded Pakistan 350 square miles area out of its total claim of 3,500 square miles (UNRIAA 1968: 569–70).

3. In the mid-1950s, for instance, the US administration even "referred Goa as one of the 'Portuguese provinces' in Asia" (McMahon 1994: 223).

4. For a diametrically opposite and competitive perspective, see Chaudhuri (2009: 841–69).

5. Pakistan demanded almost 82,000 square miles of the state's total territory of 85,000 square miles, leaving India with a very small chunk of the state (Gundevia 1984: 280). According to Major General D.K. Palit, who was then serving as director of India's military operations and assisted the Foreign Ministry to prepare five concession maps by drawing alternative lines along the CFL, India's maximum territorial concession to Pakistan was "3500 square kilometers" (1991: 371).

6. Against their collective commitment of over $500 million, the Western powers had delivered less than $100 million worth of arms and equipment to India from October 1962 to September 1965 (see Eldridge 1969: 165–67).

7. The Rann of Kutch dispute occurred weeks before the Second Afro-Asian Conference at Bandung, which also offered Pakistan an opportunity to brand India as an aggressor with China's support.

8. For full understanding of this point, see "Memorandum of Conversation between Kissinger and Huang Hua" (1999: 54–55).

9. Kissinger claimed that the White House's USS *Enterprise* move had signaled the Kremlin that India's further offensive toward West Pakistan might pull the two superpowers into an undesirable crisis (1979: 912–15).

10. If one assembles the pieces of the White House's war-time actions, diplomatic and military, it is evident that the American dispatch of the *Enterprise* was carefully timed to skip the war participation. On November 15, 1971, almost three weeks prior to the war initiation, the US decision-makers had placed clear instructions to the navy "to ready" the US attack carrier "to dissuade 'third party' involvement" in the South Asian crisis (Document 26 in NSA 2002b), but surprisingly the ship turned up only when the terms of Pakistani troops' surrender had been initiated by the Indian Army generals.

11. For instance, China withheld its promised free supply of armaments, particularly aircraft, which Pakistan desperately needed in the eastern wing (Yunus 2011: 14).

12. Since 1959, India's military capability has been directed against its two adversaries, Pakistan and China; thus India's China-related capabilities have been subtracted from its total military capability as follows: 1959 and 1960 = 15%; 1961 = 20%; 1962 and 1963 = 25%, 1964 = 30%, and 1965-72 = 35%. Percentages for 1965-72 are based on that period's data and prior to 1965 are assumed (as low as possible). To keep figures reliable, this study has considered scales that denote lower percentage(s).

13. Van Evera defines a "window of opportunity" as "a fading offensive opportunity" and a "window of vulnerability" as "a growing defensive vulnerability" (1999: 74).

14. For extensive data, see P. Mohan and Chopra (2013: Appendixes A-D, pp. 378-87).

15. During the first eleven years of independence (1947-58), Pakistan's defense expenditure was more than 60 percent of its total expenditure (cf. H.-A. Rizvi 2000: 63).

Chapter 6

1. In a personal interview with the author, Iqbal Ahmad Khan (2015), Pakistan's former ambassador to Bangladesh and Iran, also stressed that "the Indian move to occupy Siachin [was] in violation of the Simla Accord; [and] Pakistan's move in Kargil could be explained in the context of the Indian move."

2. In 1978, when India's foreign minister, Atal Bihari Vajpayee, was on a state visit to China, the People's Liberation Army (PLA) had attacked Vietnam. Later the Chinese leadership cleared the mystery surrounding the timing of the attack: "[T]hey were 'teaching Vietnam a lesson' just as they had taught another country a similar one in 1962" (Ganguly 2002: 80-81). After the Chinese provocation, New Delhi was aware of the importance of its military relationship with Moscow.

3. Under this barter agreement, "the USSR provided 200,000 tons of crude oil and 500,000 tons of diesel oil for 500,000 tons of Indian rice" (Racioppi 1994: 130).

4. Particularly after the fall of the Shah of Iran, America's strong ally in the

Persian Gulf, in the 1979 Iranian Revolution and the establishment of Soviet bases in South Yemen and Ethiopia (see Siddiqa-Agha 2001: 94).

5. On March 28, 1988, while establishing a causal link to this joint attack strategy, a Pakistani newspaper reported that India feared Pakistan would blackmail it in a regional conflict and Israel was concerned that Pakistan would share its know-how with other Arab states (*Muslim* 1988).

6. Because India's military capabilities were directed toward Pakistan and China, its China-related capabilities have been subtracted from its overall capabilities (that is, 30 percent or so). India's firm victory over Pakistan in 1971 diminished the collective Sino-Pakistani threat of slicing off its northeastern part. Thereafter India's China-related capabilities saw a minor revision, that is, a decline of 5 percent (from 35 to 30 percent). Keeping this in sight, India's Pakistan-related capabilities have been truncated by 30 percent in the post-1972 period.

7. I differ with S. Paul Kapur's understanding that "Pakistan, at . . . the beginning . . . of the 'long peace', was a nominal democracy, headed by a civilian leader, but overshadowed by the military" (2011: 73n40).

8. It is noteworthy that the Polity-IV dataset designates India stable democracy status with a polity score of seven (cf. COW 2015; S. Mohan 2016: 220n14, 222). Of late, however, this anomaly has been rectified in the Polity-V dataset, wherein India's polity score for emergency years has been lowered to six, that is, non-democratic "hybrid" regime (see Figure 6.3a, b).

9. Drawing on the framework and principles agreed at the Bandung Conference of 1955, the Non-aligned Movement (NAM) formally came into existence in 1961 in Belgrade. India was one of the founding and prominent members of the NAM. Throughout the Cold War, India's role in international affairs was largely shaped by the non-alignment doctrine and organizational cohesion through the NAM, which greatly helped it to corner the bloc politics and raise a voice for the Third World states. The formation of the NAM offered an alternative platform to the newly decolonized and neutral states to pursue a viable middle path to safeguard their national interests without linking their foreign policies with Cold War politics and compromising their strategic autonomy. Against the backdrop of Cold War politics, on the other hand, Pakistan chose to join the Western alliance system in the mid-1950s: particularly the SEATO and the CENTO (S. Mohan & Lobo 2020: 57–61). After Pakistan's devastating defeat in the 1971 war, its ruling elites were disillusioned with US alliance politics and withdrew from both SEATO in 1973 and CENTO in 1979. Meanwhile, despite the Indira Gandhi–led India's objection to its membership, Pakistan continued its attempts to join the NAM. After Pakistan's complete withdrawal from the Western alliance system, particularly the CENTO in March 1979, and India's retraction of its long-standing objection to its archrival's membership, Pakistan joined the NAM and attended its Sixth Summit as a member in September 1979 (see Ahmad 1979).

10. In a midnight address in early 1968, soon after his second release from prison, Abdullah had declared that "there was no question of compromise on the right of self-determination for Kashmir" and Indian repression would never be

able to suppress the Kashmiris' urge to be free. He further assured the Kashmiris that "he would give his life before submitting to a compromise" (Lockwood 1969: 393). However, all these commitments evaporated soon after Pakistan's debacle in the 1971 war.

11. Some observers argue that "the Indian approach was hypocritical" on Article 370 and reaffirming the terms of state's incorporation into India because "between 1954 and the mid-1970s, 28 constitutional orders 'integrating' [J&K] with India had been issued from Delhi, and 262 Union laws had been made applicable in the [state]" (Sumantra Bose 2003: 88).

12. Later G.M. Shah's deputy D.D. Thakur, a renowned lawyer, judge, and later governor, said in his autobiography that the whole act was plotted by him and Mrs. Gandhi (2005: 360–62).

13. With regard to this, Bhabani Sen Gupta, an Indian analyst, opined that "it would be correct to say that the separation of Bangladesh from Pakistan added an edge to the Kashmir conflict" (cited in S. Khan 2009: 96). In October 2015, while conducting a field survey in Pakistan I again probed to confirm from the Pakistani side whether there was any correlation between East Pakistan's secession and the Kashmir dispute, in line with Bhabani Sen Gupta's observation. A considerable majority, including policy makers, academicians, journalists, opinion-makers, and researchers, responded in the affirmative.

Chapter 7

1. According to a serving senior IAF officer, the Indian Army was reluctant to disclose the serious ground situation because it "was caught unawares and . . . wanted to retrieve the situation by asking the IAF for help without taking the issue to the prime minister" (as quoted in Lambeth 2012: 47n37).

2. For instance, on May 15, Defence Minister George Fernandes claimed that the Indian forces would throw the infiltrators out in 48 hours (*Daily Excelsior* 1999).

3. Because this was the first time that India had brought its air power into action since 1971, Pakistan termed it an "overreaction" (Musharraf 2006: 91). A similar concern was raised by Prime Minister Nawaz Sharif in his televised ceasefire address: "The use of air and land power in Kargil by India was on a scale associated with a large and regular war only." Such a "sudden escalation was unexpected" (Sharif 1999). Later Shamshad Ahmad, Pakistan's former foreign secretary, also maintained that Pakistan "misjudged the Indian ability and the will to fight back and had assumed that India would never retaliate with an all-out offensive against Pakistan" (*Times of India* 2006).

4. The "warning phase" is a vital exercise between several union ministries before resorting to the course of war.

5. Mohammad Ziauddin (2015), Pakistan's veteran journalist and the former editor-in-chief of the *Dawn* and the *Express Tribune*, confirmed this during a personal interview with the author. "Pakistan used covert armed movement in Kash-

mir till the 9 /11 attacks," he stated, but "this incident overnight tagged all its free-dom fighters as terrorists. Thereafter, the international community did not buy Pakistan's traditional argument of 'freedom fighters' anymore" (Ziauddin 2015).

6. Anam Zakaria points out that "the term working boundary is used by Paki-stan to denote that while on one side there is the internationally recognized province of Punjab (in Pakistan), on the other side is a disputed territory (that both India and Pakistan claim)" (2018: xxix). For a deeper understanding of the typology and the escalatory pattern of the Indo-Pakistani LoC and international border, see Jacob (2019).

7. To pressure New Delhi and Islamabad, the Clinton administration shuttled between the Pressler Amendment and the Brown Amendment. The Brown Amendment provided the White House sufficient room to bypass the stringent Pressler Amendment and lure Islamabad through a $368 million military package that included three P-3C anti-submarine aircraft, twenty-eight Harpoon surface-to-air missiles, 360 Sidewinder air-to-air missiles, and a range of other equipment and ammunition (Z. Hussain 1998: 42).

8. This was also partly because the US intelligence agencies had detected close connection and coordination between the ISI, the Taliban, and the mujahideen networks operating within Pakistan to target India.

9. For instance, in July 2006, after concluding the defense cooperation agree-ment (2005) and coming close to inking the civil nuclear deal with India, the Bush administration had prepared a plan to gain a double benefit through weap-ons sales to Pakistan and strike a balance in South Asia. It "presented the U.S. Congress with [a] plan to sell Pakistan F-16 fighters in a deal worth $5 billion, . . . [that would] include eighteen new F-16 aircraft with an option to purchase another eighteen planes, a support package for twenty-six used F-16s, an ammu-nition package, and an upgrade package for the current fleet of thirty-four F-16s" (Grare 2006: 14).

10. For a succinct critique of India's Indo-Pacific strategy, particularly from the standpoint of "elusive balancing," see Rajagopalan (2020).

11. The so-called Indira Doctrine of the early 1980s was loosely modeled on America's Monroe Doctrine, which reflected a general Indian consensus to oppose external intervention in "any South Asian country" with "any implicit or explicit . . . anti-Indian bias" (see Gupta 1983).

12. By "no secret," Gul (2015) refers to the past statements of Ajit Doval, now India's national security advisor (NSA); G. Parthasarathy, former high commis-sioner of India to Pakistan; and Kiran Bedi; the three were in the best experts group of *India Today*'s 2009 program, "How to Tackle an Obstinate Pakistan?" in which they said that "India should exploit fault lines within Pakistan and one such fault line is Balochistan. [India] should counter Pakistani plans in Afghani-stan" (cf. *India Today* 2009).

13. This claim was an extension of the Pakistan corps commander's May 2015 statement that "RAW [India's Research and Analysis Wing] [is] involve[d] in whipping up terrorism in Pakistan" (ISPR 2015a).

14. As a semi-autonomous tribal region in northwestern Pakistan, the Federally Administered Tribal Areas (FATA) existed from 1947 until being merged with the neighboring province Khyber Pakhtoonkhwa in 2018. This and other interviews were conducted by the author prior to the merger of the FATA with Khyber Pakhtoonkhwa.

15. For a complete understanding of this point, see Abraham (1999, 2009), Bajpai (2009b), and Chakma (2009).

16. Prior to the 1998 tests, Defense Minister George Fernandes had declared China as the greatest potential threat, but in reality it was not India's immediate target (*Times of India* 1998).

17. According to Gohar Ayub Khan, then foreign minister of Pakistan, soon after the Indian tests misperceptions were rife in Islamabad that India might strike Pakistan's nuclear sites before it could conduct tests (2007: 297–99).

18. On July 3, 1999, according to Riedel, prior to the Clinton-Sharif meeting at the Blair House, US officials received "disturbing evidence that the Pakistanis were preparing their nuclear arsenals for possible deployment" (2002: 8). The next day, President Bill Clinton reminded Prime Minister Nawaz Sharif that Pakistan was about to "plunge the world into its first nuclear exchange . . . Sharif seemed taken aback and said only that India was probably doing the same" (Riedel 2002: 11). Around the same time, an Indian journalist reported that India had been indeed "doing the same": it had "activated all its three types of nuclear delivery and kept them at what is known as Readiness State 3" (Chengappa 2000: 437).

19. Interestingly, the logistics and other requirements for such a high-magnitude operation were kept secret not only from several cabinet ministers but also from the chiefs of the Pakistan Air Force, Navy, and several senior army officers (Qadir 2002: 26).

20. Some scholars argue that the Kargil intrusion was Pakistan's "limited probe" strategy to challenge India's conventional deterrence (Ganguly & Hagerty 2005: 152). This argument, albeit powerful, does not reflect that the strategy worked out like a limited probe, because Pakistan failed to generate a controlled crisis—the mainstay of a limited-probe strategy—as India retaliated with an extensive offensive to defend its territory.

21. For a deeper understanding, see Basrur (2006); Ganguly (2008); Karnad (2002); Rajagopalan (2005); Waltz (2003a).

22. In 2018, India's Defence Acquisition Council (DAC) authorized the local construction of six conventional submarines under the "Make in India" initiative by allocating the Project 75(I) a whopping budget of $12 billion (*Economic Times* 2018e). On the other side, Pakistan has signed two pacts for upgrading its existing submarine force with China and Turkey. In 2015, it inked a $4–5 billion deal with China to procure eight Hangor (Type 042 Yuan-class) diesel-electric attack submarines with a possibly delivery of half of them by 2023 (*Express Tribune* 2016a). In 2016, it awarded a $350 million contract to a Turkish manufacturer for the modernization of its Agosta 90B-class submarines (*Nation* 2019b).

23. The US intelligence community has listed the Nasr as a deployed system since 2013 (see NASIC 2013).

24. Vipan Narang terms Pakistan's highly problematic first-use policy as an "asymmetric escalation posture" (2009-10: 39).

25. During my February 2020 field study, I conducted multiple interviews with the locals residing near the LoC areas—where the two nuclear adversaries engaged in a retaliatory aerial battle (Nowshera-Jhangar sector)—and found that at the time they were almost sure that the Indo-Pakistani crisis would escalate into a large-scale nuclear war.

26. In his second term, however, Nawaz Sharif had shown some signs of power consolidation when he replaced General Jehangir Karamat with General Pervez Musharraf. This unusual show of power could not hold for long as the new general forcibly ousted Sharif in a bloodless coup after the Kargil debacle.

27. Lal Krishna Advani, then India's home minister, had claimed that New Delhi's "decisive step to become a nuclear weapon state has brought about a qualitative new state in India-Pakistan relations, particularly in finding a lasting solution to the Kashmir problem." Thus "India is resolved to deal firmly with Pakistan's hostile activities [in Kashmir]" (cited in Swami 1998a).

28. To understand the level of threat Pakistan's overgrown terrorist and Islamist organizations pose to the country's political institutions and how they managed a deep reach within the Pakistan Army, see Ashish Shukla (2017: 114-31).

29. M.K. Narayanan, then India's NSA, had categorically stated in television interviews that General Musharraf was and remained the person with whom India "can do business" (Narayanan 2007a, 2007b).

30. In an interview, General Musharraf had categorically stated that Pakistan would give up its claim to Kashmir "if this solution comes up" (*Guardian* 2006). Later, Professor Abdul Ghani Bhat, former chairman of the Hurriyat Conference, had also expressed favorable views in an interview: "The proposal was in fact not only an acceptable solution but a very workable one too, where no party would have suffered the painful sense of defeat: neither the Indians nor the Pakistanis and not even the people of Kashmir" (Bhat 2011).

31. L.K. Advani, then the leader of the opposition, had moved an adjournment motion in the Lok Sabha that Prime Minister Manmohan Singh was keeping the nation in the dark over the back-channel progress on Kashmir (cf. Kasuri 2015: 314).

32. According to Shahid Malik (2015), then high commissioner of Pakistan to India, "it did not take off as India reneged on the commitment to discuss all issues including Kashmir during the bilateral talks."

33. This understanding is a reflection of the predominant feeling or view of the common people in Lahore and Islamabad in October 2015. During the same field study, however, I found that a majority of academicians, retired diplomats, think-tank-based area experts, and journalists had different or contrasting views about the issue.

34. Such unwavering confidence and show of authority by the prime minister-elect had posed a serious challenge to the army's traditional sphere of power. Per-

haps for this reason, the GHQ did not endorse it—a clear indication that the Sharif-GHQ relationship would follow a tense trajectory in the near future (*Hindustan Times* 2014).

Chapter 8

1. At present, a union territory (cf. note 1 in Chapter 1).

2. For a deeper understanding of how the securitization of climate change policy and increasing water insecurity in India and China are aggravating their hostility, particularly in the domain of transboundary river water disputes, see Sahu and Mohan (2022).

3. Recently, Ladakh has been split from J&K and formed as a union territory.

4. After the considerable success of the Uri-Muzaffarabad and the Poonch-Rawalakot bus services, these routes were also opened for trade in October 2008. With growing tensions between India and Pakistan, particularly after the Pulwama attack, the cross-LoC trade has been suspended since April 2019.

5. Some potential routes from J&K and Ladakh are the Kargil-Sakardu, the Noushera-Mirpur, the Rajouri-Kotli, the Pallanwalla-Chumb, and the Suchetgarh-Sialkot.

6. When I asked Pakistan's former ambassador Iqbal Ahmad Khan (2015) about it, he agreed with this perspective but approached the issue differently: "Pakistanis believe Kashmir to be a core issue in the bilateral relationship, but they are prepared to address and settle the less complicated ones such as Siachin, Sir Creek and water first in the hope that the [bilateral environment] will become conducive for the settlement of the core dispute."

7. The United States has formed bilateral and trilateral alliances with the Philippines, Japan, South Korea, Taiwan, Singapore, Indonesia, Vietnam, Australia, Saudi Arabia, Israel, and Iraq. Over the last decade or so, especially against China, it has signed an agreement with Singapore to station its combat vessels, strengthened strategic ties with the key ASEAN members, announced a $425 million Southeast Asia Maritime Security Initiative (SAMSI), signed a defense pact with India to establish a long-term strategic partnership, taken the initiative for the Quadrilateral Security Dialogue with India, Japan, and Australia, and further consolidated its already close defense cooperation with Australia by signing the US-Australia Force Posture Agreement (USAFPA) at the annual Australia–United States Ministerial Consultation (AUSMIN) (see *BBC* 2020b; Gady 2015; A. Mehta 2015; Parrish 2013; US Department of State 2014; US-China Economic and Security Review Commission 2013; White House 2021).

8. The Chinese stand in favor of Masood Azar provoked New Delhi to take a strong position against Beijing by immediately issuing a visa to the Uyghur leader Dolkun Isa, whom the Chinese government considers a "terrorist," to attend a conference in Dharamsala in April 2016. However, later the Indian government showed restraint and canceled Isa's visa without providing any justification for its diplomatic reversal (*Indian Express* 2016c).

9. From Waltz's (1981, 2003a) viewpoint, the prospects of peace increase with the spread of nuclear weapons, but the validity of this proposition as a universal norm is debatable in the Indo-Pakistani context in light of Pakistan's unstable polity, economic fragility, and military control.

10. "Personalistic" here is best understood from Kurt Weyland's definition of populism as a *"political strategy* through which a personalistic leader seeks or exercises government power based on direct, unmediated, uninstitutionalized support from large numbers of mostly unorganized followers" (Weyland 2001: 14, emphasis added).

11. Stable peace is "a situation in which the probability of war is so small" that once the rival parties attain it, they refrain from engaging in armed disputes and threats and largely pursue a course of mutual cooperation and negotiations to resolve their remaining differences (Boulding 1978: 13).

References

Aaj News (2016), "Jinnah Naval Base Being Upgraded as Alternate Port: Commander," January 7. http://www.aaj.tv/2016/01/jinnah-naval-base-being-up graded-as-alternate-port-commander/ (accessed December 30, 2018).

Abbas, Hassan (2005), *Pakistan's Drift into Extremism: Allah, the Army, and America's War on Terror*, New Delhi: Pentagon Press.

Abraham, Itty (1999). *The Making of the Indian Atomic Bomb: Science, Secrecy and the Postcolonial State*, New Delhi: Orient Longman.

Abraham, Itty (2009), "Contra-Proliferation: Interpreting the Meanings of India's Nuclear Tests in 1974 and 1998," in Scott C. Sagan (ed.), *Inside Nuclear South Asia*, Stanford, CA: Stanford University Press, pp. 106–133.

Ahmad, Naveed (1979), "The Non-aligned Movement and Pakistan," *Pakistan Horizon*, 32(4): 79–91.

Ahmed, Akbar S. (1997), *Jinnah, Pakistan and Islamic Identity: The Quest for Saladin*, Karachi: Oxford University Press.

Ahmed, Naseem (2010), "Military and the Foreign Policy of Pakistan," *South Asian Survey*, 17(2): 313–30.

Ahmed, Samina (1978), "Franco-Pakistan Relations-II: The Issue of the Nuclear Reprocessing Plant," *Pakistan Horizon*, 31(1): 35–70.

Ahmed, Samina (1979), "Pakistan's Proposal for a Nuclear-Weapon-Free Zone in South Asia," *Pakistan Horizon*, 32(4): 92–130.

Ahmed, Samina (1999), "Pakistan's Nuclear Weapons Program: Turning Points and Nuclear Choices," *International Security*, 23(4): 178–204.

Ahmed, Samina, and David Cortright (1998), "Going Nuclear: The Weaponization Option," in Samina Ahmed and David Cortright (eds.), *Pakistan and the Bomb: Public Opinion and Nuclear Options*, Notre Dame, IN: University of Notre Dame Press, pp. 89–107.

Ahmed, Samina, and Varun Sahni (1998), "Freezing the Fighting: Military Disengagement on the Siachen Glacier," Cooperative Monitoring Center Occasional Paper/1, Sandia National Laboratories, March, pp. 1–36. http://www.sa ndia.gov/cooperative-monitoring-center/assets/documents/sand98-05051.pdf (accessed February 17, 2013).

Aiyar, Mani Shankar (2012), "Misfortune Telling" (Book Review), *The Indian Express*, June 9. http://indianexpress.com/article/news-archive/web/misfort une-telling/99/print/ (accessed June 19, 2012).

Akbar, M.J. (2002), *Kashmir: Behind the Vale*, New Delhi: Roli Books.

Akbar, M.J. (2011), *Tinderbox: The Past and Future of Pakistan*, New Delhi: Harper-Collins.

Akhund, Iqbal (2000), *Trial and Error: The Advent and Eclipse of Benazir Bhutto*, Karachi: Oxford University Press.

Al Jazeera (2016), "Surgical Strikes: Pakistan Rejects India's Claims," September 30. https://www.aljazeera.com/news/2016/09/pakistan-denies-india-carried-su rgical-strikes-160929165646369.html (accessed December 31, 2018).

Ali, S. Mahmud (2005), *US-China Cold War Collaboration, 1971–1989*, London: Routledge.

Ali, Salamat (1989), "The Counter-Punch: Army Prepares for Its Biggest Ever Exercise," *Far Eastern Economic Review*, October 26.

Ambedkar, B.R. (1946), *Pakistan or the Partition of India*, Bombay: Thacker.

Ambekar, Sunil (2019), *The RSS Roadmaps for the 21st Century*, New Delhi: Rupa.

Anand, Pawan (2016), Personal Interview (translated version), president of the cross-LoC Traders Association, the Poonch-Rawalakot Sector, Poonch, July 23.

Anand, Pawan (2019), Personal Interview (translated version), president of the cross-LoC Traders Association, the Poonch-Rawalakot Sector, Poonch, April 7.

Anderson, Mary (1999), *Do No Harm: How Aid Can Support Peace—or War*, Boulder: Lynne Rienner.

Armstrong, Tony (1993), *Breaking the Ice: Rapprochement between East and West Germany, the United States and China, Israel and Egypt*, Washington, DC: United States Institute of Peace.

Asia Watch and Physicians for Human Rights (1993), "The Human Rights Crisis in Kashmir: A Pattern of Impunity," *Human Rights Watch*, New York.

Azar, Edward (1972), "Conflict Escalation and Conflict Reduction in an International Crisis: Suez, 1956," *Journal of Conflict Resolution*, 16(2): 183–201.

Baabar, Mariana (2006), "RAW Is Training 600 Balochis in Afghanistan," *Outlook*, April 24. http://www.outlookindia.com/article/RAW-Is-Training-600-Baloc his-In-Afghanistan/231032 (accessed October 10, 2014).

Badhwar, Inderjit, and Dilip Bobb (1987), "Indo-Pak Border: Game of Brinkmanship," *India Today*, February 15. http://indiatoday.intoday.in/story/when-in dian-and-pakistani-forces-positioned-themselves-along-j&k-and-punjab-bo rders/1/336697.html (accessed March 20, 2014).

Bajpai, Kanti P. (2009a), "To War or Not to War: The India-Pakistan Crisis of 2001–2," in Sumit Ganguly and S. Paul Kapur (eds.), *Nuclear Proliferation in South Asia: Crisis Behaviour and the Bomb*, New York: Routledge, pp. 162–82.

Bajpai, Kanti (2009b), "The BJP and the Bomb," in Scott C. Sagan (ed.), *Inside Nuclear South Asia*, Stanford, CA: Stanford University Press, pp. 25–67.

Bajpai, Kanti P., and Sumit Ganguly (1994), "India and the Crisis in Kashmir," *Asian Survey*, 34(5): 401–16.

Bajpai, Kanti P., et al. (1995), *Brasstacks and Beyond: Perception and Management of Crisis in South Asia*, New Delhi: Manohar.

Bajwa, Maj. Gen. Kuldip Singh (2005), "Crossing Ichhogil Canal: How Lt-Col Hayde Did It," *Tribune*, September 18. http://www.tribuneindia.com/2005/20050918/edit.htm#1 (accessed March 7, 2013).

Bakshi, G.D. (2009), "Kargil: Dynamics of a Limited War against a Nuclear Backdrop," *CLAWS Journal*, Summer: 38–51.

Barnds, William J. (1972), *India, Pakistan, and the Great Powers*, New York: Praeger.

Barringer, Richard (1972), *War: Patterns of Conflict*, Cambridge, MA; MIT Press.

Bar-Tal, Daniel (2000), "From Intractable Conflict through Conflict Resolution to Reconciliation: Psychological Analysis," *Political Psychology* 21(2): 351–65.

Bar-Tal, Daniel (2013), *Intractable Conflicts: Socio-Psychological Foundations and Dynamics*, New York: Cambridge University Press.

Baru, Sanjaya (2014), *The Accidental Prime Minister: The Making and Unmaking of Manmohan Singh*, New Delhi: Penguin-Viking.

Baruah, Amit (1998), "BJP Statements Worry Pakistan," *Hindu*, February.

Basrur, Rajesh M. (2006), *Minimum Deterrence and India's Nuclear Security*, Stanford, CA: Stanford University Press.

Basrur, Rajesh M. (2008), *South Asia's Cold War: Nuclear Weapons and Conflict in Comparative Perspective*, New York: Routledge.

Basrur, Rajesh M. (2010), "India-Pakistan Relations: Between War and Peace," in Sumit Ganguly (ed.), *India's Foreign Policy: Retrospect and Prospect*, New Delhi: Oxford University Press, pp. 11–31.

Batcher, Robert T. (2004), "The Consequences of an Indo-Pakistani Nuclear War," *International Studies Review*, 6(2): 135–62.

Bayer, Resat (2010), "Peaceful Transitions and Democracy," *Journal of Peace Research*, 47(5): 535–46.

BBC (2001), "Militants Attack Kashmir Assembly," October 1. http://news.bbc.co.uk/2/hi/south_asia/1574225.stm (accessed January 4, 2014).

BBC (2002), "Kashmir Temples Hit by Gunbattles," November 25. http://news.bbc.co.uk/2/hi/south_asia/2508531.stm (accessed January 4, 2014).

BBC (2006), "Mumbai Bombings: 400 Detained," July 13. http://web.archive.org/web/20070302203453/http://edition.cnn.com/2006/WORLD/asiapcf/07/13/mumbai.blasts/ (accessed March 28, 2014).

BBC (2008), "Zardari Distances Pakistan from Mumbai Attack," December 17. http://www.bbc.co.uk/worldservice/news/2008/12/lg/081217_zardari_nh_sl.shtml (accessed March 29, 2014).

BBC (2009), "Afghan Bomb Strikes India Embassy," October 8, 2009. http://news.bbc.co.uk/go/pr/fr/-/2/hi/south_asia/8296137.stm (accessed October 10, 2014).

BBC (2015), "Gurdaspur Attack: Ten Killed in Indian Police Station Siege," July 27. http://bbc.com/news/world-asia-india-33671593 (accessed August 15, 2015).

BBC (2016a), "Militants Attack Indian Army Base in Kashmir 'Killing 17,'" September 18. https://www.bbc.com/news/world-asia-india-37399969 (accessed December 31, 2018).

BBC (2016b), "Kashmir Attack: What's Behind the Deadliest Militant Raid in Years," September 19. https://www.bbc.com/news/world-asia-37404372 (accessed December 31, 2018).

BBC (2016c), "Kashmir Attack: India 'Launches Strikes against Militants,'" September 29. https://www.bbc.com/news/world-asia-37504308 (accessed December 31, 2018).

BBC (2016d), "India's 'Surgical Strikes' in Kashmir: Truth or Illusion?," October 23. https://www.bbc.com/news/world-asia-india-37702790 (accessed December 31, 2018).

BBC (2019), "Pulwama Attack: India will 'Completely Isolate' Pakistan," February 15. https://www.bbc.com/news/world-asia-india-47249133 (accessed February 16, 2019).

BBC (2020a), "Afghan Conflict: US and Taliban Sign Deal to End 18-Year War," February 15. https://www.bbc.com/news/world-asia-51689443 (accessed March 3, 2020).

BBC (2020b), "US-India 2+2: Crucial Defence Deal Signed," October 27. https://www.bbc.com/news/world-asia-india-54655947 (accessed October 28, 2020).

Bedi, Rahul (1999), "Paying to Keep the High Ground," *Jane's Intelligence Review*, 11(10): 27–31.

Behera, Navnita Chadha (2000), *State, Identity and Violence: Jammu, Kashmir and Ladakh*, New Delhi: Manohar.

Behera, Navnita Chadha (2006), *Demystifying Kashmir*, Washington, DC: Brookings Institution Press.

Behera, Navnita Chadha (2019), "An Abrogation of Democratic Principles," *Hindu*, August 13. https://www.thehindu.com/opinion/lead/an-abrogation-of-democratic-principles/article29035734.ece (accessed January 24, 2020).

Bell, Mark S. (2015), "Beyond Emboldenment: How Acquiring Nuclear Weapons Can Change Foreign Policy," *International Security*, 40(1): 87–119.

Bennett, D. Scott (1996), "Security, Bargaining, and the End of Interstate Rivalry," *International Studies Quarterly*, 40(2): 157–84.

Bennett, D. Scott (1997a), "Democracy, Regime Change, and Rivalry Termination," *International Interactions*, 22(4): 369–97.

Bennett, D. Scott (1997b), "Measuring Rivalry Termination, 1816–1992," *Journal of Conflict Resolution*, 41(2): 227–54.

Bennett, D. Scott (1998), "Integrating and Testing Models of Rivalry Duration," *American Journal of Political Science*, 42(4): 1200–32.

Bennett, D. Scott (2006), "Toward a Continuous Specification of the Democracy-Autocracy Connection," *International Studies Quarterly*, 50(2): 313–38.

Bercovitch, Jacob, and Richard Jackson (2009), *Conflict Resolution in the Twenty-First Century: Principles, Methods, and Approaches*, Ann Arbor: University of Michigan Press.

Bhat, Abdul Ghani (2011), "General Musharraf's Four Point Formula Can Provide an Effective Roadmap in Kashmir," Interview with Nadir Ali, *IPCS Special*

Report 99, New Delhi: Institute of Peace and Conflict Studies. http://www.ipcs.org/pdf_file/issue/SR99-BhatInterview.pdf (accessed March 13, 2013).

Bhaumik, Subir (2009), *Troubled Periphery: Crisis of India's North East*, New Delhi: Sage.

Bhola, P.L. (1988), "Indo-Pakistan Control March over Siachen Glacier," *Indian Journal of Asian Affairs*, 1(1): 28–48.

Bhutto, Benazir (2004), "Pakistan Had the Bomb by 1989," Interview with Shyam Bhatia, *Rediff*, March 8. http://www.rediff.com/news/2004/mar/09inter.htm (accessed March 13, 2013).

Bhutto, Zulfikar Ali (1969), *The Myth of Independence*, New York: Oxford University Press.

Bidwai, Praful (1999), "India/Pakistan Analysis: U.S. Brokers Kargil Peace But Problems Remain," *Asia Times Online*, July 7. http://www.atimes.com/ind-pak/AG07Df01.html (accessed January 24, 2014).

BJP (Bhartiya Janata Party) (1998), *Election Manifesto 1998*. http://www.bjp.org/documents/manifesto/national-democratic-alliance-manifesto-1999 (accessed March 13, 2013).

Blainey, Geoffrey (1973), *The Causes of War*, New York: Free Press.

Blinkenberg, Lars (1998), *India-Pakistan: History of Unresolved Conflict*, vol. 1, Sweden: Odense University Press.

Blum, Gabriella (2007), *Islands of Agreement: Managing Enduring Armed Rivalries*, Cambridge, MA: Harvard University Press.

Bobb, Dilip, and Inderjit Badhwar (1986), "Indo-Soviet Ties: The Second Honeymoon," *India Today*, December 15. http://indiatoday.intoday.in/story/india-pulls-out-all-stops-for-highly-publicised-visit-by-soviet-leader-mikhail-gorbachev/1/349219.html (accessed March 20, 2014).

Bobb, Dilip, and Ramindar Singh (1987), "Pakistan's Nuclear Bombshell," *India Today*, March 31. http://indiatoday.intoday.in/story/dr-a.q.-khans-pak-n-bomb-revelation-brings-prospect-of-nuke-arms-race-to-the-subcontinent/1/336875.html (accessed April 17, 2014).

Borders, William (1980), "Pakistan Dismisses $400 Million in Aid Offered by US as 'Peanuts,'" *New York Times*, January 19.

Bose, Pratim Ranjan (2016), "On a Railroad from Russia to Iran," *Hindu BusinessLine*, July 13. https://www.thehindubusinessline.com/opinion/on-a-railroad-from-russia-to-iran/article8843606.ece (assessed December 25, 2018).

Bose, Sharmila (2011), *Dead Reckoning: Memories of the 1971 Bangladesh War*, New Delhi: Hachette India.

Bose, Sumantra (1999), "Kashmir: Sources of Conflict, Dimensions of Peace," *Survival*, 41(3):149–71.

Bose, Sumantra (2003), *Kashmir: Roots of Conflict, Paths to Peace*, New Delhi: Vistar Publication.

Bose, Sumantra (2007), *Contested Lands: Israel-Palestine, Bosnia, Kashmir, Cyprus, and Sri Lanka*, New Delhi: HarperCollins.

Boulding, Kenneth (1962), *Conflict and Defense: A General Theory*, New York: Harper & Row.

Boulding, Kenneth (1978), *Stable Peace*, Austin: University of Texas Press.

Bowles, Chester (1971), *Promises to Keep: My Years in Public Life 1941–1969*, New York: Harper & Row.

Braibanti, Ralph (1963), "Public Bureaucracy and Judiciary in Pakistan," in Joseph LaPalomabara (ed.), *Bureaucracy and Development*, Princeton, NJ: Princeton University Press, pp. 360–440.

Brecher, Michael (1959), *Nehru: A Political Biography*, New York: Oxford University Press.

Brecher, Michael (1968), *India and World Politics: Krishna Menon's View of the World*, London: Oxford University Press.

Brecher, Michael (1979–80), "Non-Alignment under Stress: The West and the India-China Border War," *Pacific Affairs*, 52(4): 612–30.

Brecher, Michael (2008), *International Political Earthquakes*, Ann Arbor: University of Michigan Press.

Brecher, Michael, and Jonathan Wilkenfeld (1997), *A Study of Crisis*, Ann Arbor: University of Michigan Press.

Bremer, Stuart A. (1980), "National Capabilities and War Proneness" in J. D. Singer (ed.), *The Correlates of War*, vol. 2, New York: Free Press, pp. 57–82.

Bremer, Stuart A. (1992), "Dangerous Dyads: Conditions Affecting the Likelihood of Interstate War, 1816–1965," *Journal of Conflict Resolution*, 36(2): 309–41.

Bremer, Stuart A. (1993), "Democracy and Militarized Interstate Conflict, 1816–1965," *International Interactions* 18(3): 231–49.

Brines, Russell (1968), *The Indo-Pakistani Conflict*, London: Pall Mall.

Bueno de Mesquita, Bruce (1975), "Measuring Systemic Polarity," *Journal of Conflict Resolution*, 19(2): 187–216.

Bueno de Mesquita, Bruce (1978), "Systemic Polarization and the Occurrence and Duration of War," *Journal of Conflict Resolution*, 22(3): 241–67.

Bueno de Mesquita, Bruce (1981), "Risk, Power Distributions, and the Likelihood of War," *International Studies Quarterly*, 25(4): 541–68.

Bueno de Mesquita, Bruce (1990a), "Big Wars, Little Wars," *International Interactions*, 16(2): 159–69.

Bueno de Mesquita, Bruce (1990b), "Pride of Place: The Origins of German Hegemony," *World Politics*, 43(1): 28–52.

Bueno de Mesquita, Bruce, and William Riker (1982), "An Assessment of the Merits of Selective Nuclear Proliferation," *Journal of Conflict Resolution* 26: 283–306.

Burke, S.M. (1973), "The Postwar Diplomacy of the Indo-Pakistani War of 1971," *Asian Survey*, 13(11): 1036–49.

Burke, S.M. (1974), *Mainsprings of Indian and Pakistan Foreign Policies*, Minneapolis: University of Minnesota Press.

Burki, Shahid Javed (1980), *Pakistan under Bhutto 1971–1977*, London: Macmillan Press.

Burns, James MacGregor (1978), *Leadership*, New York: Harper & Row.

Business Insider (2021), "6 Billion Defence Deal Boost for HAL—Government

Approves Purchase of 83 Tejas Fighter Jets," January 14. https://www.business insider.in/defense/news/6-billion-defence-deal-boost-for-hal-government -approves-purchase-of-83-tejas-fighter-jets/articleshow/80261680.cms (accessed January 15, 2021).

Buzan, Barry and Ole Waever (2003), *Regions and Powers: The Structure of International Security*, Cambridge: Cambridge University Press.

Callard, Keith B. (1959), *Pakistan's Foreign Policy: An Interpretation* (2nd ed.), New York: Institute of Pacific Relations.

Campbell-Johnson, Alan (1951), *Mission with Mountbatten*, London: Robert Hale.

Caroe, Sir Olaf (1958), *The Pathans*, Karachi: Oxford University Press.

Carr, Edward Hallett (1940), *The Twenty Years' Crisis, 1919–1939*, London: Macmillan.

Chakma, Bhumitra (2009), *Pakistan's Nuclear Weapons*, New York: Routledge.

Chandhoke, Neera (2005), "Of Broken Social Contracts and Ethnic Violence: The Case of Kashmir," Crisis States Research Centre, London School of Economics and Political Science, Working Paper Series 1, no. 75. http://www.lse.ac.uk/in ternationalDevelopment/research/crisisStates/download/wp/wpSeries1/wp 75.pdf (accessed November 25, 2007).

Chandra, Bipan, et al. (2000), *India after Independence 1947–2000*, New Delhi: Penguin Books.

Chandra, Naresh (1998), "Growing Nuclear Family," *NewsHour with Jim Lehrer* (transcript of interview), PBS Television Broadcast, May 12. http://fas.org/ne ws/india/1998/05/amb-pbs.htm (accessed December 21, 2013).

Chari, P.R., et al. (2003), *Perception, Politics and Security in South Asia: The Compound Crisis of 1990*, London: Routledge-Curzon.

Chari, P.R., et al. (2008), *Four Crises and A Peace Process*, New Delhi: HarperCollins India.

Chatterjee, Shibashis (2008), "Intra-State/Inter-State Conflicts in South Asia: The Constructivist Alternative to Realism," in Navnita Chadha Behera (ed.), *International Relations in South Asia: Search for an Alternative Paradigm*, New Delhi: Sage, pp. 177–208.

Chatterjee, Shibashis, and Udayan Das (2021), "Indian Foreign Policy as Public History: Globalist, Pragmatist and Hindutva Imaginations," *India Review*, 20(5): 565–88.

Chaudhry, Praveen K., and Marta Vanduzer-Snow (2008), *The United States and India: A History through Archives*, New Delhi: Observer Research Foundation and Sage.

Chaudhuri, Rudra (2009), "Why Culture Matters: Revisiting the Sino-Indian Border War of 1962," *Journal of Strategic Studies*, 32(6): 841–69.

Checkel, Jaffrey T. (1997), *Ideas and International Political Change: Soviet and Russian Behavior and the End of the Cold War*, New Haven, CT: Yale University Press.

Cheema, Pervaiz Iqbal (2002), *The Armed Forces of Pakistan*, Singapore: Allen & Unwin.

Cheema, Pervaiz Iqbal (2009), "The Strategic Context of the Kargil Conflict: A Pakistani Perspective," in Peter R. Lavoy (ed.), *Asymmetric Warfare in South Asia: The Causes and Consequences of the Kargil Conflict*, Cambridge: Cambridge University Press, pp. 41–63.

Chellaney, Brahma (2001–2), "Fighting Terrorism in Southern Asia: The Lessons of History," *International Security*, 26(3): 94–116.

Chengappa, Raj (1999), "Will the War Spread?," *India Today International*, July 5. http://indiatoday.intoday.in/story/kargil-conflict-shows-signs-of-intensifyi ng-as-india-gains-pakistan-remains-resilient/1/255910.html (accessed March 13, 2014).

Chengappa, Raj (2000), *Weapons for Peace: The Secret Story of India's Quest to Be a Nuclear Power*, New Delhi: HarperCollins.

Chibber, Lt. Gen. M.L. (1990), "Siachen—The Untold Story (A Personal Account)," *Indian Defence Review*, January: 146–52.

Clary, Christopher (2012), "What Might an India-Pakistan War Look Like?," MIT Centre for International Studies, Spring. http://web.mit.edu/cis/precis/2012 spring/india_pakistan.html#.UgSg2dJHKVs (accessed on September 9, 2014).

Claude, Inis L., Jr. (1962), *Power and International Relations*, New York: Random House.

Cloughley, Brian (2002), *A History of Pakistan Army: Wars and Insurrections* (2nd ed.), New Delhi: Lancer.

Clyde, Eagleton (1950), "The Case of Hyderabad before the Security Council," *American Journal of International Law*, 44(2): 277–302.

CNN (1999), "Defense Minister: Capture of Tiger Hill 'Important Win,'" July 4. http://web.archive.org/web/20080417050230/http://www.cnn.com/WOR LD/asiapcf/9907/04/kashmir.04/index.html (accessed December 13, 2013).

CNN (2001), "Bombing at Kashmir Assembly Kills at least 29," October 1. http:// premium.edition.cnn.com/2001/WORLD/asiapcf/south/10/01/india.kash mir/index.html (accessed December 13, 2013).

CNN (2002), "Powell Criticizes Pakistani Missile Test," May 25. http://edition.cnn .com/2002/WORLD/asiapcf/south/05/25/india.pakistan/index.html (accessed May 27, 2014).

CNN (2008), "Mumbai Attacks Probed as India-Pakistan Relations Strained," December 1. http://edition.cnn.com/2008/WORLD/asiapcf/11/30/india.atta cks/index.html (accessed March 18, 2014).

CNN (2019), "Pakistan Threatens War on India and 'Any Superpower.' It's Time to Take This Nuclear Conflict Seriously," March 3. https://www.ccn.com/pakist an-nuclear-war-india-superpower (accessed March 4, 2019).

Cohen, Stephen P. (1983), "Pakistan: Coping with Regional Dominance, Multiple Crises, and Great-Power Confrontations," in Raju G. C. Thomas (ed.), *The Great-Power Triangle and Asian Security*, Lexington, MA: Lexington Books, pp. 47–63.

Cohen, Stephen P. (1984), *The Pakistan Army*, New Delhi: Himalayan Books.

Cohen, Stephen P. (1999), "The United States, India, and Pakistan: Retrospect and

Prospect," in Sleig S. Harrison et al. (eds.), *India and Pakistan: The First Fifty Years*, New York: Cambridge University Press and Washington, DC: Woodrow Wilson Center Press, pp. 189–205.

Cohen, Stephen P. (2004), *The Idea of Pakistan*, Washington, DC: Brookings Institution Press.

Colaresi, Michael (2001), "Shocks to the System: Great Power Rivalries and the Leadership Long Cycle," *Journal of Conflict Resolution*, 45(5): 569–93.

Colaresi, Michael, Karen Rasler, and William R. Thompson (2007), *Strategic Rivalry: Space, Position, and Conflict Escalation in World Politics*, Cambridge: Cambridge University Press.

Coll, Steve (2004), *Ghost Wars: The Secret History of the CIA, Afghanistan and Bin Laden from the Soviet Invasion to September 10, 2001*, New York: Penguin.

Coll, Steve (2008), "Decoding Mumbai," *New Yorker*, November 28. http://www.newyorker.com/online/blogs/stevecoll/2008/11/decoding-mumbai.html (accessed March 15, 2014).

Colman, Jonathan (2009), "Britain and the Indo-Pakistani Conflict: The Rann of Kutch and Kashmir, 1965," *Journal of Imperial and Commonwealth History*, 37(3): 465–82.

Conboy, Kenneth, and James Morrison (2002), *The CIA's Secret War in Tibet*, Lawrence: University Press of Kansas.

Congressional Research Service (2019), "Direct Overt U.S. Aid Appropriations for and Military Reimbursements to Pakistan, FY2002–FY2020," March 12. https://fas.org/sgp/crs/row/pakaid.pdf (accessed May 25, 2020).

Conrad, Justin, and Mark Souva (2011), "Regime Similarity and Rivalry," *International Interactions*, 37(1): 1–28.

Copeland, Dale C. (2000), *The Origins of Major War*, Ithaca, NY: Cornell University Press.

Corera, Gordon (2006), *Shopping for Bombs: Nuclear Proliferation, Global Insecurity, and the Rise and Fall of the A. Q. Khan Network*, New York: Oxford University Press.

COW (Correlates of War Database) (2015), "The MID4 Data Set, 2002–2010", *Correlates of War Project Dataset* (version 4.01). http://www.correlatesofwar.org/datasets/MIDs (accessed May 2, 2015).

COW (Correlates of War Database) (2020), "MID-Level and Incident-Level Data 5.0", *Correlates of War Project Dataset* (version 5.0), November 9. Retrieved from URL: https://correlatesofwar.org/data-sets/MIDs/mid-5-data-and-supporting-materials.zip/view (accessed December 11, 2020).

Cox, Eric W. (2010), *Why Enduring Rivalries Do—or Don't—End*, Boulder, CO: First Forum Press.

CPEC Portal (2018), "Chinese Investment in CPEC Will Cross $100 Billion," February 10. http://www.cpecinfo.com/cpec-news-detail?id=NDg1Mw (accessed February 11, 2018).

Craig, Tim, and Karen DeYoung (2014), "Pakistan is Eyeing Sea-Based and Short-Range Nuclear Weapons, Analysts Say," *Washington Post*, September 21.

https://www.washingtonpost.com/world/asia_pacific/pakistan-is-eyeing
-sea-based-and-short-range-nuclear-weapons-analysts-say/2014/09/20/1bd
9436a-11bb-11e4-8936-26932bcfd6ed_story.html (accessed August 28,
2015).

Crocker, Walter (1966), *Nehru: A Contemporary Estimate*, New York: Oxford University Press.

Daily Excelsior (1999), "Infiltration Will Be Pushed Out in 48 Hours: George," May 15.

Daily Excelsior (2016), "Troops on High Alert along LoC," September 22. http://www.dailyexcelsior.com/troops-high-alert-along-loc/ (accessed September 28, 2016).

Dalton, Toby, and Michael Krepon (2015), *A Normal Nuclear Pakistan*, Washington, DC: Stimson Center and Carnegie Endowment for International Peace, August 27. http://carnegieendowment.org/files/NormalNuclearPakistan.pdf (accessed August 28, 2015).

Dasgupta, C. (2002), *War and Diplomacy in Kashmir 1947–48*, New Delhi: Sage.

Dawn (1994), "'We Can Have the Bomb within 15 Days in an Eventuality,' Says Beg," April 3.

Dawn (2017a), "Nasr Pours Cold Water on India's Cold Start Doctrine: Bajwa," July 6. https://www.dawn.com/news/print/1343581 (accessed July 7, 2017).

Dawn (2017b), "Troubled Waters: India Fast-Tracks Hydro Projects in Held Kashmir," March 16. https://www.dawn.com/news/1320850 (accessed August 23, 2017).

Dawn (2018), "Pakistan's Concerns over India's Hydropower Projects Remain after Opening Round of Talks," August 30. https://www.dawn.com/news/14 29710 (accessed January 2, 2020).

Dawn (2019), "On Kashmir Attack, Shah Mahmood Qureshi Says 'Violence Is Not the Govt's Policy,'" February 16. https://www.dawn.com/news/1464205 (accessed February 16, 2019).

Denoon, David B.H. (1998), "Cycles in Indian Economic Liberalization, 1966–1996," *Comparative Politics*, 31(1): 43–60.

Desch, Michael C. (2002), "Democracy and Victory: Why Regime Type Hardly Matters," *International Security*, 27(2): 5–47.

Deutsch, Karl W., and J. David Singer (1964), "Multipolar Power and International Stability," *World Politics*, 16(2): 390–406.

Devi, Lakho (2021), Personal Interview, Survivor of the First Kashmir War (1947–48), Rawarian Tala (Uppar Bajwal) Sunderbani, J&K, October 30.

Dewey, Clive (1991), "The Rural Roots of Pakistani Militarism," in D.A. Low (ed.), *The Political Inheritance of Pakistan*, Basingstoke: Macmillan, pp. 255–83.

DGFT (Directorate General of Foreign Trade) (2019), Ministry of Commerce and Industry, Government of India. http://dgft.gov.in/ (accessed October 20, 2020).

Diehl, Paul (1985), "Contiguity and Military Escalation in Major Power Rivalries, 1816–1980," *Journal of Politics*, 47(4): 1203–11.

Diehl, Paul F., and Gary Goertz (2000), *War and Peace in International Rivalry*, Ann Arbor: University of Michigan Press.

Dikshit, Sandeep (2013), "U.S. Planes Used Indian Airbase to Snoop on China," *Hindu*, August 17. http://www.thehindu.com/news/national/us-planes-used -indian-airbase-to-snoop-on-china/article5028660.ece (accessed September 2, 2013).

Dixit, J.N. (2002), *India-Pakistan in War and Peace*, London: Routledge.

Dixon, William J. (1994), "Democracy and the Peaceful Settlement of International Conflict," *American Political Science Review*, 88(1): 14–32.

DNA (2019), "Pak in Troubled Water: India Will Stop its Share of Water Which Flows to Pakistan, Announces Nitin Gadkari," February 21. https://www.dnai ndia.com/india/photo-gallery-pak-in-troubled-water-india-will-stop-its-sha re-of-water-which-flows-to-pakistan-announces-nitin-gadkari-2722591 (accessed August 23, 2019).

Dobell, W.M. (1964), "Ramifications of the China-Pakistan Border Treaty," *Pacific Affairs*, 37(3): 283–95.

Dominguez, Gabriel (2015), "How the New India-US Defense Deal Would Impact Regional Security," *DW*, June 2. http://www.dw.com/en/how-the-new-india-us-defense-deal-would-impact-regional-security/a-18492143 (accessed December 23, 2015).

Doyle, Michael W. (1986), "Liberalism and World Politics," *American Political Science Review*, 80(4): 1151–69.

Doyle, Michael W. (2005), "Three Pillars of the Liberal Peace," *American Political Science Review*, 99(3): 463–66.

Dulat, A.S. (2015), *Kashmir: The Vajpayee Years*, New Delhi: HarperCollins.

Duncan, Peter J.S. (1989), *The Soviet Union and India*, New York: Council on Foreign Relations.

Dupree, Louis (1965), *First Reflections on the Second Kashmir War*, New York: American Universities Field Staff.

Durrani, Lt. Gen. Asad (2015), Personal Interview, Former Chief of the Inter-Services Intelligence (ISI) and Former Director-General of the Pakistan Army's Military Intelligence, Islamabad, October 13.

Economic Times (2002), "Naval Fleet Deployed on the Arabian Sea," May 22. http://articles.economictimes.indiatimes.com/2002-05-22/news/27347626 _1_naval-fleet-warships-levels-and-operational-preparedness (accessed September 29, 2013).

Economic Times (2018a), "9 Dead in Attack on Indian Mission in Afghanistan's Jalalabad," July 12. https://economictimes.indiatimes.com/news/defence /9-dead-in-attack-on-indian-mission-in-afghanistans-jalalabad/articleshow /51227213.cms (accessed December 23, 2018).

Economic Times (2018b), "Explained: Kamov Helicopter Deal between India and Russia," July 16. https://economictimes.indiatimes.com/news/defence/expla ined-kamov-helicopter-deal-between-india-and-russia/articleshow/548686 79.cms (accessed December 23, 2018).

Economic Times (2018c), "India, Russia Formally Ink the $ 5.2 Billion Deal for S-400 Air Defence System," October 5. https://economictimes.indiatimes .com/news/defence/india-russia-formally-ink-the-5-2-billion-deal-for-the -s-400/articleshow/66082930.cms (accessed December 23, 2018).

Economic Times (2018d), "Ready to Call Pakistan's Nuclear Bluff: Army Chief Bipin Rawat," January 12. https://economictimes.indiatimes.com/news/defe nce/ready-to-call-pakistans-nuclear-bluff-army-chief-bipin-rawat/articlesh ow/62478242.cms?utm_source=contentofinterest&utm_medium=text&u tm_campaign=cppst (accessed January 17, 2019).

Economic Times (2018e), "With Six New Nuclear Attack Submarines, India Officially Opens Up on its Undersea Aspirations," July 14. https://economictimes .indiatimes.com/news/defence/with-six-new-nuclear-attack-submarines-India- officially-opens-up-on-its-undersea-aspirations/articleshow/48076623.cms (accessed December 25, 2019).

Eldridge, Philip J. (1969), *The Politics of Foreign Aid in India*, New Delhi: Vikas.

Evans, Alexander (2002), "A Departure from History: Kashmiri Pandits, 1990– 2001", *Contemporary South Asia*, 11(1): 19–37.

Express Tribune (2016a), "China to Supply Pakistan with Eight New Attack Subma- rines," August 31. https://tribune.com.pk/story/1173324/china-supply-pakis tan-eight-new-attack-submarines/ (accessed September 23, 2016).

Express Tribune (2016b), "Indian Military Asks Govt to Consider 'Punitive' Cross- Border Strikes," September 19. https://tribune.com.pk/story/1184103/indian -military-asks-govt-consider-punitive-cross-border-strikes/ (accessed Sep- tember 23, 2016).

Express Tribune (2016c), "PIA Cancels Flights to Northern Areas Due to Airspace Restrictions," September 21. http://tribune.com.pk/story/1185715/pia-cance ls-flights-northern-areas-due-air-space-restrictions/ (accessed September 23, 2016).

Express Tribune (2020), "PAF Inducts 14 Dual-Seat JF-17 Aircraft into its Fleet," December 30. https://tribune.com.pk/story/2277998/paf-inducts-14-dual-se at-jf-17-aircraft-into-its-fleet (accessed January 15, 2021).

Fair, C. Christine (2014), *Fighting to the End: The Pakistan Army's Way of War*, New Delhi: Oxford University Press.

Feldman, Herbert (1972), *From Crisis to Crisis: Pakistan 1962–1969*, London: Oxford University Press.

Filipink, Richard M., Jr. (2007), "'Force Is the Last Method': Eisenhower, Dulles and American Intervention in the Suez Crisis," *Critique: Journal of Socialist Theory*, 35(2): 173–88.

Financial Tribune (2020), "Indian Budget Allocates Close to $14 Million to Chaba- har Port Project," February 2. https://financialtribune.com/articles/domestic -economy/101987/indian-budget-allocates-close-to-14-million-to-chabahar -port (accessed February 5, 2020).

Fisher, Ronald (2005), *Paving the Way: Contributions of Interactive Conflict Resolu- tion to Peacemaking*, Lanham, MD: Lexington Books.

Freedman, Lawrence (2009), "A New Theory for Nuclear Disarmament," *Bulletin of the Atomic Scientists*, 65(4): 14–30.

FRUS (Foreign Relations of the United States) (1996), *Foreign Relations of the United States, 1961–1963*, vol. 19, South Asia, Document 88. http://history.state.gov /historicaldocuments/frus1961-63v19/d88 (accessed April 21, 2013).

Furber, Holden (1951), "The Unification of India, 1947–1951", *Pacific Affairs*, 24(4): 352–71.

Gaddis, John Lewis (1997), *We Now Know: Rethinking Cold War History*, New York: Oxford University Press.

Gady, Franz-Stefan (2015), "4 US Littoral Combat Ships to Operate out of Singapore by 2018," *Diplomat*, February 19. http://thediplomat.com/2015/02/4-us -littoral-combat-ships-to-operate-out-of-singapore-by-2018/?allpages=yes& print=yes (accessed July 18, 2016).

Galbraith, John Kenneth (1969), *Ambassador's Journal: A Personal Account of the Kennedy Years*, London: Hamish Hamilton.

Ganguly, Sumit (1997), *The Crisis in Kashmir: Portents of War, Hopes of Peace*, Cambridge: Cambridge University Press and Washington, DC: Woodrow Wilson Center Press.

Ganguly, Sumit (2002), *Conflict Unending: India-Pakistan Tensions since 1947*, New Delhi: Oxford University Press.

Ganguly, Sumit (2008), "Nuclear Stability in South Asia," *International Security*, 33(2): 45–70.

Ganguly, Sumit, and Davin T. Hagerty (2005), *Fearful Symmetry: India-Pakistan Crises in the Shadow of Nuclear Weapons*, Seattle: University of Washington Press.

Garnham, David (1976), "Power Parity and Lethal International Violence," *Journal of Conflict Resolution* 20(4): 379–94.

Garver, John (2004), "China's Kashmir Policies," *India Review*, 3(1): 1–24.

Gauhar, Altaf (1996), *Ayub Khan: Pakistan's First Military Ruler*, Karachi: Oxford University Press.

Geller, Daniel S. (1992), "Power Transition and Conflict Initiation," *Conflict Management and Peace Science*, 12(1): 1–16.

Geller, Daniel S. (1993), "Power Differentials and War in Rival Dyads," *International Studies Quarterly*, 37(1): 173–93.

Geller, Daniel S. (2000), "Material Capabilities: Power and International Conflict," in John A. Vasquez (ed.), *What Do We Know about War*, New York: Rowman & Littlefield, pp. 259–77.

Geller, Daniel S., and J. David Singer (1998), *Nations at War: A Scientific Study of International Conflict*, Cambridge: Cambridge University Press.

George, Alexander, and Richard Smoke (1989), "Deterrence and Foreign Policy," *World Politics*, 41(2): 170–82.

Ghosn, Faten, Glenn Palmer, and Stuart Bremer (2004), "The MID3 Data Set, 1993–2001: Procedures, Coding Rules, and Description," *Conflict Management and Peace Science*, 21(2): 133–54.

Gibler, Douglas M. (2000), "Alliances: Why Some Cause War and Others Cause Peace," in John A. Vasquez (ed.), *What Do We Know about War*, New York: Rowman & Littlefield, pp. 145–164.

Gibler, Douglas M. (2007), "Bordering on Peace: Democracy, Territorial Issues, and Conflict," *International Studies Quarterly*, 51(3): 509–32.

Gill, John H. (2009), "Military Operations in the Kargil Conflict," in Peter R. Lavoy (ed.), *Asymmetric Warfare in South Asia: The Causes and Consequences of the Kargil Conflict*, Cambridge: Cambridge University Press, pp. 92–129.

Gilpin, Robert (1981), *War and Change in World Politics*, Cambridge: Cambridge University Press.

Gochman, Charles S., and Zeev Maoz (1984), "Militarized Interstate Disputes, 1816–1976: Procedures, Patterns, and Insights," *Journal of Conflict Resolution* 28(4): 585–616.

Goertz, Gary (1994), *Contexts of International Politics*, Cambridge: Cambridge University Press.

Goertz, Gary, and Paul Diehl (1992), "The Empirical Importance of Enduring Rivalries," *International Interactions*, 18(2): 151–163.

Goertz, Gary, and Paul F. Diehl (1993), "Enduring Rivalries: Theoretical Constructs and Empirical Patterns," *International Studies Quarterly*, 37(1): 147–71.

Goertz, Gary, and Paul F. Diehl (1995a), "The Initiation and Termination of Enduring Rivalries: The Impact of Political Shocks," *American Journal of Political Science*, 39(1): 30–52.

Goertz, Gary, and Paul F. Diehl (1995b), "Taking 'Enduring' Out of Enduring Rivalry: The Rivalry Approach to War and Peace," *International Interactions*, 21(3): 291–308.

Goertz, Gary, and Paul F. Diehl (1998), "The Volcano Model and Other Patterns in the Evolution of Enduring Rivalries," in Paul F. Diehl (ed.), *The Dynamics of Enduring Rivalries*, Urbana: University of Illinois Press, pp. 98–125.

Goertz, Gary, and Paul F. Diehl (2000), "Rivalries: The Conflict Process," in John A. Vasquez (ed.), *What Do We Know about War*, New York: Rowman & Littlefield, pp. 197–217.

Goertz, Gary, Bradford Jones, and Paul F. Diehl (2005), "Maintenance Processes in International Rivalries," *Journal of Conflict Resolution*, 49(5): 742–69.

Gopal, Sarvepalli (1979), *Jawaharlal Nehru: A Biography*, vol. 2, 1947–1956, New Delhi: Oxford University Press.

Gopal, Sarvepalli (1984), *Jawaharlal Nehru: A Biography*, vol. 3, 1956–1964, New Delhi: Oxford University Press.

Gossman, Patricia (1995), "An International Human Rights Perspective," *Asian Affairs: An American Review*, 22(1): 65–70.

GoI (Government of India) (1947a), "Mountbatten to Jinnah, 21 September 1947, F200/90A," *Mountbatten Papers*, New Delhi: Nehru Memorial Library.

GoI (Government of India) (1947b), "Jinnah to Mountbatten, 25 September 1947, F200/90A," *Mountbatten Papers*, New Delhi: Nehru Memorial Library.

GoI (Government of India) (1958), *Jawaharlal Nehru's Speeches*, vol. 3, *March 1953–August 1957*. New Delhi: Ministry of Information and Broadcasting.

GoI (Government of India) (1965), "Agreement Relating to Cease-Fire and Demarcation of Border," Ministry of External Affairs, New Delhi, June 30. www.mea .gov.in/bilateral-documents.htm?dtl/6268/Agreement+relating+to+Cease+f ire+and+Demarcation+of+Border (accessed May 10, 2013).

GoI (Government of India) (1966a), "Tashkent Declaration," Ministry of External Affairs, New Delhi, January 10. www.mea.gov.in/bilateral-documents.htm ?dtl/5993/Tashkent+Declaration (accessed May 10, 2013).

GoI (Government of India) (1966b), "Agreement on Withdrawal of Troops," Ministry of External Affairs, New Delhi, January 22. www.mea.gov.in/bilateral -documents.htm?dtl/5999/Agreement+on+Withdrawal+of+Troops (accessed May 10, 2013).

GoI (Government of India) (1972), "Simla Agreement," Ministry of External Affairs, New Delhi, July 2. www.mea.gov.in/bilateral-documents.htm?dtl/55 41/Simla+Agreement (accessed May 2, 2013).

GoI (Government of India) (1998), "Suo Motu Statement by Prime Minister Shri Atal Bihari Vajpayee in Parliament," May 27. http://fas.org/news/india/1998 /05/980527-india-pm.htm (accessed August 29, 2014).

GoI (Government of India) (1999a), "Lahore Declaration," Ministry of External Affairs, New Delhi, February 21. http://www.mea.gov.in/in-focus-article.htm ?18997/Lahore+Declaration+February+1999 (accessed January 18, 2014).

GoI (Government of India) (1999b), "Soldiers Killed during Indo-Pak Wars," Unstarred Question No. 793, Rajya Sabha, Ministry of External Affairs, New Delhi, August 12. http://web.archive.org/web/20080216231524/http://164 .100.24.219/rsq/quest.asp?qref=3798 (accessed January 18, 2014).

GoI (Government of India) (2000), *From Surprise to Reckoning: The Kargil Review Committee Report*, New Delhi: Sage.

GoI (Government of India) (2007), "PM's Convocation Address at the University of Jammu," Dr. Manmohan Singh, Prime Minister of India, Achieves PMO (Prime Minister's Office), July 15. http://archivepmo.nic.in/drmanmohansin gh/content_print.php?nodeid=544&nodetype=2 (accessed March 28, 2016).

GoI (Government of India) (2010), "India and Afghanistan: A Development Perspective," Ministry of External Affairs, New Delhi. http://www.mea.gov.in /Uploads/PublicationDocs/176_india-and-afghanistan-a-development-part nership.pdf (accessed October 10, 2014).

GoI (Government of India) (2011), "Agreement on Strategic Partnership between the Islamic Republic of Afghanistan and the Republic of India," Ministry of External Affairs, Embassy of India Kabul, October 4. https://eoi.gov.in/kabul/ ?pdf4644?000 (accessed June 10, 2017).

GoI (Government of India) (2012), "India-Afghanistan Relations," Ministry of External Affairs, New Delhi, August. http://www.mea.gov.in/Portal/Foreign Relation/afghanistan-aug-2012.pdf (accessed October 10, 2014).

GoI (Government of India) (2015), "India-US Joint Press Release on Visit of US Secretary of Defence Dr Ashton Carter to India," Ministry of External Affairs, New Delhi, June 4. http://www.mea.gov.in/bilateral-documents.htm?dtl/25

327/IndiaUS_Joint_Press_Release_on_visit_of_US_Secretary_of_Defence_Dr _Ashton_Carter_to_India (accessed November 10, 2016).

GoI (Government of India) (2017), "INSTC (International North South Transport Corridor): Express Corridor from India to Russia," Ministry of External Affairs, New Delhi, May 18. https://mea.gov.in/press-releases.htm?dtl/28470 /INSTC_International_North_South_Transport_Corridor_Express_Corridor _from_India_to_Russia (accessed October 10, 2014).

GoI (Government of India) (2018), "Country Statement by MoS for External Affairs at Geneva Ministerial Conference on Afghanistan," Ministry of External Affairs, November 28. https://eoi.gov.in/kabul/?0354?000 (accessed April 23, 2019).

GoI (Government of India) (2019), "India-Afghanistan: A Historic and Time Tested Friendship," Ministry of External Affairs, November 28. https://www .mea.gov.in/images/pdf/India-Afghanistan-Map-Book-03012019.pdf (accessed April 23, 2019).

GoI (Government of India) (2020a), "EAM's Remarks at Afghanistan 2020 Conference on 24 November 2020," Ministry of External Affairs, November 24. https://mea.gov.in/Speeches-Statements.htm?dtl/33235/eams+remarks+at+ afghanistan+2020+conference+on+24+november+2020 (accessed December 15, 2020).

GoI (Government of India) (2020b), "Joint Statement on India-Uzbekistan Virtual Summit: Close Friendship, Strong Partnership," Ministry of External Affairs, December 11. https://mea.gov.in/bilateral-documents.htm?dtl/332 81/joint+statement+on+indiauzbekistan+virtual+summit+close+friendship +strong+partnership (accessed December 15, 2020).

GoP (Government of Pakistan) (2001), *Jinnah Papers: Quaid-I-Azam Mohammed Ali Jinnah Papers*, series 1, vol. 5, edited by Z.H. Zaidi, Islamabad: Quaid-i-Azam Papers Project, Cabinet Division.

GoP (Government of Pakistan) (2003), *Jinnah Papers: The States*, series 1, vol. 8, edited by Z.H. Zaidi, Islamabad: Quaid-i-Azam Papers Project, Culture Division.

GoP (Government of Pakistan) (2022), "National Security Policy of Pakistan, 2022-2026," National Security Division, January 14. http://nsd.gov.pk/ (accessed January 20, 2022).

Gould, Harold A. (2010), *The South Asia Story: The First Sixty Years of U.S. Relations with India and Pakistan*, New Delhi: Sage.

Grare, Frederic (2006), "Pakistan-Afghanistan Relations in the Post-9/11 Era," *Carnegie Paper*, 72 (October), Washington DC: Carnegie Endowment for International Peace.

Guardian (2006), "Musharraf Offers Kashmir 'Solution,'" December 5. http:// www.theguardian.com/world/2006/dec/05/pakistan.india/print (accessed August 28, 2014).

Guardian (2019), "Dozens of Indian Paramilitaries Killed in Kashmir Car Bombing," February 16. https://www.theguardian.com/world/2019/feb/14/indian

-paramilitaries-killed-in-suicide-car-bombing-in-kashmir (accessed February 16, 2019).

Guha, Ramachandra (2007), *India after Gandhi: The History of the World's Largest Democracy*, London: Macmillan.

Guha, Ramachandra (2009), "Introduction: Travelling with Tagore," in Rabindranath Tagore (ed.), *Nationalism*, New Delhi: Penguin Books India, pp. vii–lxviii.

Gul, Imtiaz (2015), Personal Interview, Executive Director, Centre for Research and Security Studies (CRSS), Islamabad, October 14.

Gundevia, Y.D. (1984), *Outside the Archives*, Hyderabad: Sangam Books.

Gupta, Bhabani Sen (1983), "Regional Security: The Indira Doctrine," *India Today*, August 31. http://indiatoday.intoday.in/story/carnage-in-sri-lanka-spawns -indian-doctrine-of-regional-security/1/371914.html (accessed December 23, 2015).

Gupta, Shekhar (1986), "Defence Agreement: A Buyer's Market," *India Today*, December 15. http://indiatoday.intoday.in/story/indo-soviet-arms-relations hip-grows-stronger/1/349216.html (accessed March 20, 2014).

Gupta, Sisir (1966), *Kashmir: A Study in India-Pakistan Relations*, Bombay: Asia Publishing House.

Hagerty, Devin T. (1995–96), "Nuclear Deterrence in South Asia: The 1990 Indo-Pakistani Crisis," *International Security*, 20(3): 79–114.

Hagerty, Devin T. (1998), *The Consequences of Nuclear Proliferation: Lessons from South Asia*, Cambridge, MA: MIT Press.

Hahn, Peter L. (1991), *The United States, Great Britain and Egypt, 1945–1956*, Chapel Hill: University of North Carolina Press.

Haqqani, Husain (2005), *Pakistan: Between Mosque and Military*, Washington, DC: Carnegie Endowment for International Peace.

Hegre, Håvard, John R. Oneal, and Bruce Russett (2010), "Trade Does Promote Peace: New Simultaneous Estimates of the Reciprocal Effects of Trade and Conflict," *Journal of Peace Research*, 47(6): 763–74.

Henderson, Errol (2008), "Disturbing the Peace: African Warfare, Political Inversion and the Universality of the Democratic Peace Thesis," *British Journal of Political Science*, 39(1): 25–58.

Hensel, Paul R. (1996), "Charting a Course to Conflict: Territorial Issues and Interstate Conflict, 1816–1992" *Conflict Management and Peace Science*, 15(1): 43–73.

Hensel, Paul R. (1998), "Evolutionary Perspectives on Recurrent Conflict and Rivalry," paper presented at the Conference on Evolutionary Perspectives on International Relations, Bloomington, IN, December.

Hensel, Paul R. (1999), "An Evolutionary Approach to the Study of Interstate Rivalry," *Conflict Management and Peace Science*, 17(2): 175–206.

Hensel, Paul R. (2000), "Territory: Why Are Territorial Disputes between States a Central Cause of International Conflict?," in John A. Vasquez (ed.), *What Do We Know about War*, New York: Rowman & Littlefield, pp. 57–84.

Hensel, Paul R. (2001), "Contentious Issues and World Politics: Territorial Claims in the Americas, 1816–1996," *International Studies Quarterly*, 45(1): 81–109.

Hensel, Paul R., and Paul F. Diehl (1998), "Punctuated Equilibrium or Evolution? A Comparative Test of Two Models of Rivalry Development," paper presented at the annual meeting of the Peace Science Society, October, New Brunswick, NJ.

Hensel, Paul R., Gary Goertz, and Paul F. Diehl (2000), "The Democratic Peace and Rivalries," *Journal of Politics*, 62(4): 1173–88.

Hersh, Seymour M. (1990), "On the Nuclear Edge," *New Yorker*, March 29, pp. 56–73.

Hewitt, J. Joseph (2005), "A Crisis-Density Formulation for Identifying Rivalries," *Journal of Peace Research*, 42(2): 183–200.

Hill, Norman (1945), *Claims to Territory in International Relations*, New York: Oxford University Press.

Hindu (2001a), "Pak Firing in Kargil Continues," July 22. http://www.hindu.com/thehindu/2001/07/22/stories/01220004.htm (accessed March 12, 2014).

Hindu (2001b), "Protests in Jammu, Curfew Extended to Udhampur," August 9. http://www.hindu.com/thchindu/2001/08/09/stories/01090002.htm (accessed March 12, 2014).

Hindu (2001c), "Suicide Squad Storms Parliament; 5 Militants Killed; Army Deployed," December 14. http://www.hindu.com/thehindu/2001/12/14/stories/2001121400370100.htm (accessed March 13, 2014).

Hindu (2001d), "Lashkar Responsible for Attack, Says Jaswant," December 15. http://www.hindu.com/thehindu/2001/12/15/stories/2001121500310100.htm (accessed March 13, 2014).

Hindu (2001e), "Attack Could Have Been Stage-Managed: Pak," December 15. http://www.hindu.com/thehindu/2001/12/15/stories/2001121501620100.htm (accessed March 13, 2014).

Hindu (2001f), "Ready to Act If Delhi Gives Proof: Musharraf," December 16. http://www.hindu.com/thehindu/2001/12/16/stories/2001121600550100.htm (accessed March 13, 2014).

Hindu (2001g), "A Decisive Battle Has to Take Place: PM," December 14. http://www.hindu.com/thehindu/2001/12/14/stories/2001121400360100.htm (accessed March 13, 2014).

Hindu (2001h), "We Have Strong Proof: Advani," December 17. http://www.hindu.com/thehindu/2001/12/17/stories/2001121700270100.htm (accessed March 13, 2014).

Hindu (2001i), "Strike Forces Moved Closer to the Border," December 26. http://www.hindu.com/thehindu/2001/12/21/stories/2001122101130100.htm (accessed March 13, 2014).

Hindu (2001j), "Pakistan Moves Missiles Closer to Border," December 26. http://www.hindu.com/thehindu/2001/12/26/stories/2001122606070100.htm (accessed March 13, 2014).

Hindu (2001k), "U.S. Asks Pak to Act against Jaish, Lashkar," December 23. http://

www.hindu.com/thehindu/2001/12/23/stories/2001122301060100.htm (accessed March 13, 2014).

Hindu (2002a), "Former Lashkar Chief Arrested," January 1. http://www.hindu.com/thehindu/2002/01/01/stories/2002010101040100.htm (accessed March 13, 2014).

Hindu (2002b), "Crackdown Continues," January 2. http://www.hindu.com/thehindu/2002/01/02/stories/2002010201050100.htm (accessed March 13, 2014).

Hindu (2002c), "We Are Prepared: Army Chief," January 12. http://www.hindu.com/thehindu/2002/01/12/stories/2002011201020100.htm (accessed March 13, 2014).

Hindu (2002d), "30 Killed in Jammu Suicide Attack," May 15. http://www.hindu.com/thehindu/2002/05/15/stories/2002051503030100.htm (accessed March 13, 2014).

Hindu (2002e), "Pak. Asked to Recall Envoy within a Week", May 19. http://www.hindu.com/thehindu/2002/05/19/stories/2002051903410100.htm (accessed March 13, 2014).

Hindu (2002f), "We Will Not Initiate War, Says Musharraf," May 28. http://www.hindu.com/thehindu/2002/05/28/stories/2002052804100100.htm (accessed March 13, 2014).

Hindu (2002g), "Govt. Orders Withdrawal of Troops from IB," October 17. http://www.hindu.com/thehindu/2002/10/17/stories/2002101707350100.htm (accessed March 13, 2014).

Hindu (2002h), "Pak to Withdraw Troops to Peacetime Locations," October 18. http://www.hindu.com/thehindu/2002/10/18/stories/2002101804910100.htm (accessed March 13, 2014).

Hindu (2003a), "12 Killed in Mumbai Train Blast," March 14. http://www.hindu.com/thehindu/2003/03/14/stories/2003031408970100.htm (accessed January 24, 2014).

Hindu (2003b), "Blast Rips through Bus in Mumbai," July 29. http://www.hindu.com/thehindu/2003/07/29/stories/2003072906760100.htm (accessed January 24, 2014).

Hindu (2003c), "46 Killed as Twin Blasts Rock Mumbai," August 26. http://www.hindu.com/thehindu/2003/08/26/stories/2003082607640100.htm (accessed January 24, 2014).

Hindu (2003d), "India Proposes a Dozen Steps to Break the Ice with Pak," October 23. http://www.hindu.com/2003/10/23/stories/2003102307250100.htm (accessed January 24, 2014).

Hindu (2003e), "Pak Offers Ceasefire along LoC," October 30. http://www.hindu.com/2003/11/24/stories/2003112410840100.htm (accessed January 24, 2014).

Hindu (2009), "Pakistan's Nuclear Weapons Deterred India," March 10. https://www.thehindu.com/todays-paper/tp-national/ldquoPakistanrsquos-nuclear-weapons-deterred-Indiardquo/article16633492.ece (accessed December 5, 2016).

Hindu (2018), "Pak. Official Summoned," December 28. https://www.thehindu.com /todays-paper/tp-national/pak-official-summoned-over-firing/article25845 383.ece (accessed December 29, 2018).

Hindu (2020a), "Pakistan Factor behind India-China Stand-Off in Ladakh," May 26. https://www.thehindu.com/news/national/pakistan-factor-behind-ind ia-china-stand-off-in-ladakh/article31676271.ece (accessed May 28, 2020).

Hindu (2020b), "Indian Army Says 20 Soldiers Killed in Clash with Chinese Troops in the Galwan Area," June 16. https://www.thehindu.com/news/nati onal/indian-army-says-20-soldiers-killed-in-clash-with-chinese-troops-in -the-galwan-area/article31845662.ece (accessed June 20, 2020).

Hindu (2020c), "Xi Jinping's Mobilisation Order, Months of Planning Preceded Border Moves," July 13. https://www.thehindu.com/news/national/lac-stand off-xi-jinpings-mobilisation-order-months-of-planning-preceded-border -moves/article32061608.ece (accessed July 21, 2020).

Hindu (2020d), "China Has Crossed Its 1960 Claims along the LAC," July 20. https://www.thehindu.com/news/national/china-has-crossed-its-1960-clai ms-along-the-lac/article32133689.ece (accessed July 21, 2020).

Hindu (2021), "India, China Agree to Maintain Stability on Ground," April 10. https://www.thehindu.com/news/national/india-china-agree-to-maintain -stability-on-ground-avoid-any-new-incidents-in-eastern-ladakh/article342 90535.ece (accessed April 11, 2021).

Hindu (2022), "India, China Hold 15th Round of Corps Commander Talks," March 11. https://www.thehindu.com/news/national/15th-round-of-corps -commander-under-way-at-chushul-moldo-meeting-point/article65213839 .ece (accessed March 14, 2022).

Hindu BusinessLine (2019), "J&K Records 2936 Cases of Ceasefire Violations by Pakistan in 2018, Highest in 15 Years," January 7. https://www.thehindubusin essline.com/news/national/jk-records-2936-cases-of-ceasefire-violations-by -pakistan-in-2018-highest-in-15-years/article25932363.ece (accessed May 20, 2019).

Hindustan Times (2006), "Terror Strikes Varanasi; 28 Killed, No Claim Yet," March 8. http://www.hindustantimes.com/news/181_1644440,000900010004.htm (accessed March 8, 2015).

Hindustan Times (2013), "Pakistan Fires 7000 Rounds on Indian Posts at LoC in 'Biggest Ceasefire Violation,'" August 10. www.hindustantimes.com/India -news/Srinagar/Pakistan-fires-7000-rounds-on-Indian-posts-at-LoC-in-bigge st-ceasefire-violation/Article1-1106056.aspx?hts0021 (accessed August 10, 2013).

Hindustan Times (2014), "Take Cautious, Gradual Initiatives: Kayani to Nawaz on Indo-Pak Ties," May 19. http://www.hindustantimes.com/StoryPage/Print /1062504.aspx (accessed May 19, 2014).

Hindustan Times (2018), "India Takes Over Operations of Iran's Strategic Chaba- har Port, Can Bypass Pak on Way to Afghanistan," December 24. https://www .hindustantimes.com/india-news/india-takes-over-chabahar-port-operatio

ns-from-iran-will-ship-supplies-to-afghanistan/story-kWKZeStt1MfQR4s5V
oz4fL.html (accessed December 30, 2018).

Hindustan Times (2019a), "India, Pakistan Came Close to Firing Missiles at Each Other on February 27," March 23. https://www.hindustantimes.com/india -news/india-pakistan-came-close-to-firing-missiles-at-each-other-on-februa ry-27/story-rVsBjZ5qmxXMprktzDNqcM.html (accessed March 25, 2019).

Hindustan Times (2019b), "India Working on 'Priority' to Divert Water Flowing to Pakistan, says Union Minister," August 21. https:// www.hindustantimes.com/india-news/india-working-on-priority-to-divert- water-flowing-to-pakistan-says-union-minister/story- yrxnrHYTNFcrFhv12jBsxL.html (accessed August 23, 2019).

Hobbes, Thomas ([1651] 1951), *Leviathan*, New York: Penguin.

Hodson, H.V. (1997), *The Great Divide: Britain, India, Pakistan*, New York: Oxford University Press.

Holsti, Kalevi J. (1991), *Peace and War: Armed Conflicts and International Order 1648–1989*, Cambridge: Cambridge University Press.

Holsti, Kal J. (2009), "Book Review: Solving the Peace and War Puzzles?," *International Studies Review*, 11(3): 371–372.

Hoodbhoy, Pervez (2015), Personal Interview, Nuclear Physicist and Nuclear Disarmament Activist, Forman Christian University, Lahore, October 7.

Hoon, P.N. (2000), *Unmasking Secrets of Turbulence*, New Delhi: Manas Publications.

Hooson, David (ed.) (1994), *Geography and National Identity*, Oxford: Blackwell.

Hoyt, Timothy D. (2009), "Kargil: The Nuclear Dimension," in Peter R. Lavoy (ed.), *Asymmetric Warfare in South Asia: The Causes and Consequences of the Kargil Conflict*, Cambridge: Cambridge University Press, pp. 144–70.

HRW (Human Rights Watch) (1994), "India: Arms and Abuses in Indian Punjab and Kashmir," A Human Rights Watch Report, 6(10). https://www.hrw.org/re ports/INDIA949.PDF (accessed March 2, 2014).

HRW (Human Rights Watch) (1996), "India's Secret Army in Kashmir: New Patterns of Abuse Emerge in the Conflict," A Human Rights Watch Report, 8(4C). https://www.hrw.org/reports/1996/India2.htm (accessed March 2, 2014).

Huffington Post (2015), "India Will Suffer 'Heavy Losses' If It Tries to Impose War on Pakistan, Warns Defence Minister," August 31. http://www.huffpost.com /in/entry/8063172 (accessed August 31, 2015).

Hundley, Tom (2018), "India and Pakistan Are Quietly Making Nuclear War More Likely: Both Countries Are Arming Their Submarines with Nukes," *Vox*, April 4. https://www.vox.com/2018/4/2/17096566/pakistan-india-nuclear-war -submarine-enemies (accessed December 27, 2018).

Hussain, Akmal (2015), Personal Interview, Professor of Political Economy, Forman Christian University, Lahore, October 6.

Hussain, Tom (2013), "Nawaz Sharif, Pakistan's Likely Next Prime Minister, Pledges to Curb Attacks on India," *McClatchy* Foreign Staff, May 9. www.mccl atchydc.com/2013/05/09/190838/nawaz-sharif-pakistans-likely.html#.UYy SpaJHLLY (accessed October 5, 2013).

Hussain, Zahid (1998), "Deliberate Nuclear Ambiguity," in Samina Ahmed and David Cortright (eds.), *Pakistan and the Bomb: Public Opinion and Nuclear Options*, Notre Dame, IN: University of Notre Dame Press, pp. 29–46.

Hussain, Zahid (2007), *Frontline Pakistan: The Struggle with Militant Islam*, New York: I.B. Tauris.

Huth, Paul K. (1996), *Standing Your Ground: Territorial Disputes and International Conflict*, Ann Arbor: University of Michigan Press.

Huth, Paul K. (2000), "Territory: Why Are Territorial Disputes between States a Central Cause of International Conflict," in John A. Vasquez (ed.), *What Do We Know about War?*, Lanham, MD: Rowman & Littlefield, pp. 85–110.

Huth, Paul K., and Todd L. Allee (2002), *The Democratic Peace and Territorial Conflict in the Twentieth Century*, New York: Cambridge University Press.

Huth, Paul, and Bruce Russett (1993), "General Deterrence between Enduring Rivals: Testing Three Competing Models," *American Political Science Review*, 87(1): 61–73.

ICB (International Crisis Behavior) Database (2016), *International Crisis Behavior Project Dataset 2* (version 12). https://sites.duke.edu/icbdata/data-collecti ons/ (accessed December 25, 2018).

India Today (2009), "How to Tackle an Obstinate Pakistan?," October 29. http://in diatoday.intoday.in/story/How+to+tackle+an+obstinate+Pakistan/1/68505 .html (accessed December 23, 2015).

India Today (2013), "Kashmir Is Not an Obstacle for Indo-Pak Ties, Says Nawaz Sharif," May 6. http://indiatoday.intoday.in/story/kashmir-is-not-an-obstac le-for-indo-pak-ties-says-nawaz-sharif/1/269621.html (accessed October 5, 2013).

India Today (2019), "Pakistani Jets Cross LoC in Jammu and Kashmir's Rajouri, Drop Bombs," February 27. https://www.indiatoday.in/india/story/pakistan -fighter-jets-violate-loc-indian-air-force-airstrike-jammu-kashmir-nowshera -rajouri-1466040-2019-02-27 (accessed February 27, 2019).

Indian Express (2009), "India Hints at Pak Link to Kabul Embassy Attack," October 10. http://archive.indianexpress.com/story-print/527514/ (accessed April 25, 2016).

Indian Express (2013a), "Pakistani Troops Attack Indian Post along LoC, Kill Five Army Men," August 6. www.indianexpress.com/story-print/1151768/ (accessed August 8, 2013).

Indian Express (2013b), "Nawaz Sharif Calls for Warmer Ties with India," May 9. www.indianexpress.com/news/sharif-calls-for-warmer-ties-with-india/1113 225/ (accessed October 5, 2013).

Indian Express (2014a), "Upset India Calls-Off Foreign Secy Talks, Says 'Unacceptable,'" August 19, p.1.

Indian Express (2014b), "As Army Steps In to Mediate, Tahir Qadri and Sharif Play Blame Games," August 30, p. 12.

Indian Express (2014c), "Pak Army Commanders Meet as Pressure Mounts on Sharif," September 1, p. 11.

Indian Express (2014d), "Clashes Resume as Army Chief Meets Sharif," September 2, p.i.

Indian Express (2015a), "Pakistan NSA Sartaz Aziz Accuses India of Acting Like 'RegionalSuperpower,'" August24.http://indianexpress.com/article/india/india-others/sartaj-aziz-accuses-india-of-acting-like-regional-superpower/99/print/ (accessed August 25, 2015).

Indian Express (2015b), "Pak Ex-Diplomat: US Aid Will be Used against India," December 9, p. 13.

Indian Express (2016a), "Terror Attacks IAF Base and India-Pakistan Thaw," January 2, p. 1.

Indian Express (2016b), "Afghanistan: Terrorists Attack Indian Consulate in Mazar-i-Sharif," January 4. http://indianexpress.com/article/india/india-ne ws-india/indian-consulate-in-afghanistan-attacked-no-casualties-reported /99/print/ (accessed January 8, 2016).

Indian Express (2016c), "Uyghur Leader Dolkun Isa's Statement on India's Withdrawal of His Visa," April 25. http://indianexpress.com/article/india/india -news-india/dolkun-isa-statement-on-indias-withdrawal-of-his-visa-27691 35/99/print/ (accessed April 25, 2016).

Indian Express (2016d), "Rafale Deal: India Sign Agreement with France to Acquire 36 Fighter Jets," September 23. http://indianexpress.com/article/india/india -news-india/rafale-deal-france-india-sign-agreement-36-fighter-jets-3045 870/ (accessed September 23, 2016).

Indian Express (2016e), "Uri Attack: Rajnath Singh, Manohar Parrikar, NSA, Army Chief Meet to Discuss Kashmir," September 19. http://indianexpress.com/art icle/india/india-news-india/uri-attack-rajnath-singh-manohar-parrikar-nsa -army-chief-meet-to-discuss-kashmir-3038767/ (accessed September 12, 2018).

Indian Express (2016f), "Uri Attack: Jaish-e-Muhammad Suspects in Hand, Evidence Shown to Envoy," October 4. http://indianexpress.com/article/india /india-news-india/uri-attack-jaish-suspects-in-hand-evidence-shown-to-en voy-3053717/ (accessed September 13, 2018).

Indian Express (2016g), "SAARC Summit to Be Called Off as Dhaka, Kabul and Thimphu too Slam Islamabad," September 29. http://indianexpress.com/arti cle/india/india-news-india/dhaka-kabul-thimphu-too-blame-islamabad-saa rc-summit-to-be-called-off-3054953/ (accessed September 12, 2018).

Indian Express (2016h), "Blood and Water Cannot Flow Together: PM Modi at the Indus Water Treaty Meeting," September 27. https://indianexpress.com/artic le/india/india-news-india/indus-water-treaty-blood-and-water-cant-flow-to gether-pm-modi-pakistan-uri-attack/ (accessed August 27, 2019).

Indian Express (2017), "Kabul Blast: 80 Killed, At Least 350 Injured after Huge Explosion in Diplomatic Area," May 31. https://indianexpress.com/article /world/kabul-blast-near-indian-embassy-all-staff-safe-doors-windows-dama ged/ (accessed December 23, 2018).

Indian Express (2018), "INS Arihant Is Now Operational: All about India's Nuclear Deterrent in the Sea," November 6. https://indianexpress.com/article/india/ins-arihant-all-you-need-to-know-india-first-indigenous-nuclear-submarine-5435116/ (accessed December 23, 2018).

Indian Express (2019a), "J&K Records 2,936 Cases of Ceasefire Violations by Pak in 2018, Highest in 15 Years," January 7. https://indianexpress.com/article/india/jk-records-2936-cases-of-ceasefire-violations-by-pak-in-2018-highest-in-15-years-5527231/ (accessed January 25, 2019).

Indian Express (2019b), "Centre Scraps Article 370; Jammu and Kashmir, Ladakh to Be Union Territories," August 5. https://indianexpress.com/article/india/kashmir-amit-shah-proposes-scrapping-of-article-370-amid-chaos-in-rajya-sabha-5878897/ (accessed August 6, 2019).

Indian Express (2022), "India's First Indigenous Aircraft Carrier Begins Another Phase of Sea Trials," January 9. https://indianexpress.com/article/india/india-first-indigenous-aircraft-carrier-ins-vikrant-sea-trails-7714755/ (accessed January 26, 2022).

Indus Water Treaty (1960), United Nations—Treaty Series, No. 6032. https://treaties.un.org/doc/Publication/UNTs/Volume%20419/volume-419-I-6032-English.pdf (accessed March 20, 2022).

Ingram, Edward (1980), "Great Britain's Great Game: An Introduction," *International History Review*, 2(2): 160–71.

Islam, N. (1972), "Foreign Assistance and Economic Development: The Case of Pakistan," *Economic Journal*, 82: 502–30.

ISPR (Inter-Services Public Relations) (2015a), "Press Release No PR125/2015-ISPR," Government of Pakistan, May 5, 2015. https://www.ispr.gov.pk/front/main.asp?o=tpress_release&id=2868 (accessed September 9, 2015).

ISPR (Inter-Services Public Relations) (2015b), "Press Release No PR170/2015-ISPR," Government of Pakistan, June 13, 2015. https://www.ispr.gov.pk/front/main.asp?o=t-press_release&id=2913 (accessed September 9, 2015).

ISPR (Inter-Services Public Relations) (2017a), "Press Release PR34/2017-ISPR," Government of Pakistan, January 24. https://www.ispr.gov.pk/press-release-detail.php?id=3705 (accessed December 25, 2017).

ISPR (Inter-Services Public Relations) (2017b), "Press Release No PR344/2017-ISPR," Government of Pakistan, July 5. https://www.ispr.gov.pk/press-release-detail.php?id=4097 (accessed December 25, 2017).

ISPR (Inter-Services Public Relations) (2019a), "Press Release No PR-32/2019-ISPR," Government of Pakistan, January 24. https://www.ispr.gov.pk/press-release-detail.php?id=5173 (accessed March 10, 2019)

ISPR (Inter-Services Public Relations) (2019b), "Press Release No PR-37/2019-ISPR," Government of Pakistan, January 31. https://www.ispr.gov.pk/press-release-detail.php?id=5179 (accessed March 10, 2019)

ISPR (Inter-Services Public Relations) (2020a), "Press Release No PR-8/2020-ISPR," Government of Pakistan, January 23. https://www.ispr.gov.pk/press-release-detail.php?id=5592 (accessed March 20, 2020).

ISPR (Inter-Services Public Relations) (2020b), "Press Release No PR-27/2020-ISPR," Government of Pakistan, February 18. https://www.ispr.gov.pk/press-release-detail.php?id=5625 (accessed March 20, 2020).

Iyer, R. Ramaswamy (2007), *Towards Water Wisdom: Limits, Justice, Harmony*, New Delhi: Sage.

Iyer, R. Ramaswamy (2012), "Water (Interactive Session)," Conference on India-Pakistan: Civil Society Review of Strategic Relations, the Centre for Policy (in Collaboration with the Heinrich Boll Foundation and Focus on the Global South), March 29–31, New Delhi.

Jackson, Patrick Thaddeus, and Daniel H. Nexon (2009), "Paradigmatic Faults in International-Relations Theory," *International Studies Quarterly*, 53(4): 907–30.

Jackson, Robert (1975), *South Asian Crisis: India-Pakistan-Bangla Desh*, London: Chatto & Windus.

Jacob, Happymon (2019), *Line on Fire: Ceasefire Violations and India-Pakistan Escalation Dynamics*, New Delhi: Oxford University Press.

Jaffrelot, Christophe (ed.) (2009), *Hindu Nationalism: A Reader*, Princeton, NJ: Princeton University Press.

Jahan, Rounaq (1972), *Pakistan: Failure in National Integration*, New York and London: Columbia University Press.

Jalal, Ayesha (1985), *The Sole Spokesman: Jinnah, the Muslim League and the Demand for Partition*, Cambridge: Cambridge University Press.

Jalal, Ayesha (1990), *The State of Martial Rule: The Origins of Pakistan's Political Economy of Defence*, Cambridge: Cambridge University Press.

Jalal, Ayesha (1995), *Democracy and Authoritarianism in South Asia: A Comparative and Historical Perspective*, Cambridge: Cambridge University Press.

James, Patrick, Johann Park, and Seung-Whan Choi'a (2006), "Democracy and Conflict Management: Territorial Claims in the Western Hemisphere Revisited," *International Studies Quarterly*, 50(4): 803–17.

Jervis, Robert (1976), *Perceptions and Misperceptions in International Politics*, Princeton, NJ: Princeton University Press.

Jha, Prem Shankar (1998), *Kashmir, 1947: Rival Versions of History*, New Delhi: Oxford University Press.

Jha, Prem Shankar (2006), "Mani McGrill, Served Hot," *Outlook*, February 13. http://www.outlookindia.com/magazine/story/mani-mcgrill-served-hot/230164 (accessed July 30, 2016).

Jinnah, M.A. ([1940] 2001), "An Extract from the Presidential Address of M.A. Jinnah—Lahore, March 1940," in Mushirul Hasan (ed.), *India's Partition: Process, Strategy and Mobilization*, New Delhi: Oxford University Press, pp. 44–58.

JNS (*Jewish and Israel News*) (2017), "India's Modi Approves $2.5 Billion Missile Deal with Israel," February 23. https://web.archive.org/web/20170224133617/http://www.jns.org/news-briefs/2017/2/23/indias-modi-approves-25-billion-missile-deal-with-israel (accessed November 16, 2021).

Johnson, R.A. (2003), "'Russians at the Gates of India'? Planning the Defence of India, 1885–1900," *Journal of Military History*, 67(3): 697–743.

Johnston, Patrick B., and Anoop K. Sarbhai (2016), "The Impact of US Strikes on Terrorism in Pakistan," *International Studies Quarterly*, 60(2): 203–19.

Jones, Bennett Owen (2002), *Pakistan: Eye of Storm*, New Haven, CT: Yale University Press.

Jones, Daniel M., Stuart A. Bremer, and J. David Singer (1996), "Militarized Interstate Disputes, 1816–1992: Rationale, Coding Rules, and Empirical Patterns," *Conflict Management and Peace Science*, 15(2): 162–213.

Joshi, Manoj (1997), "Hardball Diplomacy," *India Today*, May 15, pp. 40–43.

Joshua, W., and Gibert, S.P. (1969), *Arms for the Third World: Soviet Military Aid Diplomacy*, Baltimore: Johns Hopkins Press.

Kak, Kapil (2017), Public Lecture, Department of Strategic and Regional Studies, University of Jammu, November 17.

Kanwal, Gurmeet (1999), "Pakistan's Military Defeat," in Air Commodore Jasjit Singh (ed.), *Kargil 1999: Pakistan's Fourth War for Kashmir*, New Delhi: Knowledge World, pp. 144–77.

Kanwal, Brigadier Gurmeet (retd.) (2016), Personal Interview, Defense Expert and the former Director of CLAWS, New Delhi, January 15.

Kapur, Ashok (2005), "Major Powers and the Persistence of the India-Pakistan Conflict," in T.V. Paul (ed.), *The India-Pakistan Conflict: An Enduring Rivalry*, Cambridge: Cambridge University Press, pp. 131–55.

Kapur, S. Paul (2008), *Dangerous Deterrent: Nuclear Weapons Proliferation and Conflict in South Asia*, New Delhi: Oxford University Press.

Kapur, S. Paul (2009), "Revisionist Ambitions, Conventional Capabilities, and Nuclear Instability: Why Nuclear South Asia Is Not Like Cold War Europe," in Scott D. Sagan (ed.), *Inside Nuclear South Asia*, Stanford, CA: Stanford University Press. pp. 184–218.

Kapur, S. Paul (2011), "Peace and Conflict in the Indo-Pakistani Rivalry: Domestic and Strategic Causes," in Sumit Ganguly and William R. Thompson (eds.), *Asian Rivalries: Conflict, Escalation, and Limitations on Two-Level Games*, Stanford, CA: Stanford University Press, pp. 61–78.

Karamat, Gen. Jehangir (2015), Personal Interview, Former Chief of the Army Staff of the Pakistan Army, Lahore, October 7.

Karbalai, Asgar Ali (2012), Personal Interview, Former Chief Executive of the Ladakh Autonomous Hill Development Council, Kargil (J&K), October 6.

Karnad, Bharat (2002), *Nuclear Weapons and Indian Security: The Realist Foundations of Strategy*, New Delhi: Macmillan.

Karnad, Bharat (2008), *India's Nuclear Policy*, Westport, CT: Praeger.

Kashmir Times (1997a), "Gujral Offers Unconditional Dialouge with Militants," July 27, p. 1.

Kashmir Times (1997b), "8 Civilian Killed, 30 Injured in Provoked Pak Shelling in Kargil," October 1, p.1.

Kashmir Times (1997c), "1 Girl Killed, 6 Injured in Pak Firing in Keran, Uri Sectors," October 2, p. 1.

Kashmir Times (1997d), "Firing in Kargil, Uri Sectors Setback to Peace Talks," October 3, p. 1.

Kashmir Times (1997e), "Over 50 Pak Soldiers Killed, 125 Bunkers Damaged in Uri, Kupwara Sectors," October 3, p. 1.

Kashmir Times (1997f), "Heavy Pak Firing in Tangdar Sector, Siachen Area," October 4, p. 1.

Kashmir Times (2014a), "Pak Troops Target BoPs, Villages on LoC, IB; 2 Injured in RS Pura," August 23, p. 1.

Kashmir Times (2014b), "Pak Firing Targets 25 BoPs, 3 Injured," August 25, p. 1.

Kasuri, Khurshid Mahmud (2015), *Neither a Hawk nor a Dove: An Insider's Account of Pakistan's Foreign Policy*, New Delhi: Penguin Books India.

Kathuria, Sanjay (2018), *A Glass Half Full: The Promise of Regional Trade in South Asia*, South Asia Development Forum, Washington, DC: World Bank. https://openknowledge.worldbank.org/handle/10986/30246 (accessed December 30, 2018).

Katju, Vivek (2016), Personal Interview, Former Ambassador of India to Afghanistan, Gurgaon, January 17. Quoted and cited in Surinder Mohan (2016), "Re-examining the Rivalry Paradigm: The India–Pakistan Conflict," PhD Thesis, University of Delhi, New Delhi.

Kavic, Lorne J. (1967), *India's Quest for Security: Defence Policies, 1947–1965*, Berkeley: University of California Press.

Khajuria, Amar Nath (2010), Personal Interview, Community Health Officer (retd.) and Survivor of the First Kashmir War (1947–48), Sunderbani (migrated from Pallandri), J&K, July 3.

Khan, Maj. Gen. Akbar (1975), *Raiders in Kashmir* (2nd ed.), Islamabad: National Book Foundation.

Khan, Ayaz Ahmed (2006), "Siachen: Problem and Solution," *News*, Karachi, July 3.

Khan, Aziz Ahmed (2015), Personal Interview, Former High Commissioner of Pakistan to India and Ambassador to Afghanistan, Islamabad, October 12.

Khan, Fazal Muqeem (1963), *The Story of the Pakistan Army*, Karachi: Oxford University Press.

Khan, Feroz Hassan (2004), "Nuclear Signaling, Missiles, and Escalation Control in South Asia," in Michael Krepon, Rodney W. Jones, and Ziad Haider (eds.), *Escalation Control and the Nuclear Option in South Asia*, Washington, DC: Henry L. Stimson Center, pp. 75–100.

Khan, Feroz Hassan (2013), *Eating Grass: The Making of the Pakistani Bomb*, New Delhi: Foundation Books.

Khan, Feroz Hassan, Peter R. Lavoy, and Christopher Clary (2009), "Pakistan's Motivations and Calculations for the Kargil," in Peter R. Lavoy (ed.), *Asymmetric Warfare in South Asia: The Causes and Consequences of the Kargil Conflict*, Cambridge: Cambridge University Press, pp. 64–91.

Khan, Gohar Ayub (2007), *Glimpses into the Corridors of Power*, Karachi: Oxford University Press.

Khan, Lt. Gen. Gul Hassan (1994), *The Memoirs of Lt. Gen. Gul Hassan Khan*, Karachi: Oxford University Press.

Khan, Ijaz (2015), Personal Interview, Professor of International and Area Studies at Peshawar University, interview location: New Delhi, March 5.

Khan, Iqbal Ahmad (2015), Personal Interview, Former Ambassador of Pakistan to Bangladesh and Iran, Lahore, October 9.

Khan, Mohammad Ayub (1964), "The Pakistan-American Alliance: Stresses and Strains," *Foreign Affairs*, 42(2): 195–209.

Khan, Mohammad Ayub ([1967] 2006), *Friends Not Masters: A Political Autobiography*, Islamabad: Mr. Books.

Khan, Saira (2009), *Nuclear Weapons and Conflict Transformation: The Case of India-Pakistan*, New Delhi: Routledge.

Khosa, Raspal S. (1999), "The Siachen Glacier Dispute: Imbroglio on the Roof of the World," *Contemporary South Asia*, 8(2): 187–209.

Kidwai, Khalid (2015), "A Conversation with Gen. Khalid Kidwai," Carnegie International Nuclear Policy Conference, Washington DC, March 23, pp. 1–21. http://carnegieendowment.org/files/03-230315carnegieKIDWAI.pdf (accessed August 2, 2015).

Kim, W. (1992), "Power Transitions and Great Power War from Westphalia to Waterloo," *World Politics*, 45(1): 153–72.

Kim, W., and J. D. Morrow (1992), "When Do Power Shifts Lead to War?", *American Journal of Political Science*, 36(4): 896–922.

Kinsella, David (1994), "Conflict in Context: Arms Transfers and Third World Rivalry during the Cold War," *American Journal of Political Science*, 38(3): 557–81.

Kinsella, David (1995), "Nested Rivalries: Superpower Competition, Arms Transfers, and Regional Conflict, 1950–1990," *International Interactions*, 21(2): 109–25.

Kinsella, David (1998), "Arms Transfer Dependence and Foreign Policy Conflict," *Journal of Peace Research*, 35(1): 7–23.

Kinsella, David, and Herbert K. Tillema (1995), "Arms and Aggression in the Middle East: Overt Military Interventions 1948–1989," *Journal of Conflict Resolution*, 39(2): 306–29.

Kissinger, Henry (1979), *White House Years*, Boston: Little, Brown.

Klein, James P., Gary Goertz and Paul F. Diehl (2006), "The New Rivalry Dataset: Procedures and Patterns," *Journal of Peace Research*, 43(3): 331–38.

Kocs, Stephen (1995), "Territorial Disputes and Interstate War, 1945–1987," *Journal of Politics*, 5(1): 159–75.

Koithara, Verghese (2004), *Crafting Peace in Kashmir: Through a Realist Lens*, New Delhi: Sage.

Korbel, Joseph (1966), *Danger in Kashmir* (2nd ed.), Princeton, NJ: Princeton University Press.

Krepon, Michael (2004), "Is Cold War Experience Applicable to Southern Asia?," in Michael Krepon (ed.), *Nuclear Risk Reduction in South Asia*, New York: Palgrave Macmillan, pp. 7–18.

Krepon, Michael (2005), "The Stability-Instability Paradox, Misperception, and Escalation-Control in South Asia," in Raaq Dossani and Henry S. Rowen (eds.), *Prospects for Peace in South Asia*, Stanford, CA: Stanford University Press, pp. 261–79.

Kristensen, Hans M., and Matt Korda (2018), "Indian Nuclear Forces, 2018," *Bulletin of the Atomic Scientists*, 74(6): 36–66.

Kristensen, Hans M., Robert S. Norris, and Julia Diamond (2018), "Pakistani Nuclear Forces, 2018," *Bulletin of the Atomic Scientists*, 74(5): 348–58.

Kronstadt, K. Alan (2008), "Terrorist Attacks in Mumbai, India, and Implications for U.S. Interests," *CRS Report for Congress*, Washington DC: Congressional Research Service, December 19.

Krupakar, Jayanna (2017), "China's Naval Base(s) in the Indian Ocean—Signs of a Maritime Grand Strategy?," *Strategic Analysis* 41(3): 207–22.

Kugler, Jacek, and A.F.K. Organski (1989), "The Power Transition: A Retrospective and Prospective Evaluation," in Manus I. Midlarsky (ed.), *Handbook of War Studies*, Boston: Unwin Hyman, pp. 171–94.

Kukreja, Veena (2003), *Contemporary Pakistan: Political Processes, Conflicts and Crises*, New Delhi: Sage.

Kupchan, Charles A. (2010), *How Enemies Become Friends: The Sources of Stable Peace*, Princeton, NJ: Princeton University Press.

Kutty, Sumitha Narayanan (2016), "India Cements Role in Iran with Chabahar Deal," *LobeLog*, May 23. http://lobelog.com/india-cements-role-in-iran-with-chabahar-deal/ (assessed December 25, 2018).

Kux, Denis (1993), *Estranged Democracies: India and the United States 1941–1991*, New Delhi: Sage.

Kux, Denis (2001), *The United States and Pakistan, 1941–2000: Disenchanted Allies*, Karachi: Oxford University Press.

Kydd, Andrew (2000), "Trust, Reassurance, and Cooperation," *International Organization*, 54(2): 325–57.

Ladwig, Walter C. (2007–08), "A Cold Start for Hot Wars? The Indian Army's New Limited War Doctrine," *International Security*, 32(3): 158–90.

LaFeber, Walter (1991), *America, Russia, and the Cold War, 1945–1990*, New York: McGraw Hill.

Lamb, Alastair (1967), *The Kashmir Problem*, New York: Praeger.

Lamb, Alastair (1993), *Kashmir: A Disputed Legacy 1846–1990*, Karachi: Oxford University Press.

Lambeth, Benjamin S. (2012), "Airpower at 18,000': The Indian Air Force in the Kargil War," Washington, DC: *Carnegie Endowment for International Peace*.

Lancaster, John (1999), "U.S. Defused Kashmir Crisis on Brink of War," *Washington Post*, July 26, p. A01.

Lavoy, Peter R. (2009a), "Introduction: The Importance of the Kargil Conflict," in Peter R. Lavoy (ed.), *Asymmetric Warfare in South Asia: The Causes and Consequences of the Kargil Conflict*, Cambridge: Cambridge University Press, pp. 1–37.

Lavoy, Peter R. (2009b), "Why Kargil Did Not Produce General War: The Crisis Management Strategies of Pakistan, India, and the United States," in Peter R. Lavoy (ed.), *Asymmetric Warfare in South Asia: The Causes and Consequences of the Kargil Conflict*, Cambridge: Cambridge University Press, pp. 171–206.

Layne, Christopher (1995), "Kant or Cant: The Myth of the Democratic Peace," *International Security*, 19(1): 5–49.

Legro, Jaffrey W. (2005), *Rethinking the World Great Power Strategies and International Order*, Ithaca, NY: Cornell University Press.

Lemke, Douglas (2002), *Regions of War and Peace*, Cambridge: Cambridge University Press.

Lemke, Douglas, and Suzanne Werner (1996), "Power Parity, Commitment to Change, and War," *International Studies Quarterly*, 40(2): 235–60.

Leng, Russell J. (1983), "When Will They Ever Learn? Coercive Bargaining in Recurrent Crises," *Journal of Conflict Resolution*, 27(3): 379–419.

Leng, Russell J. (1988), "Crisis Learning Games," *American Political Science Review*, 82(1): 179–194.

Leng, Russell J. (2000), *Bargaining and Learning in Recurring Crises: The Soviet-American, Egyptian-Israeli, and Indo-Pakistani Rivalries*, Ann Arbor: University of Michigan Press.

Levy, Jack S. (1981), "Alliance Formation and War Behavior: An Analysis of the Great Powers, 1495–1975," *Journal of Conflict Resolution*, 25(4): 581–613.

Levy, Jack S. (1988), "Review Article: When Do Deterrent Threats Work?," *British Journal of Political Science*, 18(4): 485–512.

Levy, Jack S. (1994), "Learning and Foreign Policy: Sweeping a Conceptual Minefield," *International Organization*, 48(2): 279–312.

Levy, Jack S., and William R. Thompson (2010), *Causes of War*, Singapore: Wiley-Blackwell.

Lieven, Antol (2011), *Pakistan: A Hard Country*, London: Allen Lane.

Ling, Wei (2013), "Rebalancing to De-Balancing: U.S. Pivot and East Asian Order," *American Foreign Policy Interests*, 35(3): 148–54.

Lobo, J. Susanna (2021), "Balancing China: Indo-US Relations and Convergence of Their Interests in the Indo-Pacific," *Maritime Affairs*, 17(1): 73–91. https://doi.org/10.1080/09733159.2021.1952618.

Lockwood, David E. (1969), "Sheikh Abdullah and the Politics of Kashmir," *Asian Survey*, 9(5): 382–96.

Lone, Sajad Gani (2006), *Achieveable Nationhood: A Vision Document on Resolution of the Jammu and Kashmir Conflict*, Jammu Kashmir People's Conference, Srinagar. http://docslide.us/documents/achievable-nationhood-5584536ad9c d2.html (accessed July 19, 2016).

Luard, Evan (1970), *The International Regulation of Frontier Disputes*, New York: Praeger.

Lucas, W. Scott (1991), *Divided We Stand: Britain, the US and the Suez Crisis*, London: Hodder & Stoughton.

Lynch, Michael (2004), *Mao*, London: Routledge.

Lyon, Peter (1967), "Kashmir," *International Relations*, 3(2): 111–28.

MacDonald, Myra (2007), *Heights of Madness: One Woman's Journey in Pursuit of a War*, New Delhi: Rupa.

Madhav, Ram (2015), "Is Modi's India Flirting with Fascism?," Interview with Mehdi Hasan, *Al Jazeera*, December 25. http://www.aljazeera.com/programm es/headtohead/2015/12/modis-india-flirting-fascism-151201114124802.html (accessed December 31, 2015).

Malenbaum, Wilfred (1959), *East and West in India's Development*, Washington DC: National Planning Association.

Malik, Priyanjali (2010), *India's Nuclear Debate: Exceptionalism and the Bomb*, New Delhi: Routledge.

Malik, Shahid (2015), Personal Interview, Former High Commissioner of Pakistan to India, Lahore, October 8.

Malik, Gen. V.P. (2006), *Kargil: From Surprise to Victory*, New Delhi: HarperCollins India.

Malik, Gen. V.P. (2016), "China-Pak Economic Corridor," *Tribune*, March 14. http://www.tribuneindia.com/article/news_print.aspx?story_id=208364&c atid=35&mid=70 (accessed March 18, 2016).

Mamun, Shohel (2016), "Bangladesh Signs MoU with China on Payra Deep-Sea Port Construction," *Dhaka Tribune*, December 9. https://www.dhakatribune .com/bangladesh/2016/12/09/bangladesh-signs-mou-china-payra-deep-sea -port-construction/ (accessed August 25, 2018).

Manish (ed.) (2021), *The Belt and the Road Initiative: Implications for India*, New Delhi: Pentagon Press.

Mann, James (1999), *About Face: A History of America's Curious Relationship with China*, New York: Knopf.

Mansfield, Edward, and Jack Synder (1995), "Democracy and the Danger of War," *International Security*, 20(1): 5–38.

Maoz, Zeev (1982), *Paths to Conflict: International Dispute Initiation, 1816–1976*, Boulder: Westview Press.

Maoz, Zeev (1989), "Joining the Club of Nations: Political Development and International Conflict, 1816–1976," *International Studies Quarterly*, 33(2): 99–231.

Maoz, Zeev (1997), "The Controversy over the Democratic Peace: Rearguard Action or Cracks in the Wall?," *International Security*, 22(1): 162–98.

Maoz, Zeev (2000), "Alliances: The Street Gangs of World Politics—Their Origins, Management, and Consequences," in John A. Vasquez (ed.), *What Do We Know about War*, New York: Rowman & Littlefield, pp. 111–44.

Maoz, Zeev, and Ben Mor (1998), "Learning, Preference Change, and the Evolution of Enduring Rivalries," in Paul E. Diehl (ed.), *The Dynamics of Enduring Rivalries*, Urbana: University of Illinois Press, pp. 129–64.

Maoz, Zeev, and Ben D. Mor (2002), *Bound by Struggle: The Strategic Evolution of Enduring International Rivalries*, Ann Arbor: University of Michigan Press.

Maoz, Zeev, and Bruce Russett (1993), "Normative and Structural Causes of the Democratic Peace," *American Political Science Review*, 87(3): 624–38.

Margolis, Eric (2001), *War at the Top of the World: The Struggle for Afghanistan, Kashmir, and Tibet*, New York: Routledge.

Marshall, Monty G., and Keith Jaggers (2002), "Polity IV Project: Political Regime Characteristics and Transitions, 1800–2002. Dataset Users' Manual," Center for International Development and Conflict Management, University of Maryland.   http://nd.edu/*mcoppedg/crd/PolityIVUsersManualv2002.pdf (accessed September 2, 2012).

Masood, Lt. Gen. Talat (2015), Personal Interview, Former General of the Pakistan Army and Defense Analyst, Islamabad, October 14.

Maxwell, Neville ([1970] 2010), *India's China War*, Dehradun: Natraj.

McGrath, Allan (1996), *The Destruction of Pakistan's Democracy*, Oxford: Oxford University Press, 1996.

McLeod, Duncan (2008), *India and Pakistan: Friends, Rivals or Enemies?*, Aldershot: Ashgate.

McMahon, Robert J. (1994), *The Cold War on the Periphery: The United States, India, and Pakistan*, New York: Columbia University Press.

MEA (Ministry of External Affairs) (n.d.), "Report 1963–64," Government of India. http://mealib.nic.in/reports/1963-64.pdf (accessed April 19, 2013).

Mearsheimer, John J. (2001), *The Tragedy of Great Power Politics*, New York: W.W. Norton.

Mehta, Aaron (2015), "Carter Announces $425M in Pacific Partnership Funding," *Defense News*, May 30. http://www.defensenews.com/story/defense/2015/05 /30/carter-announces-425m-in-pacific-partnership-funding/28206541/ (accessed July 18, 2016).

Mehta, Pratap Bhanu (2016), "The American Hug," *Indian Express*, April 2, p. 8.

Mehta, Pratap Bhanu (2019), "Winning Kashmir and Losing India: How Modi Is Gutting Indian Democracy," *Foreign Affairs*, September 20. https://www.forei gnaffairs.com/articles/asia/2019-09-20/winning-kashmir-and-losing-India (accessed November 20, 2019).

Mehta, Maj. Gen. Raj (retd.) (2011), "Siachen: Frozen Disengagement," *Tribune*, Chandigarh, June 6. http://www.tribuneindia.com/2011/20110606/edit .htm#6 (accessed December 23, 2013).

"Memorandum of Conversation between Kissinger and Huang Hua" (1999), in William Burr (ed.), *The Kissinger Transcripts: The Top Secret Talks With Beijing and Moscow*, New York: New Press, pp. 48–57.

Menon, Raja (2016), "The Strategic Imperative: Benefits Outweigh Costs of India, US Intimacies," *Indian Express*, April 13. www.indianexpress.com/article/opi nion/columns/benefits-outweigh-costs-of-India-us-intimacies-the-strategic -imperative/ (accessed April 13, 2016).

Menon, V.P. ([1956] 2014), *Integration of the Indian States* (rev. ed.), New Delhi: Orient Blackswan.

Meyer, Cord (1993), "Perilous Collision Course," *Washington Times*, August 20, p. F3.

Mihalka, Michael (1976), "Hostilities in the European State System, 1816–1970," *Peace Science Society Papers* 26: 100–116.

Military Balance (1965), London: International Institute for Strategic Studies and Routledge.

Military Balance (1971), London: International Institute for Strategic Studies and Routledge.

Military Balance (1996–97), London: International Institute for Strategic Studies and Routledge.

Military Balance (2016), London: International Institute for Strategic Studies and Routledge.

Military Balance (2018), London: International Institute for Strategic Studies and Routledge.

Military Balance (2019), London: International Institute for Strategic Studies and Routledge.

Military Balance (2020), London: International Institute for Strategic Studies and Routledge.

Military Balance (2021), London: International Institute for Strategic Studies and Routledge.

Military Balance (2022), London: International Institute for Strategic Studies and Routledge.

Miller, Benjamin (2007), *States, Nations, and the Great Powers: The Sources of Regional War and Peace*, Cambridge: Cambridge University Press.

Miner, Mary, et al. (2009), "Water Sharing between India and Pakistan: A Critical Evaluation of the Indus Water Treaty," *Water International*, 34(2): 204–16.

Mirchandani, G.G. (1968), *India's Nuclear Dilemma*, New Delhi: Popular Book Services.

Mirza, Mohammad Akram (2018), Personal Interview, the local NC leader and former soldier of the Pakistan Army, Sunderbani (Rajouri District), J&K, August 17.

Mohan, C. Raja (2004), *Crossing the Rubicon: The Shaping of India's New Foreign Policy*, New Delhi: Penguin.

Mohan, C. Raja (2012), *Samudra Manthan: Sino-Indian Rivalry in the Indo-Pacific*, Washington, DC: Carnegie Endowment for International Peace.

Mohan, P.V.S. Jagan, and Samir Chopra (2013), *Eagles over Bangladesh: The Indian Air Force in the 1971 Liberation War*, New Delhi: HarperCollins.

Mohan, Surinder (2016), "Re-examining the Rivalry Paradigm: The India–Pakistan Conflict," PhD Thesis, University of Delhi, New Delhi.

Mohan, Surinder, and Josukutty C. Abraham (2020), "Shaping the Regional and Maritime Battlefield? The Sino-Indian Strategic Competition in South Asia and Adjoining Waters," *Maritime Affairs*, 16(1): 82–97.

Mohan, Surinder, and J. Susanna Lobo (2020), "The Politics of Foreign Aid: Impact of Superpowers Economic Assistance on India and Pakistan during the Cold War," *Bandung: Journal of the Global South*, 7(1): 52–79.

Mohiuddin, Yasmeen Niaz (2007), *Pakistan: A Global Studies Handbook*, Santa Barbara, CA: ABC-CLIO.

Moles, Ben (2012), "'Twin Peaks' and One Long Trough: 'Operation Parakram' a Decade On," September 18. http://internationalsecuritydiscipulus.wordpress.com/2012/09/18/twin-peaks-and-one-long-trough-revisiting-operation-parakram-a-decade-on/ (accessed December 23, 2013).

Montagno, George L. (1965), "Peaceful Coexistence: Pakistan and Red China," *Western Political Quarterly*, 18(2): 309–17.

Morgenthau, Hans J. ([1967] 2001), *Politics among Nations: The Struggle for Power and Peace*, New Delhi: Kalyani.

Morrow, James D. (1986), "A Spatial Model of International Conflict," *American Political Science Review*, 80(4): 1131–50.

Mosley, L. (1978), *Dulles: A Biography of Eleanor, Allen and John Foster Dulles and Their Family Network*, New York: Dial Press.

Most, Benjamin A., and Harvey Starr (1989), *Inquiry, Logic, and International Politics*, Columbia: University of South Carolina Press.

Mountbatten, Louis, Rear-Admiral Earl (2003), *Mountbatten's Report on the Last Viceroyalty: 22 March–15 August 1947* (with additional editing and a new introduction by Lionel Carter), New Delhi: Manohar.

Mukherjee, Anit (2009), "A Brand New Day or Back to the Future? The Dynamics of India-Pakistan Relations," *India Review*, 8(4): 404–45.

Murphy, Alexander (1991), "Territorial Ideology and International Conflict: The Legacy of Prior Political Formations," in N. Kliot and S. Walterman (eds.), *The Political Geography of Conflict and Peace*, London: Belhaven Press, pp. 126–41.

Musharraf, Pervez (2006), *In the Line of Fire: A Memoir*, New York: Free Press.

Muslim (1988), "India, Israel Claimed Considering Attack," March 28, p. 1.

Nair, Pavan (2009), "The Siachen War: Twenty-Five Years On," *Economic and Political Weekly*, 44(11): 35–40.

Nanda, S.M. (2007), "Does the US Want War with India?," Interview with Ramananda Sengupta, *Rediff India News*, January 22. http://www.rediff.com/news/2007/jan/22inter.htm (accessed January 27, 2013).

Naqvi, Ali Sarwar (2015), "Seventeen Years of Deterrence," *News*, May 28. http://www.thenews.com.pk/Todays-News-9-320560-Seventeen-years-of-deterrence (accessed May 29, 2015).

Narang, Vipin (2009–10), "Posturing for Peace? Pakistan's Nuclear Postures and South Asian Stability," *International Security*, 34(3): 38–78.

Narang, Vipin (2013), "Five Myths about India's Nuclear Posture," *Washington Quarterly*, 36(3): 143–57.

Narayanan, M.K. (2007a), "India [Ha]s Invested Very Heavily in a Stable Pak: Narayanan," Interview, *CNBC-TV18*, August 1. http://m.moneycontrol.com/news/politics/india-is-invested-very-heavilya-stable-pak-narayanan_295752.html?type=politics&category=politics (accessed June, 2015).

Narayanan, M.K. (2007b), "Musharraf's Survival Will Depend on Army Chief," Interview with Karan Thapar on *Devil's Advocate*, CNN-IBN, December 16. http://ibnlive.in.com/news/musharrafs-survival-will-depend-on-army-chief/54320-3-1.html (accessed October 17, 2014).

NASIC (National Air and Space Intelligence Center) (2013), *Ballistic and Cruise Missile Threat*, Watson Way, Wright-Patterson AFB: NASIC Public Affairs Office. http://fas.org/programs/ssp/nukes/nuclearweapons/NASIC2013_050 813.pdf (accessed January 9, 2015).

Nasr, Vali (2005), "National Identities and the India-Pakistan Conflict," in T.V. Paul (ed.), *The India-Pakistan Conflict: An Enduring Rivalry*, Cambridge: Cambridge University Press, pp. 178–201.

Nation (2019a), "Pakistan Had No Choice but to Respond, says DG ISPR," February 27. https://nation.com.pk/27-Feb-2019/pakistan-has-capability-but-wan ts-peace-dg-ispr (accessed December 25, 2019).

Nation (2019b), "Pakistan to Launch Agosta 90B Soon," December 15. https://nat ion.com.pk/15-Dec-2019/pakistan-to-launch-agosta-90b-soon (accessed December 25, 2019).

National Material Capabilities Data (2021), "National Material Capabilities (v6.0)," *Correlates of War Project*, Version 6.0 (1816–2016), July 22, 2021. http:// correlatesofwar.org/data-sets/national-material-capabilities (accessed July 28, 2021).

Nawaz, Shuja (2008), *Crossed Swords: Pakistan Its Army, the Wars Within*, Karachi: Oxford University Press.

Nayak, Polly, and Michael Krepon (2011), "U.S. Crisis Management in South Asia's Twin Peaks Crisis," in Zachary S. Davis (ed.), *The India-Pakistan Military Standoff: Crisis and Escalation in South Asia*, New York: Palgrave Macmillan, pp. 143–86.

Nayar, Kuldip (1987), "We Have the A-Bomb, Says Pakistan's Dr. Strangelove," *Observer*, March 1.

Nayar, Kuldip (2003), *Wall at Wagha: India-Pakistan Relations*, New Delhi: Gyan.

Nayyar, A.H. (2015a), Personal Interview, Physicist and Visiting Professor, Quaid-i-Azam University, Islamabad (interview location: New Delhi), March 5.

Nayyar, A.H. (2015b), Personal Interview, Physicist and Visiting Professor, Quaid-i-Azam University, Islamabad, October 12.

NDTV (2013), "Gunfire Shatters Kargil, Drass Silence After 14 Years; 28 Terrorists Killed in 2 Months at LOC," August 16. www.ndtv.com/article/cheat-sheet/gu nfire-shatters-kargil-drass-silence-after-14-years-28-terrorists-killed-in-2-mo nths-at-loc-406570 (accessed August 17, 2013).

NDTV (2016a), "Uri Base Caught Off-Guard Despite Specific Intel? Army Investigates," September 20. http://www.ndtv.com/india-news/uri-base-caught-off -guard-despite-specific-intel-army-investigates-1461701 (accessed December 31, 2018).

NDTV (2016b), "PM Narendra Modi Will Not Attend SAARC Summit in Pakistan", September 28. http://www.ndtv.com/india-news/india-pulls-out-of-saarc-su mmit-in-islamabad-1467221 (accessed December 31, 2018).

NDTV (2019), "India Hits Terror Camps Across Line of Control Days after Pulwama Attack," February 26. https://www.ndtv.com/india-news/india-strikes -terrorist-camp-across-line-of-control-say-reports-official-details-awaited-19 99291 (assessed February 27, 2019).

Nehru, Jawaharlal (1961), *India's Foreign Policy: Selected Speeches, September 1946–April 1961*, New Delhi: Publications Division, Government of India.

New Indian Express (2014), "PM May Have Alluded to Musharraf's Kashmir Plan," January 10. http://www.newindianexpress.com/nation/PM-may-Have-Alluded-to-Musharrafs-Kashmir-Plan/2014/01/10/article1992068.ece (accessed August 26, 2014).

News Nation (2015), "Former ISI Chief Threatens India, Says Pakistan Will Turn Delhi-Mumbai into Hiroshima-Nagasaki," August 6. http://www.newsnation.in/article/86918-former-isi-chief-threatens-india-turn-delhi-mumbai-hiroshima-nagasaki.html (accessed August 25, 2015).

New York Times (2002), "The India-Pakistan Tension: Islamabad; Pakistan Pledges to Bar Any Groups Linked to Terror," January 13. https://www.nytimes.com/2002/01/13/world/india-pakistan-tension-islamabad-pakistan-pledges-bar-any-groups-linked-terror.html (accessed May 27, 2014).

Niazi, Lt. Gen. A.A.K. (2002), *The Betrayal of East Pakistan*, Karachi: Oxford University Press.

Nizamani, Haider K. (2001), *The Roots of Rhetoric: Politics of Nuclear Weapons in India and Pakistan*, New Delhi: India Research Press.

Noorani, A.G. (1992), "The Betrayal of Kashmir: Pakistan's Duplicity and India's Complicity," in Raju G.C. Thomas (ed.), *Perspectives on Kashmir: The Root of Conflict in South Asia*, Boulder, CO: Westview Press, pp. 254–75.

Noorani, A.G. (1994), "Easing the Indo-Pakistani Dialogue on Kashmir: Confidence-Building Measures for the Siachen Glacier, Sir Creek and the Wular Barrage Disputes," *Occasional Paper 16*, Washington, DC: Henry L. Stimson Center, April.

NSA (National Security Archive) (2001), "The Sino-Soviet Border Conflict, 1969: U.S. Reactions and Diplomatic Maneuvers." www.gwu.edu/~nsarchiv/NSAEBB/NSAEBB49/ (accessed April 9, 2013).

NSA (National Security Archive) (2002a), "Selective Genocide," March 28, 1971, U.S. Consulate (Dacca) Cable, Confidential, p. 2. http://www.gwu.edu/~nsarchiv/NSAEBB/NSAEBB79/BEBB1.pdf (accessed April 18, 2013).

NSA (National Security Archive) (2002b), "The Tilt: The U.S. and the South Asian Crisis of 1971." http://www.gwu.edu/~nsarchiv/NSAEBB/NSAEBB79/ (accessed April 9, 2013).

NSA (National Security Archive) (2005), "Nixon/Kissinger Saw India as 'Soviet Stooge' in 1971 South Asia Crisis," June 29. www.gwu.edu/~nsarchiv/news/20050629/index.htm (accessed April 9, 2013).

NSC (National Security Council, 5701) (1957), "U.S. Policy Toward South," Washington, January 10. In Praveen K. Chaudhry and Marta Vanduzer-Snow (eds.) (2008), *The United States and India: A History through Archives*, New Delhi: Observer Research Foundation and Sage, pp. 121–39.

Nye, Joseph S. (2011), "Power and Foreign Policy," *Journal of Political Power*, 4(1): 9–24.

Oneal, John, and Bruce Russett (1997), "The Classical Liberals Were Right: Democracy, Interdependence, and Conflict, 1950–1985," *International Studies Quarterly*, 41(2): 267–93.

Oneal, John, and Bruce Russett (1999), "Assessing the Liberal Peace with Alternative Specifications: Trade Still Reduces Conflict," *Journal of Peace Research*, 36(4): 423–32.

Organski, A.F.K. (1958), *World Politics*, New York: Knopf.

Organski, A.F.K., and Jacek Kugler (1980), *The War Ledger*, Chicago: University of Chicago Press.

Padgaonkar, Dileep (2016), "Dilli Ka Kashmir Ki Janata se Koyee Sanwaand Nahin ho Raha" [There is no dialogue from Delhi with the people of Kashmir], *Tehelka* (Hindi), July 31. http://tehelkahindi.com/dileep-padgaonkar-s-take -on-recent-kashmir-unrest# (accessed August 2, 2016).

Palit, Maj. Gen. D.K. (1991), *War in High Himalaya: The Indian Army in Crisis, 1962*, New Delhi: Lancer International.

Palit, D.K., and P.K.S. Namboodiri (1979), *Pakistan's Islamic Bomb*, New Delhi: Vikas.

Panigrahi, D.N. (2009), *Jammu and Kashmir, the Cold War and the West*, New Delhi: Routledge.

Paret, Peter (1992), *Understanding War: Essays on Clausewitz and the History of Military Power*, Princeton, NJ: Princeton University Press.

Parrish, Karen (2013), "Hagel Tours Forward-Based Littoral Combat Ship in Singapore," *U.S. Department of Defence News*, June 2. http://archive.defense.gov/ne ws/newsarticle.aspx?id=120191 (accessed July 18, 2016).

Parthasarathy, G. (2016), Personal Interview, Former High Commissioner of India to Pakistan and Australia (also served the Indian Army as a commissioned officer, 1963–68), Jammu, February 17.

Pattanaik, Smruti S. (2003), "Pakistan's Nuclear Strategy," *Strategic Analysis*, 27(1): 94–114.

Paul, T.V. (1994), *Asymmetric Conflicts: War Initiated by Weaker Powers*, Cambridge: Cambridge University Press.

Paul, T.V. (2009), *The Tradition of Non-Use of Nuclear Weapons*, Stanford, CA: Stanford University Press.

Paul, T.V. (2014), *The Warrior State: Pakistan in the Contemporary World*, New Delhi: Random House India.

Payari, Ram (2020), Personal Interview, Survivor of the First Kashmir War (1947–48), Seri (Mangala Devi), J&K, February 11.

PDP (People's Democratic Party) (2008), "J&K: The Self-Rule Framework for Resolution," October 2008. jkpdp.org/wp-content/uploads/2014/08/self-rule.pdf (accessed July 10, 2015).

Pehrson, Christopher J. (2006), *String of Pearls: Meeting the Challenge of China's Rising Power across the Asian Littoral*, Carlisle, PA: Strategic Studies Institute, US Army War College, July. http://www.strategicstudiesinstitute.army.mil /pdffiles/PUB721.pdf (accessed February 28, 2014).

Perkovich, George (1999), *India's Nuclear Bomb: The Impact on Global Proliferation*, Berkeley: University of California Press.

Polachek, Solomon William (1980), "Conflict and Trade," *Journal of Conflict Resolution* 24(1): 55–78.

"Policy Options toward Pakistan" (1971), Memorandum for the President, Secret, pp. 1–6 (includes Nixon's handwritten note), National Security Archive, April 28. http://www.gwu.edu/~nsarchiv/NSAEBB/NSAEBB79/BEB B9.pdf (accessed April 18, 2013).

Polity 5 Database (2018), *Polity5 Project*, Center for Systemic Peace. http://www.sy stemicpeace.org/inscrdata.html (accessed December 11, 2020).

Popper, Karl (2002), *The Logic of Scientific Discovery*, London: Routledge.

Premashekhara, L. (2008), "Three Frontiers Theory: An Explanation to India-Pakistan Animosity," *International Journal of South Asian Studies*, 1(1): 13–32.

PRO (Public Records Office) (1948), "Sargent's Minute to PM," File FO/800/470, January 6, London.

Puri, Balraj (2008), *Kashmir: Insurgency and After*, New Delhi: Orient Longman.

Qadir, Shaukat (2002), "An Analysis of the Kargil Conflict 1999," *RUSI Journal*, 147(2): 24–30.

Qazi, Ashraf Jehangir (2015), Personal Interview, Former High Commissioner of Pakistan to India and Ambassador to the US, Islamabad, October 12. Quoted in Surinder Mohan (2016), "Re-examining the Rivalry Paradigm: The India–Pakistan Conflict," PhD Thesis, University of Delhi, New Delhi.

Quackenbush, Stephen L. (2006), "Identifying Opportunity for Conflict: Politically Active Dyads," *Conflict Management and Peace Science*, 23(1): 37–51.

Quackenbush, Stephen L. (2010), "Territorial Issues and Recurrent Conflict," *Conflict Management and Peace* Science, 27(3): 239–52.

Rabasa, Angel, et al. (2009), "The Lessons of Mumbai," Santa Monica, CA: RAND Corporation.

Racioppi, Linda (1994), *Soviet Policy towards South Asia since 1970*, Cambridge: Cambridge University Press.

Raghavan, Srinath (2010), *War and Peace in Modern India: A Strategic History of the Nehru Years*, New Delhi: Permanent Black.

Raghavan, V.R. (2002), *Siachen: Conflict without End*, New Delhi: Penguin Books.

Rais, Rasul Baksh (2015), Personal Interview, Professor of Political Science and Pakistan-Afghanistan Affairs, Lahore University of Management Sciences (LUMS), Lahore, October 7.

Rajagopalan, Rajesh (2005), *Second Strike: Arguments about Nuclear War in South Asia*, New Delhi: Viking.

Rajagopalan, Rajesh (2016), "India's Nuclear Doctrine Debate," Carnegie Endowment for International Peace, June 30. https://carnegieendowment.org/2016 /06/30/india-s-nuclear-doctrine-debate-pub-63950. (accessed October 10, 2017).

Rajagopalan, Rajesh (2020), "Evasive Balancing: India's Unviable Indo-Pacific Strategy," *International Affairs*, 96(1): 75–93.

Raju, Radhavinod (2011), "Samjhauta Express Blast vs Mumbai Terror Attacks," *Institute of Peace and Conflict Studies*, no. 3328, February 10. http://www.ipcs.org/print_article-details.php?recNo=3357 (accessed March 28, 2014).

Ram, Rikhi (2018), Personal Interview, Former Indian Soldier of the 1st Battalion of Dogra Regiment (fought in the India-Pakistan wars of 1965 [the Battle of Asal Uttar] and 1971 [the Battle of Shakargarh Bulge]), Sunderbani (Rajouri District), J&K, February 17.

Ram, Sukh (2016), Personal Interview, Survivor of the First Kashmir War (1947–48), Rawarian Tala (Uppar Bajwal) Sunderbani, J&K, May 2.

Raman, B. (2007), *The Kaoboys of R&AW: Down Memory Lane*, New Delhi: Lancer.

Rashid, Ahmed (2000), *Taliban: Islam, Oil and the New Great Game in Central Asia*, London: I.B. Tauris.

Rashid, Ahmed (2008), *Descent into Chaos: The United States and the Failure of Nation Building in Pakistan, Afghanistan, and Central Asia*, New York: Viking.

Rashid, Ahmed (2012), *Pakistan on the Brink: The Future of Pakistan, Afghanistan and the West*, New Delhi: Penguin-Allen Lane.

Rashid, Ahmed (2015), Personal Interview, Author and Journalist, Lahore, October 8. Quoted and cited in Surinder Mohan (2016), "Re-examining the Rivalry Paradigm: The India–Pakistan Conflict," PhD Thesis, University of Delhi, New Delhi.

Rasler, Karen, and William R. Thompson (2001), "Rivalries and the Democratic Peace in the Major Power Subsystem," *Journal of Peace Research*, 38(6): 659–83.

Rediff (2019), "On Army Day, General Rawat Issues Stern Warning to Pakistan," January 15. https://www.rediff.com/news/report/wont-hesitate-in-carrying-out-strong-action-rawat-warns-pakistan/20190115.htm (accessed January 17, 2019).

Reuters (2016), "Militants Attack Pathankot Air Base, 7 Dead," January 3. https://www.reuters.com/article/india-attack-idUSKBN0UG01320160102 (accessed January 3, 2018).

Reuters (2019), "India, Pakistan Threatened to Unleash Missiles at Each Other," March 18. https://in.reuters.com/article/india-kashmir-crisis-page/india-pak istan-threatened-to-unleash-missiles-at-each-other-sources-idINKCN1Q Z0F1 (accessed March 20, 2019).

Rezun, Miron (1986), "The Great Game Revisited," *International Journal*, 41(2): 324–41.

Richardson, L.F. (1960), *Arms and Insecurity: A Mathematical Study of the Causes and Origins of War*, Pittsburgh: Boxwood Press.

Riedel, Bruce (2002), "American Diplomacy and the 1999 Kargil Summit at Blair House," Center for the Advanced Study of India, University of Pennsylvania, Philadelphia. http://citeseerx.ist.psu.edu/viewdoc/download?doi=10.1.1 .473.251&rep=rep1&type=pdf (accessed January 24, 2014).

Riedel, Bruce (2010), *The Search of Al Qaeda: Its Leadership, Ideology, and Future*, updated paperback edition, New Delhi: Supernova.

Riedel, Bruce (2016), *JFK's Forgotten Crisis: Tibet, China, and the Sino-Indian War*, New Delhi: HarperCollins.

Rikhye, Ravi (2001), "The Northern Light Infantry in the Kargil Operations, 1999," *Bharat Rakshak Monitor*, 3(6). http://orbat.com/site/history/historical /pakistan/nli_kargil1999.html (accessed January 24, 2014).

Riza, Maj. Gen. Shaukat Riza ([1977] 2003), *The Pakistan Army 1947-49: Pakistan's Official Report on Kashmir Operations*, Dehra Dun: Natraj.

Rizvi, Gowher (1992), "India, Pakistan, and the Kashmir Problem, 1947-1972," in Raju G. C. Thomas (ed.), *Perspectives on Kashmir: The Roots of Conflict in South Asia*, Boulder, CO: Westview Press, pp. 47-79.

Rizvi, Hasan-Askari (2000), *Military, State and Society in Pakistan*, Basingstoke: Macmillan.

Roblin, Sebastien (2020), "Pakistan Wants to Sell Its Vaunted JF-17 Fighter Jet," *National Interest*, March 4. https://nationalinterest.org/blog/buzz/pakistan -wants-sell-its-vaunted-jf-17-fighter-jet-129472 (accessed March 24, 2020).

Rock, Stephen R. (1989), *Why Peace Breaks Out: Great Power Rapprochement in Historical Perspective*, Chapel Hill: University of North Carolina Press.

Roggio, Bill (2008), "UN Declares Jamaat-ud-Dawa a Terrorist Front Group," *Long War Journal*, December 11. http://www.longwarjournal.org/archives/2008/12 /un_declares_jamaatud.php (accessed January 2, 2015).

Rosati, Jerel A. (1994), "Cycles in Foreign Policy Restructuring: The Politics of Continuity and Change in U.S. Foreign Policy", in Jerel A. Rosati, Joe D. Hagan, and Martin W. Sampson III (eds.), *Foreign Policy Restructuring: How Governments Respond to Global Change*, Columbia, University of South Carolina Press.

Rosato, Sebastian (2003), "The Flawed Logic of Democratic Peace Theory," *American Political Science Review*, 97(4): 585-602.

Ross, Robert S. (2012), "The Problem with the Pivot: Obama's New Asia Policy is Unnecessary and Counterproductive," *Foreign Affairs*, 91(6): 70-82.

Rostow, W.W. (1960), *The United States in the World Arena*, Cambridge, MA: MIT Press.

Rouhana, Nadim N., and Daniel Bar-Tal (1998), "Psychological Dynamics of Intractable Ethnonational Conflicts: The Israeli-Palestinian Case," *American Psychologist*, 53(7): 761-70.

Rubin, Barnett R. (1985), "Economic Liberalization and the Indian State," *Third World Quarterly*, 7(4): 942-57.

Rubin, Barnett, and Abubakar Siddique (2006), "Resolving the Pakistan-Afghanistan Stalemate," *U.S. Institute of Peace Special Report* 176 (October): 1-20.

Rummel, R.J. (1979), *Understanding Conflict and War: War, Power, Peace*, vol. 4, Beverly Hills, CA: Sage.

Rummel, R.J. (1995), "Democracies Are Less Warlike Than Other Regimes," *European Journal of International Relations*, 1(4): 457-79.

Russett, Bruce (1993), *Grasping the Democratic Peace*, Princeton, NJ: Princeton University Press.

Russett, Bruce, and John R. Oneal (2001), *Triangulating Peace: Democracy, Interdependence, and International Organization*, New York: W.W. Norton.

Russett, Bruce, and Harvey Starr (1992), *World Politics: The Menu for Choice*, New York: Freeman.

Sack, Robert (1986), *Territoriality: Its Theory and History*, Cambridge: Cambridge University Press.

Sagan, Scott D. (1996–97), "Why Do States Build Nuclear Weapons: Three Models in Search of a Bomb," *International Security*, 21(3): 54–86.

Sagan, Scott D. (2001), "The Perils of Proliferation in South Asia," *Asian Survey*, 41(6): 1064–86.

Sagan, Scott D. (2009), "The Evolution of Pakistani and Indian Nuclear Doctrine," in Scott D. Sagan (ed.), *Inside Nuclear South Asia*, Stanford, CA: Stanford University Press, pp. 219–63.

Sahni, Varun (2009), "A Dangerous Exercise: Brasstacks as Non-nuclear Near-War," in Sumit Ganguly and S. Paul Kapur (eds.), *Nuclear Proliferation in South Asia: Crisis Behaviour and the Bomb*, New York: Routledge, pp. 12–35.

Sahu, Anjan Kumar, and Surinder Mohan (2022), "From Securitization to Security Complex: Climate Change, Water Security and the India–China Relations," *International Politics*, 59(2): 320–45.

Sample, Susan (1998a), "Furthering the Investigation into the Effects of Arms Buildups," *Journal of Peace Research*, 35(2): 122–26.

Sample, Susan (1998b), "Military Buildups, War and Realpolitik: A Multivariate Model," *Journal of Conflict Resolution*, 42(2): 156–75.

Sample, Susan (2000), "Military Buildups: Arming and War," in John A. Vasquez (ed.), *What Do We Know about War?*, Lanham, MD: Rowman & Littlefield, pp. 166–95.

Sanjian, Gregory S. (1999), "Promoting Stability or Instability? Arms Transfers and Regional Rivalries, 1950–9," *International Studies Quarterly*, 43(4): 641–70.

Sanjian, Gregory S. (2001), "Arms and Arguments: Modeling the Effects of Weapons Transfers on Subsystem Relationships," *Political Research Quarterly*, 54(2): 285–309.

Sanjian, Gregory S. (2003), "Arms Transfers, Military Balances, and Interstate Relations: Modeling Power Balance versus Power Transition Linkages," *Journal of Conflict Resolution*, 47(6): 711–27.

Santos, Anne Noronha Dos (2007), *Military Intervention and Secession in South Asia: The Cases of Bangladesh, Sri Lanka, Kashmir, and Punjab*, Westport, CT: Praeger Security International.

SATP (South Asia Terrorism Portal) (2018), "Jammu and Kashmir Timeline 2017," Institute of Conflict Management, New Delhi. http://www.satp.org/satporgtp/countries/india/states/jandk/timeline (accessed December 31, 2018).

Sawhney, Pravin (2000), "Pakistan Scores over India in Ballistic Missile Race," *Jane's Intelligence Review*, 12(11): 31–35.

Sayeed, Khalid Bin (1959), "Collapse of Parliamentary Democracy in Pakistan," *Middle East Journal*, 13(4): 389–406.

Schaffer, Howard S. (2009), *The Limits of Influence: America's Role in Kashmir*, Washington, DC: Brookings Institution Press.

Schofield, Victoria (2010), *Kashmir in Conflict: India, Pakistan and the Unending War* (3rd ed.), New Delhi: Viva Books.

Schultz, Kenneth (2005), "The Politics of Risking Peace: Do Hawks or Doves Deliver the Olive Branch?," *International Organization*, 59(1), pp. 1–38.

Schweller, Randall L. (1994), "Bandwagoning for Profit: Bringing the Revisionist State Back In," *International Security*, 19(1): 72–107.

Sen, Amartya (2016), "Kashmir Brutality Biggest Blot on Our Democracy", Interview with Karan Thapar in *To The Point, India Today*, July 18. http://indiatod ay.intoday.in/story/amartya-sen-kashmir-situation-democracy-raghuram -rajan/1/717959.html (accessed July 19, 2015).

Senese, Paul D., and John A. Vasquez (2003), "A Unified Explanation of Territorial Conflict: Testing the Impact of Sampling Bias, 1919–1992," *International Studies Quarterly*, 47(2): 275–98.

Senese, Paul D., and John A. Vasquez (2008), *The Steps to War: An Empirical Study*, Princeton, NJ: Princeton University Press.

Shah, Aqil (2014), *The Army and Democracy: Military Politics in Pakistan*, Cambridge, MA: Harvard University Press.

Shaikh, Farzana (2002), "Pakistan's Nuclear Bomb: Beyond the Non-proliferation Regime," *International Affairs*, 78(1): 29–48.

Sharif, Nawaz (1999), "Address to the Nation by Prime Minister Nawaz Sharif," Government of Pakistan, July 12. http://acronym.org.uk/dd/dd39/39kash.htm (accessed January 29, 2014).

Sharma, B.L. (1967), *The Kashmir Story*, Bombay: Asia Publishing House.

Sharma, Gen. V.N. (retd.) (1993), "It's All Bluff and Bluster," Interview with K. Subrahmanyam, *Economic Times*, May 18 (Bombay), p. 7.

Shaumian, Tatyana L. (1988), "India's Foreign Policy: Interaction of Global and Regional Aspects," *Asian Survey*, 28(11): 1161–69.

Shlaim, Avi (2000), *The Iron Wall: Israel and the Arab World*, New York: W.W. Norton.

Shukla, Ajai (2015), "At Heart of Asia Conference in Islamabad, Swaraj Calls for Land Access to Afghanistan," *Business Standard*, December 10. http://www.bu siness-standard.com/article/economy-policy/at-heart-of-asia-conference-in -islamabad-swaraj-calls-for-land-access-to-afghanistan-11512090 (accessed April 21, 2016).

Shukla, Ashish (2017), *Pakistan Army: Institution That Matters*, New Delhi: Knowledge World.

Shukla, Saurabh (2002), "India Puts Forces in Action Mode," *Hindustan Times*, May 20.

Siddiqa, Ayesha (2012), Personal Interview, Independent Security Analyst, Location: New Delhi, March 30. Quoted in Surinder Mohan (2016), "Re-examining the Rivalry Paradigm: The India–Pakistan Conflict," PhD Thesis, University of Delhi, New Delhi.

Siddiqa, Ayesha (2015), Personal Interview, Independent Security Analyst, Islamabad, October 13. Quoted and cited in Surinder Mohan (2016), "Re-examining the Rivalry Paradigm: The India–Pakistan Conflict," PhD Thesis, University of Delhi, New Delhi.

Siddiqa-Agha, Ayesha (2001), *Pakistan's Arms Procurement and Military Buildup, 1979–99: In Search of a Policy*, New York: Palgrave.

Sidhu, Waheguru Pal Singh, and Jing-dong Yuan (2003), *China and India: Cooperation or Conflict?*, Boulder, CO: Lynne Rienner.

Singh, Jaswant (2006), *A Call to Honour: In Service of Emergent India*, New Delhi: Rupa.

Singh, Admiral Karambir (2020), "We Are Closely Watching Chinese Navy," Interview by Pradip R Sagar, *Week*, December 27. https://www.theweek.in/th eweek/cover/2020/12/17/we-are-closely-watching-chinese-navy.html (accessed December 29, 2020).

Sisson, Richard, and Leo E. Rose (1990), *War and Secession: Pakistan, India, and the Creation of Bangladesh*, Berkeley: University of California Press.

Siverson, Randolph M., and Harvey Starr (1989), "Alliance and Border Effects on the War Behavior of States: Refining the Interaction Opportunity Model," *Conflict Management and Peace Science*, 10(2): 21–46.

Smith, Charles D. (2007), *Palestine and the Arab-Israeli Conflict*, Boston: Bedford/ St. Martin's.

Smith, David O. (2013), "The US Experience with Tactical Nuclear Weapons: Lessons for South Asia," in Michael Krepon and Julia Thompson (eds.), *Deterrence Stability and Escalation Control in South Asia*, Washington, DC: Stimson Center, pp. 65–92.

Snedden, Christopher (2013), *Kashmir: The Unwritten History*, New Delhi: Harper-Collins.

Sood, Lt. Gen. V. K. (retd.), and Pravin Sawhney (2003), *Operation Parakram—The War Unfinished*, New Delhi: Sage.

Stern, Robert W. (2008), *Changing India* (2nd ed.), Cambridge: Cambridge University Press.

Stinnett, Douglas, and Paul F. Diehl (2001), "The Path(s) to Rivalry: Behavioral and Structural Explanations of Rivalry Development," *Journal of Politics*, 63(3): 717–40.

Straits Times (2015), "China, Pakistan Launch $62 Billion Economic Corridor Link," April 20. http://www.straitstimes.com/news/asia/south-asia/story/ch ina-pakistan-launch-62-billion-economic-corridor-link-20150420 (accessed May 22, 2015).

Subrahmanyam, K. (1982), *Indian Security Perspectives*, New Delhi: ABC Publishing House.

Subrahmanyam, K. (1998), "Indian Nuclear Policy—1964–98 (A Personal Recollection)," in Jasjit Singh (ed.), *Nuclear India*, New Delhi: Knowledge World, pp. 26–53.

Sultan, Adil (2011–12), "Pakistan's Emerging Nuclear Posture: Impact of Drivers and Technology on Nuclear Doctrine," *Strategic Studies*, 31–32: 147–67.

Sundarji, Gen. Krishnaswamy (1988), "I Had to Aim for the Moon," Interview with Inderjit Badhwar and Dilip Bobb, *India Today*, May 15. http://indiatoday .intoday.in/story/against-pakistan-our-dissuasive-and-riposte-capabilities -are-good-general-sundarji/1/329302.html (accessed March 12, 2014).

Swami, Praveen (1998a), "Flashpoint Kashmir," *Frontline*, August 15–28. http://in diatoday.intoday.in/story/against-pakistan-our-dissuasive-and-riposte-capa bilities-are-good-general-sundarji/1/329302.html (accessed July 19, 2014).

Swami, Praveen (1998b), "Kashmir at a Crossroads," *Frontline*, June 20–July 3. http://www.frontline.in/static/html/fl1513/15130110.htm (accessed March 12, 2014).

Swami, Praveen (2007), *India, Pakistan and the Secret Jihad: The Covert War in Kashmir, 1947–2004*, New Delhi: Routledge.

Swami, Praveen (2009), "A War to End a War: The Causes and Outcomes of the 2001–2 India-Pakistan Crisis," in Sumit Ganguly and S. Paul Kapur (eds.), *Nuclear Proliferation in South Asia: Crisis Behaviour and the Bomb*, Abingdon: Routledge, pp. 144–61.

Swaroop, Prem (2014), Personal Interview, Teacher, Poet, Refugee and Survivor of the First Kashmir War (1947–48), Seri-Seyal (migrated from Bhimber), J&K, March 28.

Tagore, Rabindranath ([1917] 2009), *Nationalism*, New Delhi: Penguin Books India.

Tahir-Kheli, Shirin R. (1997), *India, Pakistan, and the United States: Breaking with the Past*, New York: Council on Foreign Relations Press.

Talbot, Ian (2009), *Pakistan: A Modern History*, New Delhi: Foundation Books.

Talbot, Phillips (1949), "Kashmir and Hyderabad," *World Politics* 1(3): 321–32.

Talbott, Strobe (2004), *Engaging India: Diplomacy, Democracy, and the Bomb*, Washington, DC: Brookings Institution Press.

Tammen, Ronald, et al. (2000), *Power Transitions: Strategies for the 21st Century*, New York: Chatham House.

Tannenwald, Nina (2007), *The Nuclear Taboo: The United States and the Non-use of Nuclear Weapons since 1945*, Cambridge: Cambridge University Press.

Taseer, Salmaan (1979), *Bhutto: A Political Biography*, London: Ithaca Books.

Tellis, Ashley (2001), *India's Emerging Nuclear Posture: Between Recessed Deterrent and Ready Arsenal*, Santa Monica: RAND.

"Text of Joint Clinton-Sharif Statement" (1999), *CNN*, July 4. http://web.archive .org/web/20080417050230/http://www.cnn.com/WORLD/asiapcf/9907/04 /kashmir.04/index.html (accessed January 24, 2014).

Thakur, D.D. (2005), *My Life and Years in Kashmir Politics*, New Delhi: Konark.

Thapar, Romila (2002), *Early India: From the Origins to AD 1300*, New Delhi: Penguin.

Tharoor, Shashi (2012), "An India-Pakistan Thaw?," *Global Public Square*, CNN. com Blogs, April 9. http://globalpublicsquare.blogs.cnn.com/2012/04/09/th aroor-an-india-pakistan-thaw/ (accessed February 1, 2013).

Thomas, Raju G.C. (1983), "India: Balancing Great-Power Intrusions and

Regional-Security Interests," in Raju G.C. Thomas (ed.), *The Great-Power Triangle and Asian Security*, Lexington, MA: Lexington Books, pp. 65–81.

Thomas, Raju G.C. (1986), *Indian Security Policy*, Princeton, NJ: Princeton University Press.

Thompson, William R. (1988), *On Global War: Historical-Structural Approaches to World Politics*, Columbia: University of South Carolina Press.

Thompson, William R. (1995), "Principal Rivalries," *Journal of Conflict Resolution*, 39(2): 195–223.

Thompson, William R. (2001), "Identifying Rivals and Rivalries in World Politics," *International Studies Quarterly*, 45(4): 557–86.

Thomson, Mike (2013), "Hyderabad 1948: India's Hidden Massacre," *BBC News*, September 24. https://www.bbc.co.uk/news/magazine-24159594 (accessed September 25, 2014).

Thornton, Thomas Perry (1982), "Between Two Stools?: U.S. Policy toward Pakistan during the Carter Administration," *Asian Survey*, 22(10): 959–77.

Thornton, Thomas Perry (1999), "Pakistan: Fifty Years of Insecurity," in Sleigh S. Harrison et al. (eds.), *India and Pakistan: The First Fifty Years*, Cambridge: Cambridge University Press and Washington, DC: Woodrow Wilson Center Press, pp. 170–88.

Times of India (1998), "George and the Dragon," May 5.

Times of India (2006), "Kargil War: Pak Misjudged India's Ability," October 15. http://articles.timesofindia.indiatimes.com/2006-10-15/india/27787279 _1_kargil-war-foreign-secretary-shamshad-ahmad-prime-minister-nawaz-sh arif (accessed January 14, 2014).

Times of India (2010), "Pak Trashes Musharraf's 4-Point Kashmir Formula," June 30. http://timesofindia.indiatimes.com/world/pakistan/Pak-trashes-Mushar rafs-4-point-Kashmir-formula/articleshow/6109996.cms (accessed August 28, 2014).

Times of India (2019a), "India's Development Aid to Afghanistan Exceeds $3bn," January 4. https://timesofindia.indiatimes.com/india/indias-development -aid-to-afghanistan-exceeds-3bn/articleshowprint/67379066.cms (accessed April 23, 2019).

Times of India (2019b), "Tension in the Air: IAF, PAF Lose a Jet Each; Pilot in Pakistan Custody," February 27. https://timesofindia.indiatimes.com/india/tensi on-in-the-air-iaf-paf-lose-a-jet-each-pilot-in-pakistan-custody/articleshow /68192759.cms (accessed April 23, 2019).

Tipnis, Air Chief Marshal A.Y. (retd.) (2006), "Operation Safed Sagar," *Force*, October (New Delhi): 1–6.

Toon, Owen B., et al. (2019), "Rapidly Expanding Nuclear Arsenals in Pakistan and India Portend Regional and Global Catastrophe," *Science Advances*, 5(10): 1–14. https://doi.org/10.1126/sciadv.aay5478.

Tremblay, Reeta Chowdhari, and Julian Schofield (2005), "Institutional Causes of the India-Pakistan Rivalry," in T.V. Paul (ed.), *The India-Pakistan Conflict: An Enduring Rivalry*, New York: Cambridge University Press, pp. 225–48.

Tribune (2001), "Fidayeen Storm J&K House, Kill 29," October 2. http://www.trib uneindia.com/2001/20011002/main1.htm (accessed January 14, 2014).

Tribune (2006), "Hindus Massacred in Doda, Bodies of 9 Kidnapped from Udham-pur Found," May 2. http://www.tribuneindia.com/2006/20060502/main1 .htm (accessed March 28, 2014).

Trumbull, Robert (1947), "Kashmir Rebels in 13-Day Rampage Leave Baramulla in Stripped Ruins," *New York Times*, November 11, pp. 1, 6.

Tucker, Francis (1988), *India's Partition and Human Debasement*, vol. 1, New Delhi: Akashdeep.

Tudor, Maya (2013), *The Promise of Power: The Origins of Democracy in India and Autocracy in Pakistan*, New Delhi: Cambridge University Press.

UNRIAA (United Nations Reports of International Arbitral Awards) (1968), "The Indo-Pakistan Western Boundary (Rann of Kutch) between India and Paki-stan," vol. 17, February 19, pp. 1–576. https://legal.un.org/riaa/cases/vol_XVII /1-576.pdf (accessed February 10, 2022).

US-China Economic and Security Review Commission (2013), "2013 Annual Report to Congress," November 20. http://www.uscc.gov/Annual_Reports /2013-annual-reportcongress (accessed July 18, 2016).

US Department of Defense (2016), "Secretary of Defense Testimony: Opening Statement—Senate Appropriations Committee-Defense (FY 2017 Budget Request)," As Delivered by Secretary of Defense Ash Carter, Washington, DC, April 27. https://www.defense.gov/Newsroom/Speeches/Speech/Article/744 092/opening-statemen%E2%80%A6 (accessed August 23, 2018).

US Department of Defense (2019), "Indo-Pacific Strategy Report: Preparedness, Partnerships, and Promoting a Networked Region," June 1. https://media.def ense.gov/2019/Jul/01/2002152311/-1/-1/1/DEPARTMENT-OF-DEFENSE-IN DO-PACIFIC-STRATEGY-REPORT-2019.PDF (accessed June 10, 2019).

US Department of State (2014), "Joint Communiqué AUSMIN 2014," August 12. http://www.state.gov/r/pa/prs/ps/2014/230524.htm (accessed July 18, 2016).

Valeriano, Brandon (2009), "The Tragedy of Offensive Realism: Testing Aggres-sive Power Politics Models," *International Interactions*, 35(2): 179–206.

Van Evera, Stephen (1999), *Causes of War: Power and the Roots of Conflict*, Ithaca, NY: Cornell University Press.

Van Hollen, Christopher (1980), "The Tilt Revisited: Nixon-Kissinger Geopolitics and South Asia," *Asian Survey*, 20(4): 339–61.

Van Hollen, Eliza (1987), "Pakistan in 1986: Trials of Transition," *Asian Survey*, 27(2): 143–54.

Vanaik, Achin (2015), *After the Bomb: Reflections on India's Nuclear Journey*, New Delhi: Orient Blackswan.

Vanaik, Achin (2016), Personal Interview, Fellow at Transnational Institute and retired Professor, the Department of Political Science, University of Delhi, New Delhi, January 15.

Varadarajan, Siddharth (2009), "After Evidence Dossier, Direct Accusation against Pakistan Strikes Discordant Note," *Hindu*, January 8. http://www.the

hindu.com/todays-paper/after-evidence-dossier-direct-accusation-against
-pakistan-strikes-discordant-note/article370592.ece?css=print (accessed March
29, 2014).

Varshney, Ashutosh (1991), "India, Pakistan, and Kashmir: Antinomies of Nationalism," *Asian Survey*, 31(11): 997–1019.

Varshney, Ashutosh (1992), "Three Compromised Nationalisms: Why Kashmir Has Been a Problem," in Raju G.C. Thomas (ed.), *Perspectives on Kashmir: The Root of Conflict in South Asia*, Boulder, CO: Westview Press, pp. 191–234.

Vasquez, John A. (1993), *The War Puzzle*, New York: Cambridge University Press.

Vasquez, John A. (1995), "Why Do Neighbors Fight? Proximity, Interaction, or Territoriality," *Journal of Peace Research*, 32(3): 277–93.

Vasquez, John A. (1996a), "Distinguishing Rivals That Go to War from Those That Do Not: A Quantitative Comparative Case Study of the Two Paths to War," *International Studies Quarterly*, 40(4): 531–58.

Vasquez, John A. (1996b), "When Are Power Transitions Dangerous? The Contribution of the Power Transition Thesis to International Relations Theory," in Jacek Kugler and Douglas Lemke (eds.), *Parity and War: A Critical Reevaluation of the War Ledger*, Ann Arbor: University of Michigan Press, pp. 35–56.

Vasquez, John A. (1998), "The Evolution of Multiple Rivalries prior to World War II in the Pacific," in Paul F. Diehl (ed.), *The Dynamics of Enduring Rivalries*, Urbana: University of Illinois Press, pp. 191–224.

Vasquez, John A. (2004), *The Power of Power Politics: From Classical Realism to Neo-traditionalism*, New York: Cambridge University Press.

Vinayak, Ramesh (1999), "Nasty Surprise," *India Today*, May 31. http://indiatoday
.intoday.in/story/kargil-assault-pak-backed-infiltrators-occupy-snowbound
-heights-trigger-response-by-army/1/254107.html (accessed January 15, 2014).

Viswam, S., and Salamat Ali (1990), "Vale of Tears," *Far Eastern Economic Review*, February 8, pp. 19–21.

Wallace, M. (1979), "Arms Races and Escalation: Some New Evidence," *Journal of Conflict Resolution*, 23(1): 3–16.

Wallace, M. (1982), "Armaments and Escalation," *International Studies Quarterly*, 26(1): 37–56.

Walter, Barbara F. (2003), "Explaining the Intractability of Territorial Conflict," *International Studies Review*, 5(4): 137–153.

Waltz, Kenneth (1959), *Man, the State and War: A Theoretical Analysis*, New York: Columbia University Press.

Waltz, Kenneth (1979), *Theory of International Politics*, New York: Random House.

Waltz, Kenneth N. (1981), "The Spread of Nuclear Weapons: More May Be Better," *Adelphi Papers* 21(171): 1–32.

Waltz, Kenneth N. (2003a), "More May Be Better," in Scott D. Sagan and Kenneth N. Waltz (eds.), *The Spread of Nuclear Weapons: A Debate Renewed*, New York: W.W. Norton, pp. 3–45.

Waltz, Kenneth N. (2003b), "Thoughts about Assaying Theories," in Colin Elman and Miriam Fendius Elman (eds.), *Progress in International Relations Theory: Appraising the Field*, Cambridge, MA: MIT Press.

Waseem, Mohammad (2015), Personal Interview, Professor of Political Science, School of Law, Humanities and Social Sciences, Lahore University of Management Sciences (LUMS), Lahore, October 9.

Watson, Goodwin (1971), "Resistance to Change," *American Behavioral Scientist*, 14(5): 745–66.

Week (2019), "40 CRPF Personnel Killed in Pulwama Blast; JeM Claims Responsibility," February 14. https://www.theweek.in/news/india/2019/02/14/sever al-crpf-personnel-killed-in-jammu-and-kashmir-terror-attack.html (accessed July 20, 2019).

Weissman, Steve R., and Hebert Krosney (1981), *The Islamic Bomb: The Nuclear Threat to Israel and the Middle East*, New York: Times Books.

Wendt, Alexander (1987), "The Agent-Structure Problem in International Relations Theory," *International Organization*, 41(4): 335–70.

Wendt, Alexander (1992), "Anarchy Is What States Make of It: The Social Construction of Power Politics," *International Organization*, 46(2): 391–425.

Wendt, Alexander (1999), *Social Theory of International Politics*, New York: Cambridge University Press.

Weyland, Kurt (2001), "Clarifying a Contested Concept: Populism in the Study of Latin American Politics," *Comparative Politics*, 34(1): 1–22.

White House (2021), "The US Strategic Framework for the Indo-Pacific" (February 2018), National Security Council, Washington DC, January 12. https://www .whitehouse.gov/briefings-statements/statement-national-security-advisor -robert-c-obrien-011221/ (accessed January 14, 2021).

Whitehead, Andrew (2007), *A Mission in Kashmir*, New Delhi: Penguin.

Widmalm, Stein (1998), "The Rise and Fall of Democracy in Jammu and Kashmir," in A. Basu and A. Kohli (eds.), *Community Conflicts and the State in India*, New Delhi: Oxford University Press.

Widmalm, Stein (2002), *Kashmir in Comparative Perspective: Democracy and Violent Separatism in India*, Karachi: Oxford University Press.

Wiegand, Krista E. (2011), *Enduring Territorial Disputes: Strategies of Bargaining Coercive Diplomacy, and Settlement*, Athens: University of Georgia Press.

Wilcox, Wayne Ayres (1965), "The Pakistan Coup d'Etat of 1958," *Pacific Affairs*, 38(2): 142–63.

Wirsing, Robert G. (1991), *Pakistan's Security under Zia, 1977–88: The Policy Imperatives of a Peripheral Asian State*, London: Macmillan.

Wirsing, Robert G. (1998), *India, Pakistan, and the Kashmir Dispute: On Regional Conflict and Its Resolution*, first paperback edition, New York: St. Martin's Press.

Wolpert, Stanley (2000), *A New History of India*, Oxford: Oxford University Press.

Wolpert, Stanley (2006), *Shameful Flight: The Last Years of the British Rule in India*, London: Oxford University Press.

World Bank (2007), "South Asia Energy: Potential and Prospects for Regional

Trade," *World Bank Report*, November 8. http://web.worldbank.org (accessed June 15, 2011).

World Bank (2018), *World Development Indicators*, Washington, DC: World Bank. https://datacatalog.worldbank.org/ (accessed September 27, 2019).

World Bank (2019), *World Integrated Trade Solution*, Washington, DC: World Bank. https://wits.worldbank.org/ (accessed December 31, 2019).

Wright, Quincy (1964), *A Study of War*, Chicago: University of Chicago.

Yasmeen, Samina (1992), "The China Factor in the Kashmir Issue," in Raju G.C. Thomas (ed.), *Perspectives on Kashmir: The Roots of Conflict in South Asia*, Boulder, CO: Westview Press, pp. 319–40.

Yasmeen, Samina (1999), "Pakistan's Nuclear Tests: Domestic Debate and International Determinants," *Australian Journal of International Affairs*, 53(1): 43–56.

Yunus, Mohammed (2011), *Bhutto and the Breakup of Pakistan*, Karachi: Oxford University Press.

Zaidi, Mubashir (2002), "India on Warpath, Pak Steps Back; Pervez: We Must Stop Infiltration," *Hindustan Times*, May 23.

Zaidi, Mubashir, and Fred Weir (2002), "Pak Curbs on Infiltration: Deliver on Pledges, Bush Tells Pervez," *Hindustan Times*, May 26.

Zakaria, Anam (2018), *Between the Great Divide*, Noida: HarperCollins.

Zee News (2013), "Pakistan Army Chief Kayani Meets Nawaz Sharif," May 13. http://zeenews.india.com/print.aspx?nid=849407 (accessed May 13, 2013).

Ziauddin, Mohammad (2015), Personal Interview, Former Editor-in-Chief of the *Dawn* and the *Express Tribune*, Islamabad, October 15.

Zinkin, Taya (1987), "The Background to Indo-Pakistani Relations," *International Relations*, 9: 31–38.

Ziring, Lawrence (2003), *Pakistan: At the Crosscurrent of History*, Oxford: Oneworld Publications.

Index

Abbas, Hassan, 184, 252

Abdullah (Sheikh): and confederal proposal, 162; and democracy, 89, 202; drop of plebiscite push, 163; imprisonment of, 114, 115, 124, 127; and Pakistan, 125; work with India, 202-3

Abdullah, Farooq, 203-4

Acheson, Dean, 97

actor's perception approach to rivalry, 27-29, 32-33, 39-46

Advanced Warning and Control System (AWACS), 185

Advani, Lal Krishna, 334n27, 334n31

Afghanistan: attacks on Indian embassies and consulates, 248; and development phase, 180, 181-85; Durand Line, 243-45; Indian aid and development, 241-45, 247; and maintenance phase, 239-49; and military aid to Pakistan, 184, 233; and nuclear development in Pakistan, 190-91, 196, 215; and SAARC, 230-31; Soviet invasion of, 180, 181-85, 190-91, 196, 215, 233; and strategic-depth doctrine, 239-41, 244, 247, 248; Strategic Partnership Agreement, 247; and Taliban, 239-41, 247-49, 269; and war on terror, 224, 226, 236, 241

Agra Summit, 223, 268-69

Ahmad, Shamshad, 331n3

Ahmadabad: terrorism attacks in, 228

Ahmed, Samina, 169-72

airplane hijackings, 212, 235, 241

Aiyar, Mani Shankar, 241, 298-99

Akhund, Iqbal, 265

alliances: in development phase, 133-46, 167, 180-91; inhibiting effect of, 62-63; in initiation phase, 92-103; in mainte-

nance phase, 232-39; in realist theory, 62; role in rivalry framework, 4, 59, 62-63, 65-67, 72. *See also* Cold War; great powers interventions

All-India Muslim League, 18, 55-56, 76-78

All Party Hurriyat Conference, 218-19

Al Qaida, 224, 236, 241, 269

Alsace-Lorraine, 50, 284-85

Ambedkar, B. R., 111

Anand, Pawan, 290

anarchy, 5-7, 9, 11, 17-20

Ankara Defense Cooperation Agreement, 137

Arif, Khalid Mahmud, 181

arms buildups: in development phase, 133-46, 167, 180-91; and embargo on Pakistan, 180, 182-83, 192; in initiation phase, 92-103; in maintenance phase, 232-39; and peace, 63; role in rivalry framework, 59, 63, 65, 66-67, 72; and WWI/WWII, 63. *See also* military capabilities

Article 370: approach to, 331n11; revocation of, 232, 279, 288, 323n1

Asal Uttar, Battle of, 128

Asian Collective Security System, 138

Asian security architecture and prospects for termination, 293-300

Assam: clashes in, 83, 122; eviction of Muslims from, 124

asymmetries in power: and initiation phase, 103-10; and nuclear deterrence, 8-9, 13, 16; at partition, 103-4; and power transition theory, 13; and realist theory, 8, 9-10; role in rivalry framework, 64, 65; and window theory, 149. *See also* military capabilities